Re-Visioning Narcissism

OTHER BOOKS BY Gary Rosenthal
FROM POINT BONITA BOOKS

The Museum of the Lord of Shame
The You That is Everywhere: Love Poems
An Amateur's Guide to the Invisible World
Waking From an Age of Amnesia (forthcoming)
The White Latifa and its Citadel: Radical Allowing, Discipline and the Poetic Tradition's Perception of "Holy Will" (forthcoming)

Re-Visioning Narcissism

HEALING HERESIES FOR POLARIZED TIMES

Gary Rosenthal

POINT BONITA BOOKS | EPIGRAPH BOOKS
RICHMOND, CALIFORNIA | RHINEBECK, NEW YORK

Re-visioning Narcissism: Healing Heresies for Polarized Times
© copyright 2020 by Gary Rosenthal

All rights reserved. No part of this book may be used or reproduced in any manner without written permission from the author except in critical articles or reviews. Contact the publisher for information.

Paperback ISBN 978-1-948796-91-0

Library of Congress Control Number 2019916126

Book design by Colin Rolfe

Point Bonita Books
5920 Dimm Way
Richmond, CA 94805
(510) 232-1401
www.pointbonitabooks.com

Epigraph Books
22 East Market Street, Suite 304
Rhinebeck, New York 12572
(845) 876-4861
epigraphps.com

Contents

Acknowledgments ix
Prologue xiii

I.
Of Meme Warfare & Myth
& Much Ado About Nothing

1. *Ghosts* 3
2. The Obvious Target & The Deeper Work 4
3. The Roots of Polarization & the Fate of a Species 9
4. Reporting the News 18
5. Changing Waters & The Light and the Lampshade 36
6. What's to Like About Nothing: A Beginner's Guide to Non-conceptual Space 51
7. Islands 62
8. Initiation, *Meme* Warfare, and the 12 o'clock Client 70
9. Regarding Myths: *Someone Might Have Warned Us* 83
10. If Our Myths Have Failed Us... 96

II.
Clinical Takes on a Syndrome:
From the Myth Standing Behind It
To Its View by Committee

11. The Myth of Narcissus 107
12. Pools, Wells, Mirroring & Blind People Describing an Elephant 112
13. Nemesis and the Five Faces of the Narcissistic Curse 120
14. Is He a Narcissist, a Psychopath—or *Both*? And Does the President Have a Delusional Disorder? 142
15. The Mask & the Wound 169

III.
THE DEATH OF NARCISSUS & THE NATURE OF TRANSFORMATIONAL GAZES:
THE MYTHOPOEIC AND SPIRITUAL TRADITIONS WEIGH IN

16. The Baby, the Bathwater, and Narcissus's Neptunian Pool   179
17. The Death of Narcissus & the Nature of Transformational Gazes   186
18. The Threefold Sky   194
19. Meditation and "Stupid *Shamatha*"   201
20. *Trespasso*   203
21. *"Looks Like Me" & Following Your Bliss*   211

IV.
HEALING...FALLING DOWN INTO A WELL... & WALKING BRISKLY BENEATH A RIDICULOUS HAT

22. What Heals Narcissism?   219
23. Falling Down into a Well & One Insult After Another   227
24. The 12th Century's Perfect Storm & Walking Briskly Beneath a Ridiculous Hat   231

V.
LOVE, CULTURE, GODS, AND GOVERNMENT IN AN AGE OF NARCISSISM

Interlude: A Brief Primer about the Gods   247
25. Evoking, or Freshening, the Archetypes   256
26. Mythic Dissociation: The Loss of Transformational Rites & Loss of the Real Self   267
27. Cultural Narcissism: Idealization and Devaluing, Ethnocentricity & the Narrowing of God   273
28. Narcissism's Apotheosis of Fame & the Loss of Attention, *Eros*, Empathy & Altruism   279
29. Who—or What—is Echo?   285
30. Narcissism as Spiritual Dissociation; the Estrangement of Psyche from Spirit   294
31. The Ascent and Crash of the Box & What's Been Left Behind   298

VI.
COMING HOME: *The Music of What Happens*

32. The Music of What Happens   305
33. Mind, Space, and the Dislocation of the Essential Self   310
34. Egoic Will as a Feature of Mythic Dissociation   320
35. Two Roads & the "Little Two-Step"   324
36. Who *Isn't* Dissociated from Presence?   333

Epilogue: Echoing the Whole   335
Afterword: The *Gifts* of Narcissus's Pool   341

Works Consulted or Recommended   343
About the Author   349

Acknowledgments

WRITING IS A solitary activity. And yet a writer is never alone. We are accompanied by those who have gone before us. What they have seen and said informs our vision. It is good to have ancestors, visionary kinsmen.

Here I wish to acknowledge my visionary debt to *Joseph Campbell,* a true *Jnana* yogin, and one of the few produced by the West. I also want to acknowledge *James Hillman* for having alerted me to the notion that there was something about Narcissus's death scene that has commonly not been understood. (There was buried treasure there, and our differences aside, he showed me where to dig).

In addition to Hillman, I'm deeply indebted to hundreds, if not thousands of years of *the poetic tradition.* For both have stressed the primacy of the *image* in the *imagination*—and as well the *multiple* ways we might regard the images contained in mythic material. And each helped me to at least *begin* to write a psychological prose that hopefully doesn't stray too far from poetry. (In fact, the earliest incarnation of this book took the form of prose poems; and the contemplative essays of its current form were grouped into their sections much as a book of poems—by shared metaphoric themes. And so, though this book's narrative flow is not haphazard, neither is it entirely linear).

I bow as well to *Tarthang Tulku Rinpoche* for having reflected the enormous body of skillful means contained within his tradition, and for having taught me mirror gazing, and drawing my attention to the other meditative gazes employed by the Nyingma and Kagyu schools of Tibetan Buddhism. I also bow to the clairsentient empathy, humor, and wisdom of *Tsoknyi Rinpoche,* to whom I'm enormously grateful for his transmission of the Nature of Mind teachings, including the practice of The Three

Fold Sky. I feel a similar appreciation to their lineages, and in particular to *Padmasambhava.*

This is my first published book of non-fiction. With this being the case, I have had few readers till now. But the few I've had have been superb; and the generosity with which they've offered their time and attention has sustained and supported me in the writing of this book. Here I am deeply grateful to *Marie Ali*—in multiple ways. Most importantly, for her compassionate, clear-minded reflections of my own narcissism—without which, the writing of this book would have been something of a joke. I want to thank her—as well as her husband, *Hameed Ali*—for what is embedded and transmitted by their school, whose central focus *is* the spiritual transformation of narcissism—though over thirty years have passed since I took leave. I also wish to thank my golf buddy, Industrial Light and Magic's former marketing director *Rose Duignan,* as well as my other wise friends, Zen *roshi* John Tarrant, poet *Peter Fortunato,* and *Peter and Michelle Howard*—for their willingness to read parts of the book while in manuscript and offer valuable suggestions.

I have lifted many glasses of adult beverage in the company of my Irish friends—my homeboy *Peter O Hanrahan,* the late mythologist/poet *Daithi O hOgain,* plus Ireland's former Green Party MEP *Nuala Ahern, Barry Ahern,* and *Sandy and Ellen O'Malley Dunlop.* I wish to thank them all for sharing their love of mythology, their gifts of gab, and for the rather unique regard the Irish extend toward poets. Thanks to Nuala for reading an earlier draft of this book, and to her and her husband Barry for taking me to the ancient mythological sites of Ireland (when I was too afraid to drive to them myself via the unfamiliar "wrong" side of the road). These sites helped me to further recognize the impact of place and topography in understanding the mythic material that has arisen from it. Thanks to Sandy and Ellen for their marvelous Bard summer school. There is nothing quite like exploring myth, or reading poetry—when variously inspired by good companions, grog, and the breath-taking beauty of an island in the Irish Sea—an island that is inhabited by the descendants of a 16th century *lady* pirate! Love your lineage, Ellen. I love your country.

It has, in an age of sound bites, grown increasingly rare to find people willing to *read,* let alone offer feedback, for even a moderately sized manuscript. And this trend only seems to be worsening. I'm thus also grateful to fellow author *Barry Spector* for reading a manuscript that at one point had swelled to nearly 600 pages. I thank him for what has apparently become an "old school" generosity of spirit, his mythic vision, and for several suggestions that have enriched this book.

Lastly, I wish to acknowledge *those who have entrusted me to be their therapist, teacher, or guide.* Our work together has been a creative matrix, a collaboration from which many of this book's insights have arisen, and its premises tested and refined. Mine is a bastard voice that bears no stamp, no seal of lineage; but your open-ness to depth has evoked my own, thus empowering the seat I speak from.

"On some great and glorious day, the plain folks of the land will reach their heart's desire at last, and the White House will be occupied by a downright fool and a complete narcissistic moron."
—H.L. Mencken, *Baltimore Evening Sun,* July 1920

Prologue

IN A GLOBAL world, the rising tide of the sea change of Trump's election was shockingly noted—not only in the hallways of the world's governments, but in the consulting rooms of American psychotherapists. Not even 9/11 provoked such a collective wave of *anxiety* as I saw showing up for therapy in the first weeks of Trump's presidency. For many, even those not in Hillary's camp, were having post-traumatic stress reactions, as if they awoke on the morning of November 9th 2016 in a living nightmare.

Only the nightmare continued… day after day, week after week of appalling falsehoods, tweets, appointments, and executive orders; plus the mounting evidence of corruption. For many, CNN at almost any hour of any day, seemed must-watch television. As with jihadists appearing on the world stage on 9/11, here was another player on the stage trying to undo the world as we've known it.

The mythic nature of American comic books had anticipated such a nightmarish figure for years, in portraying such outlandish villains as Lex Luthor, the Penguin, and the Joker. Here were malignantly narcissistic figures—grandiose and entitled, unprincipled and obsessed with power and world-domination. These "arch enemies" seemed the shadow of Superman and Batman. For they were thoroughly lacking in empathy for the rest of humanity, and trying to change the world into one more akin to their own darkened sensibility.

Yet if central traits of narcissism are said to include a hubristic *grandiosity*, the sense of *entitlement*, and *a lack of empathy*, these traits were already politically and culturally surfacing in America long before its comic books, and long before Donald Trump.

A governmental appropriation of the lands of its native peoples certainly evidences America's sense of entitlement—an entitlement that was still being acted out in the 20th and 21st century in the hubristic regime changes America felt entitled to, and which were enacted in Iran (in 1953) and Iraq (in 2003).

And the mass abduction of Africans into slavery is earlier evidence of a historical lack of empathy, one that was also to polarize the nation. A lack of empathy that would only be continued by an immigration plan, and a plotted "Muslim ban," that would restrict displaced peoples from the Middle East's war zones from entering our country; war zones that only ensued in the wake of America's disastrous military invasion of Iraq, an invasion that was based upon lies and false premises: the putative existence of Iraq's "weapons of mass destruction;" and the equally putative collaboration between Osama bin Laden and Saddam Hussein.

America's founding fathers were concerned about this very thing. Having faced an armed colonial occupation force at the inception of our republic, they were concerned that America not follow the same path by engaging in unnecessary military adventures. Thus, Benjamin Franklin had argued against adopting the Roman legion's martial eagle as our national bird, suggesting the turkey instead. Franklin's concern turned out to be prescient. For America has been engaged in some form of warfare for every decade since its founding. (As documented in the following link: *https:// en.wikipedia.org/wiki/List_of_wars_involving_the_United_States*).

In historical hindsight, each of these features seem evidence of a hubristic entitlement that has been with us practically since the nation's inception—the often-overlooked shadow side of a nation that otherwise idealizes itself as the *greatest* on earth, "the land of the free, and the home of the brave." But *free* we might ask, in order to do *what?* And yet, for much of America's history it also *has been*, arguably the greatest of countries. And the same could be said for its democratic form of government—which is also imperfect, and subject to its own forms of pathology and dysfunction. (As can happen when one of our three co-equal branches of government runs off the rails, and the other two fail to adequately counter it).

Yet like individuals, America is neither solely all light, nor all shadow. We're more like a river that contains two tributaries, one clear running, the other muddy and foul; a nation both *noble* and *culpable*. (And often rent apart between its better and worse angels). America is a *conversation* between these two, and not just that "shining city on the hill." We lose our bearings when we lose sight of one—or the other. And when we *confuse* one for the other.

And the rise of Trump puts that conversation—and that confusion—squarely before us. If narcissism is in part an identity confusion, a confusion about who we truly are, Trump represents not only a crisis for our democracy, but *a national identity crisis.* For he leads us to ask: *Who are we as a people?* (And it's not a bad question).

However, that question has really been with us for as long as America has existed. And though much of our media has portrayed Trump as an outlier, an alien menace—as if an autocratic dictator transported from a 3rd world banana republic—what has been lost in a psychologically naïve nation with a diminished sense of history, is that Trump also embodies an archetype *as American as apple pie.* For something Trump-like is not only found in the obsessive quests of recent comic book villains, but was already spotted in the similarly obsessive quest of the monomaniacal, one-legged whale boat captain portrayed in one of the first great American novels (*Moby Dick*) which was published in 1851.

Akin to the tragic figures of ancient Greek drama, Captain Ahab is a figure who seems at first larger than life, a man who has been struck by lightning and lived, yet who is brought down by his own hubris. For he is "an ungodly, god-like" man who does not worship, or even recognize the superiority of forces beyond himself. His grandiosity is such that Ahab himself tells us he "would strike the sun if it insulted me." Yet he has the power to move people with charismatic persuasion. And through rousing speech—and the promise of gold—he solicits the support of his crew for his obsessed mission: to hunt down a white whale. For he believes there is a force within the whale that wants to injure or oppose him, to limit his role in the world. And so, he strikes out against the elemental powers of nature, and the universe—which he cannot possibly defeat—and which finally bring him down.

Yet we can track Captain Ahab farther back still… For without overlooking their "clear-running" high minded-ness, nor the noble documents they left to guide us, we might also remember that even many of our founding fathers had a bit of Ahab, a bit of Trump inside them too, a part that was "muddy and foul." For Washington, Jefferson, Madison, and Monroe—to pick just four—were slave-holders all.

And who but a version of Ahab was at the helm, as the U.S. government plowed its sea-like prairies, stole the land from its native peoples at our beginnings as a nation, and forced them onto reservations? (George Washington himself later came to regard this as the greatest failure of his presidency). And who but a sub-culture of Ahabs were responsible for sailing ships with Africans in chains in their holds; bringing them to swelter as slaves in a nation whose Declaration of Independence proclaimed in 1776 that all men were "created equal" and entitled to the rights of "Life, Liberty, and the pursuit of Happiness."

But that high-minded Declaration was to have no legal effect. And when the status of slaves—*are they people or property?*—became debated during the Constitutional Convention of 1787, the compromise that was reached was that each slave was to be counted as *3/5s of a person*. And the southern delegation had only granted slaves that *fraction* of person-hood once it became clear that the number of representatives that each state would be granted in the new Congress would be based upon population. (And so, gerrymandering and attempts to suppress and restrict voting rights of dark-skinned people is nothing new. A selfish, grandiose, and calculating *meme* has been with us forever. It comprises one of America's "twin tributaries." And this contrary pull of opposing currents has created the ongoing condition that sea captains term "confused waters." And they've made it hard to steer the ship of state on a clear, and coherent *democratic* course).

We might then jump to the 20th century, while repeating the current refrain: Who but an Abab following an obsessive, and ultimately self-destructive mission, would ever think to start a bloody, long-running war based on fake naval data in the Gulf of Tonkin, and then rain Agent Orange down upon the brown-skinned mama-sans and their families in Southeast Asia, as if they were threats limiting America's role in the world?

And who or what was the archetypal source that sentenced hundreds of thousands of Iraqis to their deaths based on charges cooked up by the neocons in George W's White House—as if it had become a death-spewing Meth House—and prosecuting *yet another war* for charges against a nation in which neither its people, nor its leader, were ever culpable? From Ahab's whale boat, through these examples, it's not a far jump to Trump's White House. Trump's just the latest of our Ahabs, an American son. (And we'll need to *own* him, as the Germans did Hitler).

And though democracies are suffering now, haunted and being hunted like an endangered species—both in America and elsewhere—*democracy* is not a great white whale. It *is* a great *ideal*, one we never quite reach—yet one we might defend when it becomes threatened. And it *does* become threatened when it is pursued in an arrogant, grandiose, monomaniacal way, a self-serving way entirely devoid of empathy. At that point what we might have is the antithesis of democracy: *malignant narcissism*. And this book will pursue *that* with its own harpoons, both now and in forthcoming chapters.

For our problem is deeper than Trump. And whether we call it Ahabism, or narcissism, a militantly obsessed *hubris* that lacks empathy has been a near continuous stream running through American politics, and unfortunately, at times at its helm. And long before Trump, people from outside the U.S. have viewed America as a crazy, gun-toting, dangerous place. And in other countries—long before Trump—the "Ugly American" had been a familiar and shadowy figure. And not only ugly, but (also *like* Trump) a dangerous bully, due to our outsized military that spends more on armaments than the other 8 or 10 most heavily armed countries *combined*.

The increasing danger of such a "military industrial complex" was already rearing its head in the 1950s, and what President Dwight D. Eisenhower tried to warn against at the end of his presidency. Like our national militancy, Trump is merely reflecting something already lurking in America's collective psyche. He's the shadow—not only of Obama and of an informed, liberal leadership—but of us all. He holds up a mirror to *a collectively suffered dissociation from the soul's deepest nature,* and all the ways that manifests: our bellicosity, racism, misogyny, and superficiality; a predatory regard toward nature; the corrupting role of money in our political system; as well as our narcissism, its entitlement, and a polarizing vision that lacks empathy…

All these unsavory traits need to be made more conscious—individually and collectively—for a people to become truly "great." *That* is the true opportunity Trump offers America. And you can't *elect* that kind of greatness—or even *recognize it*, if it remains largely obscured in *yourself*. And so, it's going to take a lot of collective effort, and not only politically. It's going to take a lot of soul searching, an increase of discernment, and a lessening of our psychological, spiritual, and political naiveté. We have to own our own shadow.

For Trump is an exaggerated mirror of what's false, polarized, obsessed, and corruptible in a human soul; and the dire consequences that can result when that polarizing corruption is not adequately recognized, let alone opposed. Opposing *that* is the true American *jihad*. Yet without adequately confronting these features in ourselves, *as well as externally*, we could just swing to someone "more liberal" in the next election cycle, while leaving the nation as gullible, and as vulnerable to a toxic divisiveness as ever. There are thus enormously important lessons to learn from this presidency—an *evolutionary challenge*, really. And if we don't learn them and evolve now, we may remain subject to the next Ahab, the next Trump in waiting, the next Joe McCarthy, the next Nixon, and be no wiser than before.

If narcissism has its *political* features and consequences as I've attempted to evoke above, a growing incidence of narcissism had been showing up in American *psychotherapeutic consulting rooms* long before Donald Trump, long before 9/11, long before even Christopher Lasch's seminal book *The Culture of Narcissism: American Life in an Age of Diminishing Expectations* was published in 1979. Not surprisingly, over the succeeding decades we've thus had a plethora of books published on the topic of narcissism.

Yet they don't seem to have helped us much. For as a psychotherapist in private practice, I've seen absolutely no diminishment in what's walking in the door for treatment. In fact, the longest running study of narcissism that had been conducted by a group of social psychologists (between 1982 and 2006 with American college students) indicated that the trend toward narcissism has been steadily increasing (by 30% over the duration of the study). And by the study's end, approximately *two thirds* of the students were scoring highly on a narcissism index.

Yet weirdly, when the latest version of the official manual of the American Psychiatric Association (*The Diagnostic and Statistical Manual of Mental Disorders, 5th edition*) was preparing for its release in 2010, it had decided to entirely *eliminate* Narcissistic Personality Disorder as a potential diagnosis. When this was announced, the uproar that resulted from many psychological professionals led the *DSM-5's* personality disorder committee to reconsider their stance. And when the *DSM-5* was finally published in May of 2013, NPD was retained as a potential diagnosis. Yet the estimate given for NPD amongst the American population was listed as a dubiously low 0% to 6.2%—which also proved to be controversial.

Certainly, the *enormous* statistical discrepancy between 0% at the low end or even 6.2% at the high end, and *two thirds* of a population being studied is quite glaring. And it seemed to reflect a polarized confusion in the minds of even many mental health professionals sent out to treat narcissism—a confusion of what the term "narcissism" truly means, or should refer to.

Clearly, if there's been a lack of coherence, a lack of agreement in our understanding of what narcissism truly *is*, then equally clearly we must begin to think outside the box in terms of what will be required for its *healing*. The need for a deeply considered re-visioning of *both* seems timely for us now—and what this book will attempt.

If a book that proposes to re-vision narcissism and its healing seems timely, this will *not* be a book of pop psychology. Its intentions are heretical, if not deadly to popular or prevailing orthodoxy. And for starters, the book will proceed from a perspective closer to that of the social psychologists. In fact, the perspective in this book goes a bit farther...

Namely, that narcissism *is deeply embedded in the human condition, has been for thousands of years, and is not just a problem suffered by a tiny fraction of the population—though it is more obvious in certain people, cultures, and times than others.* And the liberation from its encapsulating, self-centered, and polarized vision is unlikely to come from the discovery of a medical pill—or from a single this, that, or any weekend workshop. (Though saying the above may be unwelcome news for a tweeting, quick-fix, sound bite cultural epoch; and perhaps equally unwelcome by parts of a psychological priesthood that's been coasting for decades, while divided into introspective schools that seldom even read each other's literature, and that first had found narcissism to be untreatable, then tried to textually banish it, and more lately, to minimize it).

The countering narrative I would offer instead is that the transformation of narcissism has largely been the goal, the flowering of a project accomplished by those of a mystical bent—those who have had the clearest perception of what it ultimately is, and the highest standards for its healing. And these have infrequently been those with letters, like *MD* or *PhD* after their names.

And even with spiritual adepts, the liberation from narcissism is not, heroically, once and for all. Instead, they have regarded it as the work *of a lifetime*. And though humbling to consider—and as Rumi once said: *None of us have gone far*. And if we think narcissism only applies to *those* people or *that* president, this may be a case of the pot calling the kettle black.

Here, I'm beginning to mount one of this book's more controversial arguments…Namely, that we've had a diminished awareness of what narcissism ultimately is. And that it can't be fully understood, treated, or resolved from this diminished awareness because *narcissism itself* is a form of diminished awareness—and something we all suffer—*not just that guy in the White House*. In fact, it's precisely what the world's spiritual traditions have been treating throughout time, a central feature of the human condition that we might re-christen as *Self Absorbed Diminished Awareness Syndrome* (SADAS). And it's *sad as* could be. For it limits our capacity for love, empathy, truth-telling—in fact, *all* of the soul's most essential qualities.

It polarizes us politically, and interpersonally in general. Its self-absorption obscures our own deeper nature, and a deeper perception of everything else. It makes us less adaptable to the ever shifting nature of the time. It inhibits a more intelligent relationship not only to other people, and groups of people, but to the ecosystems that sustain life on our planet.

And it's not that we should in any way turn a blind eye to the narcissism (the "self absorbed diminished awareness") of Donald Trump. But if the buck stops there, we may still be blind to what needs to be transformed in *ourselves*. And so, though this book will ongoingly reflect some of narcissism's current and historically suffered political manifestations, the book's mission would be less valuable if failing to offer some hints for our personal and collective healing.

Such a "Narcissism Project" is well-worth undertaking. And at the very least we might have some fresh *conversations* about it. And to this end, this book will initiate conversations that revolve around six central and inter-connected themes…

The first and most over-arching theme will be the attempt at a "pointing out" of the soul's deeper nature—a reflection that hopes to evoke and inspire—without pretending to be comprehensive. (Which is to say, one geared for an intelligent, contemporary lay audience). For *without* a deeper grounding in this more essential nature, we *have* lacked, and *will continue to lack,* an adequate reference of what narcissism's complete opposite—and thus its full healing—even *looks* like.

Secondly, there will be a corresponding and parallel evocation—of the forms of neurotic deficiency that ensue when the essential facets of the soul have become obscured. The attempt to better embody these facets—as well as the encounter with what obscures them—can comprise a series of *initiations* for those of us presently living in a cultural epoch whose prevailing rites of passage haven't been adequately doing their intended job. For our world is peopled, if not *led*, by people who have not undergone a transformational initiatory process. And in fact, each of these facets will prove to be valuable, if not necessary, in transforming our collective narcissism.

Thirdly, the book will attempt to bridge the historical rift that has existed between professional psychology and its close cousins—the world's spiritual and religious traditions. And hopefully in the process, inspiring the psychological profession to find its footing in something ultimately more inspiring than the recognition and treatment of *pathology.* In truth, the perspectives of contemporary psychology and spiritual practice should be *allies.* Both attempt to treat what obscures our deeper nature. And nothing obscures it more than narcissism. Yet without a vision less fixated on pathology, that deeper nature remains partially obscured in even the eyes of many mental health professionals sent out to treat it.

The fourth theme in the book will occur in the attempt to initiate conversations about the nature of *myth*. In fact, this is every bit a *book about myth,* as it is a "psychological," "spiritual," or "political" book. For as Karen Armstrong writes, "every time men and women took a major step forward, they reviewed their mythology, and made it speak to the new conditions."

Since we're much *in need* of such "a major step forward," this book proposes to do *just that.* It will attempt to identify, and then initiate conversations about some of the myths which seem most urgently in need of a contemporary re-visioning—while also making contemporary, cultural reflections as to why that's the case.

Hopefully, these four themes will help provide the requisite grounding to take up the book's fifth theme—a central focus of the book. Namely, what seems a much needed re-visioning of the nature of narcissism—a re-visioning guided by *a closer reading of the myth standing behind it*, the myth of Narcissus and Echo. (For I will argue that in our current age *this* myth may be one of those *most in need* of a contemporary re-visioning).

Here, I am also suggesting that an updated understanding of narcissism, both our own, and that of our culture and its government, may comprise *a central initiatory task for the time in which we live*. (And forgive me for pounding on the same chord again, but this seems especially so given the President elected by the United States in November of 2016). In particular, we will focus on Narcissus's death scene, and the narrowly understood nature of *the vision that led to his death*. For without a *deeper, alternative,* and "heretical" view of this vision, we will continue to lack orientation to the style of vision that puts narcissism out of its misery.

In that the perspectives this book attempts to offer are multiple (personal and transpersonal, mythic and cultural, contemporary and historical) the book's opening chapters will continue to re-vision contemporary political culture, hoping this might provide readers with an easy, shared access to the book's *logos* before proceeding to the book's personal, mythic, psychological, and spiritual dimensions.

Though in truth, since each of the book's themes are interconnected I could have begun elsewhere, almost anywhere. And with this said, the last of the book's themes will be the attempt to reflect the *societal consequences* of our failures to have a better conversation about each of the above.

For me as a writer, this book has contained a further challenge—beyond that of attempting to write something with such an ambitious scope. For the book's further challenge will be the attempt—whenever feasible—to speak to the reader in an informal, conversational style; while reflecting the broad contours of these otherwise "weighty" themes (each of which could comprise a book in themselves).

Yet there are extended passages of the book where a more formal narrative style prevails—in the attempt to provide further nuance for a cultural era increasingly geared to sound bites, and text-based tweets limited to 140 (now 280) characters—a culture that is developing an increasingly diminished *attention span*. (And here too, Trump is the poster boy).

There has thus been a loss of depth in the conversations we as a culture are having—if not a failure to initiate other conversations that we've needed to have. And in an age of Trump, we've needed to re-vision and have a better conversation not only about narcissism itself, but everything narcissism has impacted—*which is quite a lot.*

We Americans have needed to re-vision and have better, collaborative conversations about our health care system, as well as about the health of our planet, and our commitment to it. We've needed to initiate better conversations—if not to "repeal and replace"—what has grown to be dysfunctional in our political system, including the need for campaign finance reform and the role of money in our political system—which strangely, keeps receding from view. For as FDR once said: "Government by organized money is as dangerous as Government by organized mob."

And when it comes to the influence of the National Rifle Association there is not *only* a direct and pernicious correlation between "organized money" and the prevalence of guns and gun violence in America, and the mass shootings and hate crimes that have increased during Trump's presidency. For as the Mueller probe played out, we discovered that a Russian operative living in the U.S. (Maria Butina) had established a back channel between the Russian government—*via the NRA*—and the Republican Party that had been part of a wider, and broadly orchestrated national security crisis. (Normally, we've looked to our president when facing a national security crisis. But to whom do you turn when the president refuses to address or even *recognize* the crisis, and when he, in fact, *is part* of the crisis?).

And in a toxically polarized political climate where there has been a loss of healthy and collaborative bi-partisanship, to whom *else* in the government can the president's *own inner circle turn*, when they have come to have grave misgivings about the president's fitness for office? The answer, unfortunately, has been nobody. Which is why there has been an unrelenting series of "leaks" from Trump's own administration to the *press*, documenting the president's unfitness for office. For our free press has recently become—more so than our congress or executive branch—the leading cultural institution capable of defending our democracy.

The U.S. is also in need of a better conversation (within its own *populace* and within its own *government*) about America's role in a rapidly changing world. For there's now a void, a largely unexplored middle ground—between *over-reach* on the one hand, and a Trumpian *abdication* on the other, as if these are the only two alternatives. And in this void, countries with autocratic, illiberal leaderships are rushing forward. The ascension of autocratic leadership in counties such as Russia, China, Iran, Syria, Turkey, North Korea, the Philippines, and Saudi Arabia, coupled with the lack of a more enlightened, updated and proactive foreign policy by the U.S. government, is certainly not going to "make America great again," nor does it auger well for the world as a whole.

The U.S. is needing to initiate better conversations about our governmental *polarization itself,* if not the lack of moral leadership that has perpetuated it. For as FDR also once said, the presidency "is pre-eminently a place of moral leadership. All our great Presidents were leaders of thought at times when certain historic ideas in the life of the nation had to be clarified." (We're in such a time *today*). And FDR suggests that when those in power *lack* such moral leadership, *we must be willing to dissent.* In such times, he says, we must dissent from *apathy*—and from *fear, hatred,* and *mistrust.* In fact, the ripples of our dissent must widen further still…

"We must dissent from a nation that has buried its head in the sand, waiting in vain for the needs of its poor, its elderly, and its sick to disappear and just blow away. We must dissent from a government that has left its young without jobs, education or hope. We must dissent from the poverty of vision and the absence of moral leadership. We must dissent because America can do better, because America has no choice but to do better."

Unless reading the sentiments of a speechwriter from a teleprompter, it's pretty obvious that Donald Trump lacks this capacity for moral leadership. And rather than uniting the nation around the historic ideas upon which our democracy is based, he's further polarized the nation with a strategy of divide and conquer—by appealing to the minority of the country that is his base—for whom he can do no wrong, though wrong is nearly *all he has done, and likely will attempt.* (For in the words of Richard Hofstadter in his prescient 1964 essay "The Paranoid Style in American Politics" that seems to *anticipate* Trump, such a leader has—*almost unfailingly*—"a greater affinity for bad causes than good"). The polarization already existent in the country has thus been further intensified.

Yet if Trump's impact has been polarizing and *dark,* his *inner* polarization and "darkness" has a further nuance: Trump was born under a uniquely rare occurrence—a *lunar eclipse.* I'll let the meaning of this be explained by the renowned astrologer Ellias Lonsdale: *"He can't resist being* thrown into the Darkness. He has to play with it—and become it. And part of his dilemma is that in a secret, faintly illuminated corner of himself he actually doubts himself enormously. Beneath his cocky exterior, in his 'secret moon self' he feels he's not for real, and caught in his own shadow."

"Yet his sun—opposite to his moon—is actually quite visionary, and why his followers are inspired by him. To them he conveys an aura of authenticity. And though a compulsive liar, his paradoxical gift is that he is also candidly honest—in that he says what he really feels, at least in his tweets. For all his nuttiness, he's also 'right there' in the flesh. And the best-case scenario is that he will finally encounter a crisis that he can no longer talk his way out of—or blame on someone else. That he may do something so undeniably stupid that he might actually learn from it, and come to see how far off he has been."

Yet if Lonsdale's "best case scenario" currently seems increasingly unlikely, there may be another one. (Though it too, currently, seems rather unlikely). Namely, that the polarized nuttiness of the Trump regime—if not its legal infractions—will finally become so appallingly unsupportable that it will lead even his own party to jump from such a floundering ship; and that the nation itself might begin to be weaned from the recent, decades-long polarization that has gripped us.

For if "polarization" is the key word for the age of Trump, this polarization is similarly evidenced now by our various forms of media—whether the Fox News Channel or Breitbart News on the one hand, or CNN and MSNBC on the other. For our widely polarized *memes* have their own sources for the day's news—and they seldom access the other's news sources. (And in Trump's case, he not only gets much of his news from Fox and Breitbart, but he then gears his tweets to those informed by the same sensibility, such that this becomes a self-enclosed conceptual tape loop—one presenting not only an alternative news source, but "alternative facts," as well as an "alternative reality;" and in many cases, an alternative *to* reality). The result is that our two political parties, and the *memes* that they represent, have become somewhat like bickering spouses in a dysfunctional marriage, each with a radically different account of why our country isn't as great as it might be, and how this should be corrected.

When this is the case, the role of a President *should be* to act like a referee, initiating conversations that can help *unify* our nation, while blowing his whistle at each evidence of either party's infractions—as a skilled licensed marriage and family counselor might do. (But when a President is so polarized himself that he cannot perform this function, and when our sources of news have also become polarized around *meme* or party lines, we should at least have *websites* that track both these infractions, as well as when a political figure acts in a way that has become freed from such a contentious polarization). For freeing ourselves from that polarization is *urgently* in need of more support now—if not a Freedom medal—as that's the direction we're needing to head in order to emerge from our dysfunctional, political gridlock.

A good example of what such a website might support would be the stirring, eloquent rebuke to President Trump's attack upon journalists—and truth itself—that Republican Senator Jeff Flake delivered from the floor of the Senate on January 17, 2018. Future presidential historians will no doubt note Flake's words. And readers might as well by following this link: *https://www.cbsnews.com/news/ jeff-flake-full-transcript-speech-senate-floor- trump-sustained-attack-on-press/*

Another example would be the now deceased John McCain, when he dramatically dissented from his party's health care plan. Yet both were left standing somewhat alone, when a faithfulness to our democratic ideals cast them as traitors to their own party, which after all is the Grand Old Party of Abraham Lincoln—who led this nation through times similarly polarized as our own. Yet this is also a party grown estranged from its own noble and principled roots, and grafted now to its shrillest of voices, at times intellectually bankrupt and ill-informed, at others morally rudderless—while at its other extreme there's the Blue *meme's** theocratic, lunatic fringe.

And evidencing *all three,* out came Alabama's Republican nominee for Jeff Sessions' former Senate seat, Judge Roy Moore… Here was a twice-disbarred judge last seen toting a gun from his horse like a senile and Tonto-less version of the Lone Ranger; a crazed Old Testament judge rocking a cowboy hat and shades, while telling us that the sexual love of gays should be prosecuted as criminal acts, that no Muslim should be allowed elected

---

* Regarding this and all future mention of *memes,* see Beck, Don Edward and Cowan, Christopher C. *Spiral Dynamics: Mastering Values, Leadership and Change.* Malden: Blackwell Publishing, 2006. See also Ken Wilber's *Boomeritis: A Novel That Will Set You Free!* Boston: Shambhala, 2003

office in the United States, and that the senseless, appalling murder of the children of Sandy Hook was God's retribution for our collective immorality, and as if God's work is now being entrusted not to the empathically wise, but to gun-toting *psychotics;* or the *slightly* less delusional religious zealots.

For if the polarizing, fundamentalist mind-set of ISIS was conceptually grounded in the theocratic, god-fearing tribalism of the 7th century, then Judge Roy Moore is a legal throwback to *the Book of Leviticus.* In fact, he'd once worked with his tribe's Vice President (Pence) on a perplexing piece of theocratic legislation, the so-called *Constitution Restoration Act.* This was an act that would've charged Congress to fire judges who refused to acknowledge our laws are based on *the words of God;* and as if there's only *one* legit version of the latter. Yet the hypocrisy of such an allegedly moral man was soon exposed when numerous *Republican-voting women* from Moore's own hometown revealed Moore had attempted to date or have sex with them while they were still in their teens, and he the local district attorney. Rather appallingly—after some initial hemming and hawing—the Republican Party then closed ranks around him, not wanting to risk the loss of a Senate seat; which they wound up losing anyhow. (I keep *trying* not to appear polarized myself, but c'mon guys, what ever happened to the separation of church and state? And as for political candidates, *where's the quality control?*).

But Judge Roy Moore is just a remnant of a party-wide moral sell-out, and the visible tip of a deeper-looming judicial iceberg. For there's been an icy flood of similarly conservative judges ushered in by the Trump administration who would not only find favor with the Christian Right, but who are also quite *young,* and thus will be having a decades-long impact upon our judicial system. In fact, under the *uber*-polarized leadership of Senate Majority Leader McConnell, the Republican Party has been attempting an end run on our democracy, whereby they've been fairly successful at steering the ship of state to the right—*not* by winning the actual votes of citizens, nor by successful legislation—but rather, through the conservative, political slant of those they've appointed to our courts.

Similarly, the Trump administration's immigration policies, and the attempt at voter suppression of minorities has been part of a calculated effort to restrict voters unlikely to side with Republicans. These degradations to our democracy are made possible when Republican legislators remain pervasively derelict in their oversight duties, by turning a blind eye to a misguided and corrupt president steering the ship of state on an ever more perilous course.

And if America has been recently losing its democratic bearings, perhaps we might remember that this nation traces its inception not from *scripture* nor the wishes of the rich, but from the dissent of its great, revolutionary forefathers, and the founding documents they left to guide us. We shouldn't forget them—and their moral courage—for if their revolution failed, each of them would have been hung. Nor should we forget that the capacity for dissent is thus a foundational part of our democracy. But so is the capacity to initiate, and then persevere in the conversations we are needing to have—so that these conversations can finally lead to a higher order resolution, and not just persist as unresolvable schisms dividing our nation—as has been the case with health care for over a half century now.

The inability to initiate such conversations is not just a *historical* and *political* problem. When we drill down a bit, this inability also has its more *mythic* and *psychological* roots. For the inability to initiate conversations *is the very problem of Echo*—a problem along with narcissism itself—that humanity has been suffering, not only now and for the past several decades, but for *thousands* of years.

And since *hubris*, like Trump, lacks a knowledge of history, and since "taking a history" is often the first step in healing processes, the sprawl of this book will in part approximate a history of narcissism itself, and how it has been viewed—and how various traditions have attempted to counter it—over the past two millennia.

My hope in writing the volume currently in your hands is to provide and *provoke* an altered perspective toward narcissism, and toward the themes (and *memes*) of this book. A perspective provided from the intersection of four avenues of vision: *mythic, psychological, spiritual,* and *historical*—rather than any one of the four. For each of the four have their own nuanced insights to offer, their own apprehensions of "reality." But each on their own can't help but provide a partial, inadequate witness, like blind people attempting to account for an elephant.

Yet for thousands of years we've been left artifacts—strange artifacts that occur at, and speak to, this intersection between the mythic, psychological, spiritual, and historical. We call these artifacts "poems." And we might profit from the breadth of the panoramic vision of those who have written them, as we explore this book's varied topics. For poets are the leading scientists of metaphor; expert witnesses of the right side of the brain. They are aboriginals, our culture's lost tribe of Zion. (And even in his own field, Freud told us that poets got there first). We have needed their continuous testimony, and in places I'll attempt to provide a little of that…

In sum, this book will evoke a sighting, a reflection, a re-visioning of our times…against the backdrop of a parallel and extended re-visioning of narcissism itself. It will mirror a widely prevailing dissociation—in our approach to *psychology, mythology, and religion*—and to *politics, love,* and *being* itself. It will be an ongoing contemplation about America, evoking its dominant *memes* and their polarizations; and the relationship between what's walking in the doors of its psychotherapy offices, and what's appearing on the news.

It will bear witness to the varied elements of a shared cultural history—those which have bewildered, and those which might lead us from our bewilderment. As mentioned, my intention is to do this in a way approachable for an intelligent lay audience, without dumbing things down, or straying far from the thematic emphasis upon *transformation*—a transformational awareness that is available *in every moment*—yet one our world is so badly lacking today.

May Day, 2020
Richmond, CA

I.
OF *Meme* WARFARE & MYTH
& MUCH ADO ABOUT NOTHING

ONE

Ghosts

AFTER SUCH A lengthy prologue, a little brevity might be welcome now. And since we'll be re-visioning American politics amongst other things, let's talk about ghosts…

Part of what's weird about America are the ghosts in its two-party-political-system. For is it not hauntingly *strange,* that no matter how horrifically and obviously flawed one party's candidate for president may be, at least 40% of the population will support him or her? (And at least 40% will oppose).

Elections thus, are not usually decided by the 40% with no eye for character who may be easily duped, nor by the 80 to 90 percent of the population already holding strong opinions on the candidates, but by the decisions made by the not previously committed, those hovering over the middle of the road, and still making up their minds. These are not quick-minded people, apparently.

They're not reading *The Atlantic,* clutching the *New York Times,* or watching CNN. Nor are they watching Fox News on a nightly basis. They're not raving MAGA, nor holding up placards that say *IMPEACH.*

Who are they?

No one in particular comes to mind. They're more faceless, and harder to recognize, or to conclusively predict which way they'll go. (Though pollsters try, often in vain). They're the *ghosts of democracy,* the wild cards in our electoral deck.

Election night in America is thus a little like Halloween, the holiday that always precedes it. Are we about to *tricked*—or treated for the next few years? For however wise or naively gullible, the fate of America's near-term political future is always placed in their impalpable hands.

May the Force be with them…

TWO

The Obvious Target & the Deeper Work

Such a large, grotesque, and obvious target as Donald Trump is easy enough to take pot-shots at. And so many have *already*, that I don't want him to take up too much of this book. Though from time to time, I have—and will continue—to find him useful in certain ways.

For what's truly significant about Trump is not the horrifically flawed man himself, but the deeper issues he raised for the culture that spawned him, the minority that elected him, and the majority who wished *he'd simply go away*. In this, he reminds me of a Gurdjieff story…

There was once a particularly repugnant man in a group that Gurdjieff was leading. Most found him hard to bear, wanted him to disappear—and had told the man as much. But when Gurdjieff saw the guy with suitcase in hand, leaving the premises—Gurdjieff ran after him, and insisted that he *stay*, even offering to pay him.

Gurdjieff's reasoning was that since the guy triggered almost everybody's issues, such a shit-stirrer was eminently useful for the group. For his abrasive "chief feature" was actually bringing to light the very issues that the group—both individually, and as a whole—were needing to work with and resolve.

In much the same way, Trump had brought a dark sort of light to all the issues that his country was needing to better address. His mocking disregard of all who disagreed with him, and his me-first/America-first orientation highlighted the importance of *collaboration*—with our allies abroad, and a healthier bi-partisanship at home. His denial of the problem was actually bringing a more urgent recognition of climate-change and greenhouse gases, and the need to better fund scientific research, and effect policies to deal with it, before it's irrevocably too late.

He was showing us the importance of core values by his very *lack* of them—the importance of truth, empathy, objectivity, and other essential facets of the soul. In this, he was an outsized mirror to our own collective narcissism (that obscures these facets). And Trump's mixture of obliviousness and disdain for our Constitution, led us to better recognize its importance, just as it fostered a deeper respect for the remarkable men who were the founders of our democracy—men, in many ways (slave-owning aside) *so different* from him. In fact, the very democratic institutions and structures left by the founding fathers—that Trump had been trying to undo—were actually showing us *what must be preserved*.

Trump, and the party he had come to lead, were intensifying our awareness of the importance of country over party, and the paralyzing impact of the political polarization that had increasingly gripped the nation for its past quarter century. They were showing us the need to address the role of money in our political system, the need to stand up to the disproportional influence of the gun, petroleum, and insurance lobbies, the need for health-care as a right of citizenship, the need to uproot racial, gender, and economic inequalities, the need to address gerrymandering, uphold voting rights for all citizens, and address the increasing politicization of our courts.

And as this book goes to press, the way the COVID-19 pandemic had been politicized not only polarized us at the moment we most needed to be unified, but had been nearly as inimical to the nation's public health as the virus itself. For it paralyzed the kind of coherent, disciplined, science-based leadership that other nation's—like South Korea, New Zealand, and Germany—had successfully followed. And Trump's impatience to "open the country up" before hardly any state had met the criteria his own science advisors had advocated, were predicted to cause as many more deaths as his weeks of negligent inaction caused at the pandemic's start.

In fact, Trump had been so *predictably* on the *wrong* side of history, the wrong side of what a democracy should foster, the wrong side of our most pressing issues, the *anti*-exemplar of true leadership, that he'd actually helped outline what right action *should* look like. (The Sufis have a saying for people like this: *Learn to behave from one who does not*).

In this light, we might read the MAGA placards held up at Trump rallies in a similarly useful—though ass-backwards way. For amidst all the chaos, Trump *really had* brought America to something great again. It's a great *question*, really. Yet a very simple one...

It's the great, simple question 40% of the American electorate had largely failed to consider. And as his presidency passed its 1000th day, a question that Trump's party leaders had been unwilling to answer: *Should the nation continue to be founded on the rule of law—or not?*

> As he left 1787's Constitutional Convention, Franklin was asked: "What have you given us, Mr. Franklin?"
> Ben replied: "A republic—if you can keep it!"

Though no individual can be blamed for a nation's polarization, it *can* become more divisively extreme when a party can win the White House, and control the senate, without having to appeal to a base that more truly reflects the American people as a whole.

And if it continues to retreat from its more centrist and moderate roots, polarization can become truly *toxic*, if that party grafts all remaining roots to the dictates of an increasingly obvious, authoritarian leader. One who *can do no wrong*. For the polarization can then present a *constitutional crisis*—when its Attorney General takes *that* now as a governing *fact*. And even tries to cloak it in the eviscerated tatters his party makes of the constitution.

And you know justice itself is partially on trial, and winding toward a bad conclusion, when a once respected constitutional scholar is trotted out to explain away both *criminal behavior*, and criminal *intent*—by a president who's amply, and repeatedly, demonstrated both. But Professor Dershowitz—like the man his hired legal gun is defending now—is not concerned with *facts*, or here to argue them (for the facts would not be helpful to his case). Instead, he's here to argue a legal abstraction.

Which is—as he explains for Republican senators badly in need of a rationalizing defense—that *anything* a president might do to become elected, if the president sees it in the public interest, can then *not* be an *abuse of power*, and hence, not subject to *impeachment*.

By this sophistic, intellectual vanishing act—in which intelligence itself vanishes—the bar is now set so low, that any moral clarity becomes insensible—if not inadmissible. For also to be inadmissible now is not only criminal *intent*, but *witnesses* and *documentary evidence*. And this—in the most historically important *trial* of our day.

Before our eyes and ears what else is vanishing now is an American *republic*. What's emerging instead is at once pre-and post-American: *a divine right of presidents*, as if the American Revolution never occurred. With the GOP devolved into an amoral cult, and the nation edging closer to a totalitarian state.

You pinch yourself, and say this must be a *dream, it couldn't happen here*. But that's what people have always felt and said when they wake up (not *from*) but *to* a real nightmare. That still could get worse...

The Republican party will one day have to own the Devil's Bargain it made with Trump. And retribution *will* come. History will judge it like the conservative, authoritarian Vichy regime that ruled France for four years, had teamed up with the Nazis, reviled and censored the press, scapegoated minorities, made abortion a capital offense, and oversaw mass deportations in which children were parted from their families.

In the eschatological mythology of one of the world's large religious groups, it is said that an anti-Christ will appear in the Last Days who must be defeated by the true Christ, who in the Last Days will come back from the dead. (Here, I'm not comparing Trump to an anti-Christ; there's no need to demonize, nor confer him with such stature).

I make this mythic reference only because if Trump is allowed to rule another four years, we really *could be* hastening the Last Days of sustainable life on our planet, and the Last Days of the American republic—at least as we've known them.

Yet even if Trump is subsequently held accountable for crimes, bested in 2020's election, or last seen carrying a suitcase (or his golf clubs) as he departs from the White House, the challenges he's raised for us as a culture will still be there for us, long after he's gone.

For the only thing *truly* on trial in his verdict by the senate was the integrity of his party's leadership. And it will either be found guilty in the court of public opinion—i.e., the 2020 elections—or the nation risks still darker days ahead.

As for now, a dark pallor already lies over the land, as do the lies spread by the old King. His tanning lights won't lift either. *We've got some work to do.*

THREE

The Roots of Polarization
& the Fate of a Species

SOME HAVE TRACED the current, "scorched earth" political polarization in the U.S. back to the Democrats' successful attempt to block Robert Bork's nomination to the Supreme Court in 1987. This enraged a junior senator from Kentucky—Mitch McConnell—who vowed never to let such a thing ever happen again. And he's been remarkably successful in keeping his vow, while ratcheting it up even further.

"The nomination changed everything, maybe forever," says Tom Goldstein, publisher of the popular SCOTUS blog, which extensively covers the Supreme Court. "Republicans nominated this brilliant guy to move the law in this dramatically more conservative direction. Liberal groups turned around and blocked him precisely because of those views. Their fight legitimized scorched-earth ideological wars over nominations at the Supreme Court, and to this day both sides remain completely convinced they were right."

Clearly, there's any number of ways to become polarized—say along issues of race, religion, or gender. And we have some statistics on this—those provided by Jonathan Haidt, a social psychologist whose main area of study has been the psychology of morality.

In researching the main areas of polarization in American culture, he found there was a 6 point polarization when it came to *gender*, 7 points of polarization regarding *religion*, 10 points regarding *economic class*, 11 points with *educational level*, and 12 points with *race*. But these all paled when it came to *politics*, which garnered 18 points of polarization on his (20 point) scale. And if the figures are dated, it's likely gotten *worse*.

In a 2008 Ted talk, in trying to tease out the moral roots separating *liberals* and *conservatives*, Haidt isolated 5 criteria drawn from his extensive research into anthropology, cultural variation, morality, and evolutionary psychology. These 5 were held in common across disciplines. He termed these 5 criteria "the foundations of morality."

The first of the 5 was *harm/care*. (We're all warm-blooded mammals, and have strong feelings about those who express caring vs. those who cause harm). The second foundation is *fairness/reciprocity*. (This too is somewhat universal, "the Golden Rule," *do onto others what you'd have them do onto you*; the foundation of many religions).

The third foundation is *in-group loyalty*. (Even animals form cooperative groups, but these groups are small, or only among siblings). It is only among humans that you find large groups who cooperate—but these groups are united to *fight other groups*; a likely outcome from our long history of tribal living, our tribal psychology. And this tribal psychology can feel very satisfying. We're no longer so alone, and can unite with others who share common values, fears, and aspirations.

The fourth foundation is (deference to, or) *respect for authority* (which is fairly self-explanatory). And the fifth foundation is *purity/sanctity*. (Any kind of sacrosanct ideology that tells that you can attain virtue by what you believe or do).

What's pertinent here is that when Haidt conducted research polls about these five criteria, he found that though both liberals and conservatives considered harm/fairness to be important, liberals scored higher here. While liberals scored notably lower than conservatives when it came to valuing *in-group loyalty, deference toward authority, and purity/sanctity*. (Liberals were basically reflecting that *they don't believe these traits are* the basis of morality). But as people become more conservative, the importance of the latter three criteria increases.

So you could say that liberals have a "two-channel" sense of morality, while conservatives have a "five-channel" sense of morality. And this breakdown has proved valid in every country Haidt studied. And this, Haidt found, brings us to the crux of the polarization between liberals and conservatives.

For liberals *reject* 3 of the foundations. They're saying, "Let's celebrate diversity, not common in-group membership," and "Let's question authority," and "Keep your laws off my body." They want change and justice ("even at the risk of chaos"). Liberals also tend to highly value a particular trait: Open-ness to experience. People who score highly on this trait like novelty, variety, travel, diversity, different cuisines, new ideas. People low on this trait like things that are familiar, safe and dependable. The main researcher of the trait of open-ness, Robert McCrae, says: "Open individuals have an affinity for liberal, progressive, left-wing political views…They like a society which is open and changing…whereas closed individuals prefer conservative, right-wing views."

Conservatives have also tended to favor institutions and traditions. Historically, they've wanted law and order, even at some cost to those at the bottom of the social structure. Plus, they recognize that order is actually hard to achieve, and easily lost.

At this point in his Ted Talk, Haidt makes a shift in vantage. He says that liberals and conservatives are *both* right, each have something to contribute, and together they form a balance on change vs. stability. And when we realize *that*, we're less prone to polarizing around the issues that each finds important. And as he points out, this understanding also lies at the heart of Asian religions.

Yin and Yang for example, aren't enemies. Both are necessary, like night and day. He likens the conservative perspective to the Hindu god Vishnu, the preserver. (Yet according to Hindu religious scriptures, Vishnu is in the heart of Shiva, the destroyer, just as Shiva is in the heart of Vishnu). They are manifestations of the same universal force that creates, sustains, and destroys all life. These seeming opposites *complete each other*. Each one is vital, and you can't have one without the other.

As another example, he offers a few lines from the earliest existent Zen document—Sengstan's *Verses on the Faith-Mind*, which I'll offer in Richard B. Clarke's elegant translation: "If you want to see the truth/ then hold no opinions for or against anything./ To set up what you like against what you dislike/ is the disease of the mind."

Haidt concludes his Ted talk by saying that when you take the great insights from Asian philosophies and religions, and combine them with moral psychology, that you come to these conclusions: That our righteous minds were designed by evolution to unite us into teams, to divide us against other teams, that then blind us to the truth.

Yet he isn't telling us to totally side with Sengstan. Nor is he advising that we cease fighting against wrongs—but instead a mixture of both. And if you want to change other people, first understand that we all think we're right, and even when you disagree with others, understand that they have some reason for doing, or believing what they do. Here, he suggests we check in with Sengstan—if for just a moment.

This is a move that Haidt terms "moral humility," a move that can protect us from the self-righteous polarizations that are, at least at present, the normal human condition; a condition grown dissociated—or yet to embody—the unifying, nondual perspective at the heart of Asian religions.

Though Haidt's given others, this Ted talk is from 2008. Since then, some of the best thinking about polarization, and the evolutionary challenges we're facing, come from Ken Wilber. Wilber, who's off the charts smart, and has read everything and everyone, Haidt included—tells us Haidt left out some important determinative factors. He also provides wider historical backdrop for our current polarization.

Wilber points out* that two or three hundred years ago, the most determinative political variables were *religion* and *power*. Those of the dominant religion held the most power. And we had ruling monarchies atop the social structure, followed in descending order by the rest of the aristocracy, a priest-hood, indentured servants, and slaves.

But with the Western Enlightenment, some entirely new elements start to emerge. There's a sudden increase in formal operational cognition—or "reason." And it gave birth to all our modern forms of science. This, in fact, became known as *The Age of Reason*.

As this kind of cognition developed, it effected a change in the way people began to regard themselves and each other. Now individuals begin to have greater agency. Correspondingly, monarchies began to decline, and democracies rose up. And along with democracies, there also arose the notion of a more universal morality—the Universal Rights of Man—rights that were now to be conferred upon all human beings, including those of other religions, women, servants, and slaves.

---

* In this sub-chapter I extrapolate from a series of podcasts on Wilber's website. If you have 2 hours of bandwidth, they're well worth listening to, and can found at *http://integrallife.com/the-four-quadrants-a-guided-tour/*

During the 18th and 19th centuries almost all Western countries had abolished slavery. Till then, not a single religion had formally objected to slavery. (Saint Paul to slaves: *Obey your master, and love Jesus*).

And this was not only an age of reason, but an age of revolution. The motto "*Liberté, Egalité, Fraternité*" first appeared during the French Revolution, 13 years after the American, and captures some of this newly emerging sensibility. (And as for kings, chop off their heads! In fact, during the Reign of Terror accompanying the French Revolution 17,000 were guillotined—a brutality of the left, that Wilber doesn't mention here, but soon will amplify).

What also is emerging now is the Orange *meme*, a developmental *stage* that is less ethno-centric. And with this, Wilber tells us, *the liberal political orientation is born*.

This is when we first have the political use of the terms "left " and "right," as these referred to where people were seated in the French Parliament in the 18th century. (Those who supported the monarchy sat on the right side of the aisle; if you supported the new wave starting to roll in—revolution and democracy—you sat on the left).

These became, and largely have remained, the two dominant political orientations. (Whigs, Liberals, Democrats on the left side of the aisle, all on guard against executive tyranny or royal prerogatives; and Tories, Conservatives, Republicans on the opposing side. Importantly, they were driven by two dominant levels of development; one, ethno-centric and mythic (conservatives)—the other, rational and more world-centric.

Wilber's view is that everybody is born at ego-centric, and will move to ethno-centric. Further evolution would lead to world-centric, and potentially to cosmo-centric, or what Wilber terms "integral."

Though Wilber makes use of Haidt's five foundations of morality, they also conceal t/his notion of *developmental stages*. And Wilber also points out that the conservative emphasis on authority, group loyalty, and purity/sanctity are all central to the *pre-rational, pre-Enlightenment world-view*. And that's what can remain hidden when Haidt reflects conservatives as possessing all 5 of the moral foundations. In other words, having 5 channels—rather than 2—doesn't make right-wingers morally superior, or more evolved than left-wingers (Though the self-righteous of either persuasion may take such a stance, and in fact, often do).

The ethno-centric aspect of conservatives *does* tend to be more racist, nationalistic, and sexist. (I'd also point out that its pre-rational, pre-Enlightenment view is also *pre-scientific*; hence the right wing's obliviousness to climate change. And today, rather than supporting a monarchy or an aristocracy, they continue to support the rich). They can also be more militaristic, jingoist, and authoritarian. And so, it's common for conservatives to say that the reason one group of people doesn't have enough is because they're lazy, and lack a work ethic. Or they don't belong here in the first place. And either way, if they don't have enough, it's their own fault.

While liberals tend to think more about what's right for all people—"world-centric" in this sense. And liberals can be one-sided and polarized in the opposite way. For they can say it's all society's fault if you don't have enough. It's because you've been oppressed, a victim. (The conservative critique reflects people's *interiors*; the liberal critique reflects *exteriors*). And it would be a narrowing of awareness to deny the reality and importance of both dimensions. For as Sengstan says elsewhere in his *Verses on the Faith-Mind*: "Deny the reality of things and you miss their reality;"

In terms of developmental stages, if the Age of Reason gave rise to the Orange *meme*, the 1960s also gave rise to a new *meme*: the Green. In 1959 it is thought that only 3% of Americans had this world-view. Today it is thought that between 20 and 25% of Americans are Green.

This is a pluralistic *meme*. (Clare Graves, Spiral Dynamics' founder, calls it a "relativistic" *meme*; a conservative client of mine calls them "tree huggers"). Green brought in multiculturalism, a postmodern relativism; and a meta-systemic approach that was able to differentiate a tremendous spectrum of variance between different cultures—yet, as Wilber has been pointing out for decades, Green didn't have the power to integrate what it had seen.

What Orange had brought in and meant by "equality"—the *Egalité* in the French revolutionary motto—was *equal opportunity*. But Green picked up that ball and ran with it—*right out of the park*. For what Green wanted was *equal outcome* for all—which is more problematic. Every child should get a trophy just for showing up. You shouldn't give one only to the winner of the race, because then each child is not being treated "equally." In pushing for its version of equality, Green is willing to give up free speech, say to speakers on college campuses, who are prevented from speaking if what they'd say might offend someone in the audience.

And perhaps minority groups should be guaranteed stipends to make up for the ways they've been victimized in the past. The national debt could skyrocket—as it had from the recent Republican legislation to favor corporations and the very rich. Yet the Green would offer an easy solution here. Since it wouldn't be very sensitive to chop off people's heads, we could at least soak the rich with a wealth tax, for it certainly isn't *fair* that a very tiny part of the population has wound up with so much of the world's wealth. (I'm not taking sides here, just saying).

Yet with only 20 to 25% of the population currently Green, even proposing such "progressive" platforms could swing national elections to the right. And so, this kind of "equality," this kind of *equal outcome* would sound crazy to the Orange *meme*. Or at least, not pragmatic.

Yet approximately a half of America's Democratic party has gone Green—its "progressive" wing—while the other half has remained grounded in the original liberal view of the Enlightenment. And thus, the political polarization we're suffering now is not just between liberals and conservatives, Democrats and Republicans; *there are schisms within each party*. (Polarization to the 2nd power!). For Republicans are also divided between those who are Orange, and those more ethno-centric, nationalistic ("America first") and now promoting a pre-rational, pre-scientific world view, and siding with what amounts to the divine right of kings.

Orange Republicans are more rational, post-Enlightenment thinkers capable of sophisticated arguing vs. doctrinal (*purity/sanctity*) polemic. Being of the same *meme*, they're not much different than traditional Democrats. Those who are politicians, sadly, have recently been cowed by a toxically enforced in-group loyalty, and obedience to dictatorial authority. (And why only 1 Republican senator voted in favor of allowing witnesses to testify in Trump's impeachment trial).

Though in polarized times it can be harder to do, Wilber makes an important point when tells us we need to be able to *recognize* it when either liberals or conservatives have gone off the rails. For when that happens the outcomes can be truly *toxic*. (Which is also why—Sengstan aside—I continually hold up an unflattering mirror to Donald Trump).

Within the past century we have already seen what can happen when conservatism's ethno-centricity, in-group loyalty, and deference to authority goes too far. It gave rise to Hitler, and the murder of approximately 7 million (gypsies, gays, and the disabled)—plus 6 million Jews. That's 13 million politically "inspired" murders. Yet following that mass regression into psychosis, Wilber reminds us that there was a significant event—the Nuremberg trials, for "crimes committed against humanity." There was a "world-centric" public reckoning. And those found guilty were hung.

And that reckoning for the Holocaust had served like an inoculation in the West, against such a thing *ever* happening again. But "ever" has become time-sensitive. And the immunizing effect of the Hitler antibody is waning. We've entered a new age; autocracies are again on the rise.

But it's not just right wing fascists who can regress into bestial genocide. (Stalin murdered an estimated 66 million, and starved to death 13 million Ukrainians alone. Mao killed an estimated 100 million. Yet these far-leftist autocrats were never tried for their crimes).

So Wilber wants us to be able to recognize it when *either* side goes beyond the pale. And he says we can recognize a tipping point for conservatives when there's an *absolutism of differences*, an ethnocentricity that promotes divisiveness or any kind of superiority amongst races or gender, such that you are not just proud of your own, but demonizing others. While the left can go too far when its extremism so exaggerates equality, that it forcefully tries to *do away with all differences*.

The Khmer Rouge, for example, killed anyone with an education. No one was allowed to be superior. There was an "absolutism of same-ness." And each Cambodian was to have an equal outcome—yet for many, that outcome was death (There are differences—if only in severity—between giving trophies to every child in a race, and *killing the winners*).

In my own mind, sometimes it seems the fate of our world is also in a race now—between a certain percentage of the world population evolving into the less-polarized perspective of 2nd tier *meme*-hood—and our planet becoming unlivable. (And if the latter happens first, *none* of us, and none of our descendants, get trophies).

Wilber says the needed tipping point of a new evolutionary paradigm *taking hold* would be 10 percent. Getting there may be do-able, if barely, within the 11 years or so that climate change scientists tell us we have, before we reach a point of no return. For ocean acidification driven by CO_2 spikes are increasing now by 5% each decade, and already threaten a quarter of all marine life.

We've also been facing the threat of global epidemics. The flu of 1918 infected between a fifth and a third of the world population, and killed 50 million. The AIDs epidemic has killed approximately 32 million, with another 38 million currently living with it. Now there's COVID-19.

Like climate change, viruses are no respecters of national boundaries. A mutation in a single gene in a single person in a single country can threaten not only *that* person or that *country*—but the entire world. (And when hundreds of millions lack adequate healthcare, it threatens us *all*).

Sadly, this is late to dawn in those still operating from a pre-scientific, ego-centric, or ethno-centric perspective. And that risk factor is intensified when those *leading us* have yet to evolve to a more world-centric or globally-centric perspective.

But just as global virus-spread is part of our equation, rapid *developmental* shifts are also more possible now. (Green grew from 3% in 1959 to between 20 and 25% of the U.S. population today). That rate-jump took less than 60 years—and occurred without the heightened necessity we have now.

Gurdjieff used to say that nothing increases the rate of development as much as *an increased necessity*. (Which may the lurking *blessing in disguise* of polarized times, or dire situations; a kind of wake-up call). And at times, he'd bring his students into war zones, to create a little…

But the political and cultural warfare raging in the U.S. today won't require anyone having to go elsewhere to feel a scary edge threatening our very foundations—moral and otherwise. That urgent sense of necessity may be both catalyst and force-multiplier for our evolution now—morally, politically, scientifically, spiritually, and in every other way.

For our political races now occur against the backdrop of other races. The human race itself is in a race now—against humanity-threatening pandemics; and the mass extinction of species (caused by CO_2 spikes) that've already occurred 5 times in our planet's history. And at this very moment, an invisible clock ticks ever closer to a deadly midnight. If that can't move the 5 and 2 channeled tribes to evolve past an inborn polarization trait (by uniting against ultimate threats to them both) then, we truly are fucked.

FOUR

Reporting the News

> It is difficult
> to get the news from poems
> yet men die miserably every day
> for lack
> of what is found there.
> —William Carlos Williams

ONE OF THE reflections from Spiral Dynamics' developmental model is that all of the world's *memes* have something of value to offer the wider "Spiral." Yet SD's extensive research (culled from first, second, and third world countries) tells us something that *should be* rather humbling: That 98.9% of those currently on our planet are operating from an assumption that their *meme* possesses the sole perspective that is most truly correct; *and thus needs to be promoted or defended.*

The polarizations of "*meme* warfare" are often the result. And this polarization seems much in evidence in the stories being reported of late, and also the ways they are *being* reported.

Here I could set the teeth of the more liberal Green *meme* on edge, by saying that the Trump administration had been quite correct—about *anything*—let alone correct in recognizing that the bulk of our mainstream media *had been* decidedly one-sided in its opposition of Trump. Even if that had been due to multiply good reasons.

Trump's chaotic administration, and a lesser form of conservatism had managed to co-opt conservative thinking itself, and as if the arrogant, yet urbane and literate intelligence of William F. Buckley, or the back-boned jovial "goodness" of Ronald Reagan had begun to seem like the "good old days." Under stress, *memes* can *regress*. Whether on Capitol Hill, in the opioid addictions of the Rust Belt, or Tehran.

In retrospect, Trump had led a formerly Blue *meme* party (with its established rules that conserve orthodoxy, and its values of discipline, duty and honor) to *regress* into the more primitive, shadow side of the Red *meme* (the impulsive lawlessness of gangs, tribal raids, and warlords; a dog eat dog world where each "dog" in the pack looks out for itself—by deferring to the alpha dog, *whatever the cost*).

Yet if conservatives of late seem a stressed breed, there seems something innately valuable about "conservatism" itself—even though it can lose its bearings, and forget what it is *that truly needs to be conserved*—say the importance of country over party, or freedom itself (when it gets moralistic and thinks to legislate social prohibitions that restrict the liberty of others).

Conservatism would look back to the past for how human beings should conduct themselves today. In Tehran we can see this in a Supreme Leader wearing the garb, and attempting to conserve the tribal religiosity of a long distant century—while inflicting it upon everyone else, even hip, tech-savvy young people with 21st century smartphones.

In Washington, this *might* retain the traditional, and long-held conservative impulse toward "fiscal responsibility," and minimizing the national debt through minimizing the role of government itself. (Which would be a more coherent and believable principle if the impulse to cut spending wasn't only attempted in programs fostered by Democrats—such as Obamacare—while the recent Republican legislation to lower the taxes for corporations and the very rich has actually *increased* the national debt.

Conservatism *needn't* be centered in policies like the mass deportations of those with dark skin, banning those from Muslim countries, attempts at voter suppression in elections, or claiming the legislative right over women's bodies by refusing abortions to women who want them.

Yet when such policies *are* the case, here's what a great poet reminds us. Rilke says: "What we choose to fight is so tiny! And even "when we win it's with small things, and the triumph itself makes us small." Rilke's perspective on "winning" would be an antidote to a president who'd seen winning as the ultimate good—regardless of whether the *cause* was good; a winning that would serve as compensation for an underlying emptiness that had seemed un-fillable, a winning that made Trump and his followers small, and certainly had *not* made America great again. And so, the wisest rejoinder to Trump's "make America great again," was provided long ago by Samuel Johnson: *"No people can be great who have ceased to be virtuous."*

Trump hadn't been entirely wrong, though, about the loss in America of something great. He'd merely been deluded about what's been lost, in fact fact he'd been *symptomatic* of it. For as Steven Brill* tells us, American *core values* have been hijacked.

There's been a loss of the social and economic upward mobility that had always been a central feature of the American experiment of democracy. There's also been the horrific loss of a once healthier bi-partisanship. With the result being that Washington had become paralyzed—and except in dire emergencies—unable to get much done.

As with the Internet, there's been something lost with a *monetization*—of democracy itself; and the growing inability of people without wealth to have anything like an equal voice. Similarly, there's been a gerrymandering of population centers, and growing inequities of the Electoral College (contributing to the fact that our last two Republican presidents have been elected while failing to win the popular vote). And with its *Citizens United* decision, an increasingly conservative Supreme Court had interpreted the First Amendment in such a way that corporations have begun to have an undue impact on politics, further degrading democracy.

There's also been a loss of governmental funding for scientific research—the very kind of funding which once *produced* the Internet (as well as penicillin). And a loss of funding for the education of the poorer parts of our population, and at a time while their healthcare had also been under threat. And with Trump in the White House, the rule of law itself had been under threat.

Along with this erosion of core values, our infrastructure had been eroding, with many of our bridges on their last legs. Yet with congress preoccupied with two year elections cycles, few had taken the long view, or gained support for the tax increases needed for infrastructure spending; much less agreement for which part of the population should pay for it.

A conclusion that many social critics have thus begun to make is that the solutions to our problems will not come from the elected officials at the top of our social order—*whether Democrats or Republicans*—that the

---

* Brill, Steven. *Tailspin: The People and Forces Behind America's Fifty-Year-Fall-and Those Fighting to Reverse It.* New York: Knopf, 2018

needed and missing perspective will now need to come from "the bottom up." (And in *that* sense, hopefully, this is a "bottom up" kind of book).

If America has been like a river that contains two tributaries, one clear-running and the other polluted and foul, then the clear-running part—which for much of its history had also inspired the rest of the world—stemmed from the remarkable men who were our founding fathers.

And here we might re-vision a warning that George Washington provided to his then fledgling nation. For the current political state of our culture suffers not only from a loss of core values, but from a loss of *historical literacy*—in failing (amongst other failings) to take adequate heed of something Washington warned us about, at the very end of his presidency.

In his Farewell Address to the American people, Washington presciently warned against political factions—and against *political parties themselves*. For these factions, he predicted, may seek to obstruct the execution of the laws created by the government, or to prevent the branches of government from enacting the powers provided them by the constitution. (*Precisely what Trump has attempted*). And though these factions may claim to be trying to answer popular demands or solve pressing problems, Washington saw their true intentions as being *to take the power from the people, and place it in the hands of unjust men*. (The italics here, and in the next two paragraphs are mine).

In this light, he argued against political parties because he felt that disagreements between political parties *weakened the functioning of government itself*. Moreover, he made the case that "the alternate domination" of one party over another and coinciding efforts to exact revenge upon their opponents have led to horrible atrocities, and "is itself a frightful despotism…that leads at length to a more formal despotism." For political parties eventually and "gradually incline the minds of men to seek security… in the absolute power of an individual."

And though Washington found that political parties at times have promoted liberties, this generally was only in *monarchies,* while he felt they needed to be *restrained* in popularly elected governments.

Washington's warning about political parties notwithstanding, their rise and the degree of their polarization in the second decade of the 21st century may have been beyond what the Founders could have foreseen when they attempted to provide in the constitution a means for removing corrupt or despotic federally elected officials from office.

Their term "high crimes and misdemeanors" which had been borrowed from English law, had always been a little vague, and wouldn't necessarily require a "crime" in the customary legal sense. It was understood broadly in terms that might include "gross negligence," or "an abuse of the public trust of one's office." The emoluments clauses—foreign and domestic—were more easily determinable.

In sum, the Founders might have been a little surprised at how *rarely* their instrument of impeachment would ever be employed. (Trump's only the 4th president to have faced formal impeachment inquiries, the third to be actually impeached—yet he's the first in U.S. history where a president's own party controlled the Senate).

And the Founders might have been more than a little surprised that a future president would one day proclaim he could shoot someone on 5th Avenue in New York, and would never be held accountable. And likely, they'd have been *horrified*, to learn that this president's Justice Department would follow a self-created edict declaring it unlawful to even investigate a president's wrong-doings. For it's fairly certain, that the Founders never intended the governmental figure *most capable of doing damage to the country to also be the person most protected from being removed from office.*

By requiring a 2/3s vote in the Senate to remove a president from office, the Founders had intended this to be a heavy lift—but not so heavy that no future president ever *would* be removed by the instrument they'd felt we might need one day.

Democracy itself is a heavy lift. And in the up-lifted freshness of the Founders' revolutionary spirit, they might've been stunned at just how hard it would one day prove to be; and at the unholy union between polarization and naiveté that would one day grip the nation—and the lawless progeny it could give birth to.

Which brings us to Donald J. Trump, and the political schisms dividing our nation. For both are everything the father of our nation tried to warn us against. And when our fathers are wise, we become unruly children when we fail to adequately listen to them.

Like a young child who wants all the toys for himself, and doesn't play well with others, narcissism itself is polarizing; as the inception of a separate self first begins to emerge in a developmental spectrum that *should* further progress: from ego-centric to ethno-centric to world-centric; leading ultimately to a radical, transformational jump into "2nd tier," the non-polarized perspective of "cosmo-centric."(Similar developmental models have portrayed the progression as: from impulsive to conformist to autonomous. Or: from pre-personal to personal to transpersonal).

In this light, we might view the current political polarization in the U.S. not only as a war of *memes*, but equally, as a case of *arrested development*. Though we're a "developed country," that development mostly applies to external things. As a culture, the vast majority (98.9%) have yet to progress to the non-polarized world-view of "2nd tier *memes*."

Though this developmental impasse, and the resulting polarizations of "tribal politics" are shared world-wide, it's become increasingly visible in the U.S. when you've had the leader of the nation operating from an *ego-centric* and *impulsive* schema—one that is also authoritarian; and his followers stuck at conformist and ethnocentrically "tribal." (Haidt's "in-group loyalty" and "deference to authority").

Here, there's very little within the tribe capable of instigating a further development. And should a more *autonomous* figure emerge, he's apt to be thrown under the bus and castigated by the ego-centric (narcissistic) and impulsive leader. Here, the tribe not only fails to evolve, it regresses into a pre-personal cult, that if inadequately opposed, can hold a whole nation captive. For here the mantra remains either ego-centrically "Me first," or ethnocentrically "My party," or "America first." (Polarizing interpersonal, domestic, and foreign relations).

The *lack of awareness* of these different developmental stages has contributed to our polarization, but also impeded strategic thinking, and the employment of skillful means for dealing with them.

And it hasn't helped when the "world-centric" Green *meme* doesn't want to recognize any stage or interpretive vantage as superior to any other. Here, the *meme* that could be *leading* the leap into "2nd tier," winds up erecting a road block. (About as helpful to accessing "2nd tier" as Trump's ethno-centric wall would be for moving into "world-centric").

※

Like an unruly child, I don't think Trump is really a Republican or a Democrat—or for that matter, a conservative or a liberal. In fact, it's hard to see him really standing for anything but his own great and insatiable need for attention—which may be the only thing "great" about him.

Yet when conservative Republicans had linked their causes with his, the result had been the crowning empowerment of a "King Baby" (which can be a *healthy* narcissistic stage—*in young children)*. But in a president who's never outgrown it, and rarely been held accountable for anything, it became a reckless and immature grandiosity that actually *threatened* both "conservatism" and what it means to be a Republican—or for that matter, an American.

Just as it threatened the proper role and functioning of numerous governmental agencies, and threatened—rather than *conserving*—fundamentals of our constitution itself, such as the separation between the Justice Department and the executive branch (constantly violated in Trump's attempt to limit, or undo FBI investigations and the Mueller probe; and by an Attorney General cherry-picked to serve and defend the legal infractions of a president and his cronies rather than the *nation* and its *laws*.

It also threatened the structure and authority of our security services, demonized journalists, degraded the State Department and any attempts at diplomacy, tilted the scales of democratic jurisprudence by giving a right-wing hue to our Courts. And threatened the proper role of Congress's oversight duties, which *should* check and balance the executive branch, and not let it run roughshod over democracy itself.

And so, it seems there's a deeper, healthier impulse within the landscape of Republicanism that hasn't adequately entered the fray. And *we need it* to stand up to, rather than cozy-up to authoritarian regimes. We need its ancestral righteousness—that of Abe Lincoln to awaken from the crypt of a decades long stupor. For conservatism's more divisive form has, since the mid 1990s,* ascended politically, and become more strident, if not having captured the Republican party. (While Trump in turn had managed a hostile takeover of *that)*.

A result is that, in the age of Trump one must trudge through miles of an arid conservative desert, before reaching the oasis of a conservative commentator who is informed by a vision of the *loftiest* of conservative values (a valuing of "the sacred spaces" and institutions that sustain healthy communities) and who has the sober *balance* and philosophical depth, the humanity and eminent good sense of a David Brooks, for example.

Other examples of principled conservative voices—those refusing to swallow the Trumpian Kool-Aid and thus averting a fall into an Echo-like swoon in which they are only able to echo a narcissistic president—are less known to liberals. But a list might include: Rick Wilson, Jennifer Rubin, Evan McMullin, Louise Mensch, George Will, and Senator Ben Sasse.

For in important ways, Trump's brand of conservatism (and Republicanism) is of a different stripe than a Never Trump Republican, a Reaganite conservative, or the *neo*-conservative brand animating the regime of George W. Bush. The Never Trump Republicans seem to have retained a memory of what their party once stood for, the Reaganites were Russia hawks, and the neo-cons formed coalitions with other nations— *already major differences.*

And after 9/11, *somebody* was going to pay for that. And so the regime of Bush (the latter) formed its coalition to launch an allegedly retaliatory military strike—not against terrorists, who are harder to track down—but against a country allegedly hosting them (Iraq), and which was much more concerned with the expression of American power abroad.

Whereas Trump's conservatism launched its strikes on the structures *within our society*, structures such as the rule of law that would limit his power domestically. And Trump resisted coalitions that would limit his power internationally—and why Trump didn't want allies—or at least not

---

* It's been argued that Newt Gingrich's ascension to House Speakership in 1995 had a pivotal and lasting impact on American politics and the health of American democracy. For he injected a "combative" approach in his party, where hateful language and hyper-partisanship became common, and where democratic norms were abandoned. Gingrich frequently questioned the patriotism of Democrats, called then corrupt, compared them to fascists, and accused them of wanting to destroy the country. He also oversaw several government shutdowns, and impeached President Clinton in a partisan fashion that has intensified ever since. His baton is carried now by Fox News, which is less the *news*, than one *meme's* hyper-polarized point of view.

those who weren't autocratic. For like Captain Ahab, he opposed anything that might limit his role in the world.

Aside from an affinity for the autocratic leaders of other countries, a desire to get U.S. troops out of the middle east, and a desire to keep people from "shit-hole" countries out of the U.S., Donald Trump didn't really come to the job of "leader of the free world" with much of a geo-political vision.

That would have required some study, the acquisition of a historical perspective and some coherent planning for the future. It would have also required a bit more humility, and the capacity to take a less grandiose, more realistic measure of his own cloth, such as knowing what he doesn't know, and a willingness to take counsel from those with more experience, rather than thinking he knows more than his generals or career diplomats—which in turn might have led to a wider consideration of unintended consequences. (And as one of America's most experienceed diplomats had put it, "the middle east *is* land of unintended consequences").

Quite importantly, a deeper geo-political vision would have also included a deeper recognition of the strategic importance of *allies*. It was, in fact, Trump's lack of regard for America's allies that caused his highly respected former Secretary of Defense, General James Mattis, to resign from his post in the winter of 2018 when Trump was first threatening to withdraw all U.S. troops from Syria.

For such an ill-considered, impulsive move would have left America's most loyal allies in the region—the Kurds—abandoned, while sure to face the hostile intentions of the Turks and Assad, and risking the release of ISIS terrorists whom the Kurds had been holding captive. This would have effectively jettisoned one of the most successful strategies of asymmetrical warfare in U.S. history, one that had degraded ISIS with the loss of very few American lives. It would also cede the region to be divvied up by Turkey, Assad, Iran, and ISIS escapees (plus the thousands who had gone to ground in Iraq and Syria)—with Russia's Putin as the new power broker in the region.

It would have also signaled the systematic continuation of an isolated, ruderless, impulsively incoherent American foreign policy that had withdrawn U.S. support for the Paris Climate Pact and from various multilateral trade partnerships, had threatened to withdraw from NATO partners, and *did* withdraw from the Iranian nuclear deal. This was accompanied by a grandstanding "love affair" with the tyrant in North Korea, that gave a rogue regime legitimacy and more time to develop its nuclear weapons system, while receiving no safeguards in return). And giving an unstable regime the wherewithal to resume developing nuclear weapons, while receiving nothing in return, is also what resulted from backing out of the Iranian nuclear deal.

This was followed by reckless brinksmanship and saber-rattling toward Iran, further eviscerations to the Department of State, and the removal of an anti-corruption ambassador in the attempt to personally profit by withholding military funding from a threatened ally in a hot war with Russia.

This wasn't "America first," or at least not the America the Founders had intended, or anyone could remember. Nor was it "playing well with others." Rather, it was narcissism's "splendid isolation," lack of empathy, entitlement, and grandiosity writ large.

More troubling than even his narcissism, what was also increasingly evident were most of the diagnostic criteria and pathological personality traits of an *antisocial personality disorder*. Here's the main ones: Failure to conform to lawful, ethical behavior; lack of concern for others—or remorse for having mistreated them; uses subterfuge to influence or control others, as well as deceit, coercion, dominance, or intimidation; dishonesty, fraudulence, misrepresentation, or fabrication when relating events; dangerous, risky, potentially damaging activities, unnecessarily and without regard for consequences; boredom proneness and thoughtless initiation of activities to counter boredom; lack of concern for one's own limitations and denial of personal danger; acts on spur of the moment in response to immediate stimuli without plan or consideration of outcomes; disregard for—and failure to honor commitments.

Psychologically, these were the very character traits that helped define Trump's foreign policy. Geopolitically, these traits were leading him and the nation he was elected to lead—to leap into an abyss prophetically warned against by Mattis: *"Nations with allies thrive, those without allies wither."*

And within a year of Mattis's resignation, as Trump's impeachment inquiry was taking place and the sordid details began to emerge of his administration's attempt to coerce the Ukrainian president to provide a false narrative exonerating Russia's role in Trump's election, and to dig up dirt regarding Vice President Biden, this is when Trump actually *did* what he'd earlier threatened to do in Syria. The outcry was immense and immediate—and rarely, even from members of his own party.

Yet, as if in denial of the personal danger he was already in, at this time Trump also publicly appealed to yet another country (China) to dig up dirt on Biden's alleged corruption (truly a case of the pot calling the kettle black).

Incomprehensibly, given that an impeachment inquiry had already begun—and in direct violation of the foreign emoluments clause in the constitution—this is also when Trump announced that the upcoming G-7 conference was to be held at Trump's own golf resort in Florida. (He then tried to walk the announcement back, but it was too late). All hell had broken loose. The abyss opened. And Trump fell into it.

And as the 45th president staggered into his 4th year in office, bellowing like a wounded dinosaur facing extinction, a few things remained uncertain: Would he launch a successful—or disastrous—Hail Mary to deflect attention from what he was about to be tried for? Would a Republican senate defend a rogue president by banning fact witnesses or new evidence, while pretending to be blind both to his glaring unfitness for office—and to their own constitutional oath to be his trial's fair-minded and unbiased jury? Would the Orange Republicans in the senate find their voice—and if so, how many? Or would they cow, cave? (And fall in step with the knee-jerk conservative leanings evoked in the last chapter: a pre-rational, ethno-centric in-group loyalty, deferring to authority—if not to the sacrosanct pre-Enlightenment "divine right of kings").

Yet the worst uncertainties were: *Just how much more totalitarian would Trump become*, in the likely case that the senate failed to convict him? Feeling bullet-proof now from a failed Democrat attempt to oust him, would he become more vindictive, more grandiose still? Would he, and his *consiglieri* William Barr attack even more profoundly the weakening vestiges of a democracy's checks and balances? And how would an isolated regime—impervious to science and oblivious to climate change—respond to a new pandemic starting to appear in China?

A lawless president can't survive without lawless followers. If both are present, democracy becomes more imperiled still, if the *followers* also wear the cloak of *leadership*. And before Trump's impeachment trial had even begun, Lindsay Graham and Mitch McConnell had already declared they'd no intention to be unbiased. With this the case, the odds seemed little to none that sufficient moral courage would suddenly appear in one side of the aisle—while the jury was still out about how skillfully that moral absence could be countered by the aisle's other side. The safest bet was that a Republican dominated Senate was never going to find Trump guilty, and thus the removal of this president would be left to the uncertainties of the 2020 election; where the further uncertainty was: Would a divided nation, in the end, wake from the nightmare of its recent peril, and decisively side against the chaotic, lawless imposter, somehow in the White House.

But you shouldn't have to be a shrink to recognize an obvious linkage between the criminal *quid pro quo* nature of Trump's Ukrainian scandal—and Trump's *antisocial personality disorder*. Aside from his equally malignant narcissism, this had been the lurking "art" behind many of Trump's "deals." And why the whiff of corruption had been such a constant in his administration.

And if so much corruption was squeezed from a deeper probe of this *one* incident involving Ukraine, what had yet come to light is how Trump's lawless character disorder might have impacted similar *quid pro quo* deals with the leaders of other countries—specifically Putin, whom Trump had mostly attempted to encounter in a hidden, unsupervised way.

For who benefitted from Trump withdrawing troops from Syria; or from withholding funding to Ukraine in its war with Russia? Who was the beneficiary of Trump's reluctance to acknowledge the nation that'd interfered in 2016's presidential election, and by siding with Putin's claims, rather than the unanimous findings of all 17 U.S. security agencies? Why did Trump advocate for Russia's readmission into the G-7, even after usurping Crimea, and invading Ukraine? Something stinks here. We've been in deep shit, and merely yet to discover it all. And no help was to be found in uncovering the truth from McConnell, Attorney General Barr, Vice President Pence, or Secretary of State Pompeo. For all the president's men were part of the cover-up. That much was certain. What wasn't was the American people; would they have the bandwidth—and discernment—to see through it?

Like the chicken and the egg, it's hard to be clear which came first—the increased polarization in American politics, or the rise of cable news. What's *more* clear now is not only the divide between liberals and conservatives, but the equally profound intellectual gulf between conservatives like David Brooks and those like Sean Hannity (which may be the first time "profound" and Sean Hannity have been linked in the same sentence).

For in Hannity's mind, the rift between *liberals and conservatives* becomes not profound but *ridiculous* when Hannity has denounced even Halloween for being a "liberal holiday because we're teaching our children to beg for something for free...we're teaching our kids to knock on other people's doors and ask for a handout."

And given such a perspective, it's often hard to watch Fox News for more than two minutes without feeling appalled, and as if delusion itself now has its own network, and its own deep-pocketed sponsors.

And deep pockets have been *necessary* at Fox, to pay off the sheer number of sexual harassment settlements—both against its cult-like founder Roger Ailes, and 13 against Bill O'Reilly alone. Until the last 5 got O'Reilly fired, leaving Sean Hannity as the station's most popular commentator.

(And speaking of *cults,* Trump and his retinue are *precisely* that. And cults—after an initial, illusory exaltation—don't end well. But in a shameful retribution for all those implicated—whose hubristic vision never saw it coming).

This *inevitable* retribution—as we'll see later, when exploring the myth standing behind narcissism—might be seen as the trans-temporal arising of the Greek goddess *Nemesis*— *"She from whom there's no escape,"* punisher of those guilty of the crime of hubris...

One of the impulses in this book is *re-visioning* ("not only narcissism, but all it impacts"). And in this chapter I've been re-visioning *conservatism* in the attempt to reflect the news and nature of our polarized time. Another impulse in the book is to mirror the intelligence (as well as the idiocy) of prevailing views—and in better moments, evoking a little of the bandwidths of human intelligence that are not so polarized—and not well-represented by journalism as a whole, mainstream psychology as a whole (and as Spiral Dynamics points out, not by *humanity* as a whole).

For in a cognitive landscape highly polarized between for and against, there's often a third perspective that is transcendent to both...And in the sensitive, liberal Green *meme* that more transcendent, less polarized perspective is often missing (as it is in all "first tier" *memes*). Yet Green can be very sensitized to what's missing in *memes* less sensitive than its own. In fact, Green was the first *meme* to recognize the limitations of Orange *meme*—the *meme* (world-view) that originated during the so-called Enlightenment, and which was pragmatically based on observable *facts*.

An achievement of Orange was that it freed itself from superstitions and narrowly-held mythic structures. What it offered instead was its science. *If you knew the scientific facts, you could begin to game the system.* No mean feat, for this fact-based worldview was capable of putting men on the moon.

But the Green recognized that the world isn't solely a realm of facts, but a realm of *interpretations*. And in recognizing the multiplicity of interpretations, the Green planted its flag in an imaginal flatland in which none of these interpretations were seen to be inherently above or beneath any other.

Yet there's ample research suggesting not all interpretative vantages are equal. Over time, some stall or regress. Others further evolve and lead to greater caring, greater empathy, greater inclusivity (from ego-centric to ethno-centric to world-centric to cosmo-centric; from impulsive to conformist to autonomous; from pre-personal to personal to transpersonal). In other words, some lead to "second tier *meme-hood*."

The Green is actually considered "a gateway *meme*" to the "second tier." But what prevents it from moving *through* the gateway, is its own *hierarchy issues*. For Green *gets red in the face* by the very notion of hierarchy; it doesn't recognize anything (or anyone) as above or deeper than its own point of view. For all its sensitivity, egalitarianism, and ecological awareness, this can render it a tourist to its own fuller depths. (When it stops short of moving through what Zen terms "the gateless gate"). Here Green becomes encapsulated by its own flatland view, and becomes spiritually unteachable—when it thinks: *No one tells me what to do.*

And in conservatives, the less polarized, more transcendent "third perspective" is often missing when the Blue *meme* of the Christian Right is willing to turn a blind eye to the moral failings of Donald Trump in what amounts to a *quid pro quo* Devil's Bargain. Namely, that the judges he installs will then overturn Roe v Wade (and as if this would be protecting

"Family Values" and the defense of "Religious Freedom"—an example of the conservative rhetoric that Corey Robin terms "a language that often *mimics* the revolutionary impulses that it's opposing").

But if Spiral Dynamics' pioneering, extensive research tells us that 98.9% of those currently on our planet are operating from the belief that their *meme* possesses the sole perspective that is most truly correct, and thus needs to be promoted or defended, then the failure to access the more rarified "bandwidths" (of the 1.1%) and a more transcendent, non-polarized "third perspective" is not just a problem with conservative news sources such as Fox or Breitbart. For the same could be said about CNN, MSNBC, *The Washington Post, The New York Times,* and *The Atlantic*. For both wings of our consensual, political reality have failed to provide adequate orientation for *the deeper evolution so urgently needed now.*

This "deeper evolution" is evoked in a conversation Andrew Harvey reports having had with the Dalai Lama, in which the latter had said of our current times: *"Prepare for the worst, but work relentlessly with peace and joy for the very best."* Harvey's takeaway from that conversation is that our planet is collectively experiencing a Dark Night of the Soul. And that the future of the planet hinges rather largely on how America responds to the multiple, interconnected challenges it is facing now—global warming, the coronavirus pandemic, an appalling political environment that keeps most in poverty, while threatening species and democracies—in both cases, beginning with our own. Yet for all the *horrors* and *atrocities* become more vivid at such a time, it is also the birth canal for a transformed humanity to be born; the beginning of a new way to live on this planet. But this will require what Harvey terms a "sacred activism," in which those of a mystical bent must wed their love of the sacred to activism, and where political activists must open to the sacred. "Otherwise," he says, "the two are just different faces of narcissism."

Yet in fairness to *The Post* and *The Times,* their armies of fact-finders have in other ways served the nation well—often more so than our Congress—by acting as a watchdog toward a fundamentally corrupt presidential administration (an administration that actually lacks the kind of discipline and well-ordered "goodness" that conservatism has normally touted, whether fiscal or otherwise).

Their reporters have been in the trenches, doing the grunt work needed to *conserve* our democracy, during a time when it has been *threatened* by the very regime elected to *lead* it. (A regime that, within itself, has been divided by a polarizing and *paralyzing* factionalism that has often rendered it dysfunctional).

Since Watergate, I've admired the willingness of news sources such as *The Times* and *The Post* for being a little edgy and even *heroic,* and each of them—at least to my own mind—possess a *far* higher truth content than *Fox* or *Breitbart.* And speaking of the latter, it should be remembered that Steve Bannon—who once touted himself as *a Leninist wanting to bring down our existing political structures*—initially thought to do this *not* by appealing to left-wing journals of discourse as a proper Leninist might do, but rather, by breaking into the Far Right's sources of news, for their standards would be lower, and thus easier for him to enter.

Though some portion of a deeper reality is also being obscured when the Green and Orange *memes* of CNN or MSNBC are polarized themselves—even when offering the occasional Trump supporter on its panels—which at times can feel like a dog and pony show.

Certainly political views arise in an imperfect world—often by siding with the lesser of two evils. Which is how much of the American electorate viewed the presidential election of 2016. Clearly—in retrospect—we wound up with the worst. And MSNBC is right to rail against it.

Yet for what is railed *against* or *for*—at either ends of a political spectrum—the news of such events come and go, as it has for centuries, while often turning a deaf ear to what lies deeper in the soul. In fact, the rise and fall of kingdoms and governments can be read as a chronicle of this obliviousness. As can the needless suffering of individuals, as this book elsewhere chronicles.

My huge red dog, whose ears are keener than mine, pays such news no attention as he puts his head against mine a few moments before going upstairs to sleep for the night. It happens like clockwork at 11 p.m., and is a gesture that moves me to immediacy, and engages my heart more than the news I'm watching on TV. It's a canine gesture I adore, and akin to the gesture of greeting or departure sometimes offered by *Tibetan gurus.* And as if to say: Though our forms are separate, *our minds are one.* And at the end of the day: we *love* each other.

And for every day's televised polemic since Trump's inaugural, something deeper was also occurring... Every day another 217,000 people in the world emerged from extreme poverty, 300,000 got clean water for the first time. 325,000 obtained electricity, and the per capita rate of deaths from warfare is way down from what it had been.

As conservative columnist Nickolas Kristof reflects the above, a great progress was transforming the world, an underlying and often unseen trend far more important than Trump's last numb-skulled action or tweet. And Kristof reminds us, that when reporters and intellectuals only report the violations and atrocities while turning a blind eye to this progress it can actually contribute to a false nostalgia (such as to make America great again). And we can wind up feeling disempowered and hopeless, while oblivious to what's deeper.

And also each day the fruit trees continue to drink deeply from the earth, from buried roots we cannot see. And God willing, each summer, they will continue to offer their fruit. And even as the genetic diversity of California's spring-spawning salmon grows extinct, other genetic strains of this majestic and totemic fish still remain, and return to what's left of their spawning grounds each fall, as they have for thousands of years.

Like young children, the salmon are neither conservative nor liberal. ("Conservative" and "liberal," "right-wing" and "left-wing" are mere human constructs, human filters, and often, human *blinders*). And in its healthy form, *democracy* is neither one, nor the other, but rather a collaborative conversation between the two; a collaboration that *should* provide balance to whatever hands are steering the ship of state.

Though in a political culture of polarized *memes,* anything—from ecology to cannabis, from healthcare to immigration—can be appropriated, spurned, or neglected in the service of a narrow brand's point of view.

And when one brand feels threatened by, and can't truly listen to the other, *the great democratic conversation fails to occur.* Instead, each brand digs in its heels and begins to *yell louder.* And we wind up deafened to what lies deeper in ourselves, and in the other.

Rather than support Donald Trump as the defender of the conservative citadel—a citadel to which he may not truly belong—Fox News might better support the salmon as a national legacy from the past to be passed down for later generations, and should speak out to *conserve* their riverine habitats and spawning grounds.

Why should the Green *meme* have to labor alone on ecology when the *conservation* of our planet's eco systems should concern us all, and properly belong in a conservative's wheelhouse?

We should better recognize—and better *conserve* what is *already* great—and in all its forms; and thus conserve them, as well as our own species, from possible extinction.

The human dead, my own extinct loved ones—at times forgotten, at times heartbreakingly missed—continue to live inside me. One day I too, and also you, will be but a memory, regardless of our political views. And later still, we'll each become completely unremembered, and finally, indiscernible; merely the frozen light that lingers in a splot of carbon.

But such impermanence—and the emptiness that lies at the heart of all things—are poignant human recognitions that might open our hearts and clear our minds. (Even if *most* of the time we're fixated on something else, furthering an agenda, and as oblivious to perennial wisdom as a dog before the evening news). Yet like being-ness itself—or good friends—we might be restored to sanity by what perennial wisdom offers, and take refuge here, a refuge *always available.*

We shouldn't forget this, though often I do: how perfectly *good* it is—just to be alive. *Even in polarized times,* and amidst the clamorous din. And how *blessed* we are, when we manage to walk through a world unburdened of blame and gain—the primordial landscape that the wisest ancestors of all faiths have known and pointed to. For the existence of this underlying landscape has been *the open secret:* a sacred world that has never gone *elsewhere.*

Unlike the latest report of bad behavior that passes for our news, this is the "*good* news" of the Gospels, whether of Jesus or Buddha: Something like Heaven is *already* here, though as Jesus said, men and women often fail to see it.

Yet when we do, it outshines all our isms. And is the most transcendent form of conservatism or liberalism. For such a world-view conserves. *And* it liberates. It *unifies.* And it *heals. It restores the world.*

And for whatever else we do—and however we get there, *that's* our job now—*to access a deeper, less polarized, and compassionate sanity.* And bring *that* forth in a time so badly in need of it.

For the Green *meme's* version of the nightly news had been clear-eyed about one thing: It was never to come from Trump's White House.

FIVE

Changing Waters &
The Light and the Lampshade

THIS BOOK'S PROLOGUE evoked recent historical "sea-changes," and a collectively suffered disorientation that has come to prevail. More so than the salmon, who still know how to return to their original home, or apple trees that have never forgotten how to bear fruit, we humans seem to have lost our bearings. And this is impacting other species now as well. Both literally and metaphorically, *things are heating up* (though our government tells us this is but "Chinese propaganda" hindering American commerce, and thus "fake news").

Yet the *facts* are that the average surface temperatures on our planet in 2016 were the warmest since record keeping began in 1880, surpassing the previous record in the two prior years. That 2016 "high water mark" has since been surpassed. According to 2018 data from the National Oceanic and Atmospheric Administration (NOAA) the hottest years on record are now *the last four.* It's getting worse...

And speaking of high water, from New Orleans to Miami, from Staten Island to Houston, American cities have been flooding. In August of 2017 while much of Houston was under water, over 41 million residents of South Asia were devastated as well. In Bangladesh, the flooding was the worst in 40 years. Here, a Red Cross spokeswoman said that many Bangladeshis had told her, *"We're used to flooding but we've never seen anything like this in our lives."*

Warming oceans give rise to more destructive "extreme weather events" such as flooding, hurricanes, droughts, and wildfires, each of these caused or worsened by greenhouse gas emissions—that's the simple science. As is the fact that global warming, as well as ocean acidification—both driven by CO_2 spikes—have been increasing dramatically. (Ocean acidification by 5% over *each* of the past 4 decades, now threatening a quarter of all marine species; CO_2 levels at a rate not seen in *tens of millions of years*).

But a president characterologically impervious to the value of scientific facts or environmental warnings, could provide but *anti-leadership* in responding to the most fundamental crises of our time. For he had attempted to roll back any existent environmental legislation, and had stymied any response to the environmental devastations already upon us.

Such was the case when Trump initially threatened to deny California federal support in response to the catastrophic fires raging in the state during the fall of 2018 (which he blamed not on global warming, but on Californians not adequately "raking their forests"—as if they were flammable sand traps on golf courses poorly maintained by those who had voted against him). And this was also the case when Hurricane Maria devastated Puerto Rico in September of 2017, and our 45th president did little more than throw paper towels at a crowd.

Trump remained steadfastly in denial, not only about global warming, but the *3000* Puerto Ricans who lost their lives—about the same number killed from 9/11. He considered his administration's inadequate response to Hurricane Maria not as a cost-cutting *failure of empathy*, but rather as an "unsung success." While he portrayed the actual number of Puerto Ricans who lost their lives as a case of "Fake News trying to make him look bad." (As if anything *else* could make him look as bad as what he himself says, does, or *fails* to do). And in policy decisions impacting the COVID-19 pandemic, the president's "leadership" was no better. In fact, it was more of the same...

On May 8, 2018, rear admiral Timothy Ziemer quit his post on Trump's National Security Council as Senior Director for Global Health Security and Biothreats. His job had been to oversee, prepare, and lead the response to pandemics. To "eliminate unnecessary costs," the position and unit he'd led were axed. There was no longer a high-ranking administrative eye watching for pandemics...

The following year, the Trump administration ceased funding an early warning program named PREDICT whose mission had been the predicting of pandemics. This was a program that for the previous ten years had been studying the interaction between the viruses of animals and their spread to humans. They'd been rather good at it.

As reported by Emily Baumgaertner and James Rainey in the *Los Angeles Times*, PREDICT had identified 1200 viruses capable of erupting into pandemics, including over 160 novel coronaviruses. The project trained and supported staff in 60 foreign labs including the Wuhan lab that would first identify SARS-CoV-2, the new coronavirus that causes COVID-19 (and that a majority of scientists suspect to have originated in bats and then jumped to humans, just like its cousin that caused the SARS epidemic in 2002 and 2003).

PREDICT's field work ceased in September 2019 when the Trump administration let funding expire, and dozens of scientists and analysts were laid off. But even so, on January 3, 2020 China had alerted the WHO of the virus, and reports soon reached both Washington and South Korea.

Yet unlike the South Koreans, Washington failed to address it in its early weeks. That proved to be a *deadly* failure. For in pandemics, their spread can be so rapid that early *detection*, and early *response* is key. But for weeks the early warnings went unheeded. Those weeks of heedlessness were a luxury the U.S. couldn't afford—yet was about to pay for.

Through January and February, the warnings had been multiple... In January Trump's trade advisor, Peter Navarro, sent the president a memo warning of economic losses that could run into trillions of dollars, and the possible loss of millions of lives. Also in January there'd been a warning from deputy security advisor Matt Pottinger, who himself had been warned early in the month by a Hong Kong epidemiologist of the spread of the virus. Pottinger, a reputed China hawk, had counseled the president to blame it on China. (And subsequently, federal agencies were instructed to always refer to it as "the Chinese," or "Wuhan virus").

On February 5, in a briefing between senators and administration officials, the senators (Chris Murphy, D-CT., among them) also warned the administration to take the threat of the pandemic more seriously, and had offered funds for increased staffing and supplies they felt were about to be urgently needed. But the offer was turned down, as the senators were told the administration had things "well under control."

The nation's top public health experts had the same warning, and they were scheduled to deliver it to Trump later in February. But that meeting was delayed, as the president had just returned from India—and he was *fuming*—over two things. The first was the stock market crashing, and the second was who he blamed for that. That person—Nancy Messonnier—was director of the CDC's National Center for Immunization and Respiratory Diseases. And she'd just made a grievous political blunder—by speaking a truth Trump wanted no one to hear. What she said was: "It's not a question of *if* this will happen but when this will happen and how many people in this country will have severe illnesses."

The same day, Health and Human Services Secretary Alex Azar was trotted out to say the virus was "contained" in the U.S. The next day Pence was appointed as the head of the coronavirus task force. Nancy Messonnier hasn't appeared at White House briefings since.

Something else quite significant happened in February of 2020—though it wasn't to surface until pre-publication passages of Bob Woodward's new book *Rage* were leaked several months later. Woodward had taped a February 7th interview with the president in which Trump revealed a surprising level of detail in his understanding of the pandemic—that it was *dangerous, airborne, highly contagious*, and "*more deadly than even your strenuous flus.*" And then in March, Trump admitted to Woodward that he chose to keep that knowledge hidden from the public—a grievous policy calculation that would lead to many more lies--and so many more unnecessary deaths. For Trump not only persistently lied to the American people about the virus, but coerced false testimony from governmental agencies that were being bent—not toward the welfare of the nation, but in favor of the president's own political ambitions. And this included agencies such as the CDC that were restricted from releasing their own scientific findings about the virus--which would have better informed and protected the nation than the doctored findings that were released instead.

Pervasive lying, the misrepresentation of events, the inability to admit fault, lack of guilt, shame, empathy, and accountability, callous disregard of the suffering of others—as well as coercion to effect self-centered ends—are all key *psychopathic traits*. And each was evident in Trump's handling of the pandemic. And another key psychopathic trait is "blame externalization." And you can sense the latter not only in the way he regarded Nancy Messonnier, but in Trump's own words: "The virus has nothing to do with me," Trump told Woodward in their final interview in July 2020. "It's not my fault. It's—China let the damn virus out."

And so, as the virus landed in deadly earnest on American shores, Trump portrayed it as "China's problem," predicting it would never become an epidemic, and *"we have it under control."*

In the ensuing months however, it grew gruesomely clear that neither the virus, nor anything pertaining to it, was under presidential control. Except the ways Trump was spin-doctoring it—by downplaying the threat, initially saying it was a hoax, and no more concerning than the flu. This was to effectively *politicize* the virus, with Republican governors grown reluctant to institute social distancing orders and the wearing of masks, for Trump had declared in a matter of *days,* not a single American would have the virus, and *anyone* who wanted a test for it could have one. But even better than that: *The tests are beautiful!*

He's saying this at a visit with the CDC, and its officials are standing behind him as he continues—*The tests are perfect,* he says—*just like the letter was perfect, the transcription...*(He's referring to the very partial account he provided of his attempt to coerce the Ukrainian president that launched his impeachment inquiry. While the CDC officials are tight-lipped, gazing into space and clearly uncomfortable. They know the president is lying. And that their tests are deeply flawed.

By the time the virus had spread exponentially through much of the nation, while needed tests, masks, and ventilators *had not,* the spinning increased in order to mask administrative failures. Trump blamed China and the WHO, while threatening to defund the latter. The response of Bill Gates (whose foundation is the WHO's 2nd largest funder) was posted on Twitter: "Halting funding for the World Health Organization during a world health crisis is as dangerous as it sounds."

By now Trump was appearing daily on TV—in lieu of his rallies which the pandemic made no longer feasible. And Pence's role, seemed now less the spear-head of a national effort against the virus, but more Trump's ceremonial spear-holder, nodding and smiling in the background of a political skit, while Trump played the role of a president.

But being Trump, the role consisted mostly of congratulating himself and his regime for the really successfully great job they were all doing, and for the months-late supplies now allegedly arriving in mass, while he huckstered instant cures, like April's warming—*it'll be like a miracle, it will just disappear!*—and "very powerful" medications known to him (whose efficacy had never been established for treating COVID-19) though Trump had "a good feeling" about them, *It'll be like a gift from Heaven!*

And though a charade of sorts, none of this was really *funny*—for a nation facing a deadly virus and in need of real leadership. Such antics led Dr. James Lawler, a member of the "Red Dawn," an email group of pandemic experts who'd been trying in vain to guide the nation on a wiser course, to post to the group: "We have thrown 15 years of institutional learning out the window and are making decisions based on intuition."

Trump's daily "progress reports" bore in no way the *gravitas* nor the *intent* of the "fireside chats" of a true war time president facing a nation in its hours of need. The only need addressed here was the *president's*—to cover his own ass as he looked ahead to the 2020 election. And even as the U.S. became the epicenter of the virus, never once did he mention there was still no coherent supply chain for getting desperately needed supplies to the people who needed them.

And when reporters asked about the baffling *disconnect* between the mountain of supplies touted in his briefings and the equally daily, dire pleas of the emergency room doctors throughout the nation, who were already working without adequate PPEs for themselves, Trump then attacked the *reporters*—for asking "nasty questions"—not the *problem* (which was the dysfunctionality of a supply chain in which individual states had to bid against each other and even against FEMA, for limited supplies, at now jacked-up prices).

While shying away from actually employing the powers of the Defense Production Act, Trump seemed content merely to bask in the image of himself as a *War Time President*—while the front-line soldiers in this war— our true heroes—were sent out to battle surging armies of an invisible Goliath, lacking both shields, locational maps, or medical grade slingshots.

I tell you, this is an interesting time to be an American on the planet Earth. In fact, it reminds me of a Buddhist curse: *May you be born in interesting times...*

As the news cycle, the new normal, became more appalling by the day, we'd entered a new, dystopian world. Now, we were in lock-down, yet everyone's well-being seemed more obviously interconnected with the well-being of everyone else. Old friends came out of the woodwork and appeared for video chats. The virus had leveled boundaries, and was a respecter of none. Nations as helpless before it as the billion Australian animals burnt to death just months before. And *all of us were in this together*—that, a constant theme—as we sheltered in place from a microbial terror, and turned on our TV screens.

The inseparable link between the shocking video images—empty streets in the great cities of the world, hospitals stuffed to the gills with people breathed by machines, a bizzaro president incapable of leading—juxtaposed with our shared vulnerability, felt like life on Earth had become an urgent lesson. Perhaps we'd forgotten, and for too long, what else to listen to, what else to steer by. In such times, Yeats tells us: "The falcon cannot hear the falconer." (*We're* the falcon, and the *transcendent source of guidance*—however else named—is the falconer).

But with the ozone layer grown thinner, so had the boundary between fact and science fiction, threatening comic book villains and presidents, reality and mass hallucination. Even *before* COVID-19 we were in challenging, polarized times. But that hadn't moved the evolutionary needle. Perhaps this would.

Writing of, and from, such a time—here's Yeats again: "Things fall apart; the centre cannot hold"..."Surely some revelation is at hand." For such times, when "The darkness drops again" also offer ripe opportunity for fresh and needed re-visioning(s) to arise; the impulse toward a broader historical, and mythic vision in order to gain our bearings...

The Sufis have a story reflecting times such as this, when a widely prevailing disorientation exists, and has become the new normal. The Sufi story may be a better, more revelatory narrative for our times than tonight's Evening News. A wise network should broadcast it, perhaps nightly. For in a metaphoric way, the Sufi story is also a rendering of the Evening

News, another way of telling it. And the story—*When the Waters Were Changed**—goes like this…

Once upon a time Khidr, the Teacher of Moses, called upon man-kind with a warning. At a certain date, he said, all the water in the world which had not been specially hoarded, would disappear. It would be replaced with different water, which would drive men mad.

Only one man listened to the meaning of this advice. He collected water and went to a secure place to store it, and waited for the water to change its character. On the appointed date the streams stopped running, the wells went dry, and the man who had listened seeing this happening, went to his retreat and drank his preserved water.

When he saw, from his security, the waterfalls again beginning to flow, this man descended among the other sons of men. He found that they were now thinking and talking in an entirely different way from before. In fact, they seemed quite mad. Yet they had no memory of what had happened, nor of having been warned. When he tried to talk to them, he realized that they thought he was the crazy one, and they showed hostility or compassion, not understanding.

At first he managed to resist the temptation to drink the new water, and instead went back to his own supply every day. But finally, he simply couldn't bear the loneliness of living, behaving, and thinking in a different way from everybody else. He drank the new water, and became like the rest.

Then he forgot all about his own store of special water, and his fellows began to look upon him as a madman who had miraculously been restored to sanity.

It seems to me that our consensual reality today is much like the time when "the waters have changed." Most of us spend much of each day in distracted exile from the true waters of life. And there's little in a secular postmodern culture to redirect this roving heedlessness. A healing aid for our madness, has yet to come from our prevailing media, its talking heads, our existing politics, which but confirm what half already believe.

---

* From Idries Shah's *Tales of the Dervishes: Teaching Stories of the Sufi Masters over the Past Thousand Years.* New York: E.P. Dutton, 1970

The kind of orientation we've been needing is more apt to come from the fringes and outskirts of our culture's understanding of things. And not from a contemporary psychological establishment, or widely prevalent *meme*. It's more apt to come from dead we've yet to fully hear, and their stories, whether mythic, mystic, poetic, or historical, or the simplest anything witnessed with the clarified eyes we've yet to see through...

A former, rather brilliant teacher of mine put it slightly differently. Rather than using the metaphor of changing waters, she said we humans possess a *marvelous light*—that's often covered by a disgusting *lampshade*.

But my teacher's brilliance didn't save her from the less savory elements of her own lampshade. And brilliance alone won't save any of us—as other teachers have told me. *We're still going to have to deal with that lampshade.*

Much of this book will explore the lampshade...But first, since we'll be traveling companions for that lengthy haul ahead, it's probably time to mention a bit about the guy who is talking to you...

I grew up in a political town. And as a kid got up at dawn to throw *The Washington Post* onto doorsteps. Later I got up at dawn to sit on round cushions in halls that smelled of incense, or to work on offshore fishing boats that reeked of diesel. I still get up at dawn—to write.

Though now I also like to whack golf balls. And suppose myself to be something of a mythologist, a therapist, a meditation teacher—and in my better moments, these banners of identity all drop away, and I'm no one in particular.

Or as a truly wise man once said: *"Love tells me I am everything. Wisdom tells me I am nothing. And between the two my life moves."*

But what does it mean to be nothing? And what does this have to do with wisdom—or narcissism? Or the metaphors of changing waters; light and lampshade? Or the evolutionary challenges of extreme times, and what *our own lives*, or *planet* are asking of us?

Glad if you wondered—but as another teacher had said, "don't tell them, *be* it, and show them..."

About 20 years ago, I was very much someone in particular—and *most* of the time. I was quite definitively a guy with *a public speaking phobia*—arguably the most common American phobia. And at this time, equally definitively—at least in my own mind—I was a poet.

In fact, about 20 years ago I'd just had published a book of ecstatic love poems called *The You That is Everywhere*. Unlike the book you're reading now, these poems had come to me in a torrent, yet so effortlessly, with almost no editing necessary. Like taking dictation from a really great Muse. And a Muse like this is hard to find!

Soon enough something problematic would arise—my lampshade. But first, well-known authors offered back cover blurbs. The most famous poet of my generation—who'd long had a policy of never writing endorsements for other poets—wrote one for my book that was so beautiful, that when I first read it I fell to my knees on the kitchen floor and cried. Book reviews began to confuse me with Rumi. The book began to sell, and at a rate uncustomary for a debut collection of poetry. It sold out its large first print run in the first 90 days. Thousands more were rush-ordered from the printer.

However, along with these fortuitous happenings, a book tour had also been scheduled. And due to my lifelong fear of public speaking, rather than being stoked about the book's initial success, I became a man *shaking in his boots*.

The love that had seemed everywhere had become the *terror* that seemed everywhere. I tried to meditate it away. It didn't work. As soon as I got off my meditation cushions, the fear was waiting for me as my unbidden and constant companion.

I called an older Sufi poet for advice—Rumi's most illustrious translator in fact. He'd earlier sent me a copy of his *Essential Rumi*—inscribed with some wise, cryptic reflections that I would only fully comprehend several years later—in response to the book of love poems I'd sent him. (In retrospect, his cryptic reflections were the most insightful critique of my book).

But while on the phone, he suggested that I "let my love lead me forward." So I gave that a try…and I also did therapy on it. But the demon of my fear seemed stronger than the words that I or anybody else seemed to know. I then did EMDR sessions to dissolve the terror. This gave some initial relief, but the terror kept coming back, and cycled on itself.

As the book tour loomed closer, any hopeful winds had fallen from my sails. I began to flounder in the Horse Latitudes of the soul, and to feel drained and hollowed out, like a shell of myself, a haunted ghost ship…It got so bad I was seriously thinking of calling the book tour off.

But the possible relief that course of action offered had its own darkness. For I realized that if I ran away from the fear by calling the book tour off, the odds were slight that I'd ever fully embody the calling of being a poet.

The Jungian notion of being a "wounded healer" had seemed a workable banner of identity for doing psychotherapy with people. It kept me in touch with my own wounded vulnerability, and in so doing, helped open my heart to the vulnerability of others. But having a fear of reading your poems in public seemed the absolute crushing shits for *the life of a poet*.

Yet I also sensed that I had actually written something—at last—that wouldn't soon feel dated or outgrown. Unlike most prior books that I never even bothered to publish, this one felt like it had integrity, and the beginnings of poetic maturity. And I didn't want to sully the integrity of the poems that had been given to me by reading them in such a terrified, debilitated condition.

I felt caught on the horns of what seemed an impossible dilemma. Caught in the tension between what I most deeply desired—and what I most feared. God had me by the short hairs. That's what it felt like, a divine *agony*. (Though I was nominally a Buddhist, and rarely thought of "God," I cried, I prayed, I railed at the source of my life: *Why would you give me these gifts, and then surround it by so much fear!*).

In retrospect, life had given me a true, natural *koan*. One that seemed more inescapably and personally meaningful than those I'd encountered in a rather unremarkable Zen career. It was a blessing in disguise—though I didn't realize it at the time.

What I did come to slowly realize was that there did seem to be some kind of *initiatory experi*ence in the offing here. But also, that I didn't seem to have the kind of personality structure that was right for the job life was now nudging forward. So if I'd be willing to walk through some kind of initiatory fire, it would require finding something inside me that was different from the structure of my ego, quite different from whom I was taking myself to be. (And *narcissism*, as we'll come to see, is "taking ourselves to be what we're not"—an unknowing fraudulence, a fundamental *identity confusion*).

I also clearly saw that if I went into the readings on the book tour trying to impress people, or make sure that they saw me as some kind of idealized figure—you know, *an ecstatic poet*—that this was not going to go well for me.

The guy who'd experienced a transformational love affair and written the poems may have been "ecstatic" at times, but if I tried to pass myself off as *that* rather than whoever I was when delivering the poems to an audience, I'd feel like a fake version of myself, a self-conscious, and probably publicly exposed fraud. (And really, not that much different from Trump).

But somehow it came to me, that if I changed the terms of engagement here to something radically different than how I'd been holding it, this might be endurable, and perhaps even with some possibility of success, though the terms of success needed to be re-framed as well. So what I hit upon was this…

Rather than trying to wow people, or fear the terrible crash if no "wow" ensued, I decided that my game plan would be that of simply saying "yes" to each moment I was on stage, *whatever* it contained—even my terror. (Encountered like this, such a "stage" is quite different than Trump's view of his "arena," where opponents fight it out in a zero sum game, as if gladiators in the Roman Coliseum, or the arenas of its more modern, staged and fake counterpart—professional wrestling. Fake wrestlers, though, are another way Trump embodies an American archetype—he's the bad guy you love to hate, the wrestler who reaches into his trunks while the clueless ref isn't looking, and smashes the likeable brawler with a weapon no one quite sees. Though the fans at ring-side are outraged, howling and pointing their fingers in vain, like the liberal media. This carny vision is in need of a corndog). But back to my own drama of years ago…

I re-framed the readings on the book tour to be an experiment in embodying a radical kind of self-acceptance, a radical kind of *allowing*—rather than trying to manufacture any other outcome. And I began to practice this in my daily life as the first reading on the book tour became more imminent. And as I did so, I began to see something interesting about all my fears and hopes that hadn't occurred to me before. They all had the quality of "future tripping." That is, these hopes and fears all pertained to the future, and if I opened instead to what was actually coming through the pipeline *now*, if there was any problem here at all, it was at least greatly diminished.

I began to see all *anxiety* as a case of losing one's grounding in presence—in becoming seduced by "coming attractions"—whether hopeful, or paranoid. It seemed that presence for human beings is like water to a fish. It's the natural "environment" for the soul to flourish, in fact to *awaken* in this dream we call "waking life." This was really Buddhism 101, of course. But sometimes you have to learn things from your own life to really know them in your bones, and not merely from the teachings of perennial wisdom. Only then does the perennial wisdom live in *you*, in your *being*, not just in your head.

I practiced letting go of everything not here, and saying yes to everything that actually was. And if what was here was fear, I said yes to that too. In this way everything arising seemed a portal to presence itself.

And when I was living from this sense of presence, nothing was really "missing," and nothing in excess—and there was nothing inside me that I needed to fear, nor anything to resist or suppress.

A kind of "basic trust" had begun to enter my awareness, replacing my fears. Admittedly, this trust at times seemed to come—and then become temporarily eclipsed by the lampshade of my conditioned mind. But at least I intuited it was always *potentially available*, and the better stance to have towards life.

Unlike the construction of a sturdy wall along the Mexican border, my lampshade—the separative *barrier* between me and the unfolding of reality had become thinner, more porous, less necessary. This was very good news.

Something had also begun to shift in my sense of *will*. Rather than trying to will what I wanted into existence, or trying to will away what I didn't want, this new sense of will was more like *thy will be done*. It had a quality of surrender—to something greater than myself; something timeless, invisible, yet quite palpable...

And I noticed this altered sense of will actually provided a subtle sense of *support*, like the image in that song, "the air beneath my wings." Or like the buoyancy of water that holds up a boat. And this subtle form of support increased my *confidence* as well.

The "increased necessity" of my life situation had shifted some lever, opened some channel in my will. Here was a dimension of the soul that was native, if not previously known, a refuge from the uncertainties of the future, and the limiting legacy of my past. As this formless support (that

Sufis term *the white Latifa*) continued to make itself known, a new poem came through its channel, a dharma talk to myself, I suppose.

If you, dear reader, find it useful, the Creative Spirit—which is quite communicable—will have hit more than one bird with the same stone...

Yes

Like a vast and gracious Host, welcome
and say "yes" to this, "yes" to this
and "yes" to every this

Your true life arrives, constantly…
when you've set up your little shop
at the intersection of Now and Yes

Relax, be simply present for every breath,
every passing car, every trilling bird…
When you look at the world
free your gaze from the mind's tiny whirling
& let each thing's uniqueness emanate forward

Consider all things as supportive Emissaries
of a greater and hidden design…Though
what is being supported may not be your ego
When you welcome each present moment
unendingly, time ceases, and your granular
self dissolves into an Ocean, at once
subtle, spacious, and buoyant
for it supports your being effortlessly
the way water holds up a boat

Yet when you abandon Presence
in order to get somewhere else
you've wandered away, an isolated figure
exiled from the tapestry of being

So let your awareness be *vast* and vastly inclusive
as the actual world—what's here and what's not—

is welcomed without quibble
Hear everything...see everything...
feel everything...with this
simple greeting inside you:
> YES*

※

And those poetry readings? For all the terror, they also brought in a blessing that outshined it; an innate support I learned I could count on, that might not have been learned in any other way.

When life turns up the heat, and we're facing extreme situations, they may be wake-up calls, mobilizing resources we never knew we had. And on this warming, threatened planet—for all the *horrors*, who knows what *else* may come in the door, along with COVID-19...

---

* Note: A version of "Yes" initially appeared in Josh Baran's anthology, *365 Nirvana Here and Now: Living Every Moment in Enlightenment*. London: Element Books, 2003. Baran's book, a lovely one for your bedside, is a collection of 365 brief statements culled throughout time, that "point directly" to the mind's Essential Nature. In addition to my poetry collection *An Amateur's Guide to the Invisible World*, "Yes" also appears in another forthcoming book that evokes the poetic tradition's perception of "Holy Will" over the past two millennia.

SIX

What's To Like About Nothing?
A Beginner's Guide to Non-conceptual Space

FOR MUCH OF the last chapter I was suffering from a lack of orientation to a deeper style of will. It had left me feeling deficiently empty, and anxiously unsupported in facing a challenge life was presenting to me. But all forms of "emptiness" are not the same.

For also in the last chapter, Nisargadatta Maharaj makes a brief appearance, and says something lovely. He says: *"Wisdom is knowing I am nothing. Love is knowing I am everything. And between the two my life moves."*

At first glance, the reader might wonder, *what's so great about being nothing?* (Let me count the ways...First off, being a "someone" *is so much work.* And perhaps why our lives seem so unnecessarily complex. Yet as we recede into being nothing, all else seems to come forward—the walls, trees, the space between things, and everywhere we look, has its own luminous aliveness).

It's like when our eyes are disrobed of preference, aversion, and the ego's near constant strategizing, all things become the secret agents of such-ness, and *this very moment* seems amply enough. And sometimes, I just fall in to it...this sufficient and enlivened stillness. And the such-ness stuns and is stunning, for out of the empty stillness, stunning insights, guidance, and epiphanies may be come.

This is the "unconfined cognizance" of *rigpa* emerging from its own "unconfined spaciousness." For as the "pointing out instructions" in Vajrayana Buddhism's Nature of Mind Teachings tell us, the spaciousness and the knowing are not separate, but an indivisible unity...

And at other times I deliberately align, say by looking out the window as I drop all thoughts and mingle my now thoughtlessly spacious mind with the spaciousness of the sky.

And sometimes I try it with my eyes shut. And notice that even the dark is alive, and less solid than I'd thought. For even with eyes shut in a darkened room, there is a visual, *spacious dimensionality*, and not a flat black wall of darkness (Try it yourself, and see if it's not so). And this spacious dimensionality is only perceptible because even in the dark, there is subtle light.

So it seems "the light of awareness" is not merely an over-used *metaphor*. For the light and the darkness peacefully exist beneath our own eyelids, as much as each revolve around each other, as they share the same ever-present sky.

I'm telling you, I'm reminding myself… the world is *subtle and profound*. But it is also so *simple* and *unadorned*, that we have to become simple and unadorned ourselves in order to recognize it, and to be blessed by inspiring glimpses—however occasional—into the mystery of life itself.

Only with an unadorned I, and naked eyes, will we recognize that the Beloved we've been waiting for, is appearing *constantly* in its unexpected and countless disguises. For S/He/It is a shape-shifter. And, like any beloved, loves to be *courted*. Which is a good way to think about spiritual practice—and how we make *ourselves more available* to the Beloved.

For, as far as I can surmise, the Beloved is *always* here—we're the ones who are less faithful, less constant. And though we're often oblivious to it, this greater, omnipresent Beloved is constantly holding us, constantly mirroring us, the macrocosm reflecting the microcosm. We're the *small* part of that equation. And "being nothing" is about as small and humble as it gets.

The Beloved seems to really love it when we get *humble* like that. Which is how we disrobe from the ways we've been disguising ourselves—not only with other people, but to ourselves. And then the Beloved responds in kind: S/He/It becomes more immanent, more palpable. So like Nisargaddata says, *"Wisdom tells me I am nothing. Love tells me I am everything. And between them, my life moves."* We just have to stop the idiot's momentum of being a fixated someone, being an ego. We just have to get out of the way.

In this chapter I'm attempting to amplify Nisargaddata's phrase "Wisdom is knowing that I am nothing." And I'm doing so because most people don't see much value in being nothing. Nor have we understood its relationship to wisdom. (Or why it is like the *antithesis* of narcissism). To the average Joe or Jill, being nothing seems worthless, like a valueless *blah*—a nothing, with nothing to recommend it.

Like if you wanted something to make you happy, say ordering a cheeseburger, and if the waiter brought you nothing you'd be pretty disappointed. And life is actually serving us nothing *all the time.* But we want something better than nothing. And we want to *be* something better than nothing. While the wisdom of Nisargadatta knows there's really *nothing better to be.*

And because we understand it differently than Nisargadatta, our lives themselves often seem bereft of meaning, or not nourishing enough. Because we fail to understand the ways that *less is really more,* we wind up disappointed, because without a better understanding of being nothing, all the "somethings" we try to get to fill us, seem in the end, not quite up to the task.

Yet Nisargadatta has "recognizing we are nothing" *right up there* with Love, as between the two, his life flows. Here, he's not saying his life moves between Love on the one hand…and a worthless, valueless *blah* on the other. That would be the perspective of someone needing to attend Sex and Love Addicts Anonymous!

Nisargadatta is speaking from a radical humility, and views "nothing" as something elemental, that Wisdom tells him he actually *is*. In truth, Nisagadatta is a big fan of being nothing. And in wiser moments, I am too. When we realize we are nothing, there's nowhere further we could possibly fall—*except in love.* And so—between the two—*our lives* might move as well.

Until we deconstruct the ego structure and become nothing we can't fit through the eye of the needle in Jesus's parable. Because he'd recognized he was a divine nothing, the Sufi saint Hallaj approached his execution *dancing* to the rhythm of the chains attached to his feet. (A feat of advanced training!). Because of nothing great Zen masters have faced their deaths with a smile on their lips. Because of nothing is the best reason for happiness! In fact, a non-conceptual spaciousness—a nothingness that *lacks* nothing—seems not only the portal for happiness and joy to arise, but *all* of our essential qualities.

Though at times we may feel unappreciated or unrecognized, they can't take our nothingness away from us—we can only fail to recognize its more ample facets. And by ample I also mean: Nothingness is elemental, primordial; was here first, gives rise to all things. In a consumer culture though, we've needed a better introduction to being nothing—a seeming poverty that actually contains riches. And I'll keep trying my best to provide one here.

But first, I can't resist a joke…

So a rabbi walks into a synagogue… and begins to talk out loud to God. *"O Lord, I am nothing!"* A few minutes later the cantor walks in, and chimes in too: *"O Lord, before you, I am nothing!"* And next the synagogue's sexton, the janitor, comes in and repeats the refrain: *"O Lord my God, you have given life to this world, and before you I am nothing!"* At this, the cantor nudges the rabbi, and whispers, *"Look who thinks he's nothing…"*

If being nothing seems paradoxically confusing, the confusion, in part, stems from this: We've been using *the same word* to describe two radically *different* encounters. On the one hand, there's a "nothing" that's experienced as lack, as if something is not here *that really ought to be.*

This is what I've come to term "deficient emptiness," and what I'd been experiencing through much of the last chapter—"hollowed out, like a shell of myself." And this deficient emptiness actually takes many forms, *depending upon which of our essential facets are currently obscured.* And besides *will,* there's also *strength, peace, compassion, curiosity* and *joy*—to name just those articulated in the Sufic *Lataif* system, which not only highlights these essential facets of the soul, but also reflects the common egoic tendencies that tend to obscure them, rendering them unavailable. And yet, there's a radically different "nothing" or "emptiness" that points to something akin to "the pearl beyond price."

If the first form of "being nothing" seems deficient and empty of value, or lacking one or more of our essential qualities, the latter form seems so valuable you can't put a price on it. Only unlike some extraordinarily rare jewel, the really marvelous nothing can be found in any moment, in any Motel 6, or any Safeway parking lot.

Though omnipresent and always open to us, *this marvelous nothingness has remained an open secret.* And open secrets can't usually be told—though

I'm trying to do so here… and so, this whole chapter could read as some abstract, valueless jive.

Often we need a lot of *training*, a lot of *emptying out*, before we're ready to receive an open secret—or what is sometimes called "a pointing out instruction." And in most real inner schools, they're not passed out before we are ready to receive them. (For that would be what my favorite rabbi once referred to as "casting your pearls before swine").

If a fettered mind could receive an open secret it wouldn't remain a secret—or be worth very much. And so, though the *marvelous* nothingness can be found anywhere, in any moment, and behind every door and gateway of time, we have to empty *ourselves* in order to recognize its more ample nature. But empty ourselves of *what?* What needs to be thrown to the frogs in order to be so empty that we can fit through that needle's eye, and by so doing, gain entrance into something akin to a primordial, metaphoric heaven, a heaven on Earth?

Nearly all of the world's great contemplative traditions tell us we need to empty ourselves of our thoughts…our judgments…our agendas and opinions—which is why they all offer various forms of meditation. Like Sengstan, the 3rd Chinese patriarch of Zen telling us, *"Quit searching for the truth, merely cease cherishing your own opinions."* He's telling us the naked truth is already self-evidently here, just beneath our conceptual filters—or what I've been terming our "lampshade."

Yet throwing even our *thoughts* to the frogs is quite a radically *different* proposition than has prevailed in the Western tradition, as exemplified by Descartes' famous, if ill-conceived maxim "I think—therefore I am."

If you went into an interview with a spiritual master to present your understanding, and told him *"I think, therefore I am,"* he might begin to laugh or weep, or maybe a mixture of both. And if he were a Zen master, he might hit you with a stick!

In order to discover the more ample nothingness, we also have to throw our self-importance to the frogs. It's really quite cumbersome, if not omnipresent, and is definitely *not* going to fit through the needle's eye.

Our emptying project has to include hopes for gain, and our fears of loss. That doesn't mean we don't try our best, or eschew excellence. It's more knowing that our well-being and sense of self-worth doesn't really depend upon the vagaries of *outcomes,* say like winning the popular vote, or delivering a kick-ass performance of some kind. Our true nature doesn't need augmentation; it's already whole and complete. And like all that's most deeply true, it can't really be *lost,* merely undiscovered and unlived.

And don't forget to throw your self-image to the frogs. What we most deeply *are* is not an *image* in the first place, but a *presence,* a human form of *being.* And *narcissism* is a case of the fundamental *identity confusion* that fails to recognize this. For by becoming overly identified with, if not in love with its own image, narcissism winds up dissociated from *being* itself. This leaves us with a fundamental hole in the soul, that "narcissistic supplies" can never fill.

Donald Trump, in a sense, has been doing us all an unintended favor. He's been showing us how distorted we humans can become when we reify divisive thoughts, opinions, and agendas—while needing constant validation for a fake and "winning" self-image. But as the Sufis remind us: *"Learn to behave, from one who does not."*

And there's really nothing more impervious to truth or wisdom than a narcissist who has gained a measure of success. Being inflated and puffed up like that is *definitely* not going to fit through that needle's eye. *Believe me, I've tried it.* And if your halo keeps going on the fritz and won't stay lit, you might need to bleed the reservoir of self-importance a bit...

For no matter how much validation or fame we might gain—even becoming President of the United States—*it's never enough* if we've grown to be dissociated from an essential nature that alone can truly light us up—*and keep us lit*—regardless of circumstance.

And when we're hooked up to that deeper nature, it doesn't seem to take so much to be happy or content. "Just this"—whatever is happening—can seem quite enough. It doesn't need to be Maui under a full moon, with some special, enchanting, somebody in tow. Nor do we need all our duckies finally lined up in a row...

As far as I can tell, the attempt to master ducky wrangling is a mission impossible. There's always something falling through the cracks, so be generous toward failure, and what falls, or gets lost. What appears to be "missing" may be feeding something you can't yet see.

In the Buddhist tradition, this "no-thing-ness" is termed *shunyata*. Yet the fact that *shunyata* has often been translated into English as "emptiness," doesn't quite do it justice. So a better way to understand *shunyata* might involve re-cognizing it as *fundamental, unpolluted spaciousness*. It's really the primordial *open-ness* through which our deepest intelligence arises. In fact, the open-ness and the intelligence are not really separate. So though "empty" of thoughts, there's nothing "deficient" about *shunyata* at all.

And thus, the encounter with this spacious, *non-deficient* "emptiness"—and the ability to recognize and *abide* in it—is also thought to demark a significant turning point in inner development (that of having become a "stream enterer").

I am writing of a perspective now, a mode of awareness long-cultivated by those of a mystical bent, if only accessed by an infinitesimal part of the world's population. But try to imagine this…

Imagine entering a mythic house with no clutter in it, an abode with no conceptual furniture at all. (This clutter-less house is making me laugh—for reasons we'll see in the next chapter). In fact, in this metaphoric abode there's not even any walls, ceiling, or divisions.

The architecture is such that—miraculously—it seems there's no inner or outer; the vistas it offers are as spacious as a cloudless sky, the mountains and trees as cozy, as intimately experienced as your own breath.

So you might conceive of this metaphoric house in terms of a completely *undivided mind*, the dwelling place of open-ness itself—the complete *absence* of "polarization." And so the concept, and even more the experience of *shunyata*, isn't an abject nihilistic blankness, but actually something quite open, panoramic, vivid, and welcoming—if not our "normal" kind of consciousness.

For "normally" our minds are stuffed with "furniture," much of it dated or of dubious quality—say like "alternative facts." Normally, our inner sky has a lot of "clouds." So our awareness itself becomes kind of cloudy, lacking in brilliance—or lacking truth itself.

Normally, like Descartes, we tend to think that what's really valuable in our minds is our clouds, or thinking. And in cartoons and comic books, a character's thoughts are usually portrayed in a cloud-like balloon above the character's head.

Though when we're especially obsessive—or frightened—our minds are less lofty than clouds, and more like a claustrophobic parade of ponderous thought elephants, with each elephant's trunk anxiously holding onto the tail of the elephant in front of it, so there's no *space, no gap* between them at all. And so our innate wisdom can't possibly break through.

Actually, our sense of what's "normal" may be more comic—or crazy—than we know. (Perhaps especially in times like these). And our sense of what's ordinary—so ordinary we don't even recognize or value it—may be quietly *extraordinary.*

For wisdom tells us that what's really more valuable than the thought-objects in our minds is the "no-thing" nature of the space itself, the space *in between the thoughts.* That's what our more rational approach has tended to devalue and misunderstand.

In this light, *meditation* is simply extending the amount of time that we manage to rest in this non-conceptual spaciousness. And its true *value* is that this spaciousness is actually *the portal to wisdom.* I've already alluded to this earlier in this chapter. But it's so central that it bears evoking again...

This intimate relationship of *space* to *wisdom* is quite central in the deepest teachings of Vajrayana Buddhism, where *rigpa*—the mind's essential nature—is elegantly defined as consisting of three things. The first is an *"unconfined spaciousness."* The second is "an unconfined capacity for *cognizance."* And the third is "the indivisible union of the first two." This is saying that though our most clarified awareness is spacious, it is not "spaced out," for such a spacious mind is unconfined in its capacity to know.

In its ultimate manifestation, such a spaciousness that is unconfined in cognizance—as with a Buddha—is said to result not only in enlightenment, or ultimate truth, but in *omniscience.* (Or what one of my teachers at the Jung Institute-Zurich—Marie Louise von Franz—once termed "the all-knowing layer of the mind").

For here, the lack of encapsulating cognitive structures may enable us to know things as intimately as if they were the back of our own hand; a condition of non-separation reflected in Hinduism by the phrase *"Thou art That."* But even lacking such a *rare* level of development, the cultivation of a more spacious mode of awareness can certainly make us more intuitive—which is that heightened capacity for "cognizance" starting to kick in.

These two facets—an empty, spacious mind, and a mind that is unconfined in its capacity to know—are thus co-emergent, two parts of the same phenomenon, like the two wings of a bird.

Though largely lacking in the Western psychological tradition, such a "pointing out" of the mind's essential nature—one that emphasizes the feature of *space*—is echoed as well in the Zen tradition. For when Zen's first Chinese patriarch, Bodhidharma—the man who brought Buddhism from India to China—was asked in an interview by the emperor of China, "what is the true nature of the mind?" Bodhidharma's famous answer was: "*Vast space, yet nothing called 'holy.'*"

Yet the *spacious* aspect of essential nature isn't something that only reveals itself in meditation—though the meditative traditions have been more apt to recognize it for what it truly is. For Western psychotherapists more familiar with it, the mind's innate and non-conceptual spaciousness can also be observed in the course of many therapy or body-work sessions—whenever a prevailing psychological or energetic obscuration suddenly releases, dissolves, becomes deconstructed. For then, what commonly seems to arise *is* this formless spaciousness, this "emptiness." And often, the client's felt-sense of spacious presence is then reported as seeming to extend well beyond the contours of their physical body.

Here, as the ego's encapsulating "psychic shell" dissolves, the expansiveness of non-conceptual space reveals itself. And though this spaciousness *seems* to arise, it's actually always available; like the vast blue sky that is always present, though it may temporarily appear obscured by clouds.

Now, it's quite possible to be helpful as a therapist, a good person, or "God's secret agent" merely by treating other beings with a reliable kindness and compassion. As my father used to say: *That ain't chopped liver!* In fact, the current Dalai Lama says *that's* his religion.

It's not actually necessary for everybody to have a keen awareness of the mind's essential spaciousness, and the subtle qualities that can then come through "the gateless gate" along with it. However, if you're in "the helping professions" and you've developed an eye for this, and can begin to help people to better recognize these states, and what opens (or closes) the gate for them, you may be helping even more; while acting as a catalyst in their future spiritual development.

Since this spacious view *is* always available, we can learn how to cultivate it, and contact it more directly, rather than just reflect what tends to obscure it—which has been more the emphasis of mainstream psychology. (And there will be numerous passages in this book where we learn how to do *just that*. In particular, the book's entire third section, where the reader will be introduced to a series of transformational gazes, that throughout history and across a range of cultures, have been employed to free vision from the encapsulations of "the narcissistic shell").

Thus far, this chapter's conversation has mostly focused on "the light" side of our equation. Though presenting the reader with occasional ontological leaps, I wanted it on our table from the onset, in part because mainstream psychology hasn't provided us with a very differentiated view of what lies deeper than our egos. And so, the evocation of a more transformational perspective is certainly important. We need it—to better understand and contextualize—what our egos obscure.

Without the awareness of an innate "light," our inner work can become fixated on fixation itself, with no real "end-game" in sight—which is perhaps why Freud once said that psychoanalysis is "interminable." Yet this might also be a critique of mainstream psychology; a tradition that initially arose as a sub-specialization of medicine, while retaining the predominant medical focus on *pathology*.

Yet an equal kind of astigmatism can prevail if we only focus on the light. (Then we can't see our own shadow). And so, it may be helpful to recognize that in the yin yang symbol, there's a little bit of light in the darkness, and a little bit of darkness in the light. I find that a very *balanced* mythic, spiritual, and psychological perspective, to see them two facets of a greater whole—life itself, and not polarized opponents in a Manichean opposition to each other; and that *you can't have one without the other.*

And so, this book—and even this chapter evoking "enlightenment"—needs to be a conversation that can include them both. And since the light and the dark exist in life, and even beneath our own eye-lids, "the lampshade" of our conditioned minds needs to be included in our conversation too—for *that's what needs to be transformed*, and held more lightly.

And we shouldn't try to just jump over it. Or reach for some version of a helium balloon that gets us "high," temporarily lifting us above the conditioning that has kept us "a prisoner of childhood." And if we try to *inhale* the helium, that doesn't help either—we just begin to sound like a cartoon character—another Donald, Donald Duck.

Thus, besides, as soon as the helium in our balloon begins to wear off, we fall right back into the same confining prison. (This can be the problem with drugs and "workshop highs"). And this is the case when the underlying ego structure hasn't been given enough light, hasn't been adequately worked with, understood, deconstructed.

And when this is the case, our spiritual states remain unstable at best, or become harder to access. And when the light and the dark have been compartmentalized like this, our development remains one-sided, and then we have the countless examples of spiritual figures who wind up in *scandals* because they've been blinded by the light, and can't recognize their own shadow. In fact, we now have a term for that kind of elevating, one-sided emphasis: *spiritual bypass.*

And with these "pointing out" reflections now in place, in the next chapters we're about to encounter a less spacious, more isolated terrain in which something feels horrifically missing. And whether we call it *dukkha*, "the human condition," or "the narcissism of everyday life," here we suffer... a more commonly experienced "emptiness."

SEVEN

Islands

I GET UP early each morning, make some coffee, and then go up to write in a little attic studio above my bedroom. It's sort of the Ellis Island of my life. It is here where refugee scribblings and books land once they've entered my house. And sometimes it takes *years* before they finally move on. And for this reason, the surface areas of Ellis Island already have settlers—and my writing studio is, in other words, a complete and unmitigated *mess*.

This is easily the most "primitive" part of my house, where empty bottles and coffee cups also compete for turf, as if rival gangs. And if a "developed person" lives under such primitive conditions, it's obviously a case of "one-sided development." And aside from books, cups, bottles, and papers, only the closest of friends are ever allowed entrance.

But most troubling are the *mounds* of words—my own and those of others—that have settled in up here, for the mounds can often get to a foot high. (Piles higher than a foot can become unstable, especially when papers are mixed in with the slippery surfaces of paperback books). And I'm a mixed pile kind of guy.

Past the tipping point of a foot, my piles are then generally divided up, and placed upon a spare chair or table, until even these over flow. At this point I either add another chair to an already cramped space, or dispatch this pile to their new residence—the floor. The last time I cleared the floor was like an archaeological dig—there were deposited writings that went back over a decade, strata reflecting completely different *eras* in my life.

Occasionally I dig down and find a lost poem that didn't manage to get included in my last collection, or there's a wake-up call kind of letter to a client, that never got sent. Sometimes I discover long-expired checks. (In one floor-cleaning year, I found over $3000 worth). It's a real grab bag down there, and collectively this layer is more like a thick, coffee-stained paper *carpet,* than something that could properly be called a pile

Aside from the time saved (for writing) in not bothering to clean, I'm not entirely unaware of what would be the alternative and more widely practiced domestic policy. Namely, that since most these pieces of paper *are* outdated, one might reasonably suppose that they could finally be tossed in the trash while repeating the mantra: *When in doubt, throw it out!*

Though I've certainly *heard* this pointing out instruction—principally from former girlfriends—I have, regrettably, yet to fully embody it in my daily life. The more disciplined aspect of my will—what some Sufis term "the Citadel"—is apparently a faulty elevator that has yet to reach the top floor of the house. And since the lovely, hard-working Mexican sisters who clean my house can't be expected to make the needed discernment between still useful papers and trash, I see no reason to deputize them to clean up Ellis Island. You know, like finally, there's a new sheriff in town. So Ellis Island continues to retain a kind of *desperado,* primitive, un-socialized vibe.

And even when I finally *do* get down to the floor level, there's still enough "potentially useful" papers down there they could easily comprise a *new* pile. The problem is simply where to put it. And so, between unconfined spaciousness, and unimaginable clutter, my life moves...

On most days I spend more time in Ellis Island than in any other room in my house, with the possible exception of the bedroom. Un-policed, messy conditions don't seem to bother me the way they can other people. I've had women friends—and even a wife, who've treated their anxiety by beginning to clean house. But I've learned to deal with my anxiety in ways that don't involve vacuum cleaners, trashcans, and such. I've discovered other technologies and work-arounds that seem more suited to me—see chapter five.

Anyhow, inside my Ellis Island, the accouterments are fairly bare—even if the clutter is not. There's just the computer, a fax/copy machine, four bookshelves crammed with books and with thumb-tacked notes pinned to their sides and shelves, and a window overlooking Wildcat Canyon.

I've also got a couple of different telephones up here as well. Though I generally don't answer either of the phones before 11 a.m.—which gives me between 5 and 6 uninterrupted hours each morning to write. My friends and clients generally know this, and seldom call before this bewitching hour.

So I'm up in my little writing studio, and right at 11 a.m. I get a call. The voice on the other end is not recognizable to me—and that voice is under a lot of stress. And the stress has a lot of momentum behind it—it took three attempts to get him to pause long enough to provide his name. He's a referral from a former therapy client—one whom I once treated for a bad bout of depression. And the guy on the phone now would like to enlist me for a similar cure, for the depression he's suffering now sounds about as bad as it gets.

He keeps descending into sobs and groans as he attempts to describe his current predicament—which he terms "a spiritual emergency." And the emergency has been triggered by multiple losses. In recent weeks he's lost his girlfriend, his job, his home…

In a *Psychology Today* article from many years ago—that may turn up when I finally clean some of the older piles—these three particular losses were included under the category of "5 point stressors" (the highest category of stress). And as if adding insult to *multiple* injuries, the man keeps blaming himself for these losses, and the groans and sobs seem to increase each time he reflects that it's *"all my fault."*

The poor guy is really undergoing what we used to call "a nervous breakdown." He's presenting an extremely regressed condition—so much so, that he's become dysfunctional and can't take care of himself. He's been passing through various friends' couches—to some kind of Sufi shelter—which is his current abode. Though he's not really sure how much longer they'll allow him to crash there.

Recently he went to a free clinic to get on some meds from a nurse practitioner. He's only been taking them a few days. So whatever impact they'll have, hasn't yet arrived. And besides, he doesn't really believe in the meds. He considers himself a spiritual person. And he suspects it's kind of a cop-out to be taking meds in in the first place. And so he's hoping I might provide the kind of *spiritual* cure that he'd really prefer.

Like most people undergoing a post-traumatic stress reaction, he feels like someone who's been abducted to an island completely cut off from the resources normally available on his mainland. (It suggests to me that he might profit from a few EMDR sessions). And so, to test out this initial hypothesis, I try to get some kind of appraisal of any resources that might still be available to him.

The answers to my questions here reveal that he is cut off from the *internal* resources I generally try to assess. In his stressed and regressed state, he's become dissociated from: his *will, strength, peace, compassion*, as well as his *curiosity* and *joy*. (In other words, the more essential facets of the soul—as reflected by the Sufic *Lataif* system—are currently all out of commission). Rather than having one or two holes in his soul where these essential facets ought to be, there are five of them—and together, they comprise one *gigantic crater*.

And the only material "resource" he can think of is, he's got the financial resources to last a few more weeks. And if he hasn't gotten his shit together by *then*, what he's facing is an even blacker Black Hole. So I'm looking at a *major* re-construction project, where the resources are minimal. And to make matters worse—the clock is ticking…

Different therapists seem to specialize as guides for different *stages* of the soul's journey. There's thus quite a wide spectrum, say from A to Z. My specialty is more at the latter parts of the alphabet. And the man on the phone has fallen down into a deep hole, a kind of personal Underworld. It's going to take *a lot* of work to even get him up to square one again.

Meanwhile, my own life is such that I've become quite selective in whom I now take on. I'm "semi-retired"—though spending 40 to 60 hours a week working at Ellis Island—and no longer want a full-on therapy practice. I still love the work—will likely continue to consult with people for the rest of my days; it brings out the best in me. But I don't really need the money any more as I once did. And I certainly don't relish the prospect of taking on somebody new that I'll worry about whenever I leave town. I've dealt with suicides in the past—and don't need any more "spiritual emergencies" like that—even if they can be the locale where spirit *is* trying, often amidst fear and trembling, to emerge.

Yet here's a suffering soul calling, and literally *crying* for help, and I want to provide what I can, yet not feel I've taken on a loose cannon that could explode at any moment into either psychosis or suicide. And so, as I speak with him, I'm trying to make an assessment, one that is soberly balanced—between *my needs and his;* which may not be the same.

Since he's already on meds, and they are beyond the scope of my license, I tell him he's going to need to find a consulting psychiatrist who can oversee his medications during the course of any treatment he enters. And he will likely also need a therapist for the psychological, emotional, and spiritual parts of the treatment—though I'm still not sure if I'm the right guy for the job (He lives two hours away, and I haven't managed to discover yet if he even has a car. I also haven't had the time yet to ask the questions that would assess the suicide threat).

I do explain that having a psychiatrist on his team could initially lessen not only *his* level of stress, but also that of any *therapist* in dealing with such "emergency" conditions. So I leave him with the task of engaging a psychiatrist before I could even consider working with him. Yet I also want to provide him with something he can begin working with on his own. And I want to present both in order to better gauge how capable he currently is to make use of whatever else I might have to offer him.

I then tell him that eventually he's going to need to find a place to live and a job. But to even have the inner strength to accomplish such adult tasks, he's first going to have to accomplish *one very important thing*. I pause…until he asks me what that might be.

And then I tell him: "You're going to need to tie a bell around that inner voice that blames you for your situation, that tells you 'all this is your fault.' That's a really strong voice inside you now, and all your strength is in this self-attack. That voice is really *angry with you,* and this 'anger turned inwards' *is what creates the psychology of depression in the first place.* Though the multiple losses you've suffered figure in too…"

I know I'm starting to throw a lot at him, with more yet to come—so I ask him to get some paper and a pen. We spend a few minutes until—with some help—he manages to write down all the points that have arisen from our conversation thus far. For I want him to have some kind of orientation he can reach for as he goes through the days ahead. Once he's gotten it all down on paper, I proceed…

"If you get better at confronting this inner attack, and can begin to disengage, or dis-identify from that blaming, guilt-tripping voice, the need for anti-depressants may certainly become reduced, if needed at all. And even while you're on the meds, you'll still need to deal with that voice differently than is presently the case."

He counters by saying that it really *is* his fault—and then *immediately* descends back into the groans and the weeping. I wait for this to subside, and then say "what just happened is the proof of what I'm saying—each time you buy into the belief that 'it's all your fault,' you become even more helpless, depressed, hopeless, and regressed."

Again, I ask him to write this down, before we go any farther. He does. But he's still so enmeshed with his inner critic that the idea of disengaging from it seems almost unimaginable. And besides it's clear to him that he's *obviously done something wrong*, or his life wouldn't now seem so hellish. (It hasn't occurred to him, and it's still too early to point out, that to the terrified inner child he's now become, it seems unconsciously preferable to have a bad, blaming inner parent on board, than to feel completely alone on the depressed island he now finds himself).

So I respond by saying: "Here's the thing you need to realize about the self-attack... *There's usually a grain of truth in it*, but that grain is wielded against you in such a toxic way that it isn't usable."

And to make this more vivid I give him an analogy. I ask: "Do you like pizza?" He does. So I ask him to imagine a pizza parlor that uses a really good sauce, with just the right balance of tomato sauce, garlic, basil, and oregano. The mozzarella is good too, and so is their crust. But along with any toppings he may like, say pepperoni or sausage, this pizza parlor also sneaks in a secret ingredient. The secret ingredient isn't very visible beneath the melted cheese. And this 'secret ingredient' is—*little pieces of shit*. And the shit invalidates the whole pizza. It makes it toxic and indigestible.

And so I say: "You've been swallowing little bits of shit each time you buy into the belief that you've committed a terrible, unforgiveable infraction, and that you are to *blame* for the life you are currently living. That blaming belief doesn't help you at all. And before anybody else can help you, you've got to stop ordering more of this pizza. You've got to stop swallowing your own shit."

My very graphic mirroring reflections seem—at least momentarily—to have stopped him in his tracks. I then ask him to write down the last points we covered. And after he's done so, there's still a gap of silence—a good sign I think. And then he wonders, "how do I do it?"

"That's a good question," I say. "And the answer is... by noticing the self-blaming *more immediately*, rather than allowing its momentum to grow and conscript you. That's what I mean by 'tying a bell around it.' And the other thing here is this: Since the self-attack is so toxic and aggressive, you're going to need to discover something inside yourself that is at least equally *assertive,* a kind of fierceness that doesn't put up with this shit."

Like poetry, dreams show us how the soul loves to speak in *images,* a language of *metaphor* and *analogies.* And since he's been living a waking *nightmare,* I give him another image, another metaphoric analogy…

"Imagine this…that you have a young boy you are caring for, maybe a son. And the two of you are in line at the checkout counter of a grocery store. And you notice that there's an older man standing behind the boy. And that older man keeps whispering negative and toxic things to the boy. He's telling the boy that he's a loser…that there's something wrong or sinful about him, and that his life will always be doomed. And each time the man whispers something dark to your child, you can see the child groan and weep, and begin to feel agitated and alarmed."

And so I ask the man on the phone what he would *feel* or *do* if he saw what was going on in the allegedly imaginary scene I'm describing. The man replies, "I'd be pissed off and put a stop to this at once."

So I say, "that's *exactly* what you must now do with the part of you who's whispering toxic beliefs in your inner child's ear. And in fact, that 'pissed off energy' is exactly what you need now in order to reverse the balance of power in your own psyche. You need to get more in touch with your own *fierceness,* and see this as part of your psychic immune system. And then to use the live, red lightning thread of your own assertive power to confront the voice that's been putting you down. Because up till now all your power has been in the blaming and the self-attack. And the result has been that you've been feeling *powerless,* while suffering an extremely debilitating depression."

We pause for him to write the last part down. (Again, I'm trying to give him something tangible he might carry and refer to—a kind of alternate reference text, and certainly a better narrative than that blaming voice in his head. Since he feels so lost, I'm also wanting to provide a map of his bereft, depressed, island terrain, and a course of action he might begin to follow as he attempts to climb out of his pit, and reconnect with the essential qualities on his mainland—his strength, his peace, his joy…).

When he finishes writing, again there's some gap, an open-ness, a silence. I let it linger for a full minute or more. And then I leave him with a parting image—from William Blake: "The fox blames the *trap,* not himself."

I look at my watch, it's 11:45, and we've been on the phone 45 minutes. I tell him there will be no charge. (But I also haven't made a commitment as to whether I will work with him in the future). In a perfect world, I'd have known of a low-fee referral source in his area code. Or taken him on regardless of his inability to pay my fee. And I'd failed to do either. As this call was about to end, he'd still be left alone, trying to find his way through the woods of a haunted, depressed island.

I suspected that he was suffering from a deeper condition than an "adjustment disorder with depressed mood." His was more likely an acute depressive order. Though I wouldn't rule out the possibility that the emptiness—that gaping hole in his soul—could also be a feature of "empty unit narcissism"(see chapter 13) which in either case could require a more extensive (and expensive) course of therapy than an adjustment disorder brought on by his multiple losses.

If he wasn't yet out of the woods, I felt slightly haunted myself. For I knew I'd just given him a little taste of something that he couldn't afford. My offering was just the provision of a little *pro bono* orientation; a few reflective seeds that might germinate, or prove useful later, on his uncertain journey home. Though here, maybe I too should take the Blake quote to heart.

In the slight chance that he calls me again, I'll want to see if he's run with the two balls I've thrown him—securing the services of a psychiatrist, and at least attempting to confront the inner attack.

I wish him well, and leave Ellis Island to go downstairs. Just enough time to read the last session's process notes for my 12 o clock client.

EIGHT
Initiation, Meme Warfare, and the 12 O Clock Client

WITH THE POSSIBLE exceptions of military boot camps, or the ordeals encountered in joining a gang, contemporary Western cultures seem to have lost the kind of *collectively induced* initiation rites that traditional, indigenous societies have possessed. Or sometimes, we've retained a rite that no longer engages the soul, has become commercialized, or denuded of meaningful training.

Fraternity hazing, corporate promotions, academic graduations, Bar and Bat Mitzvahs, Sweet Sixteen parties, *Quinceañeras,* and debutante balls, achieving a driver's license or professional licensure, all seem inadequate for the task. For people pass through such events—many of them alleged rites of passage—while remaining fundamentally untransformed. A result is: *chronological* adults; not *mature,* human forms of *being.*

One of the ways that we know we've passed through an initiation is that we feel less naïve toward some aspect of life; we feel fundamentally altered in some lasting way from what we've undergone. And yet our world today is peopled, if not *led,* by people who have not undergone a meaningful process of initiation. And for Exhibit A, I submit President Donald J. Trump...

Two great mythologists—Mircea Eliade and Joseph Campbell—tracked this loss of collective initiation back to the Middle Ages. The older, collectively induced initiatory rites, such as those profoundly celebrated at Eleusis for over two thousand years, had long since disappeared. The rise of Christianity had banished them, beginning in the tail end of 4th century.

And by the Middle Ages, the authentic and transformational spirituality of a desert mystic who shunned power, wanted little to do with politics, and had once said "give to Caesar what is Caesar's," had largely become co-opted by a lesser *meme,* and by a Church whose Popes, with the fall of the Western Roman Empire, had effectively become the new Caesar in Rome.

And during the Middle Ages the spiritual inheritance from Jesus was further squandered in two hundred years of Crusades, the so-called Holy Wars begun in 1095 AD and waged against Islamic armies for who was to control a shared Holy Land. And if the distilled teaching of Jesus was to *"love God with all your heart, and love your neighbor as yourself,"* then the love of God had become a *meme* of power and war. And a once tiny and persecuted sect had become the new persecutors.

For in 1184, on the heels of the Crusade to take back Jerusalem from the Muslims, Pope Lucius III issues the Papal Bull *Ad Abolendam*. And it had two intents. The first was to institute a parallel Crusade—only this one *within* Christendom—the so-called Albigensian Crusades, which formally begin in 1209 as military campaigns waged in the name of "heresy," and against the gnostic Cathars in Southern France. While the second intent of *Ad Abolendam* was to set up the organization of medieval Inquisitions—which were to have a foul, and long lasting legacy. (The Inquisitions began in 1231, and in Spain the Inquisition wasn't to formally end until well into the 19th century—1834—with its last execution taking place in 1826).

Though done in his name, the Albigensian Crusades and the Inquisitions do not in any way reflect the spiritual sensibility of a great teacher who'd once said, *"Judge not lest ye be judged,"* and *"let he who is without sin throw the first stone."* Rather, they are examples of the brutally polarized movements waged against other religions, or ethnic minorities, who become cast as the threatening, demonized enemy. They might also be seen as early forerunners of *the Holocaust* (and similar as well to the violently enforced religiosity of extremist cults such as ISIS that would later follow in the Islamic world). And if less draconian than the Nazis, the Spanish Inquisition went a step further than Trump's attack on minorities, for it decreed that all Muslims (*and Jews*) convert to Catholicism or be expelled from Spain. Like the campaigns of ISIS, the Albigensian Crusades were *campaigns of genocide;* ones in which particular communities—and even the populations of entire cities—were put to the torch for their religious beliefs.

Such had befallen the French city of Beziers in 1209, in which over 20,000 people were slaughtered. And here, when asked how to differentiate the Cathars from the rest of the town's Christian population, the papal legate is infamously said to have replied, *"Kill them all, God will know his own."* Over a million people were to lose their lives in the Albigensian Crusades—and henceforth, the whole of Europe was put on notice that "heretical beliefs" would not be tolerated.

The Inquisition that immediately followed the Albigensian Crusades darkened the soul life of Europe even more, and played an important role in crushing what remained of Catharism. For in 1252 AD a Papal Bull had established the legality of torture to be used by inquisitors. Then 50 years later, in one of history's worst examples of religious *hubris,* Pope Boniface delivers a Bull that declares: *"It is necessary to salvation that every human creature be subject to the Roman pontiff."* (In other words, Pope Boniface had decreed that all humans must be subject to *himself*).

Against this prevailing backdrop of religiously induced warfare and intolerance (what today we might view as a *malignant narcissism*—which I'll more comprehensively treat in chapters 13 and 14) a counter-culture with an alternative mythic perspective started to emerge, in order to counter it. And it arose from two sources. The first was the sex-positive cults of Courtly Love and their poetic troubadours. This movement was in part a reaction against the prevailing custom of arranged marriages, whereby people from landed families were being coerced into marriages with partners from other landed families—*partners they had not chosen themselves.* The result was the rise of, and in fact the institution of adulterous relationships. For in the cults of Courtly Love, the type of couple being put forward was not the *married* couple, but the "infernal couple"—which is to say, those couples not sanctioned by the Church.

The cult of Courtly Love—or *fin amour* as it was known in its own day—was really thumbing its nose at what had become of the Roman Catholic Church, and at the institution of arranged marriages. And the god they were worshipping was no longer the god of the Old or the New Testament. This god was called *Amor*—a god of the heart. A god that Dante told us could slumber in individuals for years and decades—or I might add, that could slumber in cultures for *centuries.* And as Joseph Campbell loved to point out, *Amor* is *Roma* spelled backwards.

Anyone might know that *amour* is the French word for "love." So we should pay some attention to that word *fin*. For the style of love being courted here had its own end, its own *fin*, its own *finale* in mind. Which in its more developed practitioners was really the experience of non-duality. And *fin amour* had its own technology to reach this initiatory finale, a technology of touches, visualizations, and gazes. *It was attempting to use erotic energy to arrive at transcendence.* And so, we might regard *fin amour* as a Western attempt at *Tantra*.

If *fin amour* (Courtly Love) was one of two forces of a counter culture attempting to provide an alternative mythic approach to life, the second was the Arthurian quest sagas that were now starting to appear—such as the tale of *Parsifal*, and other stories celebrating the exploits of King Arthur and the knights of his Court. Campbell notes a distinctive feature about these quest stories: The quest is an *individual* one. There's no longer such a collective emphasis, such as in obediently following a widely inculcated religious doctrine. By the Middle Ages that very approach had left Christian Europe in a metaphorical Waste Land. Instead, in the quest tales the emphasis has shifted to the importance of the individual's experience, whether of love or God. For the sensibility in these tales was, that if you've been following an already delineated path through the forest of life, then you could be sure of one thing, and one thing only—that it's not *your* path.

Another thing that both Campbell and Eliade note about these quest tales is that they're replete with *initiatory* motifs—in other words, they're replete with the very experiences that the Christian *mythos* had become increasingly unable to provide. The tale of Parsifal is a good example. And in von Eschenbach's version of the tale, Parsifal goes through a series of initiatory encounters with *women*, women of all kinds—one after another—in the course of his deepening.

One of these women is especially memorable, a veiled crone figure named Cundry, a protectress of the Grail. Behind her veil lie *tusks* and enormous eyebrows that meet at the back of her head. (Like a good Muse, women like this are hard to find! They certainly don't appear on the cover of *Vogue*, *Cosmopolitan*, or wherever women go for sex tips and fashion advice). And Cundry appears in the story to remind Parsifal of his failings, and at the precise moments others are lionizing Parsifal. Because of her, Parsifal is protected from any kind of heroic or narcissistic inflation.

A revaluing of the *feminine* is thus also a reoccurring feature of these tales, and of this emerging counter culture in general. And at this time, the old goddess religions of pre-Christian Europe seem to be re-awakening. And we see a spread of Black Madonna cults throughout Europe, which is also bringing up a lot of buried goddess material. And all of this is a very different perspective from the mythic sensibility it was attempting to counter—a *mythos* in which women had been created almost as an afterthought, and from the spare rib of a man, and created to be his *underling*, a help-mate. While divinity had been conceived as an all-masculine affair, consisting of a Father, a Son, and a Holy Ghost—and only *men* as this god's priests.

When Ken Wilber suggests that individuals (with a meditation practice) may evolve through two or more *memes* in a single lifetime, then I would concur—while also suggesting that for *cultures* this can take *hundreds*, and sometimes *thousands* of years. For today *memes* such as those reflected above, are still competing, if not at war with each other. The *meme* warfare on the part of America's two main political parties has led the government of the United States to become dysfunctional, and arguably a greater security risk than that posed by al Qaeda or ISIS.

And when our vision tilts to the Middle East, we are similarly still living in an era where competing *memes*—even within the *same* religion—violently engage in religiously inflected struggles, and proxy struggles, over who will control a shared Holy Land, and the Middle East as a whole. (Say between the Sunnis in Saudi Arabia, and the Shi'a in Iran).

Collectively, our world is still facing the problems of religious intolerance, misogyny, xenophobia, and narrowly held mythic structures that seem ill suited for the time in which we actually live. For all our technological advancements, we seem as mythically confused and polarized as those living in the Middle Ages fighting over their different inferences about God.

If Richard Hofstadter recognized an angry, paranoid, absolutist, and polarizing impulse that has resurfaced throughout history in American politics, here I'm reflecting the same in the history of religion, and certain ones in particular. Yet before I'm tarred and feathered, or a *fatwa* is declared against me, I should say that I don't view this as primarily, or only, a problem of religions. But rather, as a problem of *memes*, and their absolutist orthodoxies, and thus a problem to which all religions, all political parties, all organizations, all people are subject. (Even pizza parlors—or therapy clients, as we are about to see—may become Little Caesars).

And so, like the Middle Ages, those of us on the planet today are also facing the need for new, non-militarized forms of initiation. I'd suggest however, that it's not exactly true that initiation has entirely died out in our time. Deeper facets of our human nature have always beckoned for humans to embody them. It's just that initiations today appear in a more individualized, less collectively induced—and often, *unrecognized* way. Which is an understanding that the alternative *mythos* of the 12th to 14th centuries was trying to nudge forward.

And today, the job of those in the helping professions—as well as poets, activists, spiritual teachers, and other transformational change-agents—is to better recognize and frame the potential initiations our own lives (and *cultures*) are bringing us to face.

And with this in mind, I'll let you eavesdrop on the therapy session of my 12 o'clock client…

I like to make extensive process notes at the end of each therapy session. And then I read them just prior to the next session. It's a practice I started in my earliest clinical training. And it's a discipline I find just as useful nearly 40 years into my career.

For it helps me to track the deeper currents of my client's inner process; currents that otherwise tend to flit in and out of the client's own awareness. And without the process notes, they could easily flit out of mine.

My twelve o' clock client is in his mid-forties, and he owns a very successful business. It seems his most important relationship, though he's been married ten years, and has two young children. He really loves his kids, and is a devoted dad, but he's completely checked out of his marriage—which like those arranged marriages of the 12th and 13th centuries he'd felt coerced into entering; a marriage he only stays in now "because of the kids."

I'm also seeing the man's wife for individual sessions. While on alternate weeks, I see the two of them together for couples' counseling. And at the conclusion of our last couple's session, as I said goodbye to his wife, I asked if I might speak with the man in private for a second.

I tell him he has a homework assignment. He's to undertake an inquiry, and then email me the written results before our next individual session. And the inquiry should be entitled: *Why I Hate My Wife*. And as I'm reading my notes from this couples' session, I realize that he's yet to send me the results of his homework...

He arrives promptly at 12 for his individual session. Normally, I wait for clients to hit the opening "break shot" in our metaphoric game of pocket billiards. And if we're playing well with each other, sessions may end with relatively little still left on the table. But this session is not going to be one of those. This time *I* begin—by telling my client a story about someone else I'm working with. I tell him the therapy with this other client has taken a strange turn. That rather than being a "normal" therapy, this client is now "in training to be a saint." And that's because becoming a saint is the only way this person can remain in their marriage. For the client's spouse keeps reverting to a constant litany of complaints about not feeling loved, and it's become a broken record.

In speaking of my other client, I'm careful to language it so that even the client's gender remains non-specific. (And I certainly don't mention that the client I'm referring to is actually *his own wife).*

And in truth, I *have been* training her in how "to hold her peace," while attempting a compassionate, curious, and objective non-reactivity—while her husband remains so turned off and belligerently critical toward her. In this way she can at least have an intimate relationship with her own *being*—which down the road will also turn out to be *her* entrance ticket into having an intimate relationship with anybody else. Maybe her husband—though that remains to be seen...

Anyhow, I let what I've said linger in the room for a few moments. And only then do I say, "And by the way, since I've yet to receive your homework from last time, have you at least begun to have some insights as to why you hate your wife? And why, for example, at the beginning of each couples' session, is your bodily posture turned almost completely away from her? For the impression this gives is that she represents something potentially dangerous or harmful, something you're trying to ward off—sort of like Narcissus in the myth who turns away from Echo while saying, 'I will die before you ever throw your fearful chains around me.' "

He says I'm right, that he feels *belittled* by her. That for all the hoops he's jumped through on her behalf, *it's never enough*. And it makes him feel *powerless,* and constantly *criticized*. And even the way he fathers the kids seems to be met in such a way that his parental *authority* is continually undermined as well. And besides, they rarely have sex anymore…

I say that the belittling, the powerlessness, the hoop jumping, and the undermining of his authority are actually themes that have emerged in numerous prior sessions involving *other people,* not just his wife—and we'll return to them shortly… As for "the sex thing," that actually seems less initially complex, at least on the surface. For when a couple has two young children, it's common for sex to begin to take a backseat in the relationship—though it needn't *remain* there. Yet sex seems to be back-seated even more when a couple is constantly bickering, and critical of each other. In this way a couple's sexual relationship can sometimes be read as a barometer for the state of the relationship as a whole—and often, its *battle ground*.

And here I mention a recent study of couples. The study discovered an interesting thing regarding the frequency of complaints as compared to the frequency of appreciations. In couples relationships that are *thriving,* appreciations expressed to the partner are approximately four or five times more frequent than the expression of criticisms and complaints. And I point out that with he and his wife, that ratio had become completely *reversed.*

And to me, even his complaints about "the sex thing" seem tied to his complaints about feeling belittled, powerless, an unsatisfactory jumping through hoops, and the undermining of his authority. For in each case he's wound up feeling somewhat infantilized and frustrated—and either metaphorically, or literally *impotent.*

When he asks what I mean, I refer not only to the diabetes that has limited him sexually. I also remind him of the employee—his manager—that we worked on in our last individual session, just a couple of weeks previously.

The manager had made plane reservations to go abroad during the Christmas vacation without even clearing it with him first. My client felt his authority was being undermined here. And it really ticked him off. Yet rather than confront the employee with the possible consequences of his actions, he wound up in a power failure instead. And from his powerless stance he offered to pay for the employee's round trip plane ticket if the employee would delay his foreign travel by a few days. He was afraid a confrontation would cause him to lose his right hand man. In fact, his metaphoric impotence here was so profound that he didn't even have the juice to get up and go to work while this was unfolding. Instead he remained in bed for days while having fantasies of living a conflict-free life in sunny Spain.

I then reminded him of the work we'd done on his "very selfish and entitled sister," who too seemed to demand that he constantly abdicate his boundaries and jump through hoops in order to have any relationship with her at all. It was a completely one-sided relationship, with him doing all the giving.

Which—I point out—is not only the way he's felt about his sister—or his wife—but the way he has felt with all significant women in his life, including a *former* wife, and every past girlfriend he's ever mentioned. And perhaps most significantly, this is also precisely what he has felt with his mother.

His mom had been abandoned by her own mother at the age of two. He'd thus been raised by a mother who had never been mothered. This had left his mom with "early deficits"—as we say in the trade—and with little to give him. For his mother had a near constant neediness that could never be filled. Like whatever he did for her—and he did a lot—it was never enough.

"With you," I tell him, "relationships—especially with women—have seemed a one way highway with all the goodies travelling away from you, with very little but complaint and coercion coming back. And I think you're pissed off at that. Yet the anger comes out in a muffled, passive-aggressive way."

I let this sink in for a few moments, and then suggest we do a particular kind of meditation together, one that tends to create a more objective, witnessing kind of awareness. When I see that his awareness has shifted to a less self-referential and more objective view, I ask him to tell me how he sees himself, and the sub-personality he takes on, when he's relating to his wife in this powerless, but passive aggressive way. And the objective clarity of his response to this question seemed startling. For what he then said was: *"I become a tempestuous, little dictator."*

(Here, we might say that a little infusion of objectivity—Yellow *meme*—has just pulled the sheets on a more primitive *meme*). And after applauding him for such a marvelous, ego-pricking insight, I say the tempestuous little dictator is *his* part of "the shadow couple" that has abducted his marriage. And his wife's part of this shadowy union is to then take on the role of a dutiful but anxiously oppressed spouse, who then gets even by belittling his dictatorial grandiosity. (Her critiques—reminiscent of Cundry's toward Parsifal—are then suffered as narcissistic insults that trigger a steely, walled-off resentment for which he has no off switch. And with him walled off, *she* begins to feel emotionally cast out, all alone in her marriage).

I also suggest it would be good to tell his wife what he's come to see here, that it might begin to make the marriage a safer refuge for vulnerable self-disclosures such as this to occur, rather than re-enacting a tedious cycle of power struggles between shadowy sub-personalities, a cycle that leaves neither partner feeling appreciated by the other. And as we continue with this conversation, I point out again that his poor balance of trade, as well as his tempestuous little dictator were already *en scene* long before he met his wife. Though she's now bearing the brunt of his passive aggressiveness, an aggression that has gotten stuck. And so I tell him that he really needs to drain it off by expressing his anger more forcefully—here in his *therapy*. But first, *to see who it really is* who's caused him to feel so unloved, so angry, uncared for, and unhappy.

He counters—by saying that he doesn't see anything great about being angry. And besides, when it comes to his mother, his sister, and his past and present wives, *he's already angry a lot!* So I tell him he's right on both counts. He's angry with each of these woman, and there's nothing about anger in itself that's particularly wonderful.

However, I continue… there is something *inside* the anger that's quite useful, its distillate, in a sense. Yet the anger can't transmute into its distillate as long as the anger is being continuously expressed in a passive-aggressive way. And he needs more of this "distillate" now in his life. For its lack has been complicating nearly every part of his life, or at least the parts that he finds himself working on in his therapy—which I have just attempted to broadly reflect.

He wants to know what this distillate is. And I tell him that's a significant question. So significant, and in places subtle, that it would probably take me about fifteen minutes to even give him an overview. But it's worth doing because understanding the answer will help him to discern between mere anger on the one hand, and "essential strength"—or what some Sufi sects term "the Red *latifa*" on the other.

And the bottom line is that we can have essential strength without being angry, as is the case with any really good martial artist. Yet we can't embody the essence of "red energy" as long as we either repress our anger, act it out, or express it passive-aggressively. Anger contains the raw *energy* of the Red *latifa*, yet the energy is still being filtered and interpreted by the ego. It's thus tainted and reactive, unlike the distillate. In fact, anger is often a fake version of strength, unlike its distillate. While the distillate, I tell him, is "like having the sharp edge of a sword at your disposal, in that it provides a keen sense of discernment, and the ability to cut through anything that is not the truth."

I pause…and then say: "*And taking yourself to be the angry victim of your wife is not the truth of who you are, and this also distorts your view of your wife.*" (I scan his face to see if that last part got in). It seemingly did. And so, I continued…

"Developmentally, the Red *latifa* is the essential energy that initially kicks in at about two years of age, the 'Terrible Twos.' It's the fierce energy that initiates the important developmental stage known as 'individuation/separation,' the initial process of psychically separating from our earliest care giver, usually our mothers." I pause for a second. And then say, "*and in your case, this has yet to fully occur…*"

"For you hated your mother, but you needed her, or rather, you needed what she couldn't provide. And it kept you negatively fused with her. And this then became the template, the 'object relation' for your future relationships with women. But the thing about object relations is this: They have three components. The first is the way we wind up objectifying ourselves, the second is the way we wind up objectifying the other, and the third component is the characteristic 'emotional tone' animating these two objectifications."

I then ask him to see if he can identify these 3 components as they've prevailed in his relationships with significant females in his life. He ponders this a while… And then says he sees that he's been objectifying himself as "someone who's being neglected." The women are "takers, who neglect him." And "the emotional tone is…*anger.*"

I completely concur with his assessment. But I also point out that object relations are sort of the ego's map of relational territory, and not really the deeper truth. Human beings are not *objectifications*. And it's important to recognize that all three of these objectified components live *inside of us*. Yet when we're totally identified with an object relation, its "force field" is often so powerfully compelling and believable that we can actually pull other people in to our "object relation drama," and get them to play out a type-cast role that may not be native to them. So I tell him that where he really needs to wield his sword is upon the clunky, repetitive falseness of the *object relation itself*. That he might chop off the neck of this 3 headed monster (not his *wife's* head). But also, and quite importantly, to more clearly see how he's been characteristically neglecting *himself*.

"For the bottom line is that you need to quit putting all your juice into your business, and learn what it means to truly take care of, to truly love yourself. *And to internalize the good mom you never had*—rather than blame your wife for this. For your failure to do this has left you in a frustrated, infantile state, has had a disastrous impact on your marriage, while replicating the early dynamic with your mom. You've been waiting, helplessly, for a love that never seems to arrive, and as if it's your wife's job to provide the happiness, or supportive empathy that's been missing your whole life. And thus it would actually be more *empowering* to quit being so focused on the love or sex you feel she isn't providing, and focus instead on how much you're loving *her*, and even more importantly, to question how much you're loving *yourself*. For it's nearly impossible to feel loved if we are not yet loving ourselves."

After weeks of repetitive, unproductive bitching about his wife, today I'd wanted to mount a strong counter-narrative. And having now done so, I can see that it's shifted his assemblage point. In fact, he looks a little stunned. There would be much left on the table today. It could be months before all that was just raised got fully processed or integrated. And that's *if* he fully consented to the initiation being offered. For I know he still wonders if he's married the wrong women. And I know I don't know the answer to that. And besides, knowing *that* isn't my job. It's his. But I'm fairly certain that until he gets better at loving himself, every woman will seem "wrong." I also know that the marriage—*as he's been living it*—needs to end. It doesn't work.

It doesn't work to keep rebuffing his wife's requests to meditate together, in her hope this might make possible a following, less contentious conversation. It doesn't work to not even be on the same emotional page with a woman, and then to expect that *sex* should ensue! That sexual entitlement doesn't work. Nor does constantly collecting evidence that he's not being loved—evidence that's then turned over to his prosecuting inner attorney, who's building a case against his wife. I've told him all this before—if never in such a sustained reflection. And also, that his "career in happiness" shouldn't be put any longer on hold, projected onto Spain, or entrusted to *someone else*. And that he's an intelligent man, a rich man to boot, with two lovable kids, and generally that there's nothing interfering with our own happiness as much as the fixated parts of oneself. And besides, we've come to the end of our session...

I end it by saying: "You're in the middle of an initiation regarding both essential strength, and your capacity to give and receive love. And today we've gotten an overview of how these issues have been showing up in your life—not small potatoes. But there's more work to do in deconstructing the unconscious *narrative* you've been running for so long. For this narrative—and its starring role—hasn't made you happy...or anyone else for that matter. *That neglected little boy really needs your love.* And that angry, 'tempestuous little dictator' really needs *to be thrown to the frogs.*"

NINE

Regarding Myths:
Someone Might Have Warned Us

SOMEONE MIGHT HAVE warned us that the tribal, so-called "Holy Wars" that would be waged throughout history, were really not so holy. And that the interpersonal conflicts each of us would face, would often stem from a perspective that is far from holy. As evoked in the last chapter, these conflicts can have a long shelf-life, and may keep being re-enacted like a bickering couple in marriage counseling—or like the two parties in American politics. In either case, leaving us stymied in a frustrating game without end, a dysfunctional game that the common good suffers from, and thus, that no one truly wins.

And in particular, someone might have warned us that there can be significant and lingering implications that stem from *the narratives* that surround these conflicts—the stories we tell ourselves about ourselves, and about each other, and the world—*our myths*, in other words.

The word "myth" comes from *mythos,* the Greek word for "story." And if myths are stories, narratives that reflect a world-view, then another form of mythic structure is a nation's *foreign policies.* And in America's case, over the past decades many of its most significant foreign-policy interventions have had narcissistic features, such as the hubristic sense of entitlement in instituting regime-change in other countries—from Guatemala to Chile, from Chile to Iran, from Iran to Vietnam, from Vietnam to Iraq…

Forgetting the suffering unleashed upon other countries, the American nation has paid a tragically great cost for these interventions, and for the unrecognized narcissism of its government. The continuing ripples from these interventions will have cost *trillions* of dollars and the loss of so many lives. As with my 12 o'clock client, their narratives seem to reflect not only a short-sighted lack of empathy, but have produced a poor balance of trade. For what benefits have been gained from the coups in Central America and Iran, the Vietnam War, or the invasion of Iraq?

Since the early 1950s, American presidential administrations have struggled to find the skillful expression of American power in the world. Like my 12 o'clock client, they've often erred by being covert and "tempestuous little dictators" on the one hand, or unskillfully impotent on the other. What's *changed* since then is, for the first time in 7 decades, there's no longer a single power, or an alliance of powers, taking on the role of global leadership. And this at a moment in history when so many of the problems our world is facing—climate change, global epidemics, cyber attacks, the stability of the global economy—are such that the *need* for global leadership, and global cooperation has never been *greater*.

Yet Donald Trump's cry of "America First" is being echoed by the wider world in which every nation is increasingly only for itself. Xenophobia, isolationism, and distrust have become the new norm. We could view this as an increasingly *globalized narcissism*, the failure to evolve past an ego or ethno-centric stage—or as an evolutionary *challenge*; one capable of better recognizing our interdependence, and the skillful leadership predicated on that. Otherwise, like Trump, when the power principle prevails, empathy and *eros*—our relatedness to others—flies out the window. (Yet like my 12 o'clock client, when *eros* lacks power, Love's wings have been clipped).

Ian Bremmer in his book *Every Nation For Itself: Winners and Losers in a G-Zero World* argues that this "every country for itself" could lead to a world that has become a series of gated communities as power is regionalized instead of globalized. In fact, I'd say that *we're there now*.

For the world has been witnessing a heartbreaking, unrelenting exodus of refugees, asylum seekers, and migrants*—not only from Central

---

* There are important differences between these 3 terms. *Refugees* are people fleeing armed conflicts or persecution—and as such are protected by international law, specifically the 1951 Refugee Convention. Whereas an *asylum seeker* is someone claiming to be a refugee, but whose claim hasn't yet been evaluated. Thus every refugee is initially an asylum seeker. While *migrants* choose to move to improve their lives, find work, re-unite with their families etc.—not because of a direct threat or persecution. (Trump conflates all three, though he'd be right that the amnesty clause of our immigration policy for asylum seekers needs to be tightened up; while wrong in deporting amnesty seekers before their cases *are even considered*, and by warehousing the children of asylum seekers in concentration camp conditions. Yet in the needed revamping of our immigration policy, we should remember that excepting its native peoples, every American family stemmed from refugees, asylum seekers, or migrants).

America, up through Mexico to the U.S.—but from Africa and the Middle East desperately attempting to flee war-zones and enter Europe.

With the latter, some had to confront the Mediterranean seas, often in over-weighted dinghies. Or perilous journeys through other hostile terrains, and uncertain border crossings, while leaving their known life and possessions behind. While with the former, the recent impulse to restrict immigration to the U.S. (while planning a huge, ill-conceived wall) would effectively make the U.S. such a "gated community"—if not cause the Statue of Liberty to weep metaphoric tears for the poor, huddled masses turned away—or deported—from her freedom-loving shores.

Our *creation myths* are another genre of myth with a lingering impact, depending on what they tell is primordial, the original state of the universe, or the original state of our own souls. And there are similarly significant and lingering implications that result from our *eschatological myths*—that is, what our founding mythologies tell us will ensue at the End Times, or Last Days.

In fact, a literalistic, polarizing interpretation of the Islamic version of The Last Days has provided the underlying mythic template for the rise of ISIS—for bringing about such a world-ending apocalypse has been the end game of the so-called Caliphate of the so-called Islamic State.

And when a culture's founding mythology posits notions such as God's Word, a divine *logos,* or "original sin" at the very beginning, these notions might have come with a warning label, expiration date, or at least some mention of contraindications…

Someone might have warned us that there would be problems that come with the *Word*, problems with translation, problems with righteousness, guilt, and a *terror* yet to come; problems caused by the holy fervor of contesting *interpreters* of the Word, and fundamentalist-ventriloquists channeling their own versions of it—and the centuries of "holy warfare" that would ensue—clashes of armies inspired, whipped into a frenzy by this holy fervor.

When "in the beginning" (i.e., in *Genesis*) there is *the Word,* there will also be the problem of *literalism* in interpreting what the Word *means,* with the resulting loss of the capacity to think metaphorically, to think "mythologically." And even in polytheistic cultures—say ancient Greece—a form of literalism will lead realized beings to be executed for some version of *heresy,* a way of perceiving the world –it is feared—that might "lead people astray."

Socrates, Jesus, and Hallaj are only part of the roll call of those poisoned, crucified, or dismembered for having offended religious literalism, *or for transmitting a visionary perspective deeper than a culture's consensual reality.* And where there is literalism, there will be problems of duality, such as *us vs. them.* And the ethno-centric skirmishes of us vs. them will have a long and bloody field day… one that seems *not to have* an expiration date…

For all the prophets appearing in our version(s) of The Holy Book, one might have warned us—that the warfare fought in the Syro-Arabian desert over 3,000 years ago (between the Hebrew tribes "chosen by God" and the neighboring desert peoples who worshipped other gods)—*would not be the end of it.* Someone might have warned us of the Crusades yet to come, and the Inquisition that would follow that, and the Thirty Years' War between Catholics and Protestants that would follow that, and that would continue to erupt (in Ireland) until the end of the 20th century.

And then in the 21st century, without missing a beat, there would be 9/11, and the warfare that followed 9/11 in Afghanistan and Iraq, and later in Syria—where even two sects of the *same* religion threatened to subject the entire Middle East, if not the rest of the world, to yet another of these long-running and religiously-tinged wars.

Someone might have warned us, not only of the tribal *absolutisms* of our political parties, but of something similarly tribal and divisive in each of our monotheistic *religio*ns, and the consequences that would result. (From Christianity in believing that Jesus is *the one and only* son of God; Islam from believing Mohammed is *the last* prophet of God and thus "the last word" in religious matters; and Judaism's belief that those of the Jewish faith are God's "chosen people"). With each claiming elite, special status, is it any wonder Jerusalem remains such a hotly contested, deal-breaking turf?

Someone might have warned us… not only of the endlessness of desert warfare, *but of the mythic narratives that arise from deserts,* from landscapes that are arid, harsh, and stressful, and where Mother Nature is not to be trusted. Someone might have warned us of Patriarchal religion, and the blood-thirst of desert sand—*unquenchable and bottom-less.*

As with my 12 o clock client, someone might have warned us of *the misery* that righteousness can inflict, and the yet worse misery when an archaic, mythic vengeance becomes armed to the teeth—with the ever more toxic weaponry of modernity, which now includes biological agents, cyber hacking, and informational warfare.

Yet Joseph Campbell points out that when a myth is vital and truly useful for a culture, it's because *the myth is providing helpful orientation for the time and place in which we actually live.* And thus, when we read passages of the Old Testament in which the deity commands the Hebrews in their desert warfare with other neighboring tribes to leave nothing *still breathing* behind—not even the animals of the enemy—such a scorched earth mythic orientation might have *once* been helpful for that culture's survival—*3000 years ago.* But when applied to the 21st century, there might be some problems here, some problems with the words of God. And the same should be said for the still-occurring belief that people will ascend to Paradise if they die in the defense of their version of a religion.

And so, someone might have warned us...that even in 21st century nations sophisticated enough to possess nuclear weapons, that people would still be *stoned to death* for marrying someone they love and have chosen themselves; rather than someone their family has chosen for them. Such a Stone Age punitive-ness recently occurred in Pakistan, and right at the steps of that country's Supreme Court. (And further mythic links to the Stone Age will be discovered later in this chapter). The 12th century tried to teach us something about this, and other important things that we have either forgotten, or never quite learned—and so this book again mentions that cultural epoch, and will return to it again...

But no one warned us of "honor killings," and suicide bombers. No one warned us that a recently fading super power would be led to the brink of bankruptcy in funding armies to prosecute wars that retain a *mythological* basis—one that goes back nearly to the Bronze Age. And for these reasons alone, it would certainly be less costly if our shared world might finally cultivate a wiser way of regarding *myths,* the narratives that have been passed down to us, and that continue to shape how we've come to view the world.

So *myths*—the stories we tell ourselves about ourselves, and about each other and the world—are *important*, more important than we may have yet realized. And they are, as well, more *omnipresent*. For as I will say more than once in this book: we live right smack dab in the midst of myths, and don't even know it…

The cosmogonies of many of the world's mythologies begin with a creator god. In some, the creation of the world originates through acts of masturbation by this god, with various other gods then emerging through each other's bodily parts. But the creation story of modern science begins with a *Big Bang*, an event more literal than metaphoric, and thought to have taken place nearly 14 billion years ago.

Yet, for the updated perspective provided by modern science, two of the elements that continue to threaten our global world today seem lingering remnants of an earlier, mythic world-view. These two threatening elements are *religious intolerance* on the one hand, and a looming *environmental crisis* on the other. And I'd suggest that a narrow, outdated relationship to myth has contributed to *both*. (And so, I'm "re-visioning" them here).

In numerous passages in this book I have, and will continue to reflect the mythic facets contributing to this religious intolerance, which re-arises even today in Donald Trump's attempt to pass a Muslim ban on those coming to the United States. While now I will attempt to evoke a troubling mythic feature of our *environmental* crisis, and one not unrelated to our narcissism…

In Genesis 1:26, we are told: "And God said, let us make man in our image, after our likeness: and let them have dominion over the fish of the sea, and over the fowl of the air, and over the cattle, and over all the earth, and over every creeping thing that creepeth upon the earth." And later, in Genesis 2:19 we are told: "Now the LORD God had formed out of the ground all the wild animals and all the birds in the sky. He brought them to man to see what he would name them; and whatever the man called each living creature, that was its name."

The Judeo-Christian creation myth presents a very anthropocentric view—that is, it portrays human beings as being the central or most significant entities on our planet. (What could be more narcissistic than *that?*). For human beings have been granted "dominion" over all other species, and dominion over the Earth itself. This in itself seems *hubris,* and as Aristotle had told us, one of the contributing factors of *hubris* is its lack of knowledge of history. (And why, whenever feasible, I'll bring a historical perspective to this book—as I am doing in this chapter; but also because we Americans tend to be *historically illiterate.* And this has made America a good petri dish for *hubris*—if not more subject to electing a narcissistic president).

And this hubristic, mythic view that lacks knowledge of history has actually contributed to our current environmental crisis. *And should this inflated sense of our species' self-importance continue, it could well lead to our species becoming extinct.* For we now on this Earth live at a critical moment in time. We are the first human beings actively witnessing a significant warming of this planet, and could be amongst the last *that can do something about it,* and the cataclysmic changes that would otherwise result.

But as they say, "there is nothing new under the sun"—for cataclysms, even that of global warming, and the planet choked by carbon dioxide emissions, have happened before. (Yet if we can't learn from history—as they also say—then we are doomed to repeating it).

And when a presidential administration doesn't even believe in climate change, and considers it but "Chinese propaganda," while installing a "climate denier" to serve at the head of the Environmental Protection Agency, while peopling the EPA with over a hundred right-wing lobbyists, each day we draw potentially closer to a climatic doom.

And in truth, there has been a succession of other creatures that have reigned in "dominion" upon this planet—prior to, and for *far longer* than the relatively brief flicker of history that human beings have been here. And each of these other creatures faced an environmental crisis not dis-similar to the one we are facing today. In fact, five times over the past 500 million years some cataclysm has wiped out the dominant species, a reshuffling of the evolutionary deck that allowed new creatures to take hold. The dinosaurs being a case in point. The dinosaurs reigned for 160 million years—which in itself is just a relatively brief chapter in the history of the world, a history that spans back to the Big Bang.

And according to a prevailing scientific *theory** the dinosaurs met their end when a six mile-wide asteroid crashed upon our planet, and the following dust cloud blocked the sun. Here it is thought that temperatures initially spiked in a fire ball that roasted land creatures alive—before plummeting. And nearly every animal on Earth weighing over 50 pounds became extinct.

The reign of non-bird dinosaurs ended 66 million years ago. Over time, other creatures further evolved, like mammals, our forebears—which had previously scurried at the feet of the dinosaurs, barely eking out an existence. The first true primates begin to appear. They have forward facing eyes that allow for accurate depth perception. And also like us, with flexible hands with five digits that allow them to grasp things. Yet it would take slightly over *65 million more years* before primates could evolve enough to name *anything*.

For paleontologists tell us that it was only 200,000 years ago that a significant evolutionary advancement took place in what was becoming the human form. The larynx (or voice box) descended further down into our skeletal structure, thus allowing more complex sounds than grunts and shrieks. *We began to speak.*

For the first time information could be shared—not only between individuals, but across generations, thus giving human beings a critical advantage over every other creature on the Earth. Language transforms human beings from being like a stand-alone computer to a network computer. One's knowledge base extends beyond one's personal experience. Now we can borrow the experience of anyone with whom we can communicate.**

---

* Similar to my attempt at a countering, re-visioned view of narcissism, there's been countering theories to that of a crashing asteroid being the cause of "the fifth extinction" that killed the dinosaurs. One is that it may have been caused by a colossal series of volcanic eruptions in the Deccan Traps of India. The reportage of the controversy between these two theories—which has been described as "the nastiest feud in all of science"—is laid out in Bianca Bosker's "What Really Killed The Dinosaurs," which appeared in the September 2018 issue of *The Atlantic*. Yet a far more comprehensive account of *all 5 past extinctions* is provided by Peter Brannen in his book *The Ends of the World*—which also offers a sobering insight for us today. For each of the past extinctions were associated with *rapid shifts of carbon dioxide levels*—which are increasing *now* at a rate not seen for tens of millions, or even *hundreds of millions of years*.

** The preceding reflections of paleoecology are indebted to *The History of the World in Two Hours*, televised on the H2HD channel. See also the Smithsonian channel's fine documentary, *Mass Extinction: Life on the Brink*.

However, *every* animal has *some* form of language—and many, including all ape and monkey species have *vocal languages* that enable them to communicate with others of their immediate group about such things as the danger of a nearby predator. Similarly, even bees and ants can communicate with each other about the whereabouts of food. Yet according to the historian Yuval Noah Harari, a distinctive feature of human language, and human consciousness, is that about 70,000 years ago, a Cognitive Revolution took place. And it led humans to be capable of speaking about things that don't literally exist. *Human beings began to create myths.*

And recent archeological discoveries in Africa indicate that at approximately this time, human beings had made a technological break-through in weaponry. They discovered how to create blades out of fire-forged silcrete rock. And armed now both with their myths and their blades, roving bands walked out of the Stone Age, and out of Africa…

In Harari's view, this *myth-making capacity of Homo sapiens* is significant not only because it enabled humans to speak of things that have no objective basis in reality, but also because such common myths as the biblical creation story, the Dreamtime of Aboriginal Australians, and the national myths of modern states (to which I would add: their *political parties*) gave humans the unprecedented ability to cooperate flexibly *with large numbers of strangers, who all buy in to the same myth.* And *that*, says Harari, is "why Sapiens rule the world, whereas ants eat our leftovers and chimps are locked up in zoos and research laboratories."*

Following this Cognitive Revolution, in just another blink of an eye—a little over 5,000 years ago—another one occurred. This is when humans first began to *write*. Now what we communicated could be etched in stone, though at first this occurred in Sumer and Egypt through wedge-shaped strokes made upon wet clay surfaces, that were then left in the sun to dry.

Yet the capacity to etch dried words and concepts for posterity—or borrowing the concepts of others over one's own personal experience, while speculating about things that don't literally exist, *or not as we think*—can all have a down side. For we've been fighting over what others have told us are the ostensible words of God ever since…

---

* Harari, Yuval Noah. *Sapiens: A Brief History of Humankind*, p.24-25. New York: Harper Collins, 2015.

In the Buddhist world-view, what is seen as *primal* is not "the Word" or a heaven-sent *logos;* but instead, a primordially pre-existing "uncreated primal void," an expansively spacious and pristine "emptiness" unstructured by constructs, unfiltered by thought. Yet in Buddhism, this primal, alpha *ur*-ness is not viewed *mythically* (as part of a creation myth's cosmogony). But rather, as a valued and validate-able, (though often-obscured) aspect of *one's own psyche*—a spaciously unconfined awareness which is co-emergent with an equally unconfined capacity for knowingness; as well as compassion, generosity, and other essential *qualities.*

And as a result, in the Buddhist tradition a wiser familiarity with this formless, unconfined spaciousness (*shunyata*)—the capacity to recognize, access, and *abide* in it—is also thought to mark a significant turning point of inner development; that of having become a "stream-enterer."

(Here, if a formless emptiness is primal, it is *good* to jump in, to get a little wet…).

A semblance of this same formless and pre-existing "void" was also reflected a couple hundred years earlier than the Buddha, in another part of the world—specifically, in the cosmogony given us by the Greek poet Hesiod, a contemporary of Homer, more or less.

What's different though, is that Hesiod reflects this formlessness with a greater quasi-historical nuance—that is, as part of a mythic account of the world's origins, a *cosmogony,* in other words. And what else is significant is the *term* Hesiod uses to depict this pre-existing, formless, *ur*-ness. For as Patricia Berry notes in her book *Echo's Subtle Body*: "According to Hesiod, first there was *Chaos,* a formlessness, a nothingness. Then there was Gaia, Earth: the first form, the first principle, a something, a given."

Though there may not be much difference between *what* is being recognized here as being primordially and fundamentally pre-existent ("a formlessness, a nothingness") when "in the beginning" it is termed **chaos,** well, *who's going to want to get back to basics?*

For if formlessness, nothingness, emptiness is viewed as *chaotic,* there is something fundamentally *threatening* about it. (As if our psychic origins lie not in a peaceful, non-conceptual spaciousness "that passeth understanding," or which "gives rise to all things, and to which all things return"—but rather in a nothingness devoid of implicate order, a *chaotic nothingness* that might suck us back into itself, that might undo us and our best laid plans).

Here the *prima materia* is being viewed as a *massa confusa*, something *urgently* in need of structure, shaping, or something further *to be done about it*. It's as if our encounter with Source (or Ma Space) might render us subject to a primal regression, a descent into bleak, annihilating blankness; as if we might lose our minds, body and soul to a threatening, chaotic Death Void, a black hole, an original *vagina dentata*—*if* we were to become more familiar with, let alone abide, in the Original State for very long…

Space, space itself, has thus been regarded very *differently* by Eastern and Western cultures—whether that be the space between objects in the physical world, "outer space," or the inner, *psychic space* between the thoughts in our own minds. Western cultures have tended to have a negative perception of space to begin with, as if it is an absence lacking in value, something needed to be filled; or as with Hesiod, as if there's something *chaotic* about it. And so, whenever we encounter a gap, a lull, a space, we try to fill it up. We think, "Nature abhors a vacuum."

But in the East, space doesn't have such a negative connotation. In both the Ayurveda tradition in India, and also in Japan, space is viewed as one of the five essential elements. The Hindu term for the fifth element is *akasha* (or "aether"). In Sanskrit it can also mean "sky" or "clear space." And in the Buddhist system of the elements, the fifth element (*shunyata*) has been employed to mean "space," "void," or "emptiness."

But unfortunately, the negative perception of space that has largely prevailed in the West has resulted in another absence. Namely, an absence of "pointing out instructions" that might lead us to have a healthier regard of empty, non-conceptual space. *And our cluttered, distracted, polarized minds are the bi-product of this.* In fact we've been so bewildered and frightened of empty spaces that we've wound up in long-standing defensive skirmishes with *them too*—and seem to have trouble in allowing for them even in the course of a *conversation*.

Buddha's *Heart Sutra* tells us "form is emptiness, emptiness is form." He was telling us that all forms at their heart are essentially "empty"* and impermanent, yet even emptiness *itself* is a form; with the implication being that we needn't attach so much, nor be in aversion, to *either.*

But in the West as a whole, we've tended to be in such recoil, resistance, and fear of this lack of form that we've seldom gotten close enough to apprehend it very clearly; or to notice there are actually many subtly *different forms of emptiness.* (And why the current Dalai Lama lectured at Harvard for over 3 hours on its many varieties. And he wouldn't have devoted three plus hours to the topic if there wasn't something *quite important here* that even a *highly intelligent Western audience had yet to realize*).

And we've also come to have a frightened, *paranoid* view of the *kind* of "death" that *might* result from our encounter with this emptiness; this spaciousness that is devoid of our prior assumptions about ourselves, and even of *thought.* And so, Descartes' "I think, therefore I am" doesn't really lead us far enough back in our dying to what we are not... so that we might finally abide in what we essentially are. For we have taken even this "death" literally, and as something to be avoided at all costs, though this *metaphoric* death is *precisely* what the world's mystics have valued, and have hoped to achieve while they are *still alive.* (And this *is* "the death of Narcissus"). We have continued to face this metaphoric death with *terror,* and as literally as we have interpreted one of the myths in which this metaphoric death occurs, which keeps us from a deeper way of *reading* this myth—which happens to be the main myth this book will be treating…

With only a very slight edit, however, perhaps Western civilization—and its prevailing forms of psychology—might have evolved differently… if in Hesiod's cosmogony, or in that of Genesis, we were told that rather

---

* Beginning with Ernest Rutherford in 1911, there has also been a body of scientific support for the primacy of emptiness permeating the universe. Rutherford took a piece of gold foil, and fired alpha particles used like bullets to probe the unseen world of atomic structure. Most of the particles went straight though the foil. Only a few collided with the nuclei in the gold foil. This revealed that most of the area of the foil was, at the atomic level, empty space. In this way modern science, as it probes the nature of the physical universe, reveals the universe to be far more mysterious than our assumptions, and in many ways supporting, rather than refuting, the insight of mystics and spiritual practitioners such as the Buddha. The latter used their subtle, subjective, intuitive experience to arrive at their understanding of the universe; in other words, "the unconfined cognizance" of *rigpa*. Whereas science, predicated upon a discipline of objective observation, arrived at remarkably similar conclusions.

than *Chaos* or the *Word*, that in the beginning there was… Open-ness, a primal Spaciousness.

And it was very good, in fact, better than good. And more peaceful than anything that could have an opposite. For out of this expansiveness there was space for everything to arise and to fall away—even our confusion; space for everything to be…exactly as it is—even ourselves.

TEN

If Our Myths Have Failed Us...

If our myths have failed us, if we have been living in an age when the myths don't seem to be working, perhaps it's because we have failed to understand myths themselves; have failed to recognize their relevance, and that of the archetypes who appear in them. (Which is also to say: that if the myths don't seem to be working, that in some way we have failed to understand aspects of *ourselves*).

And if in our era the myths seem to have failed us, perhaps it's also in part because of the ambiguous way Western psychology has *handled* myths. Numerous psychologists, including Freud, Bruno Bettelheim, C.G. Jung, and James Hillman certainly recognized the importance of myths, alerting us to their psychic worth; Freud, in fact, saw in myths *the origins of culture*. Yet on the other hand, psychology has often "taken myths captive," employing them in service of its own world-view, while assuming this view of the myths to be universally true. (Nearly all *memes* tend to do this, and I too may not be blameless).

Freud, for example—who hated his father for much of his life—saw in the Oedipus myth *a universal death wish on the part of sons for their fathers.* And though this became canonized in psychoanalytic theory, it flies in the face of the myth itself.

For upon closer reading, it is the *father* and not the son, who harbors a murderous intent for the other. For at the myth's very beginning, King Laius instructs that Oedipus, his just-born son should have his feet pinned together, and then be left on a hillside to die. (From this brutal event Oedipus gets his name, which means "swollen foot"). Oedipus is rescued from the hillside, and then raised by a couple he presumes are his true parents. And later in the story, it was actually an arrogant old man who initiates the fatal duel between father and son, when on the road leading from Corinth this old man (King Laius) tries to run Oedipus off the road with his chariot. And Oedipus is only on that road in the *first* place because he has left home to *avert* killing the man he has presumed to be his father, having just heard the prophecy of the Delphic Oracle: that he would murder his father and marry his mother.

Though Freud's view of this myth might have been right *for Freud* (who might have really wished his father dead) there's no single "right," universal, interpretation of any myth. So the best way to read one may be to see what it evokes for you *now*—which may be slightly different each time you encounter it.

Long before the invention of the printing press, this was traditionally aided by hearing the story told by a bard, who might entrance the heart of his listeners with his drum beats, and then bring the story further alive by adding deftly evoked italics to the story's bare bones.

And so, if our myths seem to have failed us, perhaps it's also in part because contemporary cultures are producing *so few true bards today*—poets of the kind once referred to as "scientists of the whole" (an MFA program in poetry or creative writing being a laughably inadequate apprenticeship). And for producing transformational change-agents, the diploma mills of Western psychology and its different schools, or today's spiritual schools that churn out hundreds of "teachers" may be no better. Mastery and trade unionism are hardly the same.

A mythic loss has also occurred because monotheistic cultures have been *mono-mythic,* while often devaluing older mythologies, seeing them through "enemy glasses," and outlawing the rites traditionally linked with them, while destroying the sites of these sacred rites. (This, in fact, is precisely what happened at Eleusis* at the tail end of the 4th century; and at other sites sacred to the Greco-Roman pantheon during the reign of Rome's Christian emperor Theodosius I).

The old stories can then appear to us as denuded of meaning—even as we unconsciously act these stories out, without even being aware of the myth we are in. And the myths we're unconsciously "acting *out*" may thus be *the most pertinent myths for our time;* the very ones we've yet to

---

* And we shall return to Eleusis, and the rites celebrated there in chapter 26. For these rites offered their celebrants something quite significant that we have yet to replace.

properly *internalize*. (As has often been the case with the myth of Narcissus and Echo).

And if our myths seem to have failed us, perhaps it is also because we view them in a simplistic, fundamentalist way. That is, from *single* point of view—that precludes a more integral understanding; the same failure of understanding that we have often brought to the word "God." And this failure is no different than the confusion we experience in attempting to know ourselves in a deeper way—a confusion that leaves us dissociated from "The Great Matter."

Actually, all of the above causes, and failures, have been the case. And so, it's not so much that our myths have failed us, but rather, *that we have been failing in our relationship to myth(s)*. And the great myths often *are* about The Great Matter. They can speak to what we are, while pointing ever away from what we have taken ourselves to be until now. They may thus concern what stands in the way of coming to know ourselves more deeply, and living a true life.

And myths may reside not only in persons, or cultures, but in the very ground of a place. They may be the way that the nonhuman, or trans-human, speaks to the human; much as they are the stories we tell ourselves about ourselves, and about each other, and the world.

Myths are a way of speaking about what everything is made of, and from whence it all comes. Like our dreams, myths seem the attempt to speak to what's been missing in our perspective—the right brain's way to speak to a left-brained world. While science seems the opposite. Yet both are true, in their own ways.

Myths are also *narrative seductions* taking us back to a dream-like "once upon a time," or "a long time ago in a galaxy far, far away..." And so, properly read, they can offer a countering narrative, a metaphoric, at times animistic alternative to a literal history denuded of mystery.

The "animism" of so-called primitive peoples (Purple *meme*) possessed this sense of mystery, with numinous tales often told around a campfire. They had more an ear for the speech, and an eye for the shared being-ness of the non-human world; the sense that the entire world is of a single fabric, a fabric alive and charged with vibrancy. Such a world-view also had its archaic, pre-scientific, and primitive *superstitions* of course, but it didn't suffer from the modernist prejudices of the early, "armchair anthropologists" who first considered animism. (For example the Cartesian subject-object dualism that divides culture from nature, body from mind, and a physical world seen as distinct from humans).

Post-modern anthropologists have questioned these modernist assumptions, while reflecting that even modern people continue to have numinous, psychically-charged personal relationships with elements of the so-called objective world—whether cars, pets, and teddy bears; our lucky charms (that killer red dress); those locales closest to our heart; those sexual and fetishistic accessories that link closer to other parts of our anatomy; those equally fetishistic, erotic websites; those totemic creatures that animate our football teams, which even today American cities venerate: those Falcons, Lions, and Seahawks, our Redskins, Giants, and Bears…

In a modernist, mythically dissociated age however, it is also true that when myths *have* been employed it's often *limited* our vision, at times leading to *meme* warfare. But that's not *their* fault, or why the word "myth" has grown widely to mean "something not true." As with any metaphoric lens or mythic structure, what matters most are *the eyes through which we view them.*

And wisely read, myths can provide a view into our deeper nature. Just as they may also reflect how we lose the way, how we get lost and subsequently found. For myths are like collective dreams that may provide orientation as we navigate our way in a mysterious universe. They reveal powers—as well as obstructions—that seem to come from another world—or from a wider, more holistic sensing of our *own* world.

"Myth"—as Joseph Campbell eloquently said—"is the secret opening through which the inexhaustible energies of the cosmos pour into human cultural manifestation. Religions, philosophies, arts, the social forms of primitive and historic man, prime discoveries in science and technology, the very dreams that blister sleep, boil up from the basic, magic ring of myth."

Myths are also like breadcrumbs left by our ancestors that we might follow on our way to a metaphoric home that lies at the center of an equally metaphoric universe, a homeland akin to Jerusalem—only this homeland and the security that is experienced there is found on no map from Rand McNally. For even "homeland" and "security" are metaphoric, and ultimately refer to something in the *soul*, and if we can't find them *inside of us*, we're unlikely to vouchsafe them anywhere *else*. (And so many of the confusions our world continues to endure—in fact its fundamentalism itself—stems from this penchant to *literalize* metaphors).

If wisdom is liminal, "in this world, but not of it," the great myths occur in a liminal space, connecting two realms, such as time and eternity, the sacred and profane, wisdom and ignorance, *Nirvana* and *Samsara*, the right and left hemispheres of the brain—or different tiers of consciousness. In this way myths are *portals*, openings, like the entrance of Plato's cave, or the shape of our wounds.

And if myths are portals (somewhat like tunnels, escalators, or bridges) then like fully developed humans they have one foot of their span in literal time and history, and the other foot grounded in "trans-temporal Mystery." And so, if myths have been historically entrusted to the bards, perhaps it's because like their archetypal patron—Hermes/Mercury—they're able to bear messages back and forth between these different realms—as I'm attempting in this book.

And Hermes is a quick-minded trickster, god of both poets and *thieves*. ("Good poets borrow, great poets *steal*"). And if we imaginatively enter the mythic narratives they've transmitted, we may do so with some peril to (or enlargement of) our sense of what's real.

For like life itself, in myths we may encounter the unexpected, the unexplainable, and much that seems "unreal"—or shocking—to our normal point of view. Myths can thus serve to shift the assemblage point, the customary position of our perceptual stance. Such a shift can redirect our awareness from where we have been for so long, to where we need to go—or to experience where we have always been, but seeing it now with new eyes.

For myths contain *living metaphors*—which can make them a fresh source of *revelation*—or potentially *lethal;* for they may be differently understood depending upon the nature of the time, our stage of consciousness, or the life situation of those for whom the myth was originally told. These metaphors are like hooks that might grab you; ways for *you* to enter the story, or to recognize you've been in the story all along. Like Sufi stories or Zen *koans*, myths are booby-trapped stories for you to enter—or to awaken from. They are constructed to evoke something, to set something off, to shift something in your way of perceiving.

But for myths to work their metaphorical enchantment and help reorient us to the *Mystery* which is life itself, we may need to look at them in a new way—not like an engineer trying to figure out how something works, or like a pamphleteer or a true believer who has finally found the meaning of life, as if that could be encapsulated, now and forever. We have tried to read myths in *this* way—but also *condescendingly*, as if they were but a quaint piece of folklore having nothing to do with our own contemporary lives—and *each* of these two approaches have gotten us into trouble.

The symbolic metaphors that are found in myths cannot be concretized, once and for all; nor can the eternal *personae* of myth—the archetypes or gods. Or at least, they *shouldn't* be—for it is the concretization of the symbol that has made myths problematic.

The *symbol*, for it to remain *alive*, needs to open out, needs to be able to find new meaning, a meaning that is ever shifting, and thus capable of reflecting the time in which we actually live—which also is ever shifting. Like a great work of art, a myth may thus say something to us at one moment in our lives, and say something else at another juncture. This is what keeps a myth fresh and useful to us. As Jung once reminded us, a *symbol* is always pointing toward something *else,* a something that shouldn't be concretized, a something that is fundamentally unknown and mysterious—say like the word "God."

Poets have always been the guardian-translators of myth. Which is in part why Freud once said, *"wherever I go, I find that a poet has been there before me."* Certainly in Greek mythology the myths were told, passed on by poets, not by a priest-hood. And so we need to bring something of a poetic sensibility to our involvement with myth, *an enlargement in the capacity to think metaphorically,* to think "mythically." It is this heightened capacity for metaphoric, mythological thinking that has allowed the poetic tradition to remain relatively free from the literalisms and "mythic dissociation" that has often plagued both our religious and psychological traditions. And this is why I have—and will continue—to reference the poetic tradition often in the writing of this book.

The mythic dissociation* that has often plagued our religious traditions—as with a single-minded deity who's been posited outside of the

---

* Campbell's notion of *mythic dissociation* is more significant and far-ranging than how I allude to it in this chapter. Further nuances are reflected throughout the book; particularly in chapter 26. Chapter 33 also links it to narcissism, and the loss of presence.

self, living in "Heaven"—is also why Joseph Campbell's favorite definition of *religion* was "a misinterpretation of mythology" (while Campbell, half jokingly, defined *mythology* as "other people's religion").

But first I think, a good way to read a myth is to become completely reference-less, forgetting everything you have ever known. Whereas Coleridge spoke of a "willing suspension of disbelief for the moment, which characterizes poetic faith," here I am suggesting instead, a willing suspension of *belief*—which can lead to another kind of faith.

Like the nature of faith, reading a myth is not an entirely rational enterprise. It is a willingness to enter a conversation that might alter your perspective, *something that will mess with you,* that will speak to your imagination, allowing you to face things—including yourself—in a new way. Art, or any deep inner work—including "therapy"—is similarly not merely a rational activity, but something that should shift your perceptual mechanism, allowing you to face things—including yourself—in a new way.

Like a vital relationship, a good way to know a myth is to live with one for a long time, allowing it to seep into you, and to recognize its metaphors as they appear in your own daily life, and in the world around us. In this way a myth is not concretized or frozen in time—like a relic placed in a museum, or as something removed from its native context like an animal placed in a zoo.

The native context of myth is the human soul itself. And so a better way to read a myth is such that it becomes *a visionary matrix*, a lens through which we might see things we have never seen before.

Like a dream, a good way to enter a myth is to *temporarily identify* with every element in the story, as if each of its images is reflecting a facet of you. (Or as it is said in the Hindu tradition in its recognition of non-separation: *Thou art That*).

Like an old love, sometimes a myth will disappear for a while, having seemed to lose its spark. But they can come back and be timely again—if not come back with a *vengeance*. Like the famous dead, myths murmur from the names of our streets, and as well from Mars candy bars, Saturn automobiles, and the dreams we have at night. Even where we sit right now, supposedly awake, is mythic ground. Like bottles of wine and like ourselves, myths are *alive*. We live smack dab in the middle of myths—and don't even know it…

In my work as a therapist, for several decades I have found myself treating myths that show up as *symptoms,* and one myth in particular that has now become symptomatic in the world all around us. *This is the myth of Narcissus and Echo.* And it is a myth about being confused—about oneself, about one's own deeper nature. It is a myth about not being able to love, a myth having to do with a certain kind of arrogance. It is a myth that echoes in lonely landscapes, a myth about devaluing or being devalued.

And as with Jesus—or Mohammed—this is the story of a man who in some way never had a father. (And when the personal father is missing, how might that impact your sense of divinity?). And where the mythic hero in a religion is ostensibly not conceived via a sexual act, is never himself depicted in a sexual act, and where its priests are ostensibly *celibate,* how is sexuality itself apt to be held by the followers of that religion? And where your missing father was a *rapist*—as was the case with Narcissus—how might that impact the ways you relate to women? For *unlike* the stories which were to contextualize monotheism,* the myth of Narcissus begins with a rape, a sexual act, as does a cognate myth from its pantheon—that of Persephone and Pluto.

The myth of Narcissus and Echo is also the story of a woman who has lost part of her voice. It's a myth of curses, of what comes back to haunt us, a myth that can be read on many levels—*intra-psychically, interpersonally, geo-politically*; and in this book we shall explore them all.

This is a myth of being affected by powers seemingly beyond one's control—and the impact this has upon knowing ourselves, and those to whom we relate. And though a facet almost universally overlooked, Narcissus's story is a myth about *transformation*, a myth about a man who turns into something else than what he has been, a myth whose central image concerns a depth-vision, a vision so powerful it led to Narcissus's death.

---

* Monotheism, as Camille Paglia points out, is distinctive from nearly all other mythologies in that its cosmogony does *not* begin with a sexual act; in most others, the universe begins from a god's masturbation, incests, and rapes, gods emerging from each other's bodily parts, etc. See her *Sexual Personae*, p. 41.

The nature of this vision—and this metaphoric death—has great importance for each and every one of us now living in an age of narcissism. For here we are offered clues for how we might transform the perspective of the ego—our own, often unseen narcissism—and in so doing, lock eyebrows with the wise ancestors of all mystical religion.

II.
Clinical Takes on a Syndrome: From the Myth Standing Behind It To Its View by Committee

ELEVEN

The Myth of Narcissus

In a book that proposes to re-vision narcissism, we'd do well to include its original recognition: *the myth that stands behind it* (from where, and for whom, it was named). Yet as Karen Armstrong has told us, there is never a *single,* orthodox version of a myth. And for thousands of years poets have given us many different versions of the myth of Narcissus. And in this chapter, I'll attempt to keep that tradition alive. But first—let's look at some earlier versions…

In the version of the Narcissus myth offered by the Greek poet Conon, we're given a homoerotic moral tale, in which Narcissus dies as divine retribution for the pain he has caused a male lover.

In another version composed circa 50 BC by the poet Parthenius of Nicaea, Narcissus commits suicide. In yet another version, Narcissus loses the will to live from his inability to leave the beauty that the pool is reflecting.

Pausanias, upon evoking Ovid's telling of the tale, finds it incomprehensible that a man old enough to fall in love would not recognize his own reflection in a pool of water, and so Pausanias adds a necrophilia spin to the story. For *his* Narcissus is in love with a near identical twin sister who has died. Narcissus loves her so much he goes to a river to see what it reflects. And though he recognizes the image reflected in the water as being himself, the likeness was so similar that it evoked a living vision of his dead sister.

Yet most of these versions, to me at least, don't seem adequately useful in understanding the syndrome named after Narcissus. And the same could be said for much of the early psychoanalytic writing on the topic—in which each author has their own doctrinal axe to grind, which is argued in what now reads like an arcane cult lexicon. And so much so, that the myth itself recedes from view, losing any relevance to a human form of *being* (which Campbell tells us *should be* the overarching intent of any myth).

In the version I will offer, I leaned most heavily upon many of the psychologically apt nuances of the version provided by the Roman poet Ovid, with a few shadings, here and there, informed by other versions, as well as what's been showing up in my consulting room.

This in itself is quite in keeping with Ovid, who himself had continued the tradition of the Hellenistic poets who had preceded him in that he demonstrates his familiarity with previous versions of the myths, while giving himself the poetic license to present his own renditions. For as Karen Armstrong has also written, "every time men and women have made a major step forward, they reviewed their mythology and made it speak to the new conditions."

Ovid's *The Metamorphoses* (or "Books of Transformations") is an extended epic poem. In its entirety this master work comprised over 250 myths from the Greco-Roman world, and became one of the most influential books of Western culture, in that it had influenced Dante, Chaucer, Shakespeare and Spenser, as well as countless painters and sculptors who created art based on the classical themes of the myths contained in his book. (Spend a little time in the art museums of Florence and you'll see what I mean).

In Ovid's treatment of the myths, one myth segues (or "morphs") into the next; hence his book's title, *The Metamorphoses*. And the myth of Narcissus and Echo morphs out of the myth of Tiresias, who is quite an interesting figure in his own right. And since he's about to appear early in the myth of Narcissus and Echo, I'll give you a little background on Tiresias first, as this "back-story" was provided for readers by Ovid in the myth just prior to the story of Narcissus and Echo…

The first consultation ever offered by the blind seer Tiresias was given to Narcissus's mother and about her son. Yet a not yet blind Tiresias appears just prior to the Narcissus story. He was called in to judge a dispute between Jove and Juno (the Roman versions of Zeus and Hera).

Jove is a bit in his cups; and in joking with his wife tells her: *"You women have more joy in making love than do we men. We do all the work, while you have all the fun!"* Juno disputes this. So they call on wise Tiresias to settle the dispute. For the arguing spouses figure that Tiresias, more than anyone else, would know the truth of this matter *because he had been born a man, but then spent seven years as a woman.* And how did *that* happen?

And the answer is that Tiresias had once come upon two monstrously large snakes copulating. He then attempted to separate them with a stick—and suddenly discovers that he's been transformed into a woman. Then seven years later, he again found the huge snakes in the act of love, and in separating them this time, was turned back into his original gender.

Anyhow, Tiresias rules in favor of Jove's point of view. And Juno, "who's more offended by this than she had any right to be," damned Tiresias with eternal blindness. And then, since no god has the power to undo what another god has done, Jove tried to make up for this by giving Tiresias the gift of prophecy, an honor that made the darkness of his blinding much lighter. And with this erotic back-story in place, the myth of Narcissus and Echo begins…

The Myth of Narcissus and Echo*

Narcissus was a Thespian, son of the blue nymph Leirope, whom the river-god Cephisus had once encircled with the windings of his streams—raping her until she almost drowned. The child of this watery union was Narcissus. A boy so charming that anyone might have fallen in love with him, for even as a child he inspired others with thoughts of love.

Narcissus's mother, Leirope, went to consult with the blind seer Tiresias. And responding to her questioning, Tiresias prophesied about her son: *"Narcissus may live to a ripe old age—provided he never knows himself."*

By the time Narcissus was sixteen, his path was strewn with heartlessly rejected lovers of both sexes. For he had an arrogant pride in his own beauty, and little feeling for either girls or boys. Among those who would love him was the nymph Echo, who could no longer use her voice except in foolish repetition of another's shout; a punishment for having kept Hera

---

* My rendition of this myth, as well as its forthcoming exegesis, will employ the older, Greek names for Jove and Juno—i.e., Zeus and Hera.

entertained with long stories while Zeus's concubines—the mountain nymphs—evaded her jealous eye and made good their escape.

One day when Narcissus went out to net stags, Echo stealthily followed him through the dense and pathless forest—all the while longing to address him, but unable to speak first. At last Narcissus, finding that he had strayed from his companions, shouted: *"Is anyone here?"*

"Here!" Echo answered, which surprised Narcissus, as no one was in sight.

"Come!" Narcissus said.

"Come!"

"Why do you avoid me?"

"Avoid me?"

"Let's come together here!"

"Together here!" repeated Echo, who joyfully rushed from her hiding in order to embrace Narcissus. But cringing from her embrace, Narcissus shook her off roughly, and ran away. And as he ran from her he shouted, *"I will die before you ever throw your fearful chains around me!"*

"Chains around me!" Echo said, and then no more. For Narcissus had fled. And so, Echo began to pine away for love of Narcissus, hiding her shame and rejection by dwelling in lonely valleys and forest caves, as she fed her love on melancholic sorrow.

Depressed with ungratified longing, she now found it hard to sleep or eat. And so with the passing of time, she began to wither away, until less and less of her was visible. (At last, only her voice remained; such that now her voice—her voice alone—is heard by all who call).

The way Narcissus had rejected Echo—evoking her desire, only then to push her away—was how he played with them all, girls of the river, women of the mountains, with boys, and men. Until one boy, lovesick and spurned, cast a prayer to highest heaven. *"May he love himself alone—and yet fail in that great love."* And this prayer—a curse really—was heard by wakeful Nemesis.

Now, deep in a nearby forest there lay a pool—well deep, and whose waters were lucidly clear. This was a strange pool, one where never a shepherd came—nor goats, nor cattle, nor leaf, nor bird ever fell to its surface. In pursuing a stag, Narcissus was led to it one day, this pool that dark trees had ever kept from the sun. But the pool reflects no thing, not even the sun.

Tired and thirsty Narcissus bent to drink… Yet as he drank, another thirst arose. Beauty filled his eye, and he was caught, as if nailed to the spot. He became transfixed by a vision—that at first he thought was shadow. He bent over to peer deeper and was immobilized, as if a statue, enchanted by the charms that were his own.

Now, both worshipper and worshipped, Narcissus found himself fired by the heat of love. Again and again he tried to kiss the image in the pool, and again and again his arms embraced only elusive water. *Was his love cursed?*

Only the vision, the glancing mirror of reflections filled his eyes. And what he beheld—and kept trying to hold—seemed more real and desirable than anything he'd ever glimpsed, yet ever ungraspable…

Now, nothing could move Narcissus from the pool, where his vision continued, his love for what he beheld driving him to fevered soliloquy.

"Am I the lover or the beloved? Since I appear to be what I long for, my riches so great—yet ungraspable, do they drive me insane? Oh greatest lover, come—don't leave me here. Though it may be fate for me to look at love, and yet not grasp it."

Narcissus—whether from fatal agony or dawning bliss—then began to recede from his former likeness, as if becoming nothing himself. Only the barest wisp of what Echo had been smitten by remained. And as she perceived him—at first still resentful at his rough rejection—Echo began to pity the sight now before her.

Then suddenly, he cried out *"Oh!"* And *"Oh!"* said she. Gazing at the pool, his last words were, *"Oh darling self whose love was my undoing—goodbye!"*

"Goodbye!" said Echo.

At this, he placed his head deep in the cool grasses that lined the pool, while death shut fast the eyes that blazed with the light of their own luster.

And over time, at the very spot where he perished, there grew a flower—gold with white brimmed petals, that now—and forever—bears his name…

TWELVE

Pools, Wells, Mirroring & Blind People Describing an Elephant

> Those who come with empty hands
> will stare into the lake astonished,
> there in the cold light
> reflecting pure snow
> the true shape of your own face.
> —David Whyte

WE ARE ABOUT to begin exploring the myth of Narcissus and Echo, initially from a somewhat psychodynamic perspective—the vantage, more or less, of contemporary mainstream psychology. This has become the dominant paradigm in our view of narcissism, and so it certainly needs to be included in any re-visioning of narcissism, and the myth standing behind it.

Yet from its inception, it should be noted that modern psychology has had a somewhat limiting and ambivalent view of narcissism. And this limiting view has been a fairly prevailing constant—from psychoanalytic psychotherapy's initial belief that narcissism is *untreatable,* to the controversy that briefly flared in 2010 when the newest edition of American psychiatry's official manual was preparing for its release, and it was announced that Narcissistic Personality Disorder was about to be *eliminated* from the *Diagnostic and Statistical Manual of Mental Disorders, 5th Edition.*

Given the seeming prevalence of narcissism in our culture today, to some clinicians the proposed "textual banishment" of narcissism gave it the appearance of being a form of professional *denial.* For it would be analogous of a failure to recognize the anti-Semitism of Nazi Germany, or the racism of America's antebellum South.

It thus created a bit of an uproar amongst numerous American psychotherapists. And so, in the 11th hour, the committee entrusted to define personality disorders reversed its stance. And when the manual was finally published in May of 2013, it elected to retain NPD as a viable diagnosis.

But in doing so, its estimate of narcissism in the American population was officially listed as between 0 and 6.2 percent. Yet even this proved to be controversial. For this estimate flew in the face of what had been showing up in the consulting rooms of many American psychotherapists.

It also flew in the face of the most influential international school of transpersonal psychology (the *Ridhwan,* or Diamond Heart school) whose central focus had become the spiritual transformation of narcissism. And the *DSM5*'s estimate deviated *quite* significantly from the largest and longest running study of narcissism (among American college students) that had been conducted between 1982 and 2006.*

For the results of this study concluded that narcissism had been steadily *increasing* since the study began. And that by 2006 there had been a 30% increase in the prevalence of narcissism, with approximately *two thirds* of the students scoring highly on a narcissism index by the study's end.

Now, except for baseball, I'm not much of a statistics wonk. But I know this much: the statistical divide between 0 percent, or even 6.2 percent—and *two thirds* of a population being studied—is not insignificant. In fact, it's quite *glaring.* And to me it came to suggest several things. Firstly, the enormous statistical discrepancy over the prevalence of narcissism gives the impression of an underlying controversy about the nature of narcissism itself—as if the same *term* has been employed for somewhat *differing* things.

But what I think is more truly the case is akin to the metaphor of *blind people describing an elephant.* Namely, that there's been differing, *partial apprehensions* of a phenomenological entity that actually possesses *a greater and more nuanced contour* than commonly recognized. How else to account for such statistical variance?

---

* Twenge, Konrath, Foster, Campbell, Bushman. CHANGE IN NARCISSIM/Egos inflating over time: A Cross-temporal meta-analysis of the Narcissistic Personality Inventory.

Secondly, that the American psychological establishment may not only have had a "partial apprehension," but may have severely *underestimated it* (perhaps due to its own unrecognized narcissism). Thirdly, that we may have a largely *unreported epidemic* on our hands, an epidemic that may be showing up everywhere—in all the nooks and crannies of a culture (if not in our own psyches, and more often than we know).

And lastly, that we might be in need not only of an altered, more nuanced view of what narcissism truly *is*, but also, updated and augmented approaches to its healing. (And on *both* counts, that's what this book will attempt to provide).

And though the prevailing psychological paradigm certainly has its limitations, it also has its own *truths* to offer. And in this section of the book I will try my best to be its mouthpiece, its ventriloquist's dummy.

Though with this perspective now in the saddle, the writing may become intermittently *dense* through this, and the following two chapters. *Please bear with this*—as clinical psychology's observing ego evenly hovers—like a drone—while observing the textures and nuances of the ego's own density.

And at other times—*I can't help it*—the dummy has a mind of its own (and draws his own conclusions).

This said, if Narcissus were a therapy client, what might you think? That he had a psychopathic, absent father—a rapist; and a concerned mother who goes to fortune-tellers?

And didn't mom already begin to sense something strange about her son that led her to consult with Tiresias in the *first* place? (That Narcissus was said by the ancients to have been the topic for the first consultation ever offered by the blind Tiresias—*the* archetypal seer of the Greek mythopoeic world—suggests that the problem of narcissism has been quite a central riddle for humanity, not only now, but for *thousands* of years).

And what's it like to be raised by a single mother, while unknown by your father? How might that affect *your* sense of self? What kind of self-image, what kind of a reflection might a child take from that about himself, his worth, and his sense of world? Is there some kind of *split* in Narcissus's sense of self, a dual sense of his nature? And if so, how might this "splitting" impact upon the way he comes to view others?

And my heavens—the Greek mythic family—they've got no sexual boundaries at all! Narcissus is conceived from the rape of a river god. And in dying, he turns into a narcissus flower growing beside a pool. Echo is in love with a man who becomes this flower—but alas, she has lost part of her voice, a punishment for having attempted to distract Hera from Zeus's extramarital affairs.

Then, in a cognate myth from the same pantheon, Persephone picks a version of this very narcissus flower, which leads to her getting abducted and raped by her father's brother (Pluto/Hades). Then Demeter goes looking for Persephone (and she *also* has been raped, by the watery ocean god Poseidon/Neptune—her husband's *other* brother).

These mythic figures seem like old-time rednecks from Appalachia (where the definition of a virgin might have been: someone who can run faster than her uncles). *What's with all these rapes—and what's going on with the water here?*

Narcissus seems to like the hunt, the conquest—those stags. There's something "out there" that seems worth capturing. But from the get-go he seems incapable of being available for love, incapable of fully investing himself in a relationship to anyone else. For him, relationships seem to carry an aura of feeling trapped or engulfed, as if the love of another were "fearful chains," something that might capture *him.*

Is this narcissism's schizoid withdrawal—a disdainful retreat from other people, as well as a defense against vulnerable parts of oneself that relationships evoke? Is this saying that Narcissus, and the condition of narcissism, are reflective of a confused or unstable sense of self, a stage of development that is not yet capable of fully taking other people in—without relationships evoking the fear of being hijacked, the fear of becoming enchained, the fear of losing oneself? Is it showing us narcissism's skewed sense of freedom, its "splendid isolation?"

Do you think his single mom needed, or used Narcissus in some way, was he his mother's emotional spouse, or her idealized object? And if so, might this figure into his subsequent need to keep Echo at arm's length? Or is it that he identified with his *father*, a figure without empathy who floods and flows on, leaving others behind in his wake, as if they're nothing to him, merely debris?

What to make of his curse—that in some way he can't love others—or (except at peril) come to know himself? And aren't the two—the capacity to love, and to know oneself—related? How is it that self-knowledge is linked with his death? Or with the *metaphoric* death of what he has taken himself to be?

At first glance Narcissus seems to have fallen in love with "his own reflection"—what kind of self-knowledge is *that?* And what is it that leads to his transformation—his morphing into a flower; and is it really a *bad* thing, a less than human state?

Possibly a mistake to do psychobiography with mythological figures—yet when one sees especially narcissistic characters in psychotherapy, it's often not hard to follow the narrative breadcrumbs emerging in the consulting room *back to the myth*.

And in narcissistic characters there often *was* something disturbed about the way such people were held and mirrored by their families—and the way *that* in turn shapes their "self representation," and makes their relationships with others problematic.

To say it another way: There was often something lacking in clarity or depth about the way *most* of us were held and mirrored in our families—that in turn can skew our perception of ourselves, and make our relationships with others problematic. From this point of view, narcissism is not just a problem of *those* people. We are all blind when it comes to our own narcissism.

And when we're being "narcissistic" there is a tendency to be either idealizing ("looking up") or devaluing ("looking down") toward other people. One is seldom "on the level," which is the only ground from which a fuller, more stable relatedness might develop.

You can't relate in a true way, or from your true self, if your visionary stance is from the solitary mountaintop of a grandiose inflation—from which vantage you are only able to look down on others.

And you can't relate in a true way if you're in the pit of ontic deficiency—where you are out of touch with your own being, while looking *up* at others for something external to fill the empty holes in yourself.

Similarly, it may be hard to relate to others in a true way if how others *are seeing you* is always either idealized or devalued. (One thinks of autocratic leaders like Trump, politicians in general, pro athletes, rock stars, and other celebrities—all of whom have the reputation for narcissism). Though being viewed (by one's clients) in either an idealized or devalued way is also an occupational hazard of psychotherapists.

And in Narcissus's story, people either idealize him (for his beauty), or rejected, they begin to hate him and have a grievance for the ways they've been spurned. There are only two elements in Narcissus's myth that are offering him a clearer form of mirroring reflection.

The first is the form of reflection offered by Echo. But her "echoing" is only a partial reflection, an auditory mirroring reflecting only his own last words on any subject. And Echo winds up being devalued and spurned. As for the second element that offers Narcissus a reflection—one that is neither idealizing nor devaluing, yet which directly leads to his transformation—that (if you don't mind) I would like to hold in reserve until later...

If we have a relationship with someone in the grips of narcissistic process, sooner or later we may find ourselves being either idealized or devalued. (They wind up doing to us what was once done to them). In some way then, we're not being leveled with, as if someone is either "one up" or "one down." And so, inevitably we will come to feel that we are not being heard or seen; some part of ourselves not being recognized or valued.

For in narcissism there can be a lack of what's termed "object constancy," which means that someone seeing through a narcissistic lens will tend to have a flickering, unsteady perception of the other. (And we can certainly see this erratic *lack of constancy* in Donald Trump's regard of nearly everybody and everything, and part of why the members of his inner circle keep being so rapidly replaced, and his policies so chaotic).

Yet this same lack of constancy will likely apply as well to the self. We won't tend to see with a full range of perception, a range that includes shades of grey. Things—other people—ourselves—tend to be objectified in a more black and white kind of way, and often shifting from one to the other. And so, when seeing through a narcissistic lens not only do we not recognize the true nature of others, but become incapable of recognizing the true nature of ourselves.

Narcissism is thus thought to involve a disturbance in the sense of self, a problem with the self-image, and the tendency of not being able to accept the full range of self—all the parts that may not be included in our self-image, or what Freud termed our "ego ideal." And this often creates a painful tension between the *ideal* we hold for ourselves, and how we actually *are* in our lives.

Less commonly pointed out, however, is that who and what we *are* is not an *image* in the first place, but a *presence*, a human form of *being*. And in narcissism people confuse a distorted self-image for the *being*—identifying with former, rather than the latter. And so, as Shakespeare's Hamlet said so long ago, *to be or not to be*—really *is* the great question. For this over-concern with one's *image*—such as we find in our culture at large, with the resultant lack of orientation to one's *being*—gives rise to a sense of deficiency.

Something feels "missing." And commonly, one then tries to keep at bay that sense of ontic deficiency by reaching for "narcissistic supplies," such as for fame or wealth, "winning" exploits, erotic conquests, status-conferring possessions, the desire to appear on the cover of *Time* magazine*—or also as with Trump, on the face of Mount Rushmore! But these "supplies" can also involve a way of using others—and I think we can see this in Narcissus's story. In fact it is the way he has used and then discarded people—much like his father—that leads to the curse placed on Narcissus by wakeful Nemesis.

Taking ourselves to be what we're *not* (an image, an echo of the "real" self) leaves us in some way off-balance. We tend then to lean too far toward other people (like Echo) as if we need to connect with something "out there" in order to feel whole. Or we lean too far away from others, devaluing them (like Narcissus—or Trump). In this way both Narcissus and Echo are isolated, wounded figures. And where narcissism is prominent, empathy and true relatedness (or *eros*) *suffers*—as was the case in this myth; and unfortunately, as is often the case in our culture today.

When our narcissism is constellated, when we're confused in some way about who we really are, we thus become very vulnerable to how others see

---

* In his hilariously damming book *Commander in Cheat*, Rick Reilly mentions that fake covers of *Time* magazine (with Trump on the cover) were once left by our 45th president at his various golf courses.

us—just as in childhood our impressionability, our unbounded open-ness to the environment, led us to assume that *we are* how others see us. And where the mirroring was bad or inadequate, this lack of reflection or support for our deeper self is thought to be what creates narcissism in the first place.

There's another thing about narcissism that we can see in the myth: *Someone is cursing, opposing the self* (both the boy whose love Narcissus had spurned, and we must assume, *Nemesis*—who heard the boy's prayer/curse that Narcissus be doomed *to love none but himself,* yet fail even *there*).

And inevitably, in the struggle to free ourselves from the grips of narcissism, we come face to face with a similarly avenging, aggressive, and Nemesis-like form of self reflection—what object relations psychology has termed "the Aggressive Fused Part Object. (AFPO). Or, as I've rechristened it, the *Lord of Shame*.*

This inner critic contributes to the *vulnerability* of the ego structure, while keeping one bound and encapsulated *by* that (ego) structure. For there is an uncertain sense of self that becomes fused with a strong critic undermining it, a kind of *inner* Nemesis. And as we saw with the depressed man who called me on the phone, this devaluing inner critic can be very negative.

So though narcissism may only seem to be devaluing toward others, this devaluing inevitably will also become directed toward oneself, as well as toward reality itself. If you're unclear about your real self, it's easier to fuse with, and become confused by the critical reflection of the AFPO.

Since the *Nemesis*-like critical object comprises such an important, and often unrecognized feature of narcissism—one that can appear intermittently in almost everyone's psychology—let's expand our view of it…

---

* See my poetry chapbook *The Museum of the Lord of Shame*. Richmond: Point Bonita Books, 1997.

THIRTEEN

Nemesis and the Five Faces of the Narcissistic Curse

IN THE GREEK mythological tradition, Nemesis was a winged goddess. She was variously depicted as holding a measuring rod or scales in one hand, and a sword or scourge in the other. Her emblematic tools suggest a deity with a keen eye for proportion (the measuring rod or scales) as well as the capacity for inflicting punishment (the sword and scourge) when that proper proportion is *violated*.

Originally, Nemesis was seen as the distributor of fortune, measuring it out according to what each person deserved. She was sometimes referred to as *Adrasteia,* meaning "one from who there is no escape." And in just *this* sense, Nemesis eventually came to be seen as *the spirit of retribution* against those who succumb to *hubris*.

And *hubris* in ancient Greece was recognized all over the place (as narcissism might for us today). But in ancient Greece *hubris* was actually a civic *crime,* one perpetuated against other humans, not just against the gods. However, *hubris* was also *the primary crime* committed against the gods; a violation of archetypal, spiritual relations. And so, *hubris* usually was the *fatal character flaw* of the protagonists in Greek tragic dramas.

Aristotle noted a quality of *shame* often connected with *hubris,* such as in shaming a person and taking pleasure in this, as if by ill-treating others one's own superiority becomes greater. And a contemporary illustration of this would be Donald Trump. For even a partial listing of those he has attempted to shame and demean could fill several pages. Here I'll just mention: Hillary, John McCain, Obama, his own attorneys general Sara Yates and Jeff Sessions, the press, Gold Star parents who happen to be Muslim, Meryl Streep, his former FBI Director James Comey, our nation's security services, Senate Majority leader Mitch McConnell, most Republican primary candidates for President during 2016, and any Republican legislators who won't rubber stamp his legislative agenda, Rosie O Donnell, NFL players protesting the treatment of blacks by police, Puerto Rico, Mexicans, Vice President Pence (for his religiosity), scientists warning of an environmental crisis, a half dozen countries with Muslim majorities, NATO and the leaders of several European countries, the Democratic party leaders of his own country, and the various women he has groped and called liars. In fact, what's so disturbing is that Trump himself is so *shameless*; he seems to lack not only empathy, but conscience. For he never apologizes or admits fault, and will shame anyone who doesn't support his *hubris*.

In modern usage, *hubris* has come to mean an overbearing pride or arrogance. (Here another Donald comes to mind: Rumsfeld). *Hubris* is often associated with *a lack of knowledge of history,* and a *lack of humility*—with the accompanying sense that some suffering or punishment will follow, as in the proverb "pride goes before a fall." (Precisely what occurred with the U.S. invasion of Iraq; and likely to happen with Trump).

And so that "fall"—or retribution—links us back to *Nemesis,* who punishes the crime of *hubris.* The two concepts thus belong together. Without *hubris,* there is no following *nemesis.*

Hopefully it won't be too much of a stretch to recognize a striking similarity between the Greek perception of a prideful arrogance that shames (*hubris*) and our own perception of *narcissism.* For it was Narcissus's prideful arrogance, and the way he had spurned and shamed his lovers, that led one boy to cast a prayer to highest heaven, asking that Narcissus should ever fail at love. And this prayer was heard—by Nemesis…

I will now attempt to further reflect the shaming qualities in narcissism that Aristotle had recognized in *hubris.* I will also continue to evoke the ways that Nemesis has appeared in our contemporary, geo-political world—as is the case when Islamic *jihad* becomes the Nemesis-like response to the *hubris* of American imperialism. Or, in the case of Donald Trump, where the world's press corps functions as his Nemesis, as has America's other main political party, as well as the FBI, other security services, career civil servants, and scientists—whenever they've challenged or investigated his policies, motivations, recklessness; or the veracity of his "alternative facts."

And here I might add that the nuance of *hubris* that lacks a knowledge of history, may have also played itself out in Afghanistan—from the U.S. government's failure to have recognized from previous examples, that a costly graveyard awaits imperialistic powers attempting to exert their will upon the tribes of that proud, fierce, mountainous culture.

For Afghanistan, when facing the danger of being dominated by imperialistic invaders—from Alexander the Great and Genghis Khan, to the British, Russians, and to now—has usually then splintered into something ungovernable, a protective regression into unruly tribal fiefdoms.

And a similar *hubris* that demonstrates the lack of knowledge of history will also be reflected later in this chapter, when exploring the malignant narcissism of ISIS.

Yet one thing we might belatedly learn –whether from Afghanistan or Iraq—is, that it's a damn sight easier to invade a Middle Eastern country with military force, than to *leave* it in good shape. While a related thing that history might teach—whether from Obama's failure to back up his own "red line" ultimatum in Syria, or Trump's decision to abandon the Kurds there—is soberingly this: That almost *anything* foreign governments attempt in the Middle East runs the unfortunate risk of "unintended consequences." And that risk becomes a near-certainty, when the leader of a foreign government has the narcissistic *hubris* of thinking he knows more than he does, and then ups the risk factor by also manifesting the reckless impulsivity of a psychopath to boot.

Until the very end of the myth of Narcissus and Echo, we have seen that Narcissus bore a curse—ostensibly from Nemesis—one that would doom him to failing at love; if not from truly coming to know himself. For as Tiresias cryptically foretold of Narcissus, self-knowledge would prove to be *deadly*.

Similarly, we've been noting that in narcissism there is a critical, avenging, Nemesis-like perspective. And sometimes this critical perspective is turned on ourselves, leading us to feel shamed or deficient in some way.

While at other times, this critical and devaluing lens is turned on others—which we might recognize as a form of *hubris*. And this then, can lead other people to respond negatively toward us (i.e., *nemesis*).

Here we might also recognize that whether we inflict it upon others or suffer it ourselves, that shame or humiliation is like the underbelly of *pride*, the suffering that comes from a *lack* of humility. For if we have the virtue of humility, we can't really be humiliated.

Humility—which is one of the virtues reflected in The Enneagram of the Virtues, and the *antidote* to pride—doesn't mean that we are wearing a hair shirt. But rather, it has to do with the perspective toward the self that has been reflected in some of the quotations from Islamic, Jewish, and Christian mystics, such as when Isaac of Ninevah said the following:

"Humility collects the soul into a single point by the power of silence. A truly humble man has no desire to be known or admired by others, but wishes to plunge from himself into himself, to become nothing, as if he had never been born. When he is completely hidden to himself in himself, he is completely with God."

Here where Isaac of Ninevah speaks of collecting the soul "into a single point" and of having "become nothing," and "completely hidden" to oneself," it means that one's field of vision has become *divested of self-reference*.

Unlike people who are caught in the self-conscious headlights of narcissism and for whom it all seems "about me," with the perspective Isaac of Ninevah is speaking of there is no reference to self shading one's perception of reality. One has become *nothing, empty*—but in a good way—much like Nisargadatta Maharaj. *That* is humility.

In this way, humility enables us to see things more as they really are, for our view is no longer being shaded by self-reference or self-importance. *The self that might otherwise appear in either an idealized or devalued guise—the self that might otherwise either idealize or devalue others—has disappeared*, at least for the moment.

But lacking in humility, we thus not only are unconsciously setting ourselves up for the fall that follows pride—*nemesis*—but we are impeded from loving others, as well as prevented from knowing ourselves in a deeper way.

We might say that which impedes us from loving others, knowing ourselves more deeply, or having a genuine and healthy self-esteem—is in itself a kind of curse, and what Narcissus had been suffering until the very end of his myth.

But this is our problem too. For if we are taking ourselves to be a "concretized someone," if we have not divested ourselves of self-reference and our identification with the self-image, we will tend to *lack* the proper sense of proportion in measuring ourselves. And reflecting it mythically, the Greeks found this very lack of proportion in our regard of others, and of ourselves, to be what brings Nemesis down upon us.

While conversely, humility would be the virtue of *having this proper sense of proportion,* a proper measure of ourselves, whereby we are being neither inflated nor deflated in our self-regard, and neither idealizing nor devaluing in our regard of others.

Narcissism inevitably suffers from *both* of these pitfalls, *a lack of the right proportion in one's self-regard, as well as in our regard of others.* And for the Greeks, Nemesis came to be associated with "a resentment caused by any disturbance of this right proportion, the sense of justice which could not allow it to pass unpunished."

Like Narcissus, we are cursed by our own lack of self-knowledge, by the various ways we take ourselves to be what we're not—*which is the broadest definition I would bring to narcissism.* All our "sins" come from this, all the ways that we "miss the mark" come from this basic kind of ignorance, our ignoring of a deeper and more *selfless* nature, which leads us to fail to recognize and value the true nature of others, the true nature of everything.

And to the extent other people are also taking themselves to be what they're not, and remaining oblivious to a deeper and more selfless nature, narcissism becomes a contagious dis-ease being passed throughout a culture, and in fact, the world. (Please read this sentence again).

For in narcissism, one has identified—or more properly, become *absorbed, merged* with the self-image—without realizing one has done so—and with this *image* viewed as a stand-alone, a concretized entity apart from the rest of reality. And this isolated assumption of self-hood will tend to be inflated, or else shamed and inadequate—and either of which we then take to be our *identity.* The two main characters in our myth, Narcissus and Echo, show us these two distorted self-representations.

Narcissus has from an early age had a prideful sense of his own physical beauty, and a devaluing regard toward those who love him. Echo feels something missing inside, beginning with her own voice, and pursues Narcissus (at first in an idealizing way) as if joining forces with him would somehow enhance her.

Both of these perspectives have been "cursed" in a way that has left them erotically crippled. (Narcissus has been cursed by Nemesis; Echo by Hera). And both reflect the dissociation from a deeper way of experiencing ourselves in relationship to others—what I refer to as "presence"—which is the experience of our *being* unfiltered by the self-image.

But to the extent that the self-image is often, unknowingly, what we are taking ourselves to be, there will be a *lack* of presence. And that lack will leave us with some sense of ontic deficiency, the feeling that something both beautiful and essential is *missing—a something one can never quite grasp;* and metaphorically, perhaps what Narcissus initially experienced in failing to grasp the beauty of *his own essential nature* as reflected in a strange pool that seems to reflect *nothing else.*

Though Narcissus certainly seems fascinated, and drawn toward what he sees reflected in that mysterious pool, it's not exactly accurate to say he's *identified* with the self-image, or that the love for his self-image thus accounts for his death—which has been the more common and exoteric interpretation of his death scene.

Rather than *identifying,* he's actually quite *dissociated* from the beauty that the pool is reflecting. For what he's loving—and experiences as so ungraspable—seems "out there" to him. What thus seems more narratively accurate is, that there's an apparent split in the self—a schism that has left him *dissociated* from the beauty of his own deepest nature.

And so, it would seem an alternative—and to my mind a deeper reading of the myth—to see that beautiful image as a reflection of his own essential nature; the beauty of an essential nature that seems so foreign, so mysterious *–so previously unknown* to him. (And thus we might say that it is the encounter with *that,* and the love *for* that, which proves to be so metaphorically deadly—deadly that is, to what he has previously taken himself to be).

This I think would both be a more accurate reading of the *myth,* while also providing a more penetrating, and vivid reflection—of narcissism itself. *To view it as a condition where the deeper self is still split off, and disowned in some way.* In other words, amongst the varied metaphors he might reflect, I see Narcissus as a metaphor for the fundamental confusion experienced by humanity throughout time. A metaphor, that is, for the lack of *self-realization*—the failure to "grasp" one's own true nature.

And if this is a psychological and spiritual confusion—a fundamental *identity confusion*—it also gives rise to an *erotic confusion.* For if we can't recognize and embody the beauty of our own essential nature, then—like Narcissus—we're apt to be impeded in recognizing—or loving—that essential beauty lying in everyone *else.*

Five Faces of the Narcissistic Curse

Till now, I've been reflecting a few of the generic, yet interconnected facets common in narcissism—facets that might help us to better *define* it, while also reflecting precisely what it is that precludes us from having a more unfiltered, spiritual vision. These facets have included the following features...

- A *misappropriation of identity*—"taking ourselves to be what we are not"—whether by overly identifying with the self-image, or by the failure to recognize and identify with the beauty of our deeper nature. And in both cases, with a resultant dissociation from *being.*
- A *lack of a balanced perspective toward both the self and toward others,* which results in a loss of *eros;* that is, a loss of the sense of *relatedness* to other people, and to life itself.
- Instead, we experience ourselves as a "stand alone," a creature living in a "splendid isolation," an erotic impairment in which the relational field is seldom level, but rather, someone always either "one up" or "one down."
- Fusing with (and becoming confused by) a critical, devaluing perspective that lacks both empathy and humility; a devaluing that inevitably becomes directed towards other people, oneself, and reality itself.
- This devaluing contributes to a sense of *ontic deficiency,* precludes us from opening more fully to our own presence, and precludes us from

recognizing and valuing the presence, the true nature of others, and of life itself.
- This ontic deficiency also gives rise to the *need* for *narcissistic supplies;* for these "supplies" are employed to compensate, or defend against the *deficient* emptiness that results from the loss of *being,* the loss of *presen*ce, the lack of orientation to our own deeper nature.

And though a greater awareness of these generic facets can help us to have a more differentiated vision of the *constituents* of narcissism, as well as what narcissism tends to *obscure,* I think it can also be valuable to recognize that these facets also manifest through several *distinctively different narcissistic styles.* And the attempt to reflect these different *styles* will be my task for the rest of this chapter…

When we are in the grips of narcissism—this Hubris/Nemesis complex—our inner critic may lead us to have a very haughty way of looking at other people, as if most people are second rate and don't meet our standards.

Though this devaluing facet of narcissism can be clearly seen in Narcissus in his myth, for some reason it was the last of the four narcissistic styles to have been identified by Dr. James Masterson, who in clinical circles has been viewed as one of the leading authorities on narcissism and other "disorders of the self." It's what Masterson termed the *devaluing narcissist,* and we might recognize it in the brilliant but imperious CEO who is impossibly critical and demanding to work for. The character played by Meryl Streep in *The Devil Wears Prada* would be a good example of a devaluing narcissist. As would the role Donald Trump embodied in his TV series *The Apprentice.*

A second narcissistic style can be seen when the fusion with this critical perspective leads it to be turned against *ourselves*—leading us to feel empty in some way, empty and anxious; depressed, inadequate, and unfulfilled. (Similar to the depressed man who called me on the phone in chapter 7).

In Buddhist psychology, this *deficient* form of emptiness—which is very different from the other main genre of "emptiness" recognized by Buddhism (*sunyata)*—is called the realm of the *pretas,* the realm of the "hungry ghosts," which is one of six *realms* reflected by Buddhist psychology.

The hungry ghosts are depicted as having enormous, empty bellies, and throats no wider than a needle. So this is a metaphoric depiction of a realm of human consciousness that we enter where we feel empty inside, a perpetual state of dissatisfaction that is *structurally un-fillable.*

It's also what Masterson and object relations psychology terms *"empty unit narcissism."* And people often turn to addictions—such as for drugs, or erotic relationships *used* like drugs—in the attempt to fill this deficient type of "emptiness."

The fusion with our inner Nemesis could also take a similar, but slightly different form—one where our strategy becomes that of trying to *hide* the shamed sense of self—any time when we might be feeling wincing, fragile, cringed, and withdrawn. Here, we've "introjected" an earlier rejection by someone else, and now it lives inside us. A good example of such a shame-filled withdrawal occurs when Echo hides her shame and rejection (by Narcissus) through retreating into lonely valleys and forest caves.

Here we feel *vulnerable to exposure,* and now seek distance from the eyes of others, as if retreating into a closet. And to the extent we can't recognize the shaming AFPO now living inside us—we tend to project it *outside* of us. We thus assume other people would be looking at us the way we are secretly now viewing ourselves—and thus feel the need to hide ourselves from being viewed by others. This shame-infused perspective is what Masterson terms *"closet narcissism."* It is probably the most common narcissistic style today, though such an assessment is based purely upon what—for years now, has been showing up in my consulting room.

A fourth narcissistic style is what has been termed *"exhibitionistic narcissism."* This face of narcissism is perhaps the one that most readily comes to mind when the word "narcissism" is being employed. Here, rather than retreating into a closet so that others would not view us through our own devaluing lens, we instead attempt to pump ourselves up so as to appear larger than life. Rather than hide from other people, we now see other people as a needed audience, an audience that might provide an *idealized* reflection of self in all our "glory." (Think Donald Trump appearing at a rally in front of his base).

Here, we've become *grandiose*—and have a compelling need for this grandiose self to be witnessed and *validated* by others, as if failing to puff up in this way might lead to our not getting any notice at all. Here, like Trump, we may toot our own horn. And become identified with our "act," and with our accouterments, possessions, and various metaphoric trophies, the accomplishments of a "winning self"—in other words, with whatever might embellish the image we present to the world.

As is the case with narcissism in general, the exhibitionistic grandiosity here attempts to compensate for, or defend against, an earlier *wound*— that of our true nature not having been adequately recognized and valued. (Our true nature possesses humility, *grandeur* and dignity—*grandiosity* is the ego's counterfeit coin, an attempt to compensate for the true self that has been lost).

And anytime someone does not confirm our grandiosity, this can be experienced as "a narcissistic insult"—whereby we feel wounded, "dissed"— and then, often, wind up devaluing *them*. (Again here, Trump is a vivid exemplar, as was "the man who hated his wife" in chapter 8).

The celebrity culture of Hollywood—where people go to become stars— is a domain of exhibitionistic narcissism. It glitters with the flashbulbs of fame and conspicuous wealth. Here the self-image becomes tricked out to its ultimate deification, and now may appear—or *want* to appear—on billboards, or on the cover of magazines.

Here the sense of narcissistic entitlement seems boundless. And the profession of plastic surgery is a gold mine, with middle-aged women attempting to still appear as ingénues shopping for the splendors of Rodeo Drive with faces tight as the stitched pigskin of a football. (Think Joan Rivers). And future anthropologists may speculate about an important rite once celebrated here—the *Academy Awards*—apparently a holy day, in a narcissistic culture's worship of celebrity.

Marcel Proust—a voyeur, and the author of one of the great novels of the 20th century—would often go to a bordello, and watch other people having sex through a peephole before going home to write. (Apparently, these "gazes" shifted his assemblage point and *raised his level of psychic energy*—a libidinal wave he would then ride as he wrote).

In this light, we might view exhibitionistic narcissism as a kind of *"inverse* voyeurism," the need to have one's grandiosity stroked, one's potency viewed and admired by others. Such inverse voyeurism reigns in the porn industry—Hollywood's slightly more slutty cousin—and was once termed "phallic narcissism." And the sports world has always recognized something similar, if not identical, in those desperate for attention, and considered to be "hot dogs." Terrell Owens might be a good example of this style of narcissism, as might more contemporary exemplars: Odell Beckham Jr., and Antonio Brown. Such talented wide receivers have become pro football's *prima donnas,* the game's most narcissistic position—and thus are those most prone to violate a cardinal principle in coach-speak: *There is no "I" in TEAM.*

A fifth narcissistic style seems to want its own territory, its own Caliphate, its own base. And so, I'm about to give it its own, extensive sub-chapter. It is a style first noted by Erich Fromm, and further reflected upon later by Otto Kernberg, among others. This is what has been termed *malignant narcissism.*

There have been apparent differences in how malignant narcissism has been portrayed by the various clinicians who have recognized or used the term. Fromm, for example, considered malignant narcissism "the quintessence of evil" and the most severe of pathologies. While Kernberg, in recognizing that antisocial personality disorders are fundamentally narcissistic, located malignant narcissism at a mid-point in a spectrum of pathological narcissism, half-way between the psychopath (or antisocial personality) at the most severe end, and ordinary Narcissistic Personality Disorder at the low end.

I tend to view the perspectives of both Kernberg and Fromm as valid. For I agree with Fromm that malignant narcissism really *can be* "the quintessence of evil," and I agree with Kernberg that antisocial personality disorders *are* fundamentally narcissistic (though they *too* may be the quintessence of evil). And in the next chapter I'll argue not only a likeness between malignant narcissism and antisocial personality disorders, but that they may be reflecting the same *pathological lack of empathy*—and thus, as the *DSM 5* suggests, *both* diagnoses (NPD, or Antisocial Personality Disorder) could be validly given to the same *person.*

For people are not pie charts—and these diagnostic boundaries should not be etched in stone. In fact, one of the things that has made narcissism so difficult to more comprehensively recognize and treat, is the extent to which it often *does* seem to include elements of other disorders (as we will see in the next chapter, regarding the possible diagnoses that might be given for Donald Trump). Similarly, the narcissistic *styles* being reflected in *this* chapter should also not be etched in stone. Like Buddhism's six psychological realms–or Donald Trump—we might pass through more than one of these styles *in a single hour.*

Any form of psychological typing is ultimately a generalization—yet each of us are specifically no one other than ourselves, and include facets the generalization fails to reflect.

However, it is *also* true that to the extent we are living out of the fixated nature of any personality style, *any* ego structure, to that extent we *do* become somewhat generic. *Fixation is generic; essence is not.* And any human being is a mixture of the two.

Yet with this said, and for reasons soon to be more evident, malignant narcissism demands a deeper "re-visioning." For there are features of malignant narcissism that are especially *toxic,* and that give malignant narcissism a diagnostic importance—even if for what, fortunately, is a rather small segment of the world population.

Edith Weigert reflected one of these features: *"a regressive escape from frustration by distortion and denial of reality."* I find this a clear clinical vision—which importantly captures the *frustration* suffered by such people, and that can lead to their often-noted "unregulated" behavior. (Say like the uncontrollable impulse to post disdainful tweets in response to anyone or anything that counters or threatens one's own grandiosity).

And part of this distortion and denial of reality is maintained by a *distortive, revisionist approach to history,* while also projecting rather dreadful and unconscious facets of themselves onto others, including the cause(s) of their own frustration with life. And again, Trump is the poster boy.

For though malignant narcissists can be arrogant, insufferable, and treat other people like shit, deep down inside they may feel like shit themselves, as if they are fetid, stinky, or worthless at the core. But just as their real self has become disowned, so has this sense of deficiency. It becomes deeply buried—and then *projected onto others.* Trump's accusative smear-campaigns against others are thus actually what he deeply manifests himself, the precise reflections of his own disowned shadow.

For example, his portrayal of former FBI director James Comey as being a "grandstander" and a "nut job," Hillary Clinton as being dishonest, the press as being the purveyor of "fake news." (And in this, malignant narcissism shares something in common with devaluing narcissism, for in both cases the deficiency experienced due to the loss of the real self is being projected externally).

Hubert Rosenfeld provided another clear-eyed view into malignant narcissism: *"a disturbing form of narcissistic personality where grandiosity is built around aggression and the destructive aspects of the self become idealized."* And related to this quality of *aggression*—which is often corrosively leaking out, or exploding into the environment as a kind of resentment, or murderous, un-neutralized rage—is that malignant narcissism manifests a quality of *sadism,* and taking pleasure in one's own arrogance and cruelty. (Say the Trump administration's separation of the families of asylum-seekers at the Mexican border, and caging the children in concentration camp-like conditions—a Nazi redux lacking only the Zyklon B).

Of all the narcissistic styles I'm reflecting here, malignant narcissism is actually the one that most clearly reflects Aristotle's nuance of "shaming a person and taking pleasure in this, as if by ill-treating others one's own superiority becomes greater." And in this light, another vivid contemporary manifestation of malignant narcissism would be the soldiers of ISIS when they chop off the heads of those who don't agree with their point of view—"the sadism of ill-treating others as if this makes one's superiority the greater."

And ISIS also manifests malignant narcissism's "regressive escape from frustration by distortion and denial of reality" (as well as "the distortive, revisionist approach to history") in overlooking several centuries of evolution in Islamic thought and jurisprudence, while operating under the belief that the modern world as we know it should not even exist.

And so ISIS is dedicated to "the purification of the world"—by killing vast numbers of people. Which in itself also reflects Fromm's notion of malignant narcissism as being "the quintessence of evil."

In the Zen tradition it is said that a great and existential *doubt*—a doubt about the fundamental nature of existence—can give rise to a great *enlightenment.* (And the greater the doubt, the greater the awakening. The smaller the doubt, the smaller the awakening. No doubt, no awakening). Doubt, ridden to the end of the line, thus leads to faith. No beliefs are required. For they have been transcended in the crucible of one's own direct, spiritual experience.

Yet a *counterfeit* version of the clarity and certainty that can arise out of the probing engagement with one's own existential doubt seems the case with the soldiers of ISIS. For with the inflated sense of a Great Mission, a "narcissistic glow"* lights the faces of cultic believers, outshining the capacity for doubt. Here are not Jack-o'-lanterns, but "happy brothers fighting together in a great cause," who speak openly of the joy and *certainty* they've found in themselves (and would offer to recruits) in joining the fight against the Great Satan—a Satan that has been disowned, and projected "out there."

But Satan—God's shadow—cannot be banished or vanquished so readily as doubt. Nor can this kind of "splitting" (between God and Satan, good and evil, and us vs. them) as it is termed in contemporary psychology, where "splitting" is viewed as a rather primitive defense mechanism, a desperate attempt to keep some portion of "object goodness" alive, and thus brake the descent into a bleak, annihilating Hell.

Yet a living Hell is what many *Sunni* Muslims had endured in both Iraq and Syria—the countries from which ISIS had been spawned. I'm referring to the disenfranchisement, joblessness, and at times the brutal "ethnic cleansing" suffered by the *Sunnis* under the Maliki regime in Iraq, and under the Assad regimes in Syria.

ISIS thus offered the beleaguered *Sunni* population a ready-made and prepackaged means to express their pent up frustration and rage. Yet ironically, as ISIS attempted to undo the state boundaries in this region, one form of Hell had simply been replaced by another. For a living version of Hell is exactly what the soldiers of ISIS brought with them, wherever they managed to secure a swath of turf.

---

* You can see the same "glow" on the face of Rudy Giuliani, when he's on a mission pimping for his malignantly narcissistic president, a mission that brings a fulfilling *importance* and *delight* to Giuliani's "empty unit narcissism," as if he's relevant again, and basking in a reflected *glory*, like an ecstatic boy child at the tit of the Great Mother.

We're re-visioning *malignant narcissism* now…and if we're doing so with a greater depth than the other narcissistic styles, it's because it seems the style least understood by contemporary psychology, and not reflected by Masterson at all. And also because it is has been embodied and acted out on the world stage—both by an American president, and by an extremist cult we haven't adequately understood.

And there's a joke about another malignant narcissist that comes to mind here: Adolf Hitler. He's about to be reborn into his next life after the Hell he unloosed in his last one. (An interesting premise; one wonders if he's learned anything from his time in the after-life, has anything shifted in his perspective?). But the joke ends when Hitler says to God, "OK, I'm ready to reincarnate, but *this* time, no more Mr. Nice Guy."

And the point to be taken here is that *archetypal evil*—which remains steadfastly oblivious to its own shadow—may not be a version of psychopathology that can be reasoned with, cured, integrated, or humanized—perhaps because the fervor of what one is being gripped by, inflated by, possessed by, is not really *human*.

For if Jung once reflected Nazi Germany in the 1930s and 40s as being a collective and demonic re-arising of the archaic Germanic war god Wotan, then a desert version of a similarly archaic demonic possession has recently taken place in the modern, yet not so modern Middle East. And collectively, such archetypal evil can only be held at bay and skillfully countered—until its own *hubris* is inevitably vanquished by the collective agencies of Nemesis it elicits as retribution.

The encounter with evil—writes James Hillman—"can lead one to appreciate anew the value of morality—with what else but morality can the psyche protect itself against archetypal Evil? In this sense, all morality does come from the Devil: it is the psyche's own answer to its own evil capabilities." (The lack of *morality* is exactly what makes *this* narcissism *malignant*, and why Fromm sees it as *evil*, and I link it with *psychopathy*).

Yet cults such as ISIS are what we are left with when the tribal code of a long-distant (and psychopathically ethnocentric) past supersedes the role of *conscience*—or what Hillman has termed "the inborn capacity to feel guilt." Like Trump, such people are *shameless;* they lack a moral compass.

And we can certainly see this when the soldiers of ISIS feel ethnocentrically entitled to the sexual enslavement of Yazidi girls. Here religious doctrine becomes employed in a way that is truly Satanic, and an authentic, self-arising conscience fails to arrive or intervene. Rather than possessing a humanized empathy or *pathos*, religion becomes *psychopathic*, and *impervious to doubt*.

ISIS, the Third Reich, and Trump share malignantly narcissistic similarities, though they also have differences. Both ISIS and the Nazis practiced mass genocide—which is as *malignant* as it gets! While Trump has never gone that far. Yet his entitlement to grope women's genitals—as revealed in the infamous *Access Hollywood* tape—is analogous to the psychopathic sexual entitlement on the part of ISIS toward Yazidi girls. While the mythic underpinnings *of all three* share the premise of *purifying the world.*

The Nazi "purification" was its attempt to cleanse the human gene pool of "inferior" races such as the Jews and the gypsies. ISIS attempted its purification, *its* "ethnic cleansing," by exterminating the followers of "false religions," which is to say, any deviating from their own. Trump's purification sang its *Heil* under the banner of *Make America Great Again.* It was equally ethnocentric as the Nazis and ISIS, only his was also to be accomplished under the shadow of a multi-faceted umbrella.

From his first week in office he attempted a Muslim ban—part of an immigration policy that was also to include attempts to restrict other dark-skinned immigrants from "shit-hole" countries. Here, Trump's pet plan was to be the construction of a giant wall along the Mexican border, and deporting as many as possible who'd already entered the country.

This had the twin benefits of limiting a demographic unlikely to vote Republican, and also would appeal to a working poor base who'd felt "left behind." As Hitler had with the Jews, the immigrants had been framed as the demonized economic enemy (taking jobs from his base).

Next, purification was to be achieved by *draining the swamp* of the political operatives left in place by a demonized Democratic predecessor. This was concurrent with the attempt to systematically undo every legislative achievement of Obama, while flooding the courts with right-wing judges.

Opposition was also to be stifled, or at least minimized, by a similar demonizing of the press. And further, by removing from their posts non-political operatives happening to be experts in their field—and thus, generally holding alternate views of the President. (Who also installed as cabinet and sub-cabinet appointees, those most willing to bend or undo what those positions had historically been entrusted to *further*).

In composite, this "umbrella" covered a remarkably comprehensive agenda. And one that shared much in common with both the Nazis and ISIS. For each of the three attempted to weaken, override, ban, or deconstruct previously existent democratic structures—a commonality, if not *the game plan* in *any* totalitarian state—whether ruled by a Fuhrer, Caliph, or a President self-ascribing *unlimited executive power*.

The "purification" and demonizing being reflected here, go hand in hand. It is psychologically primitive, antithetical to democracy, and part of the malignancy that Trump, ISIS, and the Nazis have shared. However, these three aren't all on the same page in their regard of *nationalism*, nor in their regard of *history*.

With the Nazis, the nation itself—the Fatherland—is exalted, and one obtains narcissistic supplies from mythic membership—that of the Aryan race. Trump (and the skinhead followers he's refused to repudiate) share affinity here. And his central slogan—MAGA—is certainly nationalistic.

But ISIS isn't nationalistic in this way. And what ISIS exalts instead of the *Caliphate* itself, is what it would lead to—which is not of *this* world, its history, and its nation states. But rather, the heavenly Paradise that they believe will follow it, when all disbelievers are killed and left to the torments of Hell; and all believers will be rewarded for their righteousness and promptly lifted up to Paradise.

By contrast, the Nazi vision was not only nationalistic, but also *historical*. They thought they were creating a world-conquering Fatherland that would undo the collective depression (both psychological and economic) that Germany had endured in the aftermath of its losses in World War I, while creating a new world order that would endure for a thousand years or more. While the vision of ISIS is *ahistorical, unhistorical, anti-historical*. In the words of Bernard Haykel, ISIS has an "ahistorical theology, which justifies their horrific actions by essentially pretending the last several centuries of Islamic history never happened."

And if *hubris* lacks knowledge of history, Haykel views ISIS's attempt to return to the legal norms of the seventh century as "denying the legal complexity of the (Islamic) legal tradition over a thousand years." Whereas in truth, "Islamic law is a tradition that is many centuries old and extremely sophisticated, that has a multiplicity of views and opinions and is not cut and dry the way ISIS presents Islam, in an ahistorical fashion, and in a completely monolithic way…So ISIS's view of Islam is…unhistorical. They're revising history."*

The Caliphate of the so-called Islamic State was also not a cult of personality—as seen in Nazi Germany, or more recently in Trump-world, and North Korea. For even the Caliph can be found to be guilty of apostasy should he deviate from the doctrines and practices of Mohammed and his earliest followers. And finding something to *die for* has been a commonplace in a particularly *different* kind of cult than that which prevailed in Germany during the 1930s and 40's. That is, a cult where history is denied, and along with this, *the stalled evolution of religious thought*; and where Paradise is projected onto the after-life—and where the sure way to get there is through martyrdom—by dying in the "holy cause." And none of this is really questioned. Instead, the hunger of a deeper inquiry has been filled by dogma, and the selective employment of validating texts. There is a "holy fervor," but no real doubt—hence no real awakening. And so life itself is cheaply held, even one's own. For ISIS is a *death cult.*

And all deaths suffered in its cause, whether one's own, or that of one's enemies, are thus sacrifices to "God," rather than done in devoted service of an idealized leader. And make no mistake; this is a bloodthirsty and cultic desert god requiring these sacrifices—a god presumed to be the only one…

Like ISIS, Trump manifests a lack of knowledge of history**—something all great U.S. presidents have possessed. He feels no need or desire to learn from it, not even from his own past experiences.

This *inability to learn from experience* is actually a *psychopathic* trait. (And as we'll see in the next chapter, it is one of many that had been deleted from the DSM-3 in 1980 as the authors of the *Manual* were fumbling to

---

* The quotes here from Haykel appear in an interview with Jack Jenkins in which Haykel clarifies some of the issues raised by Graeme Woods in his *Atlantic Monthly* article published in March of 2015. See http://thinkprogress.org/world/2015/02/20/3625446/atlantic-left-isis-conversation-bernard-haykel/

** While touting himself "a big fan" of history, Trump provided a unique portrayal of his hero Andrew Jackson, saying that Jackson "*was really angry about the Civil War, realizing there was no need for it.*" (Fact check: Andrew Jackson died in 1845. And had thus been in his grave *for sixteen years* before the Civil War had even *begun*). Trump's historical illiteracy further led him to pay tribute to Native American veterans while standing beneath a portrait of Jackson, who signed the *Indian Removal Act of 1830*—and *then* delivered what he intended as a slur at Senator Elizabeth Warren by calling her "Pocahontas."

create its construct of the antisocial personality disorder from the scattered bones of Hervey M. Cleckley's psychopathy checklist).

And lacking a sense of history, *Trump creates his own*, a revisionist's account of the past. And here, facts don't matter. What matters is his narrative. And like a carnival barker seducing the gullible into a tent, above all, he's sought to control the narrative. And his has been one littered with lies (pervasive lying, and the misrepresentation of events are other psychopathic traits).

And it matters not that a better liar wouldn't be so *careless* with the *facts*, that what he last said would be disproved in a matter of days. (For in this time-denying revolving door of narratives, a new one will spin out as needed. And so the past doesn't really matter even when it seems to bite him in the ass.

Part of what's both interesting and *troubling* here, is not only that this assumed a form of *political amnesia* on the part of the nation—but the fact that that this calculation had actually *worked*.

Through the first three plus years of his presidency, 15,000, 20,000—or however many documented lies Trump had told—hadn't moved the needle of his approval rating one iota. It roughly remained in the low 40s for the country as a whole, and roughly 80% of Republicans.

It's too early to decisively call, but as this book goes to press, his consistent mishandling of the Coronavirus pandemic may be the game-changer for the nation's political amnesia. Touting untested malaria pills was bad enough, but suggesting we ingest disinfectants like *bleach*? By late April 2020, even most Republicans weren't buying it. And his decision to open the country before the requisite testing was in place was apt to kill *many times* more Americans than the Vietnam war.

And Death is the final wake-up call. It's so sobering, so factual. So undeniable.

The malignant narcissist I've had the most exposure to would often evidence a faint smile as he was saying, or doing something really hurtful—especially if he saw that he had just drawn blood.

Here the word "prick" comes to mind. For malignant narcissists can be thorn-like, abrasive, blood-sucking. Though often seductive, and even affable at times, these folks are largely devoid of empathy, which is why they can be *sadistic* at times without feeling remorse. They can be quite toxic for anyone drawn in to their web, even their own family, whom they profess to love—whether that be their family of origin, or their "crime family."

An example would be Jon Voight's character in the television series *Ray Donovan*, who exemplifies malignant narcissism as "the quintessence of evil," as much as Kernberg's recognition that antisocial personality disorders are "fundamentally narcissistic." In either case, these folks are not just "garden variety neurotics." They're *unforgettable*, and best avoided—as Ray Donovan keeps attempting, though unsuccessfully, with his father.

They tend to be heedless of normal human bounds and inhibitions in a way that can make them appear socially clueless, and in need of a minder. Yet they are masters of avoiding accountability, and tend to attract compliant submissives, or those who are socially deviant themselves—which in either case is to say: those willing to go along with their fixed ideas, that often result in corrupting, chaotic, or ill-advised schemes. (In fact, a diagnostic trait—though un-mentioned in the *DSM*, is: *birds of this feather often flock together*).

These people are fundamentally greedy, parasitic, and lazy. And if you're not providing "the goodie" they want from you, they can become reptilian and bite your hand off, or throw you under the bus. For you've just become another replaceable cog in their impulsive, self-centered, wheeling and dealing through life.

※

By providing "sketches" of these differing narcissistic styles, I've tried to provide something of a trait-based "differential diagnosis" within the landscape of narcissism itself. Like the many forms of coronavirus, clearly, not all are the same.

But in all five styles—from its most common and benign ("closet")—to its rarest (and most "malignant")—something in common is missing and obscured: the true nature, the very essence of what it means to be a human form of being.

Each of the narcissistic styles could be seen as strategic attempts to compensate for, or defend against the deficient emptiness that results from the *loss* of this "essence." (And you could say the same for "the fall" into ego structure; the adaptation, that is personality itself).

These adaptive, and neurotic strategies may each have similar etiology, and similar results—though they each express themselves in differing styles. Each results in a distorted self-image, coupled with the strategies adapted for defending or promoting that image. (Which overlooks that who and what we most deeply *are* is not an image in the first place, but a presence, a human form of being. Yet that being is precisely what *wasn't* adequately recognized and supported early in life, that led to the strategies.

In a sense, narcissism is the lingering and desperate "marketing strategy" formed by a young and emerging self, since the original goods—one's very being—wasn't enough to feel recognized and valued. And over time, you cease valuing your own essence, and have "left home without it." And thus are left... in a state of spiritual bewilderment.

For the effort to promote and defend a distorted self-image is akin to elaborately decorating the outhouse, even posting sentries around it; while the location of the true family jewels is entirely abandoned, grown covered with weeds and spider webs, from years of oblivious neglect.

Each strategy results in the splitting of a unitary fabric of self and world, into one divided between idealized and devalued camps. *Polarization* itself thus becomes one of its divisive hallmarks. (Where the soul that once felt devalued and neglected, now becomes the devaluer).

Yet this polarized world view has become a feature not only in the tiny fraction of those clinically-diagnosed as having a narcissistic disorder. It's now so wide-spread that I've come to think of it as part of "*the narcissism of everyday life.*"

This "everyday narcissism" may be more impactful—if only because *more omnipresent*—than the *conceptually valid* version of narcissism that the *Diagnostic and Statistical Manual of Mental Disorders* estimates to exist in only 0 to 6.2% of the American population.

Yet I'd suggest that the *DSM*'s limited view of narcissism is like having a flawed test for COVID-19. The malady may wind up underreported and inadequately treated. People could be carriers and transmitters of the affliction, without even knowing it. While the "virus" continues to spread...

And spread it has—even into domains where you'd least expect it.

Which is why both spiritual teachers and therapists can remain partially "uncooked" if they haven't also done extensive inner work in healing the lingering residues of their own narcissistic wounding.

And this helps to account for some of the scandalous behaviors on the part of gurus and teachers that spiritual schools (of all persuasions) have suffered over the years as these traditions landed and took root in American soil.

It's also why spiritual schools such as the Vipassana lineage under the leadership of Jack Kornfield in Marin County California, wisely required that its teachers also be in psychotherapy. (But it's also why psychotherapists in treating the narcissism of everyday life *ought to have* more extensive spiritual training, because narcissism suffers from deficits that are both "psychological" and "spiritual."

Seeing them as separate is *more* polarization—yet a dichotomy that has lingered (to the detriment of both) since modern psychology's inception, early in the 20th century.

But we are human beings. Not pie charts. Thus, having a psychology that isn't spiritually informed, or a spirituality that isn't psychologically savvy, isn't really optimal for the time in which we live. Nor is having a politics—and an electorate—somewhat heedless of both. Or a major political party in the 21st century that is heedless to science, such that even science becomes polarizing, as has happened in the varying responses to the COVID-19 pandemic in America.

For some, the above may sound obvious. For others, it could reek of heresy, or some kind of left-wing flakery. Or, for quite a lot of people all of this could just sound boring, and of no real concern. And these three responses are pretty much those of the American body politique: progressives, conservatives, and those who are oblivious, and have stopped paying attention.

Yet when a nation can elect a president like Trump it's saying something about the nation. Many things, in fact.

And some urgency—to explore *all of this*—is why I've written a book entitled *Re-Visioning Narcissism*.

FOURTEEN

Is He a Narcissist, a Psychopath—or **Both**? And Does the President Have A Delusional Disorder?

Author's note: Two chapters ago, I said I'd try to be a ventriloquist's dummy, allowing a prevailing psychological paradigm to speak through me. I knew this would involve the *DSM-5* entering the book more than it had, and warned the writing could thus get a little dense up ahead, asking the reader's forbearance. I was forthright in acknowledging the dummy had a mind of his own (if failing to mention the dummy might get a bit snitty at times in enacting his mission).

Meanwhile, the Trump presidency was stumbling toward the 2020 elections. A result of these factors was a chapter draft entitled "Is Trump a Narcissist, a Psychopath, or Both?" The 1st part of the ensuing chapter comes from it.

In the last chapter, Fromm's view of *malignant narcissism* led to the reflection of its similarity to *Antisocial Personality Disorder*. For *both* can embody Fromm's notion of "the quintessence of evil." And in this chapter I'd like to let the *DSM-5* weigh in on this, and related matters. Though at the considerable weight of *947 pages,* I'll have to be judicious. And I'll begin by noting the impulse that gave rise to the *DSM*...

Throughout medical history there'd been a perceived need of a *classification of mental disorders.* For equally long, there'd been a lack of agreement on *which* disorders should be included, and *how* they should be defined. Yet well into the 20th century, there'd been a lack of agreement as to whether the principle objective of classification should be for clinical, research, or administrative settings. The *DSM* thus arose as an attempt to address the need for a classification system, and these lacks of agreement.

Though it's one of the more expensive books I've ever purchased—a hardcover edition on Amazon could cost as much as $120—I don't know a single American psychotherapist who doesn't possess a current edition of the *Diagnostic and Statistical Manual of Mental Disorders*. It is considered the most significant of guides for American psychotherapists (or at the least, part of the cost of doing business). For it outlines in an official and ostensibly definitive way, the diagnoses required for compensation from medical insurance. That's mostly when I reach for it—when making out a client's initial billing to an insurance company.

And for its utility in making out insurance claims, the *DSM* is notable for something else: The *Manual* is almost completely devoid of guidance for how to *heal* the disorders it classifies. For *clinical* purposes it's thus akin to a golf manual that might define a fat or thin shot, and what a hook, slice, shank, or "the yips" are—but not how to correct them. It's a manual of defined *pathologies*, not a manual of their healing. For its visionary stance is removed from *being* itself, and from *healing's* father, Hippocrates, who famously said: *It is more important to know the person who has the condition than it is to know the condition the person has.*

The *DSM* can thus seem a dry, left-brained affair, a book written by committee, as if a coterie of the orthodox has been left *not* in the *care of the soul*, but rather, as the official definers of its mental suffering. I sometimes feel I have to turn off one part of my brain to get on its wavelength. And *sometimes* this yields helpful insights that make available part of the knowledge-base embedded in a tradition.

But unfortunately, like much of our politics, there's not much in it that seems very inspiring, eye-opening, or nourishing for the soul. And frankly, given the stature which it is granted in American psychology (and though I've found it useful at times) I don't regard it as the oracle of Delphi, even for what it's supposed to be good for.

(Parenthetically, in researching this book, I emailed a member of the *DSM*'s personality disorder committee, saying that I'd like to have a conversation with him about the committee's initial impulse to banish Narcissistic Personality

Disorder from the *Manual*, as I thought both lay and psychological professionals would be curious of the thinking behind such an impulse. Due to faculty duties, he didn't have the time. But he did have his secretary send me an article he'd written, that he thought should answer any questions I had. And it *did*—in an unintended way. For the article was a repository of academic arguments—about what I'm still not sure—for as far as I could tell, it had little to do with human beings, narcissism, or life on the planet Earth. As I finished reading it, what it brought to mind, were Dylan's lines from *Desolation Road:* "And Ezra Pound and T.S. Eliot/ Fighting in the captain's tower/While calypso singers laugh at them/ And fisherman hold flowers").

Like any text rigidly held or deferred to, the *DSM* is capable of promoting its own brand of (psychological) fundamentalism. Yet it is certainly more of a tool than a Bible, more literal than metaphoric—and perhaps why it doesn't speak so well to the soul, which seems to dream and associate via metaphoric *images*. (As Aristotle once said: *"The soul never thinks without a picture"*). And for some diagnoses, the tool is simply more useful, yields a better picture than for others.

In this chapter I will argue that the *DSM-5* doesn't do as well as it might have for Narcissistic Personality Disorder (NPD), yet it has had some shortcomings with Antisocial Personality Disorder (ASPD) as well. For with the latter, readers have been left somewhat untutored about *psychopaths*. The *DSM-5* can barely bring itself to say the word out loud. That's because *psychopathy*, for years, has been a competing construct with its own construct ASPD, and as if the former is but a subtype of the latter. (We'll get to that later). Yet for this reason, many psychologists and police profilers have been resorting to alternative sources where psychopathy is at issue. And sociopaths have been completely thrown overboard from the manual, as if they no longer exist.

And when you add NPD into the mix, things can get really curious in diagnosing America's 45th president, for he seems to embody *all* of the above, and perhaps, at least one other diagnosis as well.

Though for a *president*—and a nation founded on the rule of law—either ASPD or that chilling word *psychopath* may be the more *relevant* disorder, and politically, the more *dangerous*.

My biases aside, the *DSM-5* considers Narcissistic Personality Disorder as one of the *ten personality disorders*. And a personality disorder is characterized as "an enduring pattern of experience and behavior that deviates markedly from the expectations of an individual's culture, is pervasive and inflexible, has an onset in adolescence or early adult-hood, is stable over time, and leads to distress or impairment."

The *inflexible, pervasive,* and *enduring* features of personality disorders, as well as their degree of *deviation* from a culture's *norms* and *expectations* suggests—in layman's terms—two different things. The inflexible, pervasive, and enduring feature of these disorders, and that they are "stable over time," are all saying that personality disorders are deeply hard-wired, and not merely situationally or episodically suffered. And the deviation from norms and expectations is saying that these people aren't normal "garden variety neurotics," and that there's something a little shocking about the ways they don't meet conventional expectations for how a human being should be. In the hierarchy of mental afflictions, personality disorders are thus considered to be *more pathologically disturbed* than the rest of us *neurotics*—yet not *as* delusional as *psychotics*.

(However, personality disorders, like *all* of us at times—are subject to delusions—if sobering to admit).

In the *DSM-5*'s opening discussion of the personality disorders, each of the ten is given a thumbnail sketch. That given for NPD lists three central features: "a pattern of grandiosity, need for admiration, and lack of empathy." Yet regarding this need for admiration, some clinicians feel that the *DSM-5* misses the boat in failing to recognize that narcissists can also find disapproval equally rewarding *as long as it places them equally in the limelight*. (And Trump would be a case in point; for the lowest approval rating of any president in history during his first year in office—usually a "honeymoon" period—hadn't led him to change his course. It was too "inflexibly hard-wired," and there'd been no lack of "narcissistic supplies" when he'd been the center of attention for most major news and media outlets, whether of the left or the right).

In total, the *DSM-5* lists 9 diagnostic criteria for Narcissistic Personality

Disorder—of which, at least 5 should be met in order to give the diagnosis. (If you'd like, you could have Trump in mind, as you do your scoring from home). These 9 diagnostic criteria are:

1. Has a grandiose sense of self-importance (e.g., exaggerates achievements and talents, expects to be recognized as superior without commensurate achievements).
2. Is preoccupied with fantasies of unlimited success, power, brilliance, beauty, or ideal love.
3. Believes that he or she is "special" and unique and can only be understood by, or should only associate with, other special or high-status people (or institutions).
4. Requires excessive admiration.
5. Has a sense of entitlement (i.e., unreasonable expectations of especially favorable treatment or automatic compliance with his or her expectations).
6. Is interpersonally exploitive (i.e., takes advantage of others to achieve his or her own ends).
7. Lacks empathy: is unwilling to recognize or identify with the feelings and needs of others.
8. Is often envious of others or believes that others are envious of him or her.
9. Shows arrogant, haughty behaviors or attitudes.

I don't know about you, but to me Trump checks off all the boxes; at least the 5 the *DSM-5* requires for making the diagnosis. So the president's a narcissist. Which should surprise exactly no one.

What *might* be surprising is when we shift the focus away from Trump, and back to "re-visioning narcissism" itself. And I suggest we do it where the *DSM-5* tells us that its estimate of Narcissistic Personality Disorder in the American population (0% to 6.2%) was based upon *DSM-4* definitions, while estimating that between 50% and 75% of those suffering the condition are male. The surprise here occurs if we put these figures under a microscope, and then turn up the magnification.

For in both instances, the estimates (for all their seeming numerical specificity) are in actuality rather inconclusive, if not *useless*. For in the first instance, are we being told that NPD is so rarely encountered that it effectively *doesn't exist* in the American population—as in its low-end estimate of 0%? While in the latter instance, are we being told that NPD is equally found in men as women—i.e., 50%? Or do men comprise *three fourths* of those suffering from NPD—i.e., 75%? (How *useful* are these estimates, how clearly seen are the contours of what's being estimated; how extensive, updated—or believable, is the research behind them?).

Though the *DSM-5* fails to be more definitive about gender prevalence in narcissism, I'd have no quibble, and in fact would probably agree that men probably *are* more narcissistic (less empathic, more grandiose) than women. Yet when viewed from a more demanding standard, such as that held by some of the spiritual traditions, that men and women *equally* suffer a dissociation from their own deeper nature, while taking themselves to be what they're not—i.e., their self-image.

And though I have no quibble at all with what the *DSM-5* has *included* in its diagnostic criteria for NPD, I've felt that it hasn't been inclusive and nuanced *enough*. (Hence the attempt to add missing traits to this book).

Perhaps some on the committee entrusted to define personality disorders were so divided about including NPD in the *Manual* in the first place, that its portrayal winds up being a bit less helpful than with other diagnoses.

If so, given all that narcissism can impact—say the leadership of a country—that's a bit unfortunate. (And why I've attempted to pair political reflections with a wider range of narcissism's contours than found in the *DSM-5*; and by offering adjunct insights culled from other traditions, as well as from other practitioners within Western psychology's clinical tradition. For in the current cultural epoch, we've needed *all the help we can get)*.

And when it comes to personality disorders, the committee entrusted to handle them in the *DSM*'s 5th edition had also recognized the need for a bit more help. (And as we will see later in this chapter, that has been the case for the personality disorder's work group for its last *several* editions). In terms of the 5th edition, they were concerned about the fact that the typically personality disordered client frequently meets the criteria for other personality disorders. And that one diagnosis may be "correct"—yet a less *informative* diagnosis—as patients suffering from a personality disorder don't tend to present symptoms that correspond with one, and only one personality disorder.

For these reasons, in its latest edition the *DSM* presents both the prevailing model (for purposes of continuity) as well as a proposed Alternative Model (which is allegedly distinctive for allowing a "trait specified" diagnosis to be made, even when the *criteria* aren't met).

Also to provide more discernment in a landscape where *multiple* disorders are often the case, the *DSM-5* provides a *differential diagnosis* for the different personality disorders, which *could* be really helpful, given that personality disordered folks don't tend to present symptoms that correspond with only one personality disorder.

Since our focus now is NPD and ASPD, let's see how the *Manual* attempts to differentiate them...

"Individuals with antisocial disorders and narcissistic personality disorders share a tendency to be tough-minded, glib, superficial, exploitative, and lack empathy. However, narcissistic personality disorder does not include characteristics of impulsivity, aggression, and deceit. In addition, individuals with antisocial personality disorder may not be as needy of the admiration and envy of others, and persons with narcissistic personality disorder usually lack the history of conduct disorder in childhood or criminal behavior in adulthood."

Really? Let's get the microscope out again. And place it over the assertion that narcissistic disorders don't include characteristics of *aggression*, or *deceit*. What I then see, leads me to suggest instead: Not only is narcissism capable of aggression, but *rage*—when dealt a "narcissistic insult." In fact, *DSM-5* contradicts itself—a problem with books written by committee—where elsewhere the *Manual* tells us this very thing, that NPDs may "react with disdain, rage, or defiant counterattack" when suffering injury, criticism, or defeat. And Trump exemplifies this whenever reporters have questioned his performance, "alternative facts," or the grandiose narrative spun of his *unparalleled* and *under-reported* "success."

And as for deceit, no president, and few people in history, have lied more ongoingly than Trump. Most clinicians, and rightly so, would lay this more at the door of his ASPD (or psychopathy, if they even use the term). Yet Trump—and narcissism *at its core*—manifest a less obvious deception: the self-deception of "taking oneself to be what one is not."

And then moving through life under its false banner. And even trying to get others to buy in.

You could make a case that if or when Trump doesn't realize he's identifying with a fake self, he's merely narcissistic. And that when he knows he's being fraudulent, and tries to *mask* it, it's ASPD (or psychopathy. In fact, the seminal book on psychopathy was titled *The Mask of Sanity).* But since this seems to be going on nearly *all the time* with Trump, making a differential diagnosis becomes a more slippery slope.

I would, however, agree with the *DSM* that impulsivity, conduct disorder in childhood, and criminal behavior in adulthood are more fitting of its ASPD construct. And in the 50s and 60s, kids evincing conduct disorders, and coming from families that could afford them, were commonly sent to military schools to have instilled in them the ethical and other forms of discipline they otherwise lacked. And we know Trump was sent off to such a school; conceivably for this reason.

While his criminally fraudulent behavior in adulthood, such as the $25 million judgment against him for Trump University, the $2 million verdict for the fraudulent use of his own charity, the Donald J. Trump Foundation, and the plethora of other lawsuits against him are all at least partially documented.

By the summer of 2020 what *hadn't* been documented were his *tax returns*. There Trump had waged a desperate goal-line stand throughout his presidency—a "red line" that even Mueller's team hesitated to cross. What's hidden there is hidden for a reason. And not the dubious ones he's given for not producing them. And they *might* explain Trump's obsequious stance toward Putin.

Yet as with his conduct in life as a whole--where he appears to have cheated on everything from his wives to his taxes to his golf scores—his "charity" in itself is a case where *both* of the president's personality disorders seem equally at work. Here's an example...

The Attorney General of New York had taken action against Trump after finding that his Foundation had been employed not for charitable purposes, but rather "for persistently illegal conduct"—Trump's ASPD at work. For the Trump Foundation had been used as a tax write-off for paying debts his businesses owed, and illegally bolstering his presidential campaign, paying hush money to porn stars, etc. But it had also been used to buy expensive portraits—of himself, a billionaire's version of a selfie—which was his *narcissism* at work.

In short, at least when it comes to Trump, the *DSM-5*'s differential diagnosis that attempts to tease out NPD from ASPD is also somewhat useless, since he's such a vivid stalking horse *both* for ASPD and for several *varieties* of NPD. (In the last chapter I provided extended portrayals of 5 distinct narcissistic styles—in the attempt to provide a differential diagnosis within the landscape of narcissism itself. And in case you were interested in personalizing the results, Trump would be out of the running only for *closet narcissism*, an extremely viable candidate for *exhibitionistic narcissism* and *devaluing narcissism*, too close to call for *empty unit narcissism*, and the best exemplar I can think of for *malignant narcissism*).

Yet the *DSM-5* fails to mention, yet alone offer a portrayal of *any* of these different narcissistic styles, which is one of the ways that it lacks contour, nuance, breadth. (Just as it fails to adequately discern the important differences between *its* construct of ASPD, and sociopaths, and psychopaths—which, again, we'll get to later). And there's really quite a huge difference between what Masterson coined as "closet narcissism" and what Fromm recognized as "malignant narcissism;" and even differences between how Kernberg and Fromm viewed the latter. Those just named weren't minor league clinicians. Where in the *DSM*'s portrayal of NPD are the nuances of their clinical vision?

Not all forms of novel coronavirus are the same, each are "novel." So too with the narcissism "virus," which is also communicable. It's just in the air we breathe, and is carried and passed on through our TVs and rampant in cyber space, our dreams, our politics, our ads, the News, and its self-absorption leaves us in an isolate lock-down, as we shelter in place within an invisible shell, and gaze into our cellphones.

This disorder is not merely suffered by a tiny fraction of the population. It's spreading and nearly now the new normal. *Though it escapes notice and can remain untreated if the only standard is the valid (but very partial) diagnostic criteria contained in the DSM.* In fact, our collective narcissism is so omnipresent, that like the air we breathe, it's grown hard to clearly see. And so, it wouldn't be too much of a stretch to say our prevailing view of narcissism could stand a little…re-visioning. But for now, let's move on, and see more what the *DSM-5* says about ASPD.

Diagnostic Criteria of Antisocial Personality Disorder
A. A pervasive pattern of disregard for and violation of the rights of others, occurring since age 15 years, as indicated by three (or more) of the following:
    1. Failure to conform to social norms with respect to lawful behaviors, as indicated by repeatedly performing acts that are grounds for arrest.
    2. Deceitfulness, as indicated by repeated lying, use of aliases, or conning others for personal profit or pleasure.
    3. Impulsivity or failure to plan ahead.
    4. Irritability and aggression, as indicated by repeated fights or assaults.
    5. Reckless disregard for self or others.
    6. Consistent irresponsibility, as indicated by repeated failure to maintain consistent work behavior or honor financial obligations.
    7. Lack of remorse, as indicated by being indifferent to or rationalizing having hurt, mistreated, or stolen from another.
B. The individual is at least 18 years.
C. There is evidence of conduct disorder with onset before age 15 years.
D. The occurrence of antisocial behavior is not exclusive during the course of Schizophrenia or bipolar disorder.

Again, as with NPD, it's not that I find these diagnostic criteria to be invalid—*for ASPD*. And if you had Trump in mind, it wouldn't be difficult to come to the shocking realization that a President of the United States checks off for *all* the criteria, not merely the 3 required for the diagnosis. And that his impeachment inquiry, as well as that of Robert Mueller, had brought some of these features—the unlawful ones for example—out of the shadows and into public view. And thus, in the very unlikely event that Trump ever entered therapy, the therapist would correctly be able to give the *DSM* diagnosis for an *antisocial personality disorder*. (After which, he'd likely be *fired*, for we've seen ample evidence of how Trump deals with people whose field of expertise doesn't conform with the mask—or agendas—he presents to the world).

But is it possible that neither ASPD nor NPD was the *real* disorder being sensed by therapy clients, and causing them to freak in the immediate aftermath of Trump's election in 2016? (Just like the shark that was captured early in the movie *Jaws* and that had led the mayor of Amity to think it safe to re-open the beaches wasn't *the really menacing thing* still swimming at large).

And if ASPD in a sense is the "false shark," how did it come to be, and to be "captured" in the way that it was? And why is it that in the 5th and most recent edition of the *DSM* there's barely a mention of psychopaths? (Answers to these questions are soon to appear).

The only mention of psychopathy in *DSM-5* is found in its Alternative Model, where clinicians are advised that if a client checks off for 6 or more of the 7 characteristics listed there for ASPD, there is a further specification that can be made, *if* the client also exhibits the linkage of two traits—a *lower* degree of *anxious withdrawal* on the one hand, and a *heightened* degree of *attention seeking* on the other. Then a therapist can add a further element to the diagnosis, the "unique variant" of psychopathy, or a 'primary' psychopathy. But since the *DSM* only requires 3 of the 7 criteria to make an ASPD diagnosis, they make it far easier, and seem to prefer that you use their brand.

Now, I actually *like* the inclusion of these twin traits, for they can account for the "social potency" *psychopaths* can have. That is, devoid of an inhibiting conscience, they may not only lie or engage in fraudulence but also project the omnipotent aura of a supreme confidence that most of us lack—even if that confidence is that of the con man. One stopping at nothing to get what he wants, regardless of the wreckage left behind.

But to sleuth out such people, we're going to need far more coherently linked traits than even all seven the *DSM* provides for ASPD, plus the 2 more. For I question *DSM*'s assumption that psychopaths are merely a "unique variant" of ASPD. As we're about to see, their pathology can be more than mere "social deviancy." Thus, they can escape notice—if we're looking for them—armed only with the traits of ASPD.

※

Elsewhere I've suggested *narcissism* as perhaps the oldest of recognized personality disorders, as Greek and Roman poets had given us the myth standing behind it, and were musing about it 2000 years ago.

But *psychopathy* is also one of the more established personality disorders.

And though it's practically disappeared from the *DSM,* it too can claim some original basis.

For in the clinical tradition of American psychology it might be seen as the *prototypic* personality disorder. For the term "psychopathy," 100 years ago (in Schneider's 1923 nomenclature) referred to *all* forms of personality disorder.

With this the case, I've found it mystifying why there's so little mention of psychopaths in the 5th and current edition of the *DSM.* If you blinked, you could miss it.

Answers to this riddle, and a decades-long controversy between the *DSM*'s construct of ASPD and the alternative construct of *psychopathy* were revealed when I chanced upon an online article entitled "Psychopathy and the *DSM.*" It turned out to be more than I expected, both historical document, and a knowing form of psychological reportage. It was authored by Christina Crego and Thomas A. Widiger.

You can Google, download, and then read it yourself. But I warn you, it's dense reading. Its 10 pages took a night and a day, taking notes on the way, to plow through it, so dense was the terrain, before I could see the forest for the trees. But once I managed it, the view led to *gratitude*—for such clear-eyed and willing guides, as were Crego and Widiger.

I'll try to provide an account easier to acquire, connecting only the main dots, and culling only my main takeaways, and but a few of the further insights they gave rise to. Some will mainly interest only other psychologists. Prepare to lean into the left side of your brain… And for lay readers, I'll try to write as lucidly as I can, identifying major actors, and the unfolding plot. Enough preamble, let's jump in…

The year is 1941—11 years before the first edition of the *DSM* will appear. What appears in 1941 is a book entitled *The Mask of Sanity.* Its author, Hervey M. Cleckley, is an American-born psychiatrist. His book is about to make him the seminal figure in understanding psychopathy. Cleckley portrays psychopaths as "outwardly a perfect mimic of a normally functioning person, able to mask or disguise the fundamental lack of personality structure, an internal chaos that results in purposeful destructive behavior, often more self-destructive than destructive to others."

Cleckley derives a checklist of 21 psychopathic features (later reduced to 16). And when *DSM-1* appears in 1952, it includes a portion of these features, and links them to other contributors who are all pursuing a "sociopathic personality disturbance," one variation of which is the "antisocial reaction." Such persons were said to be "chronically anti-social."

In retrospect, what we can see already is a psychiatrist with a well-developed vision of psychopathy, and a new manual in search of what was to become an "antisocial personality disorder," though in hindsight, it wasn't to throw off its original construct of a sociopathic disorder for another 28 years.

When *DSM-2* appeared in 1968, "anti-social" was expanded, but this time, adhering closer to Cleckley's checklist. In other words, now we had the world's leading authority on *psychopaths* being used for an expanded version of a construct starting off as *sociopathy*, and now veering toward an *antisocial personality disorder*—using *Cleckley's traits* for the expansion. This was a confusing problem no one had yet recognized. It was going to get worse...

1980 was a significant marker in what I'm reflecting. Prior to *DSM-3*'s appearance in that year, the diagnosis of mental disorders was notoriously unreliable, and based on clinicians providing a narrative paragraph description of an allegedly prototypic case. No specific or explicit guidelines were provided as to which features were necessary to make the diagnosis, or how many to consider for it to be valid.

The further development of the "Antisocial" disorder had also reached a tipping point, for it finally threw its "sociopathic" construct overboard. And the further development of "Antisocial" was largely shaped and informed by L. Robins's study of 524 persons who were last seen 30 years earlier, when Robins had worked at a child guidance clinic for juvenile delinquents; which was a study that she closely aligned with Cleckley's conception of *psychopathy*.

Despite her intention of being closely allied with Cleckley (which might tell you how highly he was regarded by those toiling in what was ostensibly the same field) there were notable differences in her 19-item list. On the positive side, she eliminated at least one of Cleckley's more questionable items: "going out of their way to make a failure of life;" while retaining a number of Cleckley's key traits such as: *no guilt* and *pathological lying.* (As key *italicized* psychopathic traits enter this account, note those that mirror Trump.)

However, missing from her list were equally key traits of psychopaths that Cleckley had already captured, notably: *no sense of shame, not accepting blame, inability to learn from experience, egocentricity, inadequate depth of feeling,* and *lacking in insight.* Robins also applied an indelicate brush stroke by suggesting that *the lack of guilt* was among the *least* of valid criteria.

Forgive the editorializing, but my takeaways here are several. First, when you have Michelangelo long at work at a definitive project, you don't send a gal who flicked her brush at the juvee hall 30 years prior, to come brush over the finishing touches on the Sistine Chapel. Next is my appreciation for Cleckley's clinical vision; and that if you just read the 8 italicized traits listed in the above 2 paragraphs, it'd give you a clearer portrait of say, Donald Trump for example, than what ASPD provided—and that's *without* some of Cleckley's other psychopathic traits added to the mix.

And with Robins on board now as a member of *DSM-3*'s personality disorder work group, the group was once more trying to improve the prior group's stab at an antisocial personality disorder. And one consideration they had in mind was an important one—the previous lack of guidelines around criteria, and specifically, the requirements that should be made necessary in order for each of them to be considered valid.

But the way they went about it became limiting in its own right. For the criterion of *recklessness* that had been central to the construct of psychopathy became burdened and less useful by having to show "driving while intoxicated, or recurrent speeding." (What if a psychopathic client doesn't own or drive a car?)

Relationship infidelity became predicated upon evidence of "two or more divorces and/or separations (whether legally married or not)." While the related trait of *promiscuity* required ten or more partners within a single year. (If you only had 9, sorry, you don't make the cut). Though by this accounting, the members of almost any rock band over the past two decades would already have 2 strikes against them on an ASPD rap.

Meanwhile in 1980, as the *DSM* was struggling to successfully launch a personality disorder it could call its own, another significant figure came on the scene—the Canadian-born psychologist, Robert D. Hare. Hare had briefly worked as a prison psychologist in British Columbia, after getting his M.A. in 1960. In the ensuing 3 years while researching his PhD thesis, he encountered Cleckley's *The Mask of Sanity.* It was a pivotal encounter. For in Cleckley's pioneering book, Hare had found the field that was to be his life work, a field he was soon to lead...

But he found the other workers in the field to be few, and with the exception of Cleckley—whom he was to correspond with until Cleckley died in 1984—not having much to offer. Finally, frustrated with the lack of decent research or insight by others, Hare developed the first version of his own *Psychopathy Check List (PCL)*. In 1980—the same year that the *DSM* formally adopted ASPD—Hare released his *PCL* to a limited circulation.

It was based on and "wished to retain the essence of psychopathy embodied in Cleckley's work." Hare worked from his mentor's 16-item list while noting, as had Robins earlier, that some of them were "vague" and would "require a considerable degree of subjective interpretation." And when a 22-item version of *PCL* (in 1986) was released, it was *way* more aligned with Cleckley than the *DSM-3*, and according to my guides, "arguably a further refinement."

For it included Cleckley's *superficial charm, lack of remorse, egocentricity, and lack of emotional depth*—none of which were included in the *DSM-3*. Plus it had eliminated a number of Cleckley's more questionable items: *Absence of delusions, good intelligence, fantastic behavior when drunk (!)* and *suicide rarely carried out*. Though Hare's elimination of Cleckley's *impersonal sex life,* and *absence of nervousness* may have been two swings at psychopathy that failed to make better contact at the plate.

Yet I found it interesting that the absence of nervousness (anxiety) that Hare had banished, was a feature of Cleckley that continues to live in the *DSM-5*'s Alternate model: *lowered level of anxious withdrawal, combined with heightened attention seeking.*

But as you might see from most of these examples, Hare's *PCL* was reflective of more than a mere regurgitation of the best of Cleckley, and a deletion of the more questionable. Hare's own clinical vision is astute; and it added: *proneness to boredom, parasitic lifestyle, poor probation risk,* and *previous diagnosis as a psychopath*. (Parenthetically, *proneness to boredom* also found a home in the *DSM5*'s Alternative model, which is supposed to be more "trait based." When I first encountered it there, it struck me as one of the more deeply observed of the traits in the *DSM*'s portrayal of ASPD, like a really striking image in an otherwise unmemorable poem—though I had no idea at the time, of Hare as its source.)

Successive editions of Hare's *PCL* became—like Hare himself, a go-to source for assessing cases involving psychopathy. He's been an advisor to the FBI, and consultant to various North American and British prison systems.

And since 1980 onward, the *DSM* construct (ASPD) and Hare's *PCL* and its subsequent *PCL-R* became somewhat like Ford and Ferrari, which is to say, foils and competitors with each other. Their contentions seemed mostly about the *PCL* assessing traits, while ASPD stressed behavior. And over which was more or less useful in prison and convict populations; and whether one was sacrificing validity for reliability, or the other way around.

In terms of the last mentioned, the members of the *DSM3-R's* personality disorder work group seemed to appreciate the criticism that ASPD criteria might have been lacking in the validity vs. reliability debate. And therefore, new to the *DSM* criterion set was *lacks remorse*—which had been culled from Cleckley and Hare. Similarly, the addition of the Alternative Model in *DSM-5*, a model that was to be more "trait-specified," seems to have arisen from having the *PCL* as its foil and competitor.

By the time *DSM-4* appeared in 1994, the *PCL* also had a new version, *PCL-R* (Hare, 1991). In the latter, Hare had deleted *drug and alcohol abuse* from his former checklist, while broadening *irresponsibility* beyond parenting (perhaps having learned a lesson from the earlier edition of the *DSM* in terms of limiting *traits* when you narrow the context). The above changes in the PCL-R were part of an emerging new shape in Hare's conception of psychopathy; *one starting to form around 2 separate, broad factors.*

The first was a "selfish, callous, and remorseless use of others." This wing of the *PCL-R* was favored in the psychopathy literature, and was said by Hare to involve the traits "fundamental to the construct of psychopathy." (So you might want to read that again).

While the second of Hare's factorial "wings"—somewhat its junior partner—was a "chronically unstable lifestyle." That is, traits that corresponded to *social deviancy.*

These different wings help us to see a significant difference between Hare's construct and the ASPD of the *DSM*. For by now, ASPD had evolved into *a construct built around social deviancy.*

Of this, Hare said: "Research that uses a *DSM* diagnosis of ASPD taps the social deviance component of psychopathy but misses much of the personality component, whereas each component is measured by the *PCL-R.*"

Given Hare's critique of ASPD as lacking a wing, and now solely concerning *social deviancy*, deserves some commentary from those with no dog in the fight. My guides, Crego and Widiger, offer an alternative interpretation of the above two factors. Namely, that the first factor, the one more central to psychopathy, largely confined to traits of *antagonism* (callousness, lack of empathy, arrogance, conning manipulativeness, lack of remorse).

Whereas factor two included traits of low *conscientiousness* (irresponsibility, impulsivity, promiscuous, and poor behavioral controls, as well as antagonism). In other words, the distinction between these two factors *may* be largely *substantive* (i.e., antagonism vs low conscientiousness), not merely a distinction between *traits vs. behaviors*.

Meanwhile, studies at the time that directly compared ASPD to the *PCL-R* within prison and forensic settings consistently reported Hare's model to be more discerning. And it was also obtaining incremental validity over the ASPD in predicting criminal recidivism.

Therefore, it became the intention of the authors of the *DSM-4* to shift the diagnosis more toward the *PCL-R*. Considered for edition 4 was thus an abbreviated version of Hare's PCL-R consisting of 10 of Hare's items. Though the consideration got scrapped, when field tests revealed that for purely clinical—vs. prison settings, the *PCL-R* lost some of its edge.

And though by now ASPD had a rich empirical history of its own, by the time the *DSM-5* was in the works, there had been considerably more research taking place concerning psychopathy than ASPD. It thus again appeared the intention of the personality disorder group of the *DSM* to shift the diagnosis of ASPD toward the perspective of Cleckley and Hare. This was explicitly evident in the proposal to change the name from "anti-social" to "antisocial/psychopathic." But for other reasons, that proposal also got scrapped, and replaced by a hybrid proposal in which no reference was made of PCL-R or Cleckley.

For those who are not psychological professionals, again, my apology for spending the last pages taking you through these weeds. But my takeaways from the above history of these contending constructs are several, and have had greater cultural implications than merely the rivalry between two schools of thought on the part of shrinks.

Part of what should be inescapable though, is the extent to which the personality disorder work groups of the *DSM*, consistently, and practically since the inception of the *Manual*, had attempted to use the traits provided by two individuals—Cleckley and Hare—to augment the perceived lacks of their own group-derived construct, ASPD. (And that this had largely happened in the shadows, un-noticed by the vast majority of psychological professionals).

The unrecognized controversy between these dueling diagnostic constructs contributed to a widely experienced confusion on the part of lay people and psychological professionals alike. And had led lay people to use "psychopath" and "sociopath" interchangeably—only to have a psychological priesthood rap their knuckles with a ruler for not using the "correct" term (*antisocial personality disorder*)—a term that Big Tony at the shipyard has never gotten his head around. Though Big Tony knows damn well what a sociopath is. ("The dudes are ganged-up, and do bad shit to people, and don't even feel bad about it").

Yet even many psychologists continue to be confused in sorting out the following terms: *sociopath, psychopath, antisocial personality disorder*. Most just know that "sociopath" has fallen out of favor, and can no longer be used in a diagnosis, for it has disappeared from the *DSM*, along with "psychopath," as both have become blanketed under the *DSM*'s term "antisocial personality disorder." Yet in common usage—even among American psychotherapists—there's still not wide-spread agreement, nor much discernment between these similar, but differing constructs.

For example, when Trump's niece, the clinical psychologist Mary L. Trump published her book *Too Much and Never Enough: How My Family Created the World's Most Dangerous Man*, she characterized the progenitor of the family's pathology, the president's father Fred, as being a "high functioning *sociopath*." Yet an hour after her first televised interview, Harvard psychiatrist Lance Dodes, appeared on same station (MSNBC) and diagnosed both Trump and his father as *psychopaths*. (Just two years prior however, in an interview with Chauncy DeVega published in *Salon*, Dodes had also diagnosed Trump as being a sociopath). So what to make of this—*is there no difference between sociopaths and psychopaths*?

Perhaps the clearest discernment between sociopaths and psychopaths was offered by Hare, who didn't dismiss the term *sociopath* as if it were merely an outdated label. He considered them as different, though, than *psychopaths,* in that the former were caused by growing up in an antisocial or criminal sub-culture, rather than from a fundamental lack of social emotion or moral reasoning (as is the case with *psychopaths*).

In other words, Tony Soprano is a *sociopath,* not a psychopath. So is Ray Donovan. For neither would exploit their own children, the way Ray Donovan's father did. Ray's dad I see both as a malignant narcissist, and as well as a psychopath. He's more chaotic. And it's all about *his* needs, chaotic needs that lead him to commit self-destructive acts, that also become destructive for his kids. And Ray is constantly trying to protect both his brothers and his kids from the destructivity he knows his father leaves in his wake.

Tony and Ray aren't great role models for their kids, and in that way "irresponsible." (As we've seen though, in 1994 Hare had broadened the trait of *irresponsibility,* in order to free it from parenting as its definer). Plus Tony and Ray aren't totally absent of traits with a redeeming humanity, though sometimes they're obscured.

Whenever his brothers face difficulties, for example, Ray stops whatever he's doing, and speeds in his black sedan to fix things. Being a "fixer" is what he does, and he's good at it. It's a craft and a craftiness that goes back to having to fix things in a broken family with a psychopath for a father.

Tony and Ray grew up in families with criminal fathers, and as Hare told us, being shaped in such gangland environments is what *creates* sociopaths. But they're not totally lacking in any accountability toward others. They feel family obligation, and are capable of feeling guilt—*unlike* psychopaths—as well as failed responsibility, and remorse. They're capable of speaking the truth, even crying, Tony's actually in therapy. (Could anything in the last 3 sentences apply to Donald Trump?).

Squat Peter Clemenzo in the *Godfather* is at once a good family man, yet he's also a killer. That's just what you do, if you're in *this* "family." When Clemenzo oversees Paulie's murder in *his* black sedan by the side of the road, he's not only thinking of the responsibility he'd just carried out for his crime family, but his responsibility to his personal family, as he—now famously—says: *Leave the gun, take the cannoli.*

Back to Hare...While he didn't disregard *sociopathy,* neither did he disregard the *DSM* term *antisocial personality disorder* either. Though he did view it as separate from his construct of *psychopathy,* as the two constructs didn't list the same personality traits (though that to me, seems not entirely true, for the *DSM* did import some of Hare's and Cleckley's traits, while sensing the need for *more* of them, throughout the years).

Actually, Hare thought the *DSM* construct of ASPD *would validly apply* to *many more people* than the disorder he and Cleckley had been profiling. And though there are no statistics for sociopaths—the *DSM* had thrown them all overboard in 1980—Hare's belief has been that *many more people* would be covered by *that* term than ASPD.

Though my amplifications surrounding sociopathy weren't contained in the Crego / Widinger article, a takeaway is that since *sociopathy* actually covers the *largest* population of these similar but separate disorders, the *DSM* might return to its earlier roots in supporting and publishing research about sociopathy in forthcoming editions; rather than leaving its cupboard so bare, or turning a snobby nose at those who continue to use the term.

And though the term *psychopath* would truly only apply to the *smallest* population amongst the various but similar constructs being explored here, that population has had an impact upon society, and the world, far beyond its numbers. And so, it too should command its own full and rightful presence in a manual that purports to be American psychiatry's official manual of mental disorders.

For when pathologies—whether personality disorders or viruses—fail to be adequately recognized, their destructivity can increase, until their full force catches us by surprise, with consequences truly *disastrous*.

In fact, I'd suggest that our lack of recognition of psychopathy *has had* a disastrous consequence. Which brings us back to Cleckley, psychopathy's seminal authority. If you'll remember, he ended his thumbnail depiction of psychopaths by evoking their internal *chaos* "that results in purposeful destructive behavior, often more self-destructive than destructive to others." But what he failed to evoke there, I'd like to add now. It's this...

The Mask of Sanity was published in 1941, as an Austrian-born psychopath was unleashing a destructivity that would result in the death of tens of millions of people. Decades later, my country also found itself with a chaos-driven psychopath at the seat of power. That too had resulted in the unnecessary deaths of many people.

As for my other takeaways, the first is the easiest to say, and should be obvious: The destructivity of psychopaths can also be *even more perilous* to others, even globally so.

For this reason, just as our survival as a species would be aided by more awareness of climate change, and better planning for pandemics, we've similarly been in need of a better recognition of psychopathy. Its inadequate presence in the current edition of the DSM is akin to having an inadequate test for the coronavirus. It's a failure of psychological vision and leadership that might have better warned us that a Trojan Horse had entered our gates: *a psychopath running for president.* For like the pandemic, his psychopathy was to effect, and infect the nation.

And so, this may be when the bill comes due for our lack of discernment. The time we too begin to suffer the limitations of what our planet can bare. Already the dying has begun—a billion animals burnt to death in a single Australian summer. American democracy attacked from within, just barely alive. *How bad does it need to get?* And who knows how many deaths the pandemic will claim? Were they alive now, I imagine the Old Testament prophets blowing ram's horns, and wailing warnings to wake the people. Such is the spiritual and mythic obliviousness of these times, and the urgent evolutionary shift our planet needs us to make. In a time of psychopathic lies told from on high, we must become those prophets now —the kind who speak uncomfortable truths. For as Dylan once sang—inspired by a biblical passage from Isaiah: *So let us not talk falsely now /the hour is getting late.*

Though psychopaths and narcissists share central traits in common—egocentricity, lack of empathy, being interpersonally exploitive—I'm quite used to encountering narcissism. Its numerous features—more extensive than those contained in any edition of the *DSM*—are also like the different strains of a virus passed on, and widely pervasive in many parts of American culture (Check out the *Millionaire Matchmaker*, the *Real Housewives* of *every* city, or almost anything *else* on the Bravo channel and you'll see narcissism on the hoof. Even if professional psychology wouldn't be able to recognize or ascribe validity to many of its traits, by sleuthing through the *DSM* for them with a magnifying glass, and wearing a Sherlock Holmes hat).

But having previously borne some of narcissism's strains myself, I can better recognize it now, and have a bit of immunity. And so, though it can still feel insufferable at times, with the exception of *malignant* narcissism, none of this *scares* me. Narcissism seldom gets under my skin. If it's not there already...

But psychopaths are a different, more rarely encountered breed. There's something distinctively missing in their foundational makeup. The kind of socialized human restraints and accountability you'd expect *as a given* in another human being, just aren't there, and it can be palpable, shocking. And so, whenever a psychopath has entered my life, however briefly, it's been unsettling. It *scares* me, and can keep me up at night.

Similarly, the therapy clients I mentioned in this book's prologue—who were having anxiety-filled reactions in the wake of Trump's 2016 election—*weren't freaking over his narcissism*. Though under-reported at the time, the psychopathy about to emerge then, didn't escape the notice of Oxford University psychologist Kevin Dutton. Though it wasn't able to be adequately identified by many others, from the manual left to them by the American Psychiatric Association.

In the run-up to the presidential election of that year, Trump had mostly been identified in the media as a narcissist, a text book exemplar of Narcissistic Personality Disorder. Though Tony Schwartz, who'd ghost-written Trump's *The Art of the Deal*, described Trump's herky-jerky attention span ("like a kindergartner who can't keep still") in terms suggestive of an Attention Deficit Hyperactivity Disorder.

But as the election of 2016 was drawing toward the homestretch, Dutton explored something else: *To what degree do the candidates resemble psychopaths?*

As reported in a "Mind" guest blog by Claudia Wallis, published in *Scientific American*, Dutton compared Trump and Clinton, as well as each party's runner up (Ted Cruz and Bernie Sanders) to 16 historical leaders in terms of their scores on the short form of the Psychopathic Personality Inventory, which measures individually and in composite, eight central psychopathic traits.

For the historical leaders—some going back over 2000 years—the form was completed by biographers or other scholars, and for contemporary candidates by a seasoned political reporter.

In terms of the contemporary candidates Trump outpaced them all for psychopathic traits, just as he wound up outpacing them all in the election. And for one of the traits, "Machiavellian Egocentricity," (where narcissism can place a bit of a thumb on the scale) Trump had to step up in class to have any real competition.

And even there, he was almost beyond compare, and bested only by Adolf Hitler, while outscoring near rivals Saddam Hussein, Idi Amin, *and every other world leader over the past 2000 years.*

Though in fairness to Trump's psychopathic attributes, in his *total score* when all eight traits were combined—and as close as psychopaths come to having a decathlon, its form of Olympic equivalent—Trump outdid even Hitler. Though the gold medal here was carried away by Saddam Hussein. Though it's possible the scoring was skewed...

For Trump's score in Blame Externalization seems artificially low. Unlike Saddam who'd led his nation for decades, Trump hadn't been given equal time to show what he was made of. If scoring had been done later, and not before his presidency even began, the ways he blamed all but himself for his failures, would have led to higher scores in Blame Externalization, and psychopathy as a whole. (Just in the early months of the COVID-19 pandemic he blamed his failures on the Obama administration, the Chinese, the WHO, CDC, the Press, states that have complained too much).

In the composite scores of the women—Elizabeth I, Margaret Thatcher, and Hillary Clinton—all finished in the bottom half of the 20 contestants. My takeaway is, that though I'm a big fan of equality opportunity, women simply can't compete with men when it comes to psychopathy. (Though in truth, none of the women came in last).

For bringing up the rear—as if competing in events for which neither had adequately trained—there was a tie between two men: Abraham Lincoln and Mahatma Gandhi.

Though I'd prefer having a more truly *psychopathic* diagnosis than ASPD available, as well as a more differentiated version of NPD, I'd remain confident of a paired diagnosis of both for our 45th president. I also wouldn't rule out the further possibility of a *delusional disorder*. For though Trump is a compulsive liar, an underlying question many have had is whether he actually *believes* the myriad untrue things he's said, or merely employs them in support of his agendas—and in support of an underlying *fraudulence* and *grandiosity* that is more adequately reflected by other disorders.

However, these other disorders (NPD and ASPD) may fail to reflect the presence of *delusional* features. Yet by "delusional," what exactly is meant? The psychological literature considers delusions to be *false beliefs based upon incorrect inference about external reality that persist despite evidence to the contrary*. (Say Trump's view of climate change, to pick just one example).

Those suffering from a delusional disorder are thought *to make conclusions based on insufficient information, attribute negative events to external personal causes, and have difficulty in envisaging others' intentions and motivations*.

And though their delusions are based upon insufficient information, part of what is striking about this is the *certainty* they seem to have about the conclusions they've reached. For example, one study reports that those with a delusional disorder made probability decisions *based on lesser data than normal controls, yet remained as certain of the accuracy of their perceptions as those who are not delusional*.

There are multiple categories, or subtypes of delusional disorder. Regarding Trump, two would seem primary: *persecutory* (the belief that individuals, organizations, or groups are trying to harm them—say the Press in Trump's case, with its "fake news" that is trying to make him look bad); and *grandiose* (such as the belief in one's "exceptional abilities").

People of the grandiose type believe they possess some great and unrecognized talent, have made important discoveries or break-throughs, and have great and special relationships with prominent people. (Say, the leaders of North Korea and Russia). Yet many patients of the paranoid (or persecutory) type *also show some degree of grandiosity in their delusions*.

Of the various categories of delusional disorder, the persecutory type is the most common. Yet in contrast to the persecutory delusions of schizophrenia (which may be fundamentally *bizarre*) those suffering from persecutory delusional disorder have delusions which are *systematized, coherent, and defended* (with at least some semblance of *logic*). *No obvious deterioration of social functioning and/or personality is observed*. (And the lack of more florid deterioration may contribute to delusional disorder being unrecognized, and thus under reported).

Though appearing normal in their social functioning, persecutory delusional types may pursue formal litigation, and at times, *multiple* litigations against their perceived persecutors; and with a determination to succeed against all odds, and whatever the cost. (Before the Mueller probe ever commenced, Trump had been involved in over **3500** litigations— if not the world record, first ballot qualifications for the Litigant's Hall of Fame).

These folks tend to be big on "conspiracies." (Say, of a "*Deep State*;" or in the 1950s Joe McCarthy ranting at a communist conspiracy. In fact, the paranoid aspect of persecutory delusion may cohere with what Richard Hofstadter portrayed in his famous essay "The Paranoid Style in American Politics"). They often identify barriers to justice as being a conspiracy, and thus often feel *they can't get justice.*

While in Trump's case, it should be evident that he's actually the one who's *conspired* to erect barriers to justice. (But that's the paranoid element *itself* at work: projecting externally what is actually the case within oneself).

In this way, individuals with persecutory disorders wind up doing battle with their own shadow. And so, their battles and lawsuits can be "ongoing, and omnipresent;" as is the ever-looming and "unfair" nature of the enemy they feel is opposing them.

Those with a persecutory delusion can thus exhibit "an endless drive to right a wrong." They manifest "quarrelsome behaviors," "saturating the field" with multiple complaints, accusations, and suspiciousness (that might be contained in an avalanche of tweets). Plus, they often experience a degree of emotional distress such as irritability, anger, and resentment. In extreme situations, they may resort to violence against those they believe are threatening them.

And so, clinicians are advised that some care should be mustered around their access to *weapons.* (An ominous detail of psychological reportage— should a person with a persecutory delusion happen to be Commander and Chief of a nation's military forces).

Because those with delusional disorders still possess intact cognitive organization, some capacity for reality testing, and many other psychosocial abilities, delusional disorder has sometimes been described as "partial psychosis." (And it's "partial" to the extent it doesn't exhibit the auditory or visual hallucinations characteristic of severe psychotic disorders).

And so, the mental status examination of people with a delusional disorder usually appears somewhat normal, other than the presence of their abnormal, delusional beliefs. And in general they are well groomed and well-dressed without evidence of gross impairment. But people with delusional disorders do not have good insight into their pathological experiences. And insight-oriented therapy seldom works for them. And besides, only rarely do they seek help. If they are grandiose, they don't think they need any. Trump for example, considers himself "a stable genius." And also like Trump, if their delusions are persecutory and paranoid, they are more apt to resort to *lawyers*, rather than psychiatrists.

In considering the diagnosis of a delusional disorder, clinicians are reminded that it can be difficult to tease out a delusion from a firm belief, or an overvalued idea. And thus it is often *the extremeness and inappropriateness of the person's behavior* associated with a given belief—rather than the simple truth or falseness of the belief itself—that indicates a truly *delusional disorder*. (So in the case of Trump, an argument could be made that though he has firm beliefs, and overvalued ideas that aren't really true, what may confirm him as having a delusional *disorder* is "the extremeness and inappropriateness" of his *behavior*—which has been fairly unrelenting).

Modern psychology's ethical codes and standards have largely protected it from the "extreme and inappropriate behavior" exhibited by delusional disorders. For psychologists who run afoul here have their licenses yanked.

Yet modern psychology's own "firm beliefs" may at least mimic something delusional—when psychologists overestimate what it is we think we know. And then support each other's limiting hypotheses, definitions and beliefs, even confirm them as universally valid, the correct way to be thinking, and better than all others. For psychologists too are reflective of, and often limited by *meme*-hood.

And here we might consider that the prevailing view of the *prevalence* of delusional disorder may not be truly known. The view of it may be as limited as its estimates within the population (which the *DSM-5* estimates as only 0.02% of the American population).

But if you don't truly know what a phenomenological entity *is*, how can you possibly or accurately estimate its prevalence? And in truth, the prevailing view of delusional disorders is much occluded by a lack of understanding. We don't know its *etiology*. Coherent, successful treatment plans remain largely *undiscovered*, or at best, merely anecdotal. (Further research has been complicated by the fact that *delusional patients seldom present for treatment*, and thus seldom make themselves available for research studies).

And consistent with modern psychology's lack of knowledge of this syndrome, even its *definition* has been changing over time, and continues to be "a work in progress."

Yet I've been suggesting that similar limitations may apply to our understanding of narcissism, and its prevalence; which shares the same grandiosity found in both persecutory and grandiose types of delusional disorder, and where the prognosis for it has also changed over time. (The early psychoanalysts believed it untreatable).

In fact, when a higher standard of mental health is employed—or the perspective of a different *meme*—the vast majority of us, in any moment of any day, may have a delusive view, and take even ourselves to be what we're not.

The above sub-chapter is much indebted to the excellent article *Delusional Disorder: Overview, Diagnosis, Epidemiology* written by James A Bourgeois, MD, OD, MPA and David Bienenfeld, MD and which can be found online at *https://emedicine.medscape.com/article/292991-overview#a5*

FIFTEEN

The Mask and the Wound

> "The purpose of poetry is to remind us
> how difficult it is to remain just one person."
> —Cszelaw Milosz

I LIKE IT that the *DSM* allows for multiple diagnoses, when appropriate. It reminds me not only of the above quote by Milosz, but the title of a book of poems by the objectivist poet George Oppen: *Of Being Numerous*. And aside from the *DSM* and the poetic tradition, other psycho-spiritual traditions have also reflected a like multiplicity.

Such is the case in Buddhist psychology's recognition of the six psychological realms that we move through in the course of our days. There's a fluid dynamism here, if a lessened focus on *pathology* (as most of these traditions did not originate from a *medical* schema). For example, this fluid "multiplicity" can also be seen in the Enneagram of the Personality where, along with a fallback type, people are viewed as manifesting another type when under stress, another as they begin to move closer to their essence, and yet another in "the wing" lying next to their dominant type. Here, the understanding is that in any moment we might be dwelling in one of *several* perceptual domains.

And aside from this horizontal *breadth*, there's a further dimensional *depth* in an enneagram that addresses what lies deeper in humans than the fixated nature of our *personality structures*. And the reflection of this deeper, *spiritual* dimension* is largely what Western psychology *lacks;* it's entirely *missing* in the *DSM-5*. Here, I'm referring to the less widely

---

* I've argued that lack of adequate *mirroring* and *support* for this "deeper dimension" IS "the narcissistic wound." And that narcissism can't be fully *treated* from such a spiritually dissociated perspective.

understood Enneagram of the Holy Ideas, where it is thought that an embodied understanding of the "holy idea" for one's dominant type is not only the corrective (or "psycho-catalyst") for one's dominant personality style, but amounts to *a facet* of *enlightenment.** (Not a small thing to say). While an embodied understanding of *all nine* of the Holy Ideas is a far rarer, more comprehensive form of self-realization.

Archetypal astrology also contains this understanding "of being numerous," in that all the planetary archetypes also reside in us, yet in a unique constellation for each of us. And Spiral Dynamics' reflection of the various *memes* gives us a way of differentiating the prevailing world-views not only of individuals, but also of cultures and sub-cultures. (And here, both individuals and cultures might embody the perspective of one *meme* in a particular part of life, and quite another *meme* when it comes to another part of life. Not dissimilar to C.G. Jung who considered himself Apollonian *before* dinner, and Dionysian after dinner, once he'd had a few glasses of wine).

All forms of psychological typing and diagnoses have their unique virtues. For this reason having reference to *multiple* diagnostic systems can yield a more differentiated x-ray of the soul. And I happen to like the diagnosis of narcissism, in part because "the narcissistic wound" (of not having our essential nature adequately mirrored and supported) may be the *original, deepest,* and *hardest to treat* wound in the soul. This is a condition widely suffered throughout cultures, and exhibited by *all* enneagram types. We can hit a lot of what collectively ails us with the "stone" of this diagnosis. And given the state of our culture, I'm trying to do something in this book that I can't achieve in one to one therapy sessions: I'm trying to address a culture; and hit all the "birds" that I can.

I also find it important to be writing about narcissism not only because it holds up a mirror to an American president and at times to domestic or geo-politics, but also because it's one of the *oldest* diagnoses known. Narcissism has been recognized for thousands of years. Yet to my mind, it's also been inadequately understood—and part of why it's been so *pervasive* for thousands of years. And I like it because there are mythic facets

---

* See A.H. Almaas's *Facets of Unity: The Enneagram of Holy Ideas*. Though there are now thousands of enneagram teachers, a deep embodiment of one's own Holy Idea is rare enough; I doubt if there's more than a handful capable of transmitting each of the Holy Ideas. Almaas (Hameed Ali)—is one who's managed it.

available with this diagnosis that provide *hints for its healing*—that we also have not adequately understood.

We humans are capable of a great clarity, which in itself has many *facets* inadequately reflected by Western psychology's mainstream. (And for this reason I also like the Sufic *lataif* system, which both highlights these different "facets," and contains teachings that address what *obscures* them). In other moments we are dense, confused, and layered with complexity. And the layered, often repetitive features of egoic density may continue for *years* even in a "good enough" therapy.

And should the therapy have a transpersonal orientation, still there is a continuing dialectic between what is spacious and what is dense; between what is innate and what is conditioned or fixated. Whether in "spiritual work" or a more ego-centered approach, there is something "interminable" about narcissism, our penchant to take ourselves to be what we're not.

And we take *others* to be what they're not, when we view them through the distortive lens of idealizing or devaluing. And splitting the world into two such polarized camps has become the interminable view not only of jihadists, or the sectarian squabbles between Shi'a and the Sunni in the Middle East, but also of America's two main political parties. This has left us with a fragmenting, destabilized Middle East; and in America it has left us in a divided nation, with a psychopathic narcissist in the White House.

And we take *ourselves* to be what we're not to the extent that we continue to identify with the self-image—*any* self-image. Similarly, we take ourselves to be what we're not when we fail to identify with the beauty and "enough-ness" of our own underlying being. And we also take ourselves to be what we're not to the extent we remain fused with "the aggressive fused part object"—which can take the form of being overly aggressive toward others, or showing up as our own inner critic. For the inner critic holds up a distorted mirror of self, a shame-filled, *deficient* self-image. Just as our critical judgments towards others distorts a deeper perception of them.

And *intra-psychically*, this form of critical reflection contributes to *the fragility of one's sense of self,* while leading us to feel that anything *else* which challenges or confronts our self-image is an *attack* that must be immediately defended against, lest we be left feeling truly bewildered or awful about ourselves.

In this way, narcissism—which I see in part as an "identity-confusion"—can be a *very defended and self-enclosed perceptual system* (and part of why psychoanalytic psychotherapy initially considered narcissism to be untreatable). And we can certainly see this defensively self-enclosed quality in Trump—who never admits fault, and who'd be quite a handful for even the world's greatest *team* of therapists, even if outfitted with state of the art clinical armor, to deflect the devaluing insults sure to come their way. And though Trump considers himself a stable genius, there is something innately fragile and *unstable* in identifying with—and attempting to promote or defend—*anything that is not true.*

Yet the *fragility* lurking beneath this self-enclosed and enshelled brittleness is also why clinicians such as Masterson feel that narcissistic disorders can't be strongly *confronted*—as one might attempt with borderline personalities; they need to be *mirrored* instead. For it is thought that only through "empathic mirroring" that narcissistic characters can begin to stitch together a fuller sense of self.

In keeping with Masterson, I too find empathic mirroring interventions useful in the treatment of narcissism. As with the employment of fairy tales, teaching stories, and myths, mirroring interventions can *bypass the defenses* we might normally have in place. And yet—Narcissus's myth seems to suggest that *verbal mirroring alone is not apt to be fully adequate for the transformation of narcissism.* (Echo was *constantly* mirroring Narcissus's last words on any subject—yet she wound up being devalued and spurned, as had each of Narcissus's previous lovers).

What actually led to Narcissus's transformation was a *visionary experience of his own*, not something that someone else had *said* to him. (And to this end, the next section of this book will reflect induced visionary experiences that have been employed—throughout history—in order to deconstruct "the narcissistic shell").

※

The lack of awareness of the internalized critic, the extent to which we are still fused with it—the extent to which it has yet to be *adequately deconstructed*—leads its critical vantage to be projected onto the outer world. In this way the outer world is experienced as a locale where it is not safe to reveal how we really feel or are. (Which often mimics what was felt in childhood).

People suffering from the features of narcissism—a *much* greater number than 0 to 6.2 percent of the population—thus often feel at some risk, as if hiding a more genuine (though vulnerable) self-hood behind a rock. This phenomenon perpetuates as a lack of *basic trust*—both toward one's more authentic underlying being, and toward the world as a *topos* (space) that might welcome or receive us.

To the extent our more innate and indigenous being was—or continues to be—inadequately recognized, mirrored, or supported, we also tend to *lose touch with it*. And then feel a rootless loss of origin, and a sense of shame about the "real yet impaired" self we secretly think we are.

And then, rather than come forward with what feels real but impaired, we may feel we need to be perfect in some way, present a more idealized image to the world, or to lead with something else than how we actually *are*. And so we adopt *a false self*–which, in a sense, is what the personality *is*.

Here, I'm "re-visioning" *personality*… The very word comes from *persona*, the Latin translation of the Greek word for "mask" (*prosopa*) –which refers back to the large masks worn by the actors in Greek tragic dramas so that the people sitting in the cheap seats could see the faces of the characters being portrayed. The word *persona* has also come to mean an *assumed* personality that masks one's true thoughts and feelings. With Jungian psychology the term *persona* was employed to denote the "outward or social personality," but also "the set of attitudes adopted by an individual to fit himself or herself for the social role seen as his or hers; the personality (or mask) an individual presents to the world." (Say like how Trump presents himself when reading from a teleprompter, vs. the tweets that reflect how he really feels).

As a term of literary criticism the poet Ezra Pound employed *persona* (or its plural *personae*) as an "assumed identity or fictional I" assumed by a writer in a literary work. Today, both the words "mask" and "persona" suggest not only a "fictional I," but *those facets of a person that are presented to the world for its approval*. For both terms reflect the attempt to negotiate a region of our psychology where who we innately *are* collides with whom or what we think we ought to *appear to be*.

And narcissism, at least in the way I view the phenomenon, is largely an identification with the mask; a mask that unknowingly we put on long ago in order to seek recognition from those ill attuned to their own deeper nature, and thus incapable of recognizing ours. And like "the tail wagging the dog," this is a mask *that has come "to wear us."* Inner work is thus a continual process of "un-masking."

For this masked *objectification* of the self obscures the underlying and more native *being*. And the *loss* of the underlying and more native *being* limits the capacity of a parent—or any human being—to more fully recognize, mirror, and support the *being* of others. And in this way, narcissism and its dissociation from *being,* can be perpetuated throughout generations of a family, as well as through governments, *cultures,* and the world at large.

Just as we've noted multiple layers of association behind our conception of the personality, in my view of narcissism it's as if there are several layers here. There's the false or adapted self—the *persona*. Underneath that is the "real but impaired self"—the self which has been narcissistically wounded and that remains partially fused with a rejecting inner Nemesis; yet which is capable of developing into a more integrated or healthy ego. And deeper still is a transpersonal self—what the spiritual traditions sometimes call "true nature," or "essence," the innate state of being free from conditioning.

But in a spectrum of development that spans from pre-personal to personal to transpersonal, something will remain clunky, limping, or lacking in stability from any attempt to jump from the pre-personal to the more transpersonal ("true nature") without first having healed what's been genuinely *wounded,* what's "real but impaired," what never got a chance to adequately develop.

If inadequately processed, these *early wounds* continue to limit one's sense of *basic trust.* These wounds thus persist: as delusions about the nature of the *world,* and corresponding delusions about *oneself*—thus making genuine spiritual realization(s) less *accessible*—as well as less *stable*—than would otherwise be the case. And these early, *unprocessed narcissistic wounds,* also make *relationships themselves* less *accessible,* as well as less *stable,* than would otherwise be the case.

And with a narcissist in the White House—one with a floridly, full-blown Narcissistic Personality Disorder, not merely "narcissistic features"—the one coherent result from Trump's presidency has been the fragmentation of our previous relationships to other countries, a fragmentation of trade partnerships,* and even a growing rupture *within* his own administration. For narcissism is polarizing, and does not play well with others.

Its lack of "object constancy" creates *chaotic fluctuations* in the regard of other people, nations, and societal institutions. Its "entitlement" leads it to have a confused sense of boundaries, and so, it often violates them. It can feel "unfairly treated" (each time its grandiosity or fraudulence is punctured). It sees relationships as either transactional opportunities to further one's interests, or otherwise in a limiting light, as if offering only "fearful chains"—a "bad deal."

And so, narcissism often retreats into a "splendid isolation"—say Mar-a-Lago, or surrounding itself only with sycophants, and the comforting cocoon of "alternative facts." And in the case of Trump this self-absorbed isolation then plays itself out *geo-politically,* when his abrasive character disorder, and his "America first" foreign policies, continue to alienate America's traditional allies.

To the extent that the nature of our *being* was not adequately recognized, mirrored, valued, or related to as one's sense of selfhood was being formed, as adults when we are in the grips of narcissism—which could be much more often than we realize—we will tend to be *out of touch* with our being, as instead we attempt to fabricate something *else*—whatever it *was* that once seemed to be mirrored back or valued.

---

* Having shot down the Trans-Pacific Partnership on the first day of his presidency—a trade agreement that would have opened American businesses to the markets of the fastest growing economies in the world, while limiting their tariffs, guaranteeing worker rights, and environmental protections—Trump, in one of the worst American foreign policy decision since Obama's walking away from his own "red line" ultimatum in Syria, then further damaged America's credibility and leadership by walking away from the Paris climate pact. Plus he's wavered on endorsing NATO, NAFTA, and pulled out from the Iran nuclear deal. The result has been not only a divisive split within his own administration (hence a good deal of "the leaking") but America's traditional allies have been left in an awkward state of limbo. And for his self-idealization as being a great businessman, Trump's unwillingness to enter multilateral trade agreements has left an abdicated void in Asia that the Chinese have been quite happy to fill. The lack of trade agreements, coupled with Trump's castrated State Department, leaves only military options in effecting foreign policy. Yet rather than educate himself about, or devise a coherent foreign policy, Trump left this to his generals. But he's even been replacing them, leaving policy decisions to be made with no adults in the room. If the 20th was "America's century," Trump has unwittingly insured that the 21st will now likely become China's.

Maybe as children we were adorable to look at like Narcissus. Or perhaps as children we were athletic, "winners," helpful, smart in school—or "the toughest kind on the block." In any case, it was often some manifestation, some act, a trait, a strength—some *objectification* of the self that seemed to be valued, not the innate being itself.

When the essence of a child—the innate being—is not adequately recognized or valued, yet when some talent or trait *is* recognized and praised, it can create a *split in the sense of self*. Some part of the self feels worthless and unrecognized, and another part quite grand. The tension between these two extremes can lead people who've been narcissistically wounded to approach life as if it were a slippery slope, as if trying to manifest or have recognized the more idealized perception of self—yet ever in danger of slipping down the slope into a shamed pit of ontic deficiency should we fail to manifest our "ego ideal." And this metaphor of "the slippery slope" seems to mirror not only the split sense of self that is encountered in narcissism, but also *the nature of its vulnerability*.

And to the extent the early environment failed to adequately value, resonate with, or mirror *being* itself, we may not only become narcissistically wounded by this and feel *unseen*, but we tend to grow up *heedless toward our own being*, as if there's nothing there that we might value or better relate to. And without the receptive attunement toward our own sense of *being*, something really *is* missing, and this ontic deficiency begins to complicate our relationship with others, and with life itself.

Like Narcissus flailing in the pool, we may become uncertain about boundaries, confused about our place in the space; longing for what can't quite be grasped, because what we long for is what we already *are*—but have failed to recognize or more fully embody. Or like Echo, we begin to look at relationships in an idealizing way, as if they might provide for us the thing that would make us feel whole—while we continue to suffer from the lack of our own fuller voice...

With this section's psychological amplifications now in place, it is time to disembark from the densities of a primarily psychodynamic perspective, as we prepare to approach the central image in our myth—Narcissus's transformational depth-gaze into a reflecting pool. And how this relates to the myth's curious conflation of self-knowledge with death.

III.
The Death of Narcissus:
The Mythopoeic and Spiritual
Traditions Weigh In

SIXTEEN

The Baby, the Bathwater, and Narcissus's Neptunian Pool

> "A clear, attentive mind
> Has no meaning but that
> Which sees is clearly seen"
> —Gary Snyder

WE'VE HAD A zillion books on narcissism published over the past several decades. Their profusion correctly registers a disturbing trend. Yet as I've suggested, they don't seem to have helped us much. For narcissism remains as rampant in our world as ever. It has thus become my perspective that the transformation of narcissism will require a more comprehensive understanding than we've had thus far. And for starters, we'd profit from a better dialogue, initiating more of a conversation—between the *psychological, spiritual,* and *mythological* traditions.

For if the failure of America's two political parties to initiate a better conversation with each other has left our government in a state of political gridlock, then something similar has prevailed between the psychological, spiritual, and mythological traditions in their differing perspectives on narcissism. (In fact, this *inability to initiate a conversation* is the very problem of Echo; and thus central to the myth standing behind narcissism, and narcissism itself).

Though the psychological, spiritual, and mythological traditions each provide valuable nuance and insight, each (on their own) have tended to be successful only in transforming the narcissism in a few individuals, more rarely their *cultures.* Hence, narcissism has lingered as a central problem of humanity for thousands of years. Yet today, in our increasingly global world, the effect of all that narcissism can impact changes the calculus in a more urgent way. *The transformation of our collective narcissism becomes a central initiatory challenge for the time in which we live.* (And *why* I'm attempting to give narcissism such an extensive, nuanced, and *multi-angled* re-visioning).

To this end, the last section of this book at first accessed the myth standing behind narcissism, while using some of the key images in the myth as lenses to reflect narcissism's multiple nuances; and then, accessed an alternate text (the *DSM*) in order to reflect what I've found useful (though often less useful) in understanding narcissism. I was trying in other words, *to initiate more of a dialogue between the mythic and psychological traditions,* while reflecting how their mythic and psychological nuances are showing up in our contemporary world. (And for *that* at least, Trump has been a useful poster boy).

Though in our contemporary world they've become largely divorced from each other, the mythopoeic and psychological traditions really *belong* together. For until the tail end of the 4th century AD Greek and Roman poets had, over the course of approximately 2,000 years,* inherited and transmitted a mythology that effectively mapped the various archetypes that people the human psyche. Here was a living "archetypal psychology"—thousands of years *before* C.G. Jung or James Hillman. And these poets had not only given us various versions of the myth that stands behind narcissism, but many of them had done a good deal of thinking about narcissism's *hubris* that we've ignored to our own detriment.

Here, in the book's following section, I'll attempt to initiate a better dialogue between the *mythic* and *spiritual* traditions. For when combined, the perspective gained provides hints for the *transformation* of narcissism's vision. Such a "transformational vision" occurs *in the myth itself*—where such a visionary gaze into a lucidly clear pool of water was *deadly* to Narcissus.

And as I will argue, kindred forms of transformational gazes may be deadly to narcissism itself—and precisely *why* they've been employed in an initiatory way throughout history.

---

* It's hard to conclusively date the origins of the Greek myths. Some sources find them to have been acquired during the Mycenaean era, the last phase of the Bronze Age in ancient Greece (approximately 1600 to 1100 BC) and to have been transmitted by poets and minstrels. Others contend the Greek myths were already fully developed 2700 years ago, as reflected by the written works of poets such as Homer and Hesiod. Though many of the myths likely had an older origin, with the earliest Greek legends thought to have spanned back to 1900 BC.

In "An Introduction to Archetypal Astrology" Rick Tarnas suggests that the Narcissus archetype correlates with astrological Neptune. And Neptune, in itself, correlates with all things watery, beginning with "the intrauterine condition in which the child's being and consciousness are not yet differentiated from the mother's, where there is a symbiotic union, a melting oceanic feeling." And of course, there's the watery nature of Narcissus's visionary pool…

In Tarnas's view, Neptune "governs the ideal world, whether this be defined as the perfect all encompassing maternal womb, the spiritual world of ideal reality, or one's highest dreams and aspirations. Yet, like every other planetary archetype, Neptune has opposite sides, light and shadow. For it can both illuminate one with the highest spiritual truths that transcend the everyday world, and yet also lead one into escapist fantasy, illusion, and deception."

In other words… "Neptune represents Nirvana, the supreme state of mystical bliss where all the divisions and structures of this world are transcended; yet it also represents Maya, the divine play which produces the many illusions of reality that enchant consciousness. Neptune relates to both madness and mysticism, and the line is often hard to draw."

Yet the healing of narcissism involves drawing that very line, just as it also must involve the deeper aspects of Neptune; that is, the inner work involved in *dissolving* the illusions and deceptions that have enchanted human consciousness throughout time—*which can give rise* to the supreme state of mystical bliss.

The spiritual traditions have also done a good deal of thinking about what transforms narcissism that we ignore at our own peril. In fact, the lack of curiosity, and the failure of mainstream, modern psychology to make anything like adequate use of the spiritual traditions' insights and narcissism-reducing practices is, in itself, a form of *hubris*. In other words, this constitutes evidence of professional psychology's own narcissism—and why, historically, it has been less equipped to fully *treat* it.

For historically, as part of its initial attempt to establish itself as a legitimate scientific and medical enterprise, there has been the tendency on the part of Western psychology to dissociate itself from religion and spirituality—if not to pathologize religion and spirituality, while viewing them as illusive. And the roots of this go way back, and have had an unfortunate, limiting, and lingering effect. For example, in his 1927 work, *The Future of an Illusion,* Freud sees religion as an outgrowth of the Oedipal Complex, and reduces God to a childish "longing for a father." "Religion," wrote Freud, "is comparable to a childhood neurosis."

Even Jung thought that yoga shouldn't be seriously considered by anyone having a telephone. (Which at the time he said it meant: most of us Westerners). And in my student days at the Jung Institute-Zurich during the early 70s, the prevailing regard toward anything which eroded the ego structure—whether meditation, yoga, or psychoactive substances—was certainly suspect, and as if even Jungian analysts were still doing business under the banner of Freud's maxim: *"Where id is, there shall ego be."*

Even James Hillman, the most poetic of psychologists, and a writer I respect, seemed to have had an uncomfortable stick up his ass when it came to spiritual experiences that dethrone the ego, as if he'd never recovered from the freak-out he experienced in the Himalayas through his encounter with the yogi Gopi Krishna. Ever since, he argued for the "vales of soul," while shunning the "peaks of spirit." (And when Gopi Krishna was invited by Hillman to speak to our small study group in Zurich, just moments before he arrived Hillman warned us not to be taken in by the *dangers* this yogi offered, that Gopi Krishna was quite "psychotic").

And though religion and spirituality certainly *have* evidenced their own delusional, Neptunian features, such a perspective *throws out the baby along with the bath water.* In other words, (and whether with Freud, Jung, or Hillman) the psychoanalytic attempt to separate itself from the illusive, watery nature of Neptune, also dissociated itself from Neptune's more spiritual and enlightening nature. This overly "dry" semblance of rationality also left spiritual matters *outside of psychology's purview.* And unfortunately, one of the societal consequences of this has been, that it has left our psyches—*and many of our psychologists*—in a "spiritually dissociated" condition. Yet narcissism itself—as I argue—is also a spiritually dissociated condition. And thus, *its healing must include elements of a* (Neptunian) *spiritual cure.*

Narcissism gets its name from Narcissus—whose myth is thus the *ur*-story standing behind narcissism. And as we have seen, Narcissus perishes in the immediate aftermath of a depth-vision into a strange pool of water. But how to understand the pool in which he becomes entranced? This pool seems hypnotically "other worldly" in some way—as if removed from ordinary, temporal, mundane life. For the world of ordinary things that come and go—shepherds, goats, cattle, leaves, and birds never appear—are not what this pool reflects. At the point Narcissus discovers this pool, we are told the pool has never reflected *any* of these things, not even the sun.

The most common way of looking at this pool psychologically has been as a symbol for Narcissus's *self-absorption,* a self-absorption that precludes him from being able to "take in the rest of the landscape"—in other words, for the very thing that we have come to call "narcissism"—as if he only has eyes for himself, and has yet to emerge from a stage or style of consciousness that is completely self-encapsulated, completely ego-centric, completely self-absorbed. And on one level, that *might* be an accurate reflection of what we have seen in Narcissus—*until* this point in his myth—as well as an accurate, if partial reflection of narcissism in general. But what this pool does and does not reflect was already the case *before* Narcissus ever encountered it.

And besides, is it really the reflection of his own *self-image* that Narcissus falls in love with in the pool? Or is it instead the reflection of a beauty so alien, so utterly *ego dystonic* to what Narcissus has previously taken himself to be, that at first it seems to be reflecting someone *else?* What else could this be but the beauty of his own deeper nature; a radiant being that both sees and is seen, that is both lover and beloved? This certainly seems a version of self-hood that Narcissus has never recognized before, a beautiful Self that in being glimpsed for the first time still seems *confusing* in some way.

Here we might recall again the prophecy Tiresias had revealed to Narcissus's mother—that Narcissus would live to a ripe, old age—*provided that he never comes to know himself.* In this light, that the still youthful Narcissus perishes *immediately after* his vision in this pool, suggests that the vision he's just had *is* a vision having to do with "self-knowledge." If so, the further suggestion we might take from this is that in-sight of our deeper nature—*and the love for it*—can be the death knell for our more narcissistic perspective.

We should remember, however, that just as there is never a single orthodox version of a myth, neither is there a single "correct" way to interpret mythic material. Generally, different *memes* have interpreted nearly everything having to do with consciousness or culture—myths, religion, psychology, politics, even science—in the single way most syntonic with their own world-view. Which has led to doctrinal controversy in even the followers of the *same* religion—say the Protestant Reformation; or the same *political party*. And the same could be said for the view of narcissism, and the myth standing behind it.

Regarding the latter, some of the different versions of the myth of Narcissus have shaded the myth in such a way that gives even Narcissus's depth-vision in the pool a "narcissistic" patina—as if he dies due to the love of his own self-image. But to me, since such self-absorption had already been the case *throughout* his life, it would make little sense for this to suddenly lead to his death.

In the version of the myth that I've employed, the nature of the self being reflected by this mysterious pool is a version *so foreign and unknown*, that Narcissus doesn't even identify with it at first. He assumes a visage so lovely must belong to someone *else*.

And if I bang on this chord (repeatedly) it's because the mirroring of a beautiful (yet largely unknown, dis-owned) version of self-hood *is so pivotal for transforming the condition of narcissism*, and its characteristic form of vision. In fact, such a vision may be "deadly," in that it leads to the metaphoric death of whom we more commonly have taken ourselves to be. And the gazes about to be reflected in this section of the book will be attempts to mirror this largely unknown selfhood for readers, just as the strange pool in the myth seemed to mirror it for Narcissus…

The more conventional, exoteric interpretation of Narcissus's death scene (that he perishes due to an unhealthy "self love") would actually violate the evocative hint laden early in the myth's structure—Tiresias having said that *it is self-knowledge* that would be deadly for Narcissus (as it *is,* in fact, for narcissism).

In that Narcissus *does* perish in the wake of his visionary experience, we might entertain the possibility once suggested by Hillman—*that the true nature of his vision has yet to have been adequately portrayed.* (Here—to my mind at least—Hillman's mercurial, wonderfully developed capacity for mythic, metaphorical thinking led him to insightfully recognize that the true nature of this vision—or at least a deeper view *of* it—had yet to be adequately portrayed. Yet Hillman's own ambivalence toward "spirituality" inhibited him from taking his insight further—a task thus left for someone else to do).

Certainly, there's really nothing very transformational about Narcissus's death scene if all Narcissus is seeing is the reflection of his self-image, just another form of the self-absorption he has already demonstrated throughout the myth. For as Lou Andreas Salome once concluded, if it were only his more familiar sense of self that he was viewing in this pool it wouldn't have seemed so *arresting* for Narcissus; he wouldn't have continued to be so *fascinated,* he wouldn't have continued to *gaze* at it.

Since other poets, mythologists, and psychologists have yet to be more convincingly forthcoming in suggesting what might have transpired through Narcissus's gazing into that lucidly strange pool of water, I would now like to make a run at this. And I would like to do so by exploring the notion of *transformational gazes*—different ways of using our eyes that can alter our perspective, and transform our accustomed sense of self, as well as our accustomed sense of world. Gazes, in other words, that might approximate the transformational vision that Narcissus seemed to have experienced at the end of his myth…

SEVENTEEN

The Death of Narcissus & the Nature of Transformational Gazes

Throughout history, and across a wide range of cultures, gazing practices have been employed to effect a shift in consciousness, a shift that gives rise to a deeper form of knowing, or an altered way of experiencing oneself. From the Zulus in Africa, to ancient Greece and Rome, as well as in Polynesia, Siberia, and Tibet, we find such practices.

Nearly as far back as 2,000 B.C. in Greece, but also amongst the Celtic, druid priests, people have practiced various forms of *scrying* (from the English word *descry*, meaning "to make out dimly" or "reveal") in which water—as well as beryl, crystal, mirrors, polished quartz, and other light-catching surfaces—have been employed to activate a deeper, more revelatory kind of vision. And as I will explore more fully later in this section of the book, similar gazing practices have also made use of the sky, religious images—or the eyes of a partner.

Pausanias, the noted Greek travel writer and cultural geographer writing under the auspices of the Roman Empire, notes: *Before the Temple of Ceres* at Patras, there was a fountain, separated from the temple by a wall, and there was an oracle, very truthful, not for all events, but for the sick only.*

---

* Ceres (which has the same root from which our word "cereal" originates) was a goddess of agriculture, grain crops, and fecundity. She, along with her daughter Proserpina, were the Roman counterparts of the Greek goddesses Demeter and Persephone—whose myth formed the basis for the rites celebrated at Eleusis. For over 2,000 years *these were the greatest transformational rites of the pre-Christian world*, and they will be discussed at greater length in chapter 26.

The sick person let down a mirror, suspended by a thread till its base touched the surface of the water, having first prayed to the goddess and offered incense. Then looking in the mirror, one saw the presage of death or recovery, according as the face appeared fresh and healthy, or of a ghastly aspect.

Though there's been some disagreement amongst various biographers, the 16th century French seer Michel Nostradamus is also said to have practiced water gazing—as a means of clairvoyance.

In his own referencing of the techniques he employed to produce his various predictions, Nostradamus writes of two things. The first: *"emptying my soul, mind and heart of all care, worry and unease through mental calm and tranquility."*

But he also makes reference to a bronze tripod filled with water. And here the controversy seems to center around whether Nostradamus actually gazed into such a water-filled bowl held by a tripod, or whether he was merely using the water-filled bronze tripod and its employment by the oracles of ancient Greece as an *analogy* to his own visionary process.

The above image from a wall in Pompeii is another illustration from the ancient world of gazes being employed—in this case, to induce a transformation in the sense of self. On the left hand side of this work of art there is a boy being initiated. In front of him is his initiator, and behind him the initiator's assistant.

As Joseph Campbell explains the scene: "The boy is told, 'Look in this bowl, and you will see your own face, your own true face.' The bowl is of such concavity inside that what he is going to see is not his own face at all but the face of old age held behind him. And isn't that a shock! He is being introduced to what our American Indians call the 'long body,' the whole body of your life from birth to death."

This is quite a different perception of "the self" than that held by those who lack initiation, those lacking an awareness of impermanence, those who are still identifying with the self-image.

The poetic tradition seems especially replete with examples of transformational gazes being employed to induce a deeper form of vision. For example, when Rilke was a young man he moved to Paris, and had the good fortune of not only living in that great city, but having secured a really great job. He was hired to be the personal assistant to the great sculptor Rodin. During his time with Rodin Rilke experienced a major writing block, and so he brought the problem to the older, more experienced artist. And what Rodin advised him to do was to go to the zoo during his lunch hour. But what was he to *do* there?

He was to go there and look, *just* look at the animals, at first the large cats. That is, he was to attempt to gaze at the animals without a conceptual filter intervening. This practice not only helped free Rilke from his writer's block, but also gave rise to a very penetrative form of vision, one that helped him to more deeply and empathically enter what it was he was gazing at. This less encapsulated form of vision ushered in a new phase of his poetic career, one that Rilke came to regard as "the work of seeing," and the first result of this was his famous poem "The Panther."

But learning how to gaze at *anything* without a conceptual filter intervening is also precisely what the Japanese poet Basho had hoped to induce in his students four hundred years earlier, when he told them that if they wanted to write about bamboo, they first "must *become* the bamboo."

Though transformational gazes have often been intentionally induced, they can also occur randomly, quite naturally—yet in a way that also profoundly shifts what Toltec shamanism refers to as "the assemblage point."

Between the 12th and 14th centuries when Courtly Love and its poetic troubadours were in flower, love poems began to flood practically the whole of Europe as well as the near East. At this time it was not an uncommon thing for men to have had profoundly transformational visionary experiences in gazing at particular *ladies*.

Dante (and his Beatrice) and the Sufi poet and sheikh Ibn Arabi (and a lady he gazed upon named Nizam) are two well-known examples. And another concerns the Italian poet Petrarch—who would later be credited as one of the fathers of the Italian Renaissance.

On April 6, 1327, the sight of a woman named Laura in the church of Sainte-Claire d'Avignon awoke in Petrarch a lasting passion. But a passion that would not be consummated in a physical sense—Laura was to refuse *that*, though on grounds that hadn't impeded many other lovers of this time; namely because she was already married. And so, the love for Laura becomes internalized by Petrarch—as a kind of divine *ache*.

As was the case with Beatrice for Dante (or Shams for Rumi) Petrarch's beloved also dies in mid-adoration—while continuing to inspire the poet throughout his life. Here the beloved lives on as an eternal flame capable of lighting the candle of the poet's own vision, a Muse that brings guidance and joy. But a joy that is also an ache—an ache in the words of Petrarch *"whose lovely sting pierces me so, till I feel it and weep."*

The very sight of such medial figures seemed to have illuminated both the *eye* and the *heart* of the beholder, shifting their assemblage point. Love—beauty—or wisdom—especially in conjunction, can *do* that. It's as if there's secret channel between the eyes and the heart that Western medical science has yet to discover. The visionary radiance of the beloved moves through that passageway, becomes blinding in some way, outshining all mundanity—and out of this blinding, *the eyes of the heart may begin to see...*

The form of vision that transpired for Ibn Arabi, Dante, Petrarch, and Rumi, was a form of epiphany. The incarnated person, the "local beloved," becomes a portal to newly glimpsed facets of divinity. While in the case of the latter three, even after death the *imaginal presence* of the beloved endures as continuing *inspiratrix* or *mediatrix*, guide to invisible realities, radiant portal into the beauty of transcendence itself. And henceforth, the whole world seems to glint a little from this radiance, as when our vision is enlightened by love, the whole world becomes illumined with us.

There's a subtle truth here that poets and writers have experienced or expressed in similar, if slightly different ways. Oscar Wilde, for example, once said, *"looking at something is not seeing it, and seeing it is seeing its beauty."*

In Ibn Arabi's case, he realized that we couldn't see God or "the Uncreated" directly. But when we are "alone with the Alone" we can see God in the beauty of His creations, as if they were the more visible ray of a greater, all-surrounding Light; in this case the beauty of human beings such as Nizam, who inspire us to love.

In a year of my life that flooded me with love poems, one ended with the lines "and the crust / that had covered my heart? /—*trampled / by wild hooves / of your beauty.*" And for some poets, the rippling shockwaves of such an *eros*-inspired vision may linger far longer than a single year. In Dante's case, even an illuminated childhood *glimpse* of the beauty of Beatrice Poltinari, will go on to inform, guide, and perfume the rest of his days.

Something rather similar seemed to have occurred not so long ago as the Middle Ages, but for the Russian cosmonauts and American astronauts when first gazing at the planet Earth from outer space. The only difference was that in these cases "the beloved" was not a human being, but Gaia, the Earth itself.

In my friend Kevin Kelly's book *The Home Planet,* he juxtaposed photographs of extraordinary beauty—images of our "home planet" as seen from outer space—with quotes from the cosmonauts and astronauts themselves that evoked what they actually experienced in looking at the Earth for the first time from the theater seat of outer space. What they saw was a beautiful, uniquely blue planet, spinning in space. This evoked, and *should* evoke a protective feeling about the environment of our planet. It helped us to see it as a single undivided organism: Gaia.

This, as cultural historians had noted, became a potent symbol for an emergent, if not urgently *needed* ecological vision; one that includes the entire human race, all the animals and plants on our planet, and its air and seas. Like ourselves, each of these elements are uniquely *themselves,* yet not truly *separate*. And long before space travel, nondual spiritual practitioners have told us the same.*

For as we will see, they too possessed gazes evoking a more unitary perception of things, giving rise to mystery and awe. (Which as Joseph Campbell has told us, *should also be* the primary intent of *myth*).

These cosmonauts and astronauts were not poets or mystics by training or sensibility—most of them were *engineers*. And yet, so many of them seemed to have had a transformational vision, a mystical epiphany brought about by the sudden shift of perspective, a more global and unitary perspective—now become an evolutionary and ecological *imperative*.

And in a sense, the grunt work of a poetic—or spiritual—life, is to do *whatever we can* to make ourselves more *available* for such an epiphanic vision; gazes through which the ego becomes outshined, illuminated, or *annihilated*—by something more profound and less divisive… than what we had been taking ourselves, other beings—or our world, to be.

My own experience of *gazing* comprises one of my earliest memories, and also my first spiritual practice. For when I was three or four years old, I developed the habit of spinning around and around until I fell down on my back—and dazed, I then gazed up at the sky. When I did this the feeling I had was that I was communing with "God."

The clouds would shape-shift, and pass across the sky—and God was there: in the clouds, in the blue vastness behind the clouds, and in the resonant connection I was feeling as I gazed—all of this unfolding at what seemed the true speed of the Universe.

Sometimes I would think heartfelt thoughts toward God, and sometimes I thought I sensed some kind of response. But more important than anything either real or imaginary that might have transpired here, was the felt-sense of communion itself, a child's intuition that there is something exalted, some Majesty in the world—that I was not apart from—and that I could resonate with it through lying on my back and gazing at the sky.

---

* Apollo 14 astronaut Edgar Mitchell found his experience in space so powerful that when he got back to Earth he began digging into various literatures to understand what had happened. He found nothing in science literature, but eventually discovered in the spiritual texts from ancient India that "the descriptions of samadhi, Savikalpa Samadhi, were exactly what I felt: it is described as seeing things in their separateness, but experiencing them viscerally as a unity, as oneness, accompanied by ecstasy." Other astronauts such as Neil Armstrong and Buzz Aldrin had similar experiences.

In my early twenties I spent a number of years in a monastery—gazing still—at a bare, white wall. And just a few years later, I received a scholarship to attend a summer-long training that Tarthang Tulku Rinpoche used to give for Western mental health professionals in Berkeley, California—the Human Development Training Program.

A *tulku* is a re-incarnate *lama,* or teacher. In the Tibetan tradition these are spiritual teachers who, following their deaths and subsequent rebirths, are searched for and located through clairvoyant means by psychically gifted lineage holders. Then they are generally given certain tests to verify that they are, in fact, the *tulku* being searched for.

Having been identified, they are then given a rigorous and extraordinary training—often by those who had been their teachers or disciples in their previous lifetime. In this way, the flame of wisdom present in the tradition continues to manifest as it is carried forward by the *tulkus* from generation to generation. Tarthang Tulku is such a person, and one of the first lamas to publicly teach in the United States, a fortuitous outgrowth of the otherwise sorrowful Tibetan diaspora, that followed the occupation of Tibet by the Chinese communists in 1959.

In the Human Development Training Program Tarthang Tulku attempted to transmit some portion of the extensive range of skillful means contained within the Nyingma tradition of Tibetan Buddhism—that in some way it might begin to seed a deeper wisdom that would hopefully take root in the Western approach to mental health. For as he baldly challenged us, *"you would guide others to a deeper sense of what's true—but what or who, is going to guide* **you***?"*

One day Rinpoche was teaching about the self-image, and how to see past it, how to cease *identifying* with it. And for this he gave us all mirrors, and had us gaze into them until we could simply view what we were seeing—but without getting trapped in the mirror*—that is, without our knee-jerk tendency to *identify* with the self-image.

To a passing observer, a room filled with people all gazing at themselves in a mirror might seem the very height of narcissism—rather than people

---

* A similar attempt to counteract "getting trapped in the mirror" –while assisting a fundamental shift into a non self-referential mode of awareness—occurs in the Zen tradition. For during *sesshin* (intensive meditation retreats) all bathroom mirrors are covered over with paper for the entire duration of the *sesshin*.

engaged in a practice intended to *deconstruct* it. But truly, the sensibility behind this practice was not dissimilar from other meditative practices he'd been teaching. For we had already seen that we could view our thoughts without identifying with them, that we could simply observe them arising like clouds, and them watch them dissolve.

He was teaching us in both instances that we aren't the *content* of our minds—neither self-image, nor thought—but instead, the spaciousness of pure *content-less awareness itself,* the context out of which thought objects arise, and dissolve back to their source.

Rinpoche was guiding us, in other words, to a radically altered perspective toward cognition (and identity) than that more widely held in the West and most notably reflected by Rene Descartes's famous maxim, "I think, therefore I am." (A maxim that reflects the over-rationality that has prevailed in the Western tradition—and for anyone with a meditation practice, *clearly wrong-headed!).*

Somewhere in this teaching about cultivating an altered sense of view, I related to Tarthang my early experiences as a child in gazing up at the sky. "Yes," he replied, "we have such gazes in our tradition."

EIGHTEEN

The Threefold Sky

Practitioners of The Three Fold Sky* are guided to imagine that they have just come home from a very productive day in which everything one had hoped to accomplish had been achieved. One is to imagine coming home with nothing left undone, nothing one has to think about any longer, to imagine that one is about to settle into a favorite old armchair, or a comfortable couch—and that we might use the ground beneath us to be that armchair or couch.

And in the process of leaning back or lying down, we might exhale a deep *"Ah,"* the seed syllable almost all cultures associate with the release into a natural comfort and ease, a syllable which in the case of Buddhism is also associated with the *Dharmakaya*—the thoughtless, vastly spacious, yet knowing aspect of our own most primordial nature.

… Lying with my back on the ground in a pasture by the Eel River in Northern California, several decades have passed since my initial childhood practice of gazing at the sky and communing with "God." There is a voice—that of another Tibetan lama, Tsoknyi Rinpoche—guiding us to just gaze up at the spacious blue vastness of the summer sky….and to mingle the thoughtless spaciousness of our own minds with the spaciousness of the sky.

Our own thoughts might arise and pass like clouds, but we need do nothing about them, just let them pass. The clouds in the sky, we are

---

* In the context of Tibetan Buddhist teachings, "threefold" indicates a tripartite reflection being offered; namely an *outer,* an *inner,* and an *innermost*. Here, the *outer* refers to the empty space of the sky before you; the *inner* space being simply the empty quality of your own mind; the *innermost* space refers to the empty nature of *rigpa*—that is, non-dual awareness itself—which is being directly pointed out by the vajra master or teacher guiding the practice. This is a specific practice to enhance *trekcho,* the "thorough cutting through" (of all cognitive obscurations) unique to the *Dzogchen* teachings—and thoroughly *lacking* in Western psychology.

reminded, do not threaten in any way the spacious blue vastness that lies behind the clouds. And in the same way, the spaciousness of our own minds needn't be disturbed by the thoughts that temporarily appear.

Tsoknyi points out to us that the spaciousness of the blue sky is just like the spaciousness of the mind's *essence*. However there is one difference. The spaciousness of the sky does not have a cognizant quality. It is spacious without having the capacity to recognize that it is spacious. Our mind's essence, however—what the Tibetans call *rigpa*—has the spacious quality, as well as the cognizant capacity of being able to recognize its own spaciousness. And so, we are merely to cultivate the following view: that of resting in the recognition of space, the recognition of "emptiness."

> "Do not"—he said—"try to hold on to the recognition of this spaciousness. Allow it to naturally arise. At first you may only actually experience this natural, spacious view for a second or two at a time, and that is fine. When a thought, or some form of commentary arises, that is fine too. Don't make your thoughts –the cloud-like obscurations to 'vast sky mind'—into a problem. Just let thoughts pass like clouds, and eventually the essential nature of the mind will naturally reappear, as the blue sky eventually reappears once the clouds have passed—though in truth, like the blue sky lying behind the clouds, mind's essence—*rigpa*—is actually always here."

Such spiritual practices as the form of gaze induced by The Threefold Sky *may not be adequately transmitted through the written page*. Usually the ego must first be pacified, and attention re-routed from its "idiot's momentum" before such exercises can bear their intended fruit. For the capacity of words to actually guide us into any initiatory intent, much depends on our receptivity, our capacity to receive and embody. (No receptivity, no Transmission). And usually, our thoughts need to be thinned out as well. There needs to be some kind of purification first, like weeding a garden before introducing a rare and valuable plant.

For this reason, Vajrayana Buddhism's uniquely initiatory "Nature of Mind" teachings have been traditionally offered only after a significant preparatory phase (a phase in which a series of preliminary practices termed *ngöndro* are performed, usually in increments of a *hundred thousand* each).

For otherwise, the prevailing cognitive and emotional obscurations are such that until they have been substantially "purified" we can't readily access—let alone *"sustain the view"* of fruition stage practices such as The Threefold Sky.

This principle was driven home for me—in an egg on my beard kind of way—the first time I attempted to employ this practice (as part of a cycle of gazing practices*) in leading a spiritual retreat. The retreatants were all people I had been working with for a number of years, and everybody thus had a number of years of meditative training—and so I had hoped the "ground" would be sufficiently prepared to receive what I was attempting to plant. But nobody quite "got it." The practice didn't really shift the collective assemblage point; nobody was left resting in the vastness of non-conceptual space.

When we convened for our next practice period I asked each retreatant to describe in vivid detail what they actually *did* experience in attempting to do this practice. These descriptions amounted to a very precise portrayal of the specific form of "idiot's momentum" customarily suffered by each of the retreatants.

The more obsessive people were having an experience of "trying to do it right," the same thing that captures their awareness in their daily lives. The man who was obsessed about the difficulties he was currently encountering with his girlfriend (the same man who'd later "hate his wife" in this book's chapter 8) would look up at the sky, but all he saw was his unhappy girlfriend, and rather than the unbounded luminosity of space, what he experienced instead was the dark specter of an imminent abandonment depression.

My folks weren't having a *meditative* experience, they were experiencing the very cognitive and emotional obscurations that *prevent* true meditation from occurring. I was thus forced to abandon the initial road map I had constructed for the rest of this retreat. And for the next two practice periods what we did instead was work with the very "obscurations" that each of the retreatants were encountering in their mind-stream.

---

* Videos of the others in this cycle of gazing practices can currently be viewed at www.gary-rosenthal.net/video-audio/; later, I hope to offer a larger compendium of such gazes in a DVD entitled *That Which Sees is Truly Seen.*

Once each person had become very clear about what his or her characteristic form of "idiocy" was, and had gained more insight into how they could hold it differently, we then went back to the practice of The Threefold Sky. But this time nearly everybody succeeded in shifting his or her assemblage point. They were able to effortlessly rest in non-conceptual space without latching onto the mental content that formerly had been *filling* the space. (And meditation, truly, is simply extending the amount of time that we manage to rest in this *content-less* spaciousness).

The form of gaze obtained by looking into a mirror without identifying with our *image,* as well as the form of gaze achieved in The Three Fold Sky, both entail an experience of self-hood that is completely "empty," completely spacious. For in both cases our *intrinsic awareness* has managed to pry itself away from the *self-image,* and the ideation which tends to surround it.

And thus, a kind of alchemical *separatio* occurs, that no longer confuses this image with (being) the seat of *identity.* And this may be very different from the way we customarily regard ourselves. This is also very different from the perspective of *narcissism*—where self-image is mistakenly *conflated* with identity.

A like form of gaze, and a like resulting shift in the sense of identity—a metaphoric "death of the old self"—seems to have occurred in the depth-vision Narcissus had at the end of his myth.

And if so, it would resonate not only with the prophesy Tiresias had made about Narcissus to his mother—that self-knowledge would be "deadly" in some way—but with the words of the mystics encountered in almost every spiritual tradition, as they each speak of a kind of cognitive shift in which they have so entered themselves, that they've passed beyond themselves, as if they had died or no longer existed (in the old way).

The attempt to die to one's former sense of self—such that "self" becomes no longer anchored to the self-*image, any* self-image —tends to be a steeper and more narrow passage than Western psychology commonly aims for, a needle's eye.

But it is also a true standard for the mystics of every religion, for the self-image can't fit through this needle's eye, nor anything else we might think we own, nor anything circumscribed by time, nor anything that's been created, or has arisen as a compound from something else. The only thing that can pass through the needle's eye is an empty, spacious mind, a mind that clings to *nothing*, not even this spaciousness itself.

> "No eyes, no ears, no nose, no tongue, no body and no mind, nor any thing the mind can grasp," says *the Heart Sutra* in reflecting the mind's essential nature. And I'll leave it to the reader whether this is a stretch… but a deeper reading of the myth of Narcissus might recognize a similar reflection—that given by the strange and lucid pool that led to Narcissus's (metaphoric) death: "No shepherds, goats, cattle, leaf or bird ever fell to the pool's surface. The pool reflects none of these—no thing—not even the sun."

My perspective on inner development (which is as well my perspective on the transformation of narcissism) has come to be that it is not enough to merely reflect or have knowledge about what we are not—the ego, and the self-image that we conflate with *identity*.

Psychotherapies of all kinds over the past hundred years have tended to be variously adequate at an analysis, an interpretation, a mirroring of the egoic personality—that sense of self shaped and reflected through our conditioning process, whether in this life-time, or as a retained residue from others. And they've variously succeeded in reflecting the nature of the ego structure, replete with its complexes, traumas, and defenses, its transference projections, and the various object relations that tend to shape our perception of self and of world.

But coming to understand more about what we're not—the ego structure, and its projective (and defensive) mechanisms—though extremely *valuable,* is not *enough*. To fully free ourselves from the visionary perspective of narcissism, we seem to need a yet deeper kind of reflection, a deeper mirroring, a deeper pointing out—of an essential nature that the ego structure has been *obscuring*. And for this deeper aspect to be most usefully *mirrored* it also needs to be *embodied* in some way.

However, at the beginning—and even well along the path of inner work—there can be a problem here. For people tend at first to be so disoriented to their deeper nature that it doesn't seem recognizable. We're still often functioning with an assumption of self-hood akin to Narcissus before his "fatal" vision in the pool. We've grown so identified with a familiar and encapsulated version of self, become so identified with the perspective of the ego, that we don't know *what else might be available,* as if the egoic perspective is the only option, and "as good as it gets."

Our deeper nature is often quite obscured, as if covered over by clouds, or by a subtle kind of psychic shell. These "clouds" and this "shell" are comprised of the various mental structures that create our "veil," a veil that blocks our perception of what exists *beneath* the veil—which is the transcendent, and spaciously non-conceptual nature of "pure awareness" itself. Yet even when it might briefly appear—like the blue sky emerging from behind the clouds—without some "pointing out" or mirroring, people would be less likely to recognize it.

Our obscurational "clouds" may not only include the self-image (whether inflated, anxious, depressed, or defended). But also the superego—which is often running us ragged, as it commands, negates, or second-guesses us. Our "clouds" are also comprised of the various other object relations that keep us in duality by splitting our relational field into tenaciously familiar typecast dramas for two players (such as what we saw with my 12 o clock client and his wife in chapter eight).

Our minds might be similarly clouded by a near incessant sub-vocal inner monologue; by grasping and aversion; our attempt to avoid pain or latch onto pleasure; by dwelling upon either the past or the future. Our possibilities for cloudy moments, hours, days, and *lives,* seem nearly endless. For nearly endless are the mental constructs, habits, and assumptions that fill, shape, and *confine* the otherwise prevailing *vastness* of psychic space.

Our cloudy minds may also include the belief that *something must be done,* or done urgently *first,* before we can fully exhale, or experience a natural ease or contentment; but also our belief in another mental structure: that there is a "particular someone" who must do this something, and that who we are *is* this "someone," a someone who is a stand-alone, and separate from everything and everyone else.

Without some cessation from all of the above, without some gap or opening, it is hard for our deeper nature to be glimpsed or experienced—and so it can't really be optimally *mirrored* yet. (And in truth, all spiritual practices are the attempt to create such a "gap" in awareness, an attempt to render the ego passive, so that our deeper nature can begin to shine through).

For as long as we don't have an alternative way of experiencing ourselves, it can be hard to have much faith that something deeper is actually available as an option. And so, if our more essential nature were to be spoken of without some form of actual experience (and without the preparatory training that makes actual experience more possible) it would tend to remain a less meaningful abstraction, sounding like "pie in the sky."

And so, as part of "the work," a spiritual teacher, transpersonal therapist, or guide must gradually begin to orient the other to their deeper nature, continually mirror essential nature should it appear, but also ongoingly mirror "the idiot's momentum" that keeps one dissociated from presence, while identified with the ego.

This latter form of mirroring is a pointing out of exactly what it is that needs to be worked with, de-potentiated, and ultimately dis-identified from, in order to connect with an underlying depth.

Here the guide must lie in wait—like Pluto beneath Persephone—for moments where it may be possible to "abduct" the other, to smuggle them past the boundary of their more familiar and prevailing ego structure; in the process providing for them a beginning taste, a growing familiarity, with their own deeper nature.

NINETEEN

Meditation and "Stupid Shamatha"

IN ADDITION TO mirroring the actual contours of ego structure as it reveals itself in daily life—and as part of the attempt to *pacify* the ego structure so that the deeper lying essential nature can begin to become more accessible—I've often found myself either giving my clients some orientation to meditation, or supporting the importance of meditating if the client already has some form of meditative practice.

But one of the things I have learned from many years of working with people is that for beginners at least, it may take quite a number of *years* before meditation can give a more ready, potent, and distilled experience. This is not to say that the tranquil, calming aspect of *shamatha* practice can't kick in fairly soon; and thus people can certainly begin to get some of the benefits of "stress relief" from their meditation without much lag-time from the point that they begin to practice meditation.

But as a whole, when people are in the early stages of establishing a meditation practice, most of the time that we are ostensibly "meditating," we are still filled with all manner of thoughts and daydreams—such as what my retreatants experienced the first time they attempted the practice of The Threefold Sky.

Often we are still subliminally self-absorbed within the construct, the image we have of ourselves as "the meditator"—whether inflated, virtuous, anxious, or striving—and few moments of real meditation are generally occurring; so there still may not be much of the deeper (and more "selfless") self there to reflect, mirror, or point out.

For while ostensibly meditating, people are often attempting to launch themselves into their imagined version of an ideal state, or to *duplicate* some *previous* experience of meditation. But this is putting the wily fox in charge of the hen house, and such a willful approach to meditation only keeps in the saddle what really needs to fall away.

We may attempt to use our meditation as a defense against something in our mind-stream that feels threatening. We may be trying "to do it right." We may be holding on so tight to our "meditation object" that it becomes impossible to recognize and rest in the effortlessly spacious, non-conceptual presence we already *are*.

In other words, our "meditation" may reflect the same "idiot's momentum" that captures us when we're *not* meditating—for the ego can get ahold of almost anything, even "meditation."

The somewhat humorous, somewhat derogatory term that is thus sometimes employed by *Dzogchen* practitioners in referring to most of what passes for meditation is "stupid *shamatha.*"

However, I have found one form of meditation—a type of gaze, interestingly—to be quite efficacious even with beginners to meditation in providing some opening access to *sunya* (or *non-deficient* "emptiness"). And this is the practice of *trespasso*.

TWENTY
Trespasso

THE SPANISH WORD *trespasso* is most commonly used as a real estate term. It denotes "lease," as in a property or locale one doesn't purchase or come to own, but instead, a locale being *rented*. Yet, for English speakers, it is hard not to hear a secondary undertone in the word, the sense of "trespass," *to pass beyond* (a customary boundary).

The practice of *trespasso* might thus be thought of as giving us a lease into a dimension of experience that one does not own. For in this exercise, the separate self (that might otherwise claim ownership) seems to *evaporate*, or recede from view. And in just *this* sense, the practice leads us to "trespass"—to pass beyond—the narcissistic shell, the characteristic bounded-ness of the egoic perspective.

Though the word *trespasso* is of Spanish origin, we may recognize the practice as belonging to a category of spiritual exercises recently alluded to—those Romanized as *shamatha* (from the Pali and Sanskrit word *samatha*), which is often translated as "calm abiding." For *shamatha* practices are those designed to calm, cool, or pacify the mind.

And earlier in this book, when Michel Nostradamus spoke of "emptying my soul, mind, and heart of all care, worry, and unease through mental calm and tranquility," this description identifies Nostradamus's practice as a version of the "calm abiding" intended by any *shamatha* practice. (While the *clairvoyance* this gave rise to, reflects the "unconfined cognizance" aspect of *rigpa,* which was developed more fully in chapters 6 and 18, and also reflected at the bottom of the footnote on p. 94).

The *intent* behind such practices stems from the recognition that normally our minds are like a whirlwind of agitation, whereby we're engaged with an obsessive concern about the past, a *belief* about the present, or an anxious concern for the future—and so, *our minds are rarely experiencing the naked fullness of the present moment itself.* And when distracted and agitated in this way, it prevents us from accessing our deeper nature—and the *intuitive insight* it can give rise to (*vipassana*).

Shamatha practices are divided into two broad categories—*shamatha* with support, and *shamatha* without support. Here the word "support" refers to the object that one is using as a kind of meditation target, that which is used to calm and stabilize the mind, and to bring it into presence. Common examples that make use of the support of an "object" would be meditative practices that focus on the breath, a mantra, or a visualization, such as of a deity. Though useful for anyone, in Mahayana and Vajrayana Buddhism these are usually the *initial* meditative practices given to beginners.

"*Shamatha* without support" refers to a more advanced style of meditation, where one is no longer employing an object to calm and focus the mind, but simply resting the mind in the boundlessness of non-conceptual space—which usually can't be done unless one has first developed sufficient concentrative stability through *shamatha* practices that employ an object.

Dzogchen's sky gazing, or Zen's *shikan taza* ("just sitting") are examples of *shamatha* without support. While *trespasso* is a practice that makes use of a "support." But in the latter instance, the object being employed to calm and support the mind and bring it to presence is not the breath or a mantra, etc., but instead, *the left eye of a partner.*

The fact that *trespasso* is done with a *partner* makes it distinctive from most other meditative practices of which I'm familiar (though tantric sexual practices also come to mind). And as I've suggested, the fact that of all the various *shamatha* practices I've employed over the years in my own inner work, as well as in my work with clients, the fact that this practice is often one that readily gives access to fruitional (nondual) states, even with beginners to meditation, also makes it distinctive.

I cannot state with any authority why *trespasso* gives such a ready "lease" into nondual states, even with beginners to meditation. But this question has intrigued me enough to ask those whom I've taught it *why* it works so well for them.

Some of the answers I've received are: there's "more energy" available by virtue of doing it with another person; since it's a shared experience, people report feeling a greater accountability to stay present than is often the case when meditating on their own; of all the senses many people are "more visual" these days—especially men perhaps, and the closeness of the partner's eyeball often seems a more compelling meditation target, say, than one's own breath or a mantra; Westerners may be more "relationally oriented"—especially women perhaps, and with *trespasso* there is a built-in sense of mirroring and accompaniment being provided by the eye of one's partner, and hence a sense of being held—with a lessened anxiety thus about disappearing, or becoming "lost" in the meditation; it "just seems more fun."

In gazing into the left eye of one's partner there should be a willingness to let go of *everything else*—a letting go of past and future, and importantly, *a letting go of any of the ways we may have objectified either our partner or ourselves*. We thus allow ourselves to become somewhat reference-less, such that our only reference point becomes the left eye of our partner.

This sense of reference-less-ness is a letting go of any fixed position, any fixation, anything we might normally cling to or carry forward from one moment to the next—anything which perpetuates a habituated sense of self—usually one estranged from our deeper nature.

In practicing *trespasso* thoughts may continue to flicker in a way that can mildly distract us. We may briefly go off with these thought objects— but more importantly, we *keep coming back* to our partner's left eye—as if we've begun to commit to a kind of psychic monogamy.

As concentration begins to stabilize, at a certain point the edginess of egoic structure often begins to collapse or dissolve; a more undivided and unitary sensing of the world begins to prevail. And with this, the passing away of a subtle level of anxiety or defensiveness that we may not have even realized was there.

Trespasso is thus a practice that leads to "the dissolution of the binary"— the very *coniunctio* that Jung wrote about as the apotheosis of the alchemical process; the experiential encounter of the state of unity (that exists behind seeming opposites, and behind the dualistic mind itself).

Here we no longer have a sense of ourselves as being encapsulated within a psychic shell, a defining structure that would have an edge, a periphery, a boundary—such that something has become less defined about exactly where we might end or begin. We have "trespassed" our customary ego boundaries and entered a field of shared resonance, a true state of "intimacy." And rather than this feeling threatening, when *trespasso* yields its characteristic fruit, this actually feels like we've "come home" to ourselves, as if we've reconnected with something natural and innate.

The kind of dissolution, boundless-ness, or merging that can happen in *trespasso* is very "Neptunian." Yet it's different than what takes place with *projective identification* (an often confusing psychological phenomenon that occurs when one person begins to internally experience disowned, and projected features of another's inner world).

In *trespasso,* your mind comes to a *one-pointedness* through concentrating solely on your partner's left eye. This "one-pointedness" is the very feature that Isaac of Ninevah was pointing to (on p. 123) when, in speaking of humility, he says it consists of collecting the soul "into a single point" such that one's field of vision has become *divested of self-reference...* "The self that might otherwise appear in either an idealized or devalued guise—the self that might otherwise either idealize or devalue others—has disappeared, at the least for the moment."

Something quite similar happens in *trespasso.* For in its one-pointed focus, we are neither distracted by, nor identifying with our own customary psychological phenomena (i.e., "divested of self-reference"). And neither are we distracted by another's psychological phenomena, let alone living it vicariously in being granted a first-hand experience that properly belongs to another (as in the case of projective identification).

In fact, the mind dwelling on the single point of a partner's left eye may enable our self-consciousness to have thankfully fallen out of the picture; no longer on the scene bifurcating a unitary field into a squirmy drama for two players. This is, in other words, a higher order of "merging."

You're not trying to save face, or embellish or defend your self-image. You're just gazing, free of self-reference. It's a pleasure—just to be. To be here in a body wide-open and attentively present with another person kind enough to offer their left eye as your meditation target (which is simultaneously an opportunity to let go of all your conceptual baggage, and the clunky, habituated ways you've related to people in the past).

There's absolutely nothing you need to know, do, or believe. *Nothing,* in particular, *is* what's happening here. But *this* nothing is quite vibrant and *sufficient.* For though *nothing* is happening, *nothing* is in *excess,* and *nothing* whatsoever is *lacking.* This "no-thing" is a welcome vacation from

Too Much Information, and from subliminal Acquisition Campaigns and Defensive Campaigns of all kinds. It's the secret prize the wise walk home with, while all the rubes are leaving this carnival walking briskly beneath a ridiculous hat, or clutching kewpie dolls that have already lost their luster.

As we've seen, this nothing, or "emptiness"—what Buddhism refers to as *shunyata*—is the very matrix out of which our essential qualities arise; their portal in a sense. And so, the encounter with this *non-deficient* form of emptiness—and the capacity to abide in it—demarks a significant turning point in inner development, that of having become a "stream enterer." (A merit badge one should hold lightly; for our career in idiocy has not come to an end, even if other options *are* now more available).

And as marvelous and efficacious as *trespasso* can be—once one gets the hang of it—still, it could be a little inconvenient to have to carry a partner around in order to trespass the mundane bounded-ness of the egoic perspective. For this reason, in my work with people I often employ *trespasso* to provide some initial familiarization with an alternative "view," while later introducing other attentional practices and deconstructive conversations just beyond the scope of this book. Some of these "attentional practices" are gazes almost identical to *trespasso*—yet that don't require "lugging a partner around." We have already alluded to a couple of them—sky gazing, and mirror gazing.

Though there's any number of ways to employ a mirror that might lead to an alteration of one's customary perspective, and one's customary assumption of self-hood, one way is to use the reflected image of one's own left eye as the meditation object one is calmly abiding with, in exactly the same way as one might in doing *trespasso* with a partner.

※

At timely moments (and right timing is essential) the practice of *trespasso* can be quite useful in doing *couples counseling*—or for anyone in an intimate relationship. For *trespasso* gives couples—and quite literally—*another way of looking at each other.*

In the process, the practice of *trespasso* can begin to give a couple a taste of the very *intimacy* that has often been in short supply when their relationship is going through doldrums, or at the point that they've been led to enter couples therapy. It can help them to find a less enshelled way of experiencing themselves, and a less aversive, critical, grasping, or oblivious way of experiencing their partners.

Once the prevailing conflicts have been sufficiently voiced and explored, *trespasso* can then give the couple an alternative perspective, a way to unhook from the impasse that has captured them. It gives couples a means to SHIFT out of who has been living their relationship when it's the shits—what I term "the shadow couple." For at the point a couple initially comes to seek counseling, often "the *shadow* couple" has abducted the relationship, leaving it in a kind of uninspired, recrimination-filled Waste Land.

And as we saw with my 12 o'clock client and his wife, when the shadow couple is on stage, the drama is rather predictable, as are the protagonists: there's a fixated, endarkened version of the other being perceived, as well as a somewhat endarkened and reactive version of oneself, a self that is in recoil from the other, and *blaming* the other for this contracted recoil in oneself.

But *trespasso* provides a gap, an opening in the field of awareness, through which *the Lovers* can again emerge and begin to re-inhabit the landscape of a relationship. It can bring the couple back into real, present-time contact with each other again, rather than continuing to relate to some *image* of our partner that we have formed and are still carrying from the past, some way we have concretized them, some way we have "put them in a box." And thus, through the practice of *trespasso* we can more freely and freshly encounter our partner(s) rather than continuing to butt heads in a defensive or habitually reactive way.

As the less defended, less bounded, more intimate experience of self and other begins to emerge, the shift in perspective often brings with it a correspondingly altered *type of voice*. A voice that is less shrill, less polarized—and more resonant with the tonality of *being*, a voice less edgy, softened yet fuller; a voice like a well-tuned cello, *a voice no longer dissociated from presence.*

And with these less pressured and less polarized voices, a couple might now explore any of the issues they've recently been experiencing, but as now seen from an altered perspective. For now the couple has removed their "enemy glasses," and ceased experiencing the partner as having "fearful chains." Rather, these partners have entered a state of awareness that possesses a native freedom and contentment.

From this more contented posture, it's also easier to see one's *own* prior reactivity, and how *that* had been contributing to the difficulties, whereas previous to this shift, all that can generally be seen is the reactivity or limitations of one's *partner*. (Re-read the previous paragraphs about "the shadow couple" while imagining the *political* consequences of such a shift, should Democratic and Republican legislators receive training in polarizing-reducing gazes such as *trespasso*. For *any* relationship becomes subject to a dysfunctional gridlock when it is being experienced through the divisive perspective of the shadow couple).

Finding a voice that hadn't previously seemed available may signal the release from the archetypal perspective of Echo. It may signal a couple's emerging from the echo-chamber of the myth of Narcissus and Echo, a myth in which the protagonists are either devaluing or feeling devalued—a mythic structure within which true relatedness seems perpetually doomed.

And so, when I am working with a couple to help them reconnect in a more intimate way, I often suggest that the couple make regular *"trespasso* dates" with each other, and use the shift in perspective brought about by this practice to become more sensitized toward what takes them *out* of intimacy, and to speak about whatever else that might be voiced now, such that people can begin to feel better heard, more expressed, better accompanied, in their relationships.

Many couples report using the practice of *trespasso* as a way of reconnecting when they've been apart for a while, either geographically or emotionally. And as an added bonus, couples often report incorporating *trespasso* into their lovemaking, where the disruption of ordinary left-brain awareness can give rise to all manner of tantric phenomena...

I have also come to use various gazes in working with groups, and in leading retreats. For example, it's often been a wonderfully eye and heart opening thing to begin a retreat by having us all welcome each other through the practice of *trespasso*. For I have found that if a retreat is begun, by first doing a couple of minutes of *trespasso* with each person in the room, some of the isolative and self-conscious social edginess that can be present when a group first gathers, quite readily transmutes into a shared depth, and the most lovely group resonance is thus formed rather quickly.

For retreatants have been given some immediate grounding in an alternative way of experiencing themselves, which is as well an alternative way of experiencing other people, and Reality itself. And this is because the temporary *collapse* of the narcissistic shell gives rise to a radically altered view; a nondual mode of awareness that is no longer so egocentric. For this is a style of vision, and a mode of awareness, that has no *center*—nor *edge*, no *boundary* at all—and so is connected in some way to everything, and everyone else.

TWENTY-ONE

"Looks Like Me"
& Following Your Bliss

THERE'S ANOTHER GAZING practice that's been continuously employed for over twelve hundred years. And though it doesn't require the use of an embodied partner, it does make use of another pair of eyes—the eyes of Padmasambhava as captured in a sculpture of him that came to be known as "Looks Like Me."

For the sculpture was so life-like, and so captured the mind-essence of Padmasambhava that when he first viewed it in the eighth century, his comment was "Looks like me." And then he blessed it, empowering it, saying, "Now it is the same as me!" And from that time forth, *Vajrayana* practitioners have employed representations of this sculpture as if they were having a visionary, meditative audience with Padmasambhava himself.

The eyes in particular have a special, portal-like quality. They reflect—and may transmit—the brightened, and stable immediacy of an awakened mind. But also, like the pool in Narcissus's myth, they seem to give a true reflection of the essence of the beholder. If you gaze into these eyes, *he's seeing you*, and as deeply as anyone could. The left eye (appearing on the right side of the image, as you face it on the following page) seems especially illuminating. And if you bring your own gaze into a one-pointed focus on this eye, it may become a portal into the depths of non-conceptual space, a spacious nondual awareness in which "that which sees is clearly seen." Such a transformational gaze may "cut-through" (dissolve) who you last took yourself to be. And in its place, the "perfection" of your own naked awareness.

If the reader will Google "Looks Like Me," there will be links to several good color photos of the sculpture that can then be downloaded and printed on decent photo stock paper and framed. You could download the photo's file and take it to the local print or copying center if you don't have a color printer at home. It will only cost you a few dollars to have a very serviceable reproduction of this marvelous work of art, which is as well a wonderful portal into meditation. I've found a *color* photo of approximately eight inches by ten inches to be excellent for this gazing practice, though if much smaller, or not in color, something may be "lost in translation." Once you have a decent photograph of "Looks Like Me," you can gaze into Padmasambhava's eyes in a similar manner as in doing *trespasso* with a partner.

The numerous intentionally induced gazes evoked in this section of the book are but a few of a larger body of practices that have been employed throughout history in the attempt to deconstruct "the narcissistic shell"—such that our deeper nature might stand more revealed. Several of those evoked here have been formal practices—passed down through time—gifts from the past. *Which shouldn't stop us from discovering and employing practices of our own;* practices that are similarly capable of relaxing or dissolving this shell.

For this can be experienced in countless ways, some uniquely suited to you, where something in you just goes "ah," drops its burden, and steps out of time, its deadlines, and of being the doer. Maybe just being in the presence of a place you love, a certain hill or part of a river; listening to the sound of the rain on the tin roof of a little retreat hut, or a particular piece of music; walks on a trail with your dog; turning off the electric lights, and lighting some candles. There are countless ways of taking refuge.

Ultimately, we each need to find our own way to the soul's sacred waterfall, where we too are letting it all go, yet being constantly filled. This is soul work, the deeply fulfilling work of embodying that wonderful phrase Joseph Campbell left us: *following your bliss*. And he told us we should devote at least an hour of every day to this, to dwelling in a particular room or locale where we can simply experience, and bring forth what we are, and might be. And though nothing may seem to be happening at first, he confidently promises us that if we have a sacred place, and make use of it, "something will happen…"

But I think Campbell used the word "bliss" to point us to more than *just* a heightened joy (though *including* that too). For there's a myriad of other subtle qualities and "flavors" that may spontaneously arise here: a peaceful spaciousness, a humble gratitude, an effortlessness, a tender-hearted compassion; a supportive buoyancy, an allowing-ness, a sudden confidence, or strength; an objectivity, a knowingness, an undefended-ness, etc. It's like there's a wine that begins to flow within us, and we might "know what we like"—say an uplifting quality—but may not at first have the vocabulary yet to identify the subtle taste we're actually experiencing. (The teachings contained in the Sufic *lataif* system reflect both these subtle qualities of our deeper nature, as well as the common psychological fixations and conflicts that preclude their arising. In this way, "formal" teachings can also lead to "bliss"). And being a bliss fan-boy, I'll take it, wherever, however, I find it.

In a *therapy* setting, the growing familiarity with these qualities of essential nature—and the growing familiarity with what commonly *obscures* them—lends a depth, a further dimensionality to the work. There begins to be more a dialectic—more of a conversation—between what's fixated and what's not. And as our fixation(s) become less ongoing and pervasive, a therapist or teacher thus has something else now which it is their task to resonantly mirror back. For if we have crystallized into fixation in part through a lack of mirroring or support for our essential being, then when that deeper being *begins to reappear*, it now *quite importantly* needs to be recognized, mirrored, supported—to be included now as a significant element in the therapeutic conversation; in a sense, the leading edge of an emerging spiritual development.

And the development—and dimensionality encountered here—is *every bit* as nuanced and varied as the stunted landscape of our personality fixations. It's like entering a land you'd become oblivious toward—or a world made new—now that a subtler form of awareness is in the saddle, and capable of recognizing it. And so, there may be a lot to talk or share notes about, a lot to notice here that our fixation(s) had been obscuring. Yet like our growing clarity itself, our fixations seem to *keep coming back*, if in subtler forms. (Or sometimes, not so subtle). It's like we have dual citizenship. Or contending world-views—within our own *inner* Congress.

And though it's a developmental achievement to possess greater awareness of our fixations (which can make our freedom from them more likely) a merely psychological knowledge of the contours of ego structure—say, by knowing one's enneagram type—is but a booby prize *if* we continue to remain oblivious to the nuances and dimensionality that the ego structure obscures.

It is the job of the transformational change-agent to have one foot in each of these two realms, and thus to serve as a kind of bridge, while being capable of reflecting the nuances of *both*. (And it's far easier to recognize and reflect fixation. Clinical psychology is rather good at it). But it can't be overstated, that a clear, receptive mirroring of another's *essential nature* requires that one be grounded in, and adequately familiarized with, essential nature oneself.

Like the pool in Narcissus' "fatal vision," such a transformational vision that mirrors the beauty and riches found in the soul's depths is properly *Plutonic*—as much as it is Neptunian). For our essential qualities come more fully alive in us, and thus, can be more truly *mirrored*—the more the larvae-like shell of ego structure has begun to erode, perish, or molt away. This perishing ("the death of Narcissus") is really the intent that precipitates the flowering of psycho-spiritual work. Here nothing is *added* to attain fruition. Instead, a radical subtraction may occur—the "thorough cut" of *trekcho*. That is, *a transformative deconstruction of what we have taken ourselves to be, and as well a radical deconstruction of what we have taken the world to be*.

And though there've been *rumors*... I'm personally unfamiliar with human exemplars, where anything here is *permanently* achieved. What's more certain is, that with adequate orientation, mirroring, support, and practice, we're all capable of experiencing a psychic deconstruction in which the ego—and the ego's world-view—becomes dethroned, no longer so firmly in the saddle, no longer the sole perspective that's living, filtering, or ruling one's life...

In sum then, the various gazes spoken of* in this section of the book, each lead to a dis-identification from an otherwise habituated sense of identity. Thus allowing an altered, less *inflationary* (and less *deficient*) sense of self to now be encountered and *lived*; if only for moments or hours at a time... For here we might come to experience in our own bones the effects of a depth-vision, perhaps one akin to that experienced by Narcissus at the end of his myth.

---

* "Speaking of something" is different than its *transmission*. And spiritual practices are seldom optimally transmitted through the written page. The pacing, and spacing of words and silence, is simply quite different in a practice setting. For this reason, again I suggest that readers may want to watch videos of some of these gazes being led and practiced in a group setting by going online to: www.garyrosenthal.net/video-audio/ under Meditations.

IV.
Healing...
One Insult After Another
& Walking Briskly Beneath a Ridiculous Hat

TWENTY-TWO

What Heals Narcissism?

THERE'S NO SIMPLE, single answer to what heals narcissism. Just as there's no simple, single answer for how to be a fully developed, human form of being. At best we can offer evocative hints and metaphors that will always leave something out of the equation.

Yet if the "N word"—as well as the myth that stands behind it, have been in need of a re-visioning—so too has the notion of its healing. And if the ways we've thought about this thus far have seemed inadequate for the task, it suggests we must begin to think "outside of the box."

The ego structure itself is a kind of box. Though this is hard to recognize if we're still mostly encapsulated by it. As mentioned, the ego structure is also *a developmental achievement*, a necessary *station* in development, not its end point. It's akin to the larvae-like shell, from which a butterfly—or the soul's deeper nature—might later emerge and take flight. But in humans, that requires the metaphoric death of what we have previously taken ourselves to be.

And so, in the last section of the book I was presenting quite a number of gazing practices that have been employed throughout history, that not only echo Narcissus's gaze into a mysteriously lucid pool, but also give rise to an equally metaphoric and transformational "death." Such gazes—in fact any form of meditation or prayer—are allies in narcissism-reduction.

But it is not just a small part of the population whose vision is largely encapsulated by "the narcissistic shell." And so our re-visioning of narcissism might include seeing it less through the clinical lens of a particular personality disorder, which allegedly only pertains to 0 to 6.2 percent of the American population. And instead, to have a bit more humility—by recognizing that we *all* have "narcissistic features"—if not a full-blown "Narcissistic Personality Disorder." Humility, *in itself,* helps us to reduce our narcissism. For it helps us to see things, as well as ourselves, more as both truly are.

Yet there also seems something *correct* in professional psychology's notion of narcissism being a *personality disorder*—even if I don't consider its estimates within the population of Americans to be useful. For a personality disorder is considered to be something that is not episodic or of a limited duration like an "adjustment disorder," but rather it is understood as a condition with a lengthy trajectory—"an idiot's momentum" if you will—that is, a deep-seated condition that persists over a *long* range of time, and which had its onset by adolescence or early adult-hood.

In this sense, as I've suggested, narcissism is rather like an addiction, and not something that can be healed once and for all, but rather a "one day at a time," or a *one moment at a time* kind of encounter.

Yet in this way, the *healing* of narcissism is also akin to enlightenment itself, for in only the rarest of cases—if ever—is it a permanently achieved perspective. (Hence, as one of the shortest of Zen *koans* goes: *"The clearly enlightened person falls into a well"*).

Like the eternal dialogue between *guru* and *chela*, the "light" of awareness and what *obscures* it, are in an ongoing dialectic, an eternal dance. And similarly, the encounter with our own narcissism may be in play for the *entirety* of our lives—which is rather *humbling*.

Yet with adequate orientation and practice, the capacity to come to a transformational clarity is also *potentially* available—*in every moment*, and for the entirety of our adult lives—which is rather *empowering*. (As is the recognition that whatever is "unreal"—each of our illusions, however reoccurring—are fundamentally empty and impermanent, and thus subject to deconstruction. For were this not the case, any kind of psychological or spiritual development would be impossible).

And for these reasons, I think it might be helpful to quit pathologizing narcissism so much. And to quit regarding it as something that only exists in *those* people; which unknowingly, could be "a case of the pot calling the kettle black". And so, it might be better to regard narcissism as a *fundamental confusion*, and thus a fundamental *challenge* we encounter simply in being human.

And the challenge has to do with getting more in touch with the *being* component of what it means to be a "human being." That's what we essentially are, or should be: a *human form of being*. Yet as I've been reflecting it, narcissism is what results when we've become *dissociated* from our being, and taken ourselves to be something other than that.

And from this point of view, anything that helps us to get hooked up more to our *being* is transformative for a collectively shared estrangement from an underlying deeper nature. And this estrangement really *is* a collectively transmitted "dis-ease" (not a *disease,* which would be to further pathologize it). For there's something uncomforting about this estrangement from being, and it *is* socially communicable—not merely an intra-psychic phenomenon. There are cultures, and cultural epochs, which are simply more narcissistic than others. And we seem to be in one now.

And when a whole culture is largely fallen from wisdom, or dissociated from being, its influences are pervasive, subliminal, just in the ether of an epoch. Yet like the air we breathe, these influences can escape our notice, or be hard to clearly see (as I feel has been the case; and part of why I've written this book).

For this reason, and for thousands of years, human beings have not only employed transformational gazes, but gone on *wilderness retreats* in order to disengage from the culturally transmitted features that tend to shape and encapsulate our vision.

In this regard, when I was 21 years old I lucked into a fairly rare, yet wonderful initiation. It was an initiation into a radical solitude in the natural world, a radical alone-ness. I'd been hired by the New Hampshire Forestry Service to be its fire lookout ranger on top of Smarts Mountain, about 14 miles from the college town of Hanover. I lived in a little one-room cabin four miles from the nearest road. That meant that any food or supplies I would need had to be carried up the mountain in my own backpack.

Except for the occasional lightning strike, there was no electricity up there. Nor running water. What there was: a nearby Indian spring once used by the Mascoma tribe, a cast iron wood stove once carried up the mountain (in pieces) by two of my burly predecessors, plus plenty of downed firewood to buck-saw and chop for the stove. And during day-lit hours (when the mountain wasn't socked in by clouds) I'd ascend a high tower next to my cabin and scanned the adjoining White Mountains for forest fires.

Positioned up in the lookout tower, there was an Osborne Fire Finder. It consisted of a topographic map of the surrounding terrain that was oriented and centered on a horizontal table with a circular arm graduated in degrees, with two sighting apertures above the map that could be rotated until the sighting holes aligned with the fire.

In actual practice, a much more conclusive location of a fire was obtained by intersecting my single angle of vision to the fire with the angles provided by two or three other lookout towers in the nearby mountains. (And I've attempted something similar in this book, in trying to view its topics from the intersection of *multiple* angles of vision—those provided by the psychological, spiritual, mythic, and historical perspectives).

But the most significant thing here—and why I'm writing about it now—is that I'd sometimes go ten days without seeing another person. And this experience of solitude was very instructive. I'd fallen into a natural harmony with nature, both my own and that surrounding me. And this was a harmony—a state of being—that I hadn't yet learned to metabolize around other people.

I'd been given an extended taste of aspects of my essential nature, yet without really having to do any inner work to uncover them. And this extended solitude in nature had shown me how much of the neurotic anxiety I'd often experienced was *socially determined*. For without any other humans around, I could let go of the ways I'd bent myself out of shape in order to socially adapt.

There are a couple of teachings here that point to, and amplify what I'm trying to convey. One is from the great English pediatrician and psychiatrist D.W. Winnicott, and the other from the Zen tradition. Winnicott said that what people need to learn from psychotherapy is "how to be alone while in the presence of others." For commonly, we're editing ourselves in order to fit in, and can thus wind up estranged from our deeper nature, as if that's somehow the cost we must pay to have other people in our lives. Which simply isn't the case. And the Zen teaching is nearly identical: *"Be with others the way you are when by yourself. And be with yourself the same way you are with others."*

The extent to which therapy clients have learned how to embody these teachings—by remaining grounded in their being regardless of whom they're interacting with—provides a helpful indicator of how "cooked" they've become, and how ready they may be to take leave of being in therapy. Yet in my own case, it would take me at least another *twenty years* before I learned how to access this unedited naturalness around other people. And sometimes, I'm still working on it…

Human beings have always retreated into nature—often either the mountains or the desert—as a means of reconnecting to their own being. But what might help us to keep that naturalness alive, when we come back into the complexities of living with other people?

I think it really helps if we have some kind of community in which authentic being-ness is shared, recognized, valued, and supported. And this is perhaps especially important when the wider culture is especially "narcissistic" (that is, estranged from their own being). If our retreat has brought us more deeply in touch with the truth of our being, or our sense of *dharma,* then the communal aspect—the *sangha*—is equally important.

For one of the things we have seen from re-visioning the myth of Narcissus and Echo is how fundamentally alone Narcissus was. He was living in what has been ironically termed a "splendid isolation." This is very different from *solitude.* It's an isolation that in truth is not very "splendid" at all, but rather an isolated island of self-hood…that enabled Narcissus's grandiosity, as well as his devaluing of others to remain unchallenged.

Deep and sustained interpersonal relationships can thus help heal our narcissism. Which is to say, the experience of loving, and of being loved, the experience of caring *for* others, and of being cared for *by* others.

Yet this brings to mind two things that Gurdjieff had once said. He was once asked what needed to happen to increase the rate of one's spiritual development. And asked by someone else, how could she learn how to have more loving relationships with other people. And Gurdjieff's succinct answer to the first person was *"increased necessity."* And his answer to the second person was *"start with animals and plants—they're easier!"*

The sense of "increased necessity" is actually an important component in transforming our narcissism—and in fact, an important component in transforming *anything*. (Say, the warming of our planet). For as Jung once similarly said, *"without necessity nothing budges."*

When (in chapter 5) I was facing the then terrifying prospect of having to read my poems in public, that situation was providing an increased necessity. The man (in chapter 8) "who hated his wife" was starting to be confronted with an increased necessity, as was the man I spoke to in the previous hour (in chapter 7). Whenever life seems to turn up the heat we are facing an increased necessity, a potentially initiatory experience.

America's two political parties have been facing an increased necessity for many years now. The question is, do we take on the necessity of changing something in *ourselves*—say becoming less polarized—or do we continue to attempt to get by without truly taking up the challenge? For part of the idiocy of what I term "idiot's momentum" is just continuing to do the same old thing.

And when Gurdjieff says that if we want to learn how to love other people that we might start with plants and animals—because they're *easier*—that seems to suggest a couple of things. First, that learning how to love is not *easy*. And here I'm not talking about "falling in love"—that divine madness! Any idiot can do *that*, as if it's nature's trick to propagate the species.

I mean instead, learning how to be reliably kind and loving toward other beings in general. And learning how to care for plants and animals is good training. Animals seem to exist more in the timeless present—which is one of the reasons why we love our pets. We love their immediacy, their being-ness, their heart-full innocence, and their capacity to give and receive love. And when we commune with them (as with entering wilderness areas) we may step out of time. And be given back a portion of unpressured, intimate vastness...

Yet in caring for plants and animals you have to become aware of their needs, putting your own aside. Domesticated plants can't water or prune themselves; they're dependent on you. Your dog can't buy his own kibble, or take himself to the vet. There's thus an *empathy* involved, a caring, and the capacity to feel into the other's situation, to see things from *their* point of view. (Which can help you to know what your dog is saying when he barks, or what a plant is saying when it wilts). Yet that sense of empathy is largely what narcissism *lacks*—a self-absorption where it's "all about me."

In this regard, I think being a good parent is anti-narcissism training; and being a good *single* parent may be *advanced* training. Being a good friend is anti-narcissism training. Learning how to hold *ourselves* in a compassionate way is anti-narcissism training. Anything that increases our level of awareness is anti-narcissism training. Being generous is anti-narcissism training. Learning how to trust and open fully to the present moment—that is, to harmonize with how reality is actually transpiring now—is anti-narcissism training; while discovering the "enough-ness" of our own presence and continuing to abide in it, regardless of circumstance and outcomes—is anti-narcissism training.

Letting go of fixed agendas, and our "cases" against others is anti-narcissism training. Most of the precepts, and spiritual teachings contained in our religious traditions are anti-narcissism training; in siding with our egos instead, we've simply failed to embody them. Going on spiritual retreats is anti-narcissism training, a time set aside from "the ten thousand things" that we might attempt (with an increased necessity) to get more hooked up to "the Great Matter" of our own deeper nature.

Yet ultimately, we need to learn how to provide our own sense of "increased necessity" as if our very life depends upon it—because it *does*—and not only when life seems to turn up the heat, or when we go on retreat.

To this end, I've found it helpful to have a few spiritual practices that have been honed while on retreat. And with our neural pathways thus already primed and familiarized through intense practice, we then can do these practices *for as little as 10 or 20 seconds* at a time, and *throughout* the day.

The various gazing practices I've discussed in this book not only seem to echo Narcissus's "death-dealing gaze" into that lucid pool of water, but *seem ideal for these "mini meditations,"* which can interrupt the stream of fixation, and thus create gaps, or openings for an unfiltered awareness to arise. *And perhaps even to stay for a while...*

For our contemporary lives are often so over-scheduled and complicated by "the ten thousand things," that it's hard for people to go on extended retreats very often, or even to find a 30 or 40 minute chunk of time to meditate in a busy day. But *ten seconds* can certainly be found, and often, *if* we have a sense of increased necessity.

And in this way, we can learn how to shift our own assemblage point—eventually at will—whenever we remember to do it, rather than relying solely upon a teacher, a therapist, a retreat, or some dramatic, challenging situation to help do this for us. In fact, the times we don't feel we "really need it," may be the most significant times to apply the sense of increased necessity. Which reminds me of a story...

So there's this Taoist master gardener. Or maybe he's a Sufi, a Hindu, a Baptist, or a Mormon—I can't remember that detail, and it doesn't matter. Anyhow, he's training an apprentice about the care involved in pruning a particularly high tree. He gives some climbing instructions, and then tells the apprentice to climb all the way to the top.

The apprentice then mindfully climbs to a dangerously high hundred feet up. His ass is really at risk, and this is unmistakably obvious. And so, the higher he climbs, the keener the apprentice's attention becomes. Finally, when he gets to where he could prune the very tip of the tree, "the ten thousand things" have completely fallen from his mind, and his state of awareness become very one-pointed and clear. Perhaps this was the true "pruning" the master had in mind, for at this point he tells his apprentice to forget about topping off the tree, and to begin his descent.

The apprentice gets down to 80 feet, and then to 60, and the master says nothing. The apprentice descends further, to 40 feet, and then 20. And still the master says nothing.

Finally, when the apprentice has descended to just 10 feet above the ground, the master shouts with great urgency: *Careful now! This is where accidents happen!*

TWENTY-THREE

Falling Down into a Well & One Insult After Another

IN A PAPER she published in the psychoanalytic journal *Imago* in 1921, Rilke's former girlfriend Lou Andreas Salome put forward the notion of Narcissus having a "dual nature." In her paper—*Narzissmus als Doppelrichtung* (The Dual Nature of Narcissism)—she writes: "Bear in mind that the Narcissus of the legend gazed, not at a man-made mirror, but at the mirror of Nature. Perhaps it was not just himself that he beheld in the mirror, but himself as if he were still all."

Here Salome notes a form of Narcissus that is what she calls "just himself," and then there is "himself as if he were still all." She suggests that if it were just the smaller, more encapsulated sense of self which he encounters in his fateful vision in the pool—that which is "just himself"—that he wouldn't have been so fascinated with the vision he was experiencing, that he wouldn't have continued to linger before it.

Narcissus, in other words, sees reflected and falls in love with a (transpersonal) version of self-hood that is "still all." Thus what dies, what ceases to live on, is his *former* sense of self, a self-representation that had been separate from, or dissociated from "the all"—*which is what the ego takes itself to be*.

For this reason, I've been suggesting that a deeper way of reading the myth might be to say that *until* that final ("fatal") vision in the pool, Narcissus had been—well, narcissistic. And the vision he then has at the end of his story is the death knell of his former perspective. For here at last in that strange pool Narcissus' deeper nature is being reflected—and with it, a way of knowing himself that till then had evaded him—and it is *this* that does his old self in.

With human beings, however—unlike mythic figures—the depth-vision that is the death knell of the narcissistic perspective tends *not* to be a once-and-for-all kind of thing. We don't irrevocably transform into something closer, or more in touch with the ground of being—say like that flower Narcissus morphs into.

The insight into what some spiritual traditions have called "true nature" (i.e., "self realization") though a kind of ego-death, is rarely—if ever—some final fruition, not the end of our spiritual labor—as if we've died and gone to some heaven. Though it *may* be a version of existence that at times can seem more colorful, fragrant, tasty, or vivid with immanence, as if all of our senses have awakened from a cloudy trance.

This deeper vision that comes to our eyes is a seeing-through, or a seeing-*past* (a ceasing to *identify* with what till then we had taken ourselves to be). And if it is a "death," something that is dissolving or passing away, it is as much a fresh beginning, an awakening to a more immediate and less egocentric way of sensing the world.

It is finding oneself grounded in a more timeless mode of being, a continuously new unfolding—not the *end* of the work. For our struggle to remain free from the more narcissistic vantage proves to be an ongoing project, *a life-long project,* even *after* "self-realization."

When Chogyam Trungpa once said that the job of the spiritual teacher is to insult your ego, and that the spiritual life is thus "one insult after another" it suggests that part of the process, part of the *function* of a "spiritual life" is to repeatedly see-through our identification with the ego, and the continuing ways that we take ourselves to be a self that could *become* insulted.

Quite similarly, the desert fathers in certain Christian monastic orders used to pay people to come out to their monasteries to insult them! This wasn't a *mea culpa* masochism. It was a practice that assisted the monks in freeing themselves both from the accusative inner object (the superego or AFPO), as well as from the self-importance that might otherwise be easily offended by what other people think or say.

Such an understanding also appears to have been clearly articulated by the Toltec shamans of ancient Mexico. For regardless of the vacillating regard of Carlos Castaneda, the words he attributed to the shaman Don Juan Matus seem right on point: *"Self-importance is man's greatest enemy. What weakens him is feeling insulted by the deeds and misdeeds of his fellow men.*

Self-importance requires that one spend most of one's life offended by something or someone." (A tweeting president again the poster-boy).

Our often self-important, egocentric personality structures were not formed overnight, and perhaps not even over a single lifetime—and thus the process that begins to transform them is not an all at once kind of affair. It's not a "now I've got it," or "now I've arrived" kind of deal—what could be more self-congratulatory and self-important than *that?* Nor is it a "now I am saved" kind of deal—such as we find in evangelical religion.

In our impatient, sound-bite, fast-paced, fast-food, instant gratification culture, people may not want to hear that the inner work that addresses our central disorientation to reality is not for the faint-hearted—nor something that's going to be resolved in a few weeks or months, nor in a weekend workshop—nor in a single shining moment of "enlightenment." It's the work of a lifetime.

For even a spiritually vivid insight into our "true," our eternal nature, our "face before our parents were born" (as it's been put by Zen) can still, at some later point, be appropriated by the ego and used to further embellish our narcissism, as if now we were even more special and have wisdom—or God's Grace—in our back pocket.

Even genuine spiritual experiences become a breeding ground for narcissism when our egos then want to claim a pride of ownership for whatever experiences or insights that might have taken place during the ego's temporary absence from the scene. Over the past several decades as the quest for spiritual enlightenment has become a cottage industry in America and Western Europe, there have been too many cases to catalogue of spiritual "luminaries" still tinged or motivated by such unrecognized narcissism.

In this way our narcissism is like a flower garden that keeps needing to be weeded. And we don't even need to go *looking* for the weeds. Each time we find ourselves feeling grandiose—*or* slighted, deficient, and insulted by life—or each time we fall prey to idealizing or require that we ourselves be seen in an idealizing kind of way, or each time we slight or devalue others, and even ourselves—*our weeds have found us.*

And so—as that other Zen *koan* goes—it is still possible, and in all but the rarest of cases *inevitable,* that "the clearly enlightened person falls into a well." That is, falls back into the more confined perspective, the enshelled perspective of ego structure. As Stephen Mitchell has suggested, *becoming* enlightened isn't all that hard... but continuing to refine one's insight—*while staying out of that well*—takes a bit of work.

And in a sense, we get wet with well water the second we objectify ourselves, others, God—or *anything,* the second we attempt to grasp for a self-image, even a radiant or "enlightened" one.

In fact, we might say that's the very thing Narcissus first attempts to do with the onset of his deeper vision—he grasps for the radiant image, the beautiful self he has glimpsed—but only gets his hands wet. And needless to say, there are many guides, spiritual teachers, therapists—and I sometimes am one of them—who are often still wet with well water.

TWENTY-FOUR

The 12th Century's Perfect Storm & Walking Briskly Beneath a Ridiculous Hat

In the last chapter we began to develop Lou Andreas Salome's notion of there being *two very different versions of Narcissus reflected in his myth*. And in a sense, the notion of two very different versions of selfhood lies at the heart of the transformational undertaking found in deep inner work. For each of us have both a conditioned, as well as a more essential version of self. And correspondingly, two different perspectives—two different modes of awareness—have comprised the timeless dialogue between *guru* and *chela*.

At times, two very different voices of "God" appear even in the same religious text; as if reflecting altered ontological views. The voice that speaks from the Whirlwind in the book of Job, for example, is a different kind of voice than we often find elsewhere. In fact, the book of Job itself clearly has two very different voices, two different *authors,* two different perspectives, as well as two different ways of *writing,* poetry and prose.

And in the spirit of such "two-ness," since we've been re-visioning the myth of Narcissus and Echo, a myth that concerns a relationship, I would now like to explore something about couples—and love in general. Namely, two very different ways we tend to experience the beloved in our intimate relationships…

I remember once being at a somewhat drunken, rowdy evening with a bunch of male psychotherapists. Kind of a guy's night out. Somehow, the topic turned to romantic love, a phenomenon that one of the therapists then related to narcissism. From here I have little memory of what I or anybody else subsequently said—which is probably just as well. I do remember, however, feeling suddenly very sorry both for the man and his wife.

Now sober, and years later, there's something I might have said...

My friend, I think you may be right. There *may* be a connection between narcissism and romantic love. Though a connection here wasn't evident to me at first. For until the very end of the myth of Narcissus—when he finally falls in love with what he sees reflected in that strange pool—the one thing we are constantly shown about Narcissus is how impervious and disdainful he has been towards love, for he constantly evidences narcissism's penchant for *devaluing* potential love objects. And perhaps this is why Freud once said: *"Those who love have, so to speak, pawned a part of their narcissism."*

At first glance then, narcissism would seem to be equated not with *falling* in love, or romance, but with the *inability* to love, the inability to fully take in the reality of another (or even, fully, the reality of oneself) without the fear of becoming hijacked or enchained. And thus, if there's a link between narcissism and romantic love, I think it may involve what we were exploring in the previous chapter—specifically, in Lou Andreas Salome's perspective on Narcissus's "dual nature." And here's another way we might view it...

Should we fall in love, a shift in our dual nature may become activated—and what Lou Andreas Salome called "the all" nature can begin to bleed into our experience. Here, *love begins to melt our ego boundaries,* and so we may feel more unbounded, but in a delicious, authentic way. The narcissistic shell has begun to dissolve, and we are no longer warding the other—or the world, off—as if they threaten us with fearful chains. Instead, we may begin to have the experience of *merging* with the beloved, if not with the world at large.

A memorable illustration of this once occurred when I got a phone call from someone who apparently knew me well—so much so, that he didn't feel it necessary to give his name. I was initially struck by how soulful and authentic his voice sounded. He sounded like someone I would really *like* to know—yet I couldn't place him. It was only after he mentioned the recent birth of his child that I realized I was speaking to a family member, and one of the most narcissistic people I've ever known. The birth and love for his child had profoundly, if temporarily, shifted his assemblage point, so much so that energetically he became totally unrecognizable to me.

Like honey, "the all nature" of merging love can seep into our perception of beloved and world, and we ourselves become exalted from this sweet, unitary alchemy. With our boundaries thinner or more permeable, *the beloved gets under our skin,* starts to live inside us in some way, as if we are pregnant now with new life, and its suddenly more ample-seeming possibilities.

Here love seems an altered state; affects us as if we're in the presence of a goddess or god. And when we have "chemistry" with a lover, this could be more than a metaphor. It could be the literal release of a heady cocktail of neurotransmitters: norepinephrine, dopamine, serotonin, and oxytocin.

Though there's no single right way to interpret the dream-like experience of falling in love, it *could* also be empty unit narcissism's wet dream: of having finally secured an idealized other to ride off with into the sunset. But whether we interpret such love as a temporarily pawning away of our narcissism, or as evidence of narcissism itself, when love's potently tipped arrow has penetrated us, the world in some way seems *changed.*

And it may lead us to wonder if maybe our prior life—all the time that we *weren't* in love—was the "altered" state; and now we're sensing things more as they truly are, a bestowal from an ample, generous, and mysterious Source. For the Great She or the Great He has for the moment taken up residence on Earth; the Muse or some deeper reality awakening in and around us. Lou Andreas Salome herself seemed to have been perfumed with something of this intoxicant in her effect upon men. Nietzsche, Rilke, Wagner, Freud—the men inspired by her very presence reads like a cultural Who's Who of early 20th century Europe.

But a point I've been rambling toward is this: Surely we run the risk of narcissism if we only have an *idealized* perception of the beloved—and then want to merge with "the idealized object" as if to bask in a reflected glory, or augment what feels lacking in us. And possibly the point my drunken friend was trying to make...

But just as we run the risk of narcissism (and so fail to have a "real" relationship with the other) if we only have an idealized perception of our beloveds, there's the danger of narcissism if we *fail to recognize* the god or goddess-like nature of our partner, if we objectify them in some way that keeps them small, devalued, or encased within a box.

And when we do so, we ourselves wind up inside a box. For then, a greater dimensionality is nowhere to be found, and "the all nature" (perhaps with all those heady neurotransmitters) fails to appear. And then, the common lament people report in their intimate love relationships is, that "something feels missing." Even if it's not what they think...

In this regard, I once had a brief correspondence with the poet Robert Bly in which we were exploring why *so few love poems are being written today.* What was this saying? Bly wondered if this was due to the loss of what he termed "the Large She"—i.e., the loss of the archetypal perception of the beloved. For it seems *that* is more common today.

And pondering the contemporary lack of love poems, I've wondered if that wasn't also an outgrowth of our culture's mythological narrowing, its loss of a *poly*-mythic perspective. For monotheism is mono-mythic; there is only one God, one creation story, one basic myth that accounts for everything. But in the process we wind up losing the so-called pagan gods, and the different nuances of divinity they offer—which includes different nuances, *different ways of loving.*

As I've come to understand it, the troubadour sensibility—and the sudden profusion of love poems that began to rain down between the 12th and 14th centuries—was really part of an attempt to regenerate its cultural era by providing *an alternative* to its prevailing mythological underpinnings—and the ways they had been *narrowing* the perspective on love. But what actually triggered the medieval flood of *eros,* as exemplified by the troubadours? And what cut it off?

And are there insights we might glean from reflecting back upon this cultural epoch and *the type of* **eros** *it engendered*—gleanings that might help us in facing our own cultural era, and its prevailing narcissism?

Here's what I've pieced together...

The Perfect Storm

Somewhere during the 11th century, it seems that women are beginning to be noticed in a different way—"different" that is, from a reigning mythological perspective in which women had been created almost as an afterthought—from the spare rib of a man—and created to be his *underling*, his helpmate. For this is also a *mythos* in which, for the previous seven centuries, Europeans were being taught to conceive of divinity as an *all-masculine* affair—consisting of a Father, a Son, a Holy Ghost; and only *men* as God's priests. But by the tail end of the 11th century, the long-missing feminine aspect of divinity began to resurface, and in part from an unexpected source. For 1095 brings the beginning of the Crusades.

There are to be nine of these military campaigns, and they are to span approximately 200 years. And as part of the 200 years of warfare between the Christian crusaders and the knights of Islam for who is going to control a shared Holy Land, there will be ongoing *negotiation counsels* between the rival camps. And these negotiation counsels apparently contain a bit of a newsflash for the Christian crusaders.

For the Islamic ambassadors are not so "heathen" after all. They make quite an impression upon the Christian crusaders, in fact, and give the appearance of being rather refined human beings, actually. As it turns out, almost all of them are *poets*. And in addition to negotiating the customary terms of military engagement, the Islamic ambassadors begin to transmit something else...

Though Islam, of course, is also a monotheistic tradition, the Islamic poetic ambassadors aren't burdened by the uniquely Christian, anthropomorphic conception of divinity—all that Father and Son business that began to be codified as the official version of Christianity from the time of the Council of Nicea in 325 during the reign of Constantine I, and further strengthened later in the 4th century during the imperial reign of the Christian emperor Theodosius I (which violently attacked the sacred sites of the male and female deities, as well as the customs and practices of traditional Hellenistic religion that the Romans had inherited from the Greeks).

And perhaps for this reason, a different kind of *eros* could come through the Islamic poetic ambassadors. Namely, a transmission of the sensibility found in certain strains of ecstatic Arabic and Persian *love poetry* that had remained embedded within their cultural reference. And this sensibility becomes transmitted to one of the more refined and mobile conduits of European culture, who are also knights, warriors mounted on horseback.

We begin to see what amounts to a poetic, cultural dissemination that has come up from the south—up from Moorish Spain, over the Pyrenees and into France. (And the French word for "horse"—*cheval*—figures into the medieval "chivalry" that animates the *eros,* and poetry of this period). Yet at approximately the same time, coming down from the *north,* we suddenly find a re-emergence of buried remnants of Celtic and Germanic goddess worship. This is also when we're beginning to see cults of the Black Madonna spreading throughout Europe, and this too is bringing up a lot of buried goddess material.

If "the goddess" is re-arising in the collective psyche of Europe, and women are beginning to be seen as having a more "elevated" possibility, we're already getting the sense that there is no *single* factor that gives rise to this—and to all the love poems that begin to flood Europe, and even the near East, between the 12th and 14th centuries.

For this was the time of the Provençal troubadours in France, and in Italy the time of Dante (and his Beatrice) and Petrarch (and his Laura). In Germany there were the minnesingers, those troubadours including Wolfram von Eschenbach, whose version of *Parsifal* we've already alluded to. In Moorish Spain there were troubadours writing love lyrics in Spanish, Arabic, and even in Hebrew. And farther east, this was also the same general time-frame of poets such as Rumi and Hafiz, and of the Sufi sheikh and poet, Ibn Arabi—whose transformative vision of a woman named Nizam, was quite similar in effect to Dante's vision of Beatrice some eighty years later. And even farther east, born the same year as Hafiz, in 1320—a year before Dante died—there was the great ecstatic lady poet, Lalla, who moved through Kashmir without the benefit of clothes. As I've suggested, a perfect storm arising from many fronts had gathered, all at the same time.

And taken together, all of these elements seem to reflect what a contemporary Jungian historian might call a collective awakening of the *anima* in European consciousness, an awakening of what Goethe termed "the eternal feminine"—which Ean Begg in his book, *The Cult of the Black Virgin,* notes as "the Muse of all true poets." Women are beginning to be seen in the light of "transformational portals," portals into transcendence.

And the initiatory themes associated with this, that the Arthurian quest sagas are so replete with, are significant. And they're significant—as both Joseph Campbell and Mircea Eliade point out—because the Middle Ages had become a time in which *initiation had practically died out.* So Europe must have been starving for viable forms of initiation, for their lack had left the cultural climate in the condition of a Waste Land. But the European soul must have also been starving for the type of goddess consciousness that had fallen into forgetfulness ever since Europe had been "Christianized at sword-point"—to quote Joseph Campbell—during the fourth century.

The 12th century also gives rise to medieval romances such as Tristan and Isolde where there's an erotic love triangle,* just as there's a similar love triangle between King Arthur, Guinevere, and Sir Lancelot. In medieval times, this theme of love triangles—or adulterous love—reflects in part a *revolt* against the custom of arranged marriages, whereby landed families had used their sons and daughters as proxies in order to form alliances with other landed and politically prominent families.

These arranged marriages thus had more to do with following *convention,* following what was expected of you—rather than *following your heart.* They had more to do with power than love; and when the power principal prevails, *love flies out the window.* And when love flies out the window, it has to appear elsewhere. And thus, love triangles—or adulterous love—figures prominently not only in the new stories, the new *mythos* arising, but also in the cult of *Courtly Love,* which is *also* starting to emerge now.

As mentioned earlier, the followers of Courtly Love (*fin amour*) worshipped another god, Amor, the often-slumbering god of the heart—a god different than that of the Old or New Testament. And they were really thumbing their nose at the Roman Catholic Church, and at the prevailing institution of arranged marriages. But in southern France, it was not only the courts of *fin amour* that in giving rise to a new sensibility did so while thumbing its nose at the Roman Catholic Church. There were also the gnostic Cathars. But unlike the Catholic Church with its tripartite sense of divinity, the Cathars had a *dual* sense of divinity.

They believed there were actually two kinds of deity encountered here on Earth. There was a god of spiritual purity, and its countering force—an evil demiurge that was only concerned with power. And this evil demiurge, to the Cathars, seemed to be expressing itself via *the Roman Catholic Church*—which of course didn't sit very well with the Church.

---

* Later in this book I'll further reflect a similar erotic love triangle as part of the "back story" in the myth of Narcissus and Echo—namely between Zeus, Hera, and Zeus's concubines—the mountain nymphs. And that it was Echo's duplicity in trying to hide from Hera her husband's extra-marital affairs that led Echo to be cursed by Hera with the inability to initiate conversations.

So the Church launched what became known as the Albigensian Crusades. Which when followed by the Inquisition, proved to be successful strategies on the part of the Church in turning the tide against "heretical beliefs." For by the 14th century heretical groups such as the Cathars and the Waldensians had either been silenced, slaughtered, or forced to recant. This effectively marked the beginning of the end of the perfect storm that had begun to flood Europe with love poems. Now another kind of storm was about to descend...

The 14th century would eventually give rise to the Italian Renaissance, a "rebirth" partially midwifed by a poet mentioned earlier—Petrarch—whose contribution was to be part of a broader cultural rediscovery and valuing of classical sources, which would later spread to the rest of Europe.

But the 14th century was also to be a ferocious time of spiritual agony, a world plunged into chaos. And it wasn't just love poems that began to dwindle. The Black Death of 1348-1350 was to wipe out *over a third of the population between Iceland and India*—and the Bubonic Plague was to return four more times before the end of that anguished century.

The ideal of *chivalry* that had lent its distinctive flavor to the romantic sensibility of the 12th and 13th centuries was starting to erode, in some part due to advances in weaponry. In Europe there was a "hundred years' war" that no one, not even the combatants could stop. There were peasant revolts—and the answering panic and repression on the part of the landed classes. There was a schism in the Catholic Church with the Papacy removed to Avignon (the very city where Petrarch had received his initial vision of Laura, his family having moved near to Avignon in order to follow Pope Clement V who himself had moved to Avignon in 1309 in order to begin the Avignon Papacy).

And just seven years earlier, in one of history's most outrageous statements of religious *hubris*, Pope Boniface in 1302 delivers a papal Bull that declares: *"It is necessary to salvation that every human creature be subject to the Roman pontiff."*

In such a climate, people of mystical insight often had to operate with one eye peeled for the punitive fundamentalism—if not the malignant narcissism—that reigned in high places all around them. In 1328, for example, and within seven years of the last Cathar being burnt at the stake,

Meister Eckhart—himself a Catholic cleric—disappears from the world just as he's about to be tried for heresy...

Fin amour and its poetic troubadours had attempted to light up an alternative path that the West might have taken, one not lit by a mob's fiery torches, witch and heresy trials, or the glint of swords wielded in God's name. For encountering something ecstatically transcendent was the *fin*, the end or goal for *fin amour's* more spiritually inclined practitioners.

There was really an emotional alchemy in all this, one that humbled men in relation to women, and "brought them to their knees." It was only then that a lady might confer her favors, her *merci*. And only from this more humbled stance might a man come know the slumbering god in his own heart.

Fin amour thus intended a transformational process, a form of *initiation* that the Middle Ages had come to otherwise lack. And here the masculine ideal was a lovely triumvirate of Warrior- Poet-Lover, a leaning back into old Celtic sources, such as the *Fianna*—a mythical cadre found in Irish mythology and for whom admission required a series of initiations—not only being able to demonstrate various forms of physical prowess, but also an apprenticeship in *poetry*, and not insignificantly, that one *treat women well*. (The latter facets no doubt contributed to all the love poetry of this era).

Although something rather revolutionary and potentially enlivening had occurred in regards to love between the 12th and 14th centuries, we should be clear that this phenomenon and its attendant idealization of the feminine was not a culture-wide feature, even in southern France where the troubadours briefly flourished. The troubadour sensibility of *fin amour* actually seems a corrective reaction to the then dominant wider culture, a wider culture that had for hundreds of years been extremely dismissive and chauvinistic towards women; a wider culture where women were routinely beaten by their husbands—as wife abuse was more common then than child abuse.

And so, at this time women commonly *feared* their husbands, even when they loved them. And this is another reason, among others, that in *fin amour* "real love" was seen as something that existed *outside* of marriage. For as earlier mentioned, in the courts of *fin amour* the type of couple being put forward was not the *married* couple, but instead "the *infernal* couple"—those unions that took place outside the sensibility, and *sanctioning*, of the Church. (Yet even many medieval cardinals and popes of the Church enjoyed these "infernal unions"—the Borgias being a rather vivid example).

Aside from its widespread adulteries, a critique that has been leveled at *fin amour* (and its poetry) concerns what has been seen as *the idealization of the beloved*. And we *could* of course, make a psychological critique of "idealized love"—and at several places in this book I attempt to do so. But there's also something *lovely* to be found in placing another above oneself, in bowing down before another, in being brought to one's knees—in holding someone with such *reverence*. In this regard, I once found myself asking…

> Is it strange
> to regard your lover
> as a kind of god?
>
> Or is not doing so
> the thing that is strange?*

Such reverence could be an antidote to narcissism, and certainly the opposite of how Narcissus regarded *his* lovers. Such devotion or reverence can allow something very pure to rise up in us that's at least a close cousin to wisdom. For this can be a wild, unbounded kind of love—a love that may not only melt your heart, but blow out the walls of your ego structure. *Encountering the goddess can do that.* The beloved "becomes your everything," a portal into ecstasy…

But we should understand that what could seem "idealized" to us here may not be entirely *personal*. It may be the encounter—or worship—of something divine, a *mythological being*, really—which may suddenly emerge out of the encounter with the personal beloved. That's "the large She" that Robert Bly spoke of. And the more humbled heart that comes from contact with *Her*—or the more humbled stance that *allows Her to*

---

* This excerpt from the poem "Is it Strange?" occurs in *The You That is Everywhere: Love Poems*. Richmond: Point Bonita Books, 2000. Here, the regard of the beloved is somewhat akin to the teaching "if you see your teacher as limited, you will only get a limited blessing; if you hold your teacher as a Buddha, you may get the blessings of a Buddha." (Something we might bear in mind, as we gaze upon our girlfriends, boyfriends, husbands and wives…).

appear—can activate a deep vein of feeling, not at all dis-similar to the devotional feelings that can come up in Guru Yoga, or in any spiritual path or practice with a devotional inflection.

Such "divine encounters," however, may in themselves have a "dual nature." On the one hand, they may trigger, re-stimulate, or evoke a phase in development wherein there *has yet to have arisen* any separation between self and other. For however humbled and devoted our union with the beloved may feel, this could still be some form of "pre-personal regression," or the longing of "empty unit narcissism." It could indicate not only a regression, but a failure to have ever fully *emerged* from a more infantile, symbiotic, if not an *amniotic,* and womb-like state. (The less evolved side of Neptune).

At the same time, such encounters *might* be a more *trans*-personal form of experience, a different (developmental) level of "non-separation" (the "nondual"). And accessing *that* was really the ultimate *fin,* the end intended by the most evolved practitioners of *fin amour.* Yet what can make discernment here a bit fuzzy is that the kind of *language* often employed to describe such experiences tends to sound similarly "oceanic"—like something is flooding us (Neptune again)—regardless of where one is actually stanced on Ken Wilber's pre/trans divide. And it's actually possible to write wonderfully ecstatic love poems with a *doofus* for a Muse. (Trust me: sometimes love really *is* blind).

Though there's a lot of similarity between the medieval love poetry in praise of the lady, and the devotional poetry from Eastern cultures that's been written in praise of the guru, or devotional poetry addressed to Jesus or *any* religious figure, these forms of devoted appreciation don't seem to play so well, or occur so frequently in a more "ruggedly individualistic," "me first," narcissistic culture such as our own.

And we shouldn't lose sight of the issue of narcissism. For in our own cultural era probably nothing has been as limiting to the erotic climate—or helping to account for the rarity of our love poems—as our rampant narcissism. Rather than viewing our lovers as portals into transcendence, or "divinity in drag," we often view them the way Narcissus viewed Echo. Then something indeed feels "missing."

Yet like Echo, the more we chase after what seems to be lacking in ourselves, the more the object of our desire only seems to evade us. Narcissism is really a very *anti-tantric* schema. It has thus become my perspective that the work involved in deconstructing our narcissism offers us something potentially similar to what *fin amour* offered its practitioners between the 12th and 14th centuries. Namely: *a viable form of initiation for a cultural epoch in which viable, collective forms of initiation have largely disappeared.*

By conferring what we now take for granted—that individuals, and not their families or church, should dictate *whom* or *how* we love—*fin amour* and its medieval troubadours helped shape our modern conception of romantic love; giving love unions a more individuated basis.

Another, though more problematic vestige retained from *fin amour,* is the lingering, subliminal expectation that many people seem to have today—namely, that our intimate love relationships *should* bring us face to face with what amounts to a transcendent, mythological being—what the troubadours termed *Amor.* Yet I also find something *real* in this expectation, a whole realm of sacred *eros* that might open for us—at least that *possibility*...

But the fact remains that we've largely lost the mythopoeic perspective of *fin amour.* And unfortunately, we've also lost almost all of its spiritual *practices.* In this way, contemporary lovers are often left with *erotic expectations* that they lack the training to either embody, or *sustain*—thus contributing to a widespread erotic discontent*—a discontent that in men which now commonly settles for *Internet porn* as the readily available, but *counterfeit version* of the epiphany inducing gazes upon a beloved evoked elsewhere in this book.

For these reasons, in order to free our contemporary relationships from the difficulties caused by our prevailing narcissism, there's often *a lot* of psychological work needing to be done even *before* we can fully address The Mother of All Wounds—that is, the wound formed when our essential nature was not adequately recognized, mirrored, or valued.

We may also need to discover or invent our own "love practices"—or borrow and employ practices from spiritual traditions possessing the

---

* Since 2006, Durex, the world's leading manufacturer of condoms, has annually commissioned a worldwide Sexual Wellbeing Survey. The initial survey polled 26,000 adults from 26 countries, and found that the U.S. ranked 23 out of the 26 countries in sexual well being. And though the majority of Americans (80%) believed that sex is a vital part of life, less than half of us were feeling sexually fulfilled. The studies helped highlight both the emotional and physical facets needed for healthier outcomes. Yet in both the initial and the latest surveys, less than half the people polled world-wide regularly experience orgasm, with the number of women who regularly experience orgasm less than one third.

skillful means that have historically helped free their practitioners from the mundane bounded-ness of "the narcissistic shell."

As we began to see in the third section of this book, there have been countless practices employed throughout history that can enable people to pass beyond this "shell," practices that may employ any, or several of the senses. And as I've mentioned, I often employ the practice of *trespasso* in working with couples—precisely *because* it is done with a partner, and where each partner *can* become a portal to something sacred and transcendent.

But *accessing* states of awareness in which the narcissistic perspective becomes outshined is only *part* of the work. To *stabilize* in such a view is really the project of a lifetime, an ongoing *demolition* project. And perhaps nothing offers us such a clear and ready view of what needs to be deconstructed as the forms of enshelled reactivity that show up for us—and *as* us—in our relationships with other people.

For those who have the curiosity and willingness to see, our relationships are continually showing us the ways we take ourselves to be something other than our true nature; for *un*transformed, our relationships continue to suffer in the failure to recognize the divine nature dwelling within our beloveds and within ourselves. (Just as we may continue to suffer from another kind of perceptual loss, when we fail to more keenly recognize the more finite guy or gal).

Or perhaps, we might say it like this…

> The goddess
> and the actual woman
> are *both* real
>
> And when either
> appears
> try to sense
>
> always
> behind the one
> the often invisible other.

For when a man
follows one
—*one alone*—

he has been tricked,
walking briskly
beneath a ridiculous hat*

---

* The above poem, "Walking Briskly Beneath a Ridiculous Hat," is from the author's poetry collection *An Amateur's Guide to the Invisible World*. Readers wishing to further steep themselves in the material presented in this chapter can read an interview with the author at www.garyrosenthal.net/interviews/ or watch a video of a poetry reading Gary Rosenthal gave at the California Institute of Integral Studies entitled *When Lovers Dissolve*, which can be found at www.garyrosenthal.net/video-audio/ under Poetry Readings. An earlier, initial treatment of this material also occurs in the keynote address Gary gave to the International Enneagram Conference in 2000. An audiotape of this address—"Love and the Poetic Tradition"—can be heard at www.garyrosenthal.net/video-audio/ under Presentations.

V.
Love, Culture, Gods, and Government
In an Age of Narcissism

INTERLUDE

A Brief Primer about the Gods

W E'VE DONE SOME heavy lifting, and covered a good bit of ground. Perhaps this is a good time for an interlude—one in which the reader is commended for having gotten this far—and where I might briefly relax the formal strings that have been holding this book together; and maybe thus, allowing something not previously intended to come through…

In the rites of certain Native American traditions, at a high point of solemnity the Trickster (or Coyote figure) would often appear, and humorously ape the gestures of the hierophant leading the ritual. This might suggest that a heightened solemnity—when coupled with a humorous, carefree irreverence—may provide the right *balance* in approaching matters of the spirit. That is, a perspective that acknowledges sanctity alive in the world, yet without allowing the religious superego to claim it, or taking ourselves too seriously…

In just this spirit, as we prepare to begin the next section of the book, I'd like to offer the following brief primer—which may be one part *gnosis,* and one part (tongue in cheek) playful riff. The long (and sometimes *not* so noble) history of god-talk generally *has been* a mixture of something real and something fanciful—as the gods are not easy to talk about without running afoul, or adding our own inferences about invisible presences.

And yet, part of a poet's duty is the attempt to be "a scientist of the whole." And so the rights—if not the duty to offer you something like this—have been traditionally granted in any poet's contract with life. (See contract clause involving "Poetic License").

A Brief Primer about the Gods

Though it's part of a bard's job
to serve as a custodian of remembrance
for a culture's storehouse of myths

What I know about the gods is not very much…
And whenever we talk about a god, intelligent people
may be correct in not taking us seriously.

For gods are hard to speak about conclusively
—yet for this reason, we may be confused
about nearly everything else.

This much seems certain:
Our bodies die. The gods don't.
(Though they do become forgotten).

And being humble or awed before a god
is both proper etiquette
and its own reward.

The gods known in pre-Christian antiquity
—and resurrected in Renaissance art—
have grown dim to us again…

Though we suffer them as ever
we can barely hear them now
(in the echoed whispers of astrology).

But is it the gods
—or our own mythic awareness—
that remains on life-support?

The gods have attributes, virtues
—and strangely, just like us—
they may exhibit psychopathology.

And the same should be said for religious fanatics
(though either part of this understanding
could get you strung up & tried for heresy).

The gods are shape-shifters, uniquely pliable
and give the appearance of shaping
themselves to our own beliefs

—Though this may be illusory
while giving rise to doctrinal strife
or crazed people preaching on the street.

But when we deny
*the **reality** of a god,*
*we become blind to **that** god's reality*

They seem to like it
when our hearts melt or
the hairs stand up on our arms

any time we seem electrified
or less dense & more pliable
—more like they are.

*It is scientific hubris to search
for biological markers that might prove
or disprove the reality of a god*

*(or the psychopathologies that may
come in the door with them).
The gods must find this laughable, a searching*

*under the wrong street light
for where our own keys have been lost.
Like being itself, the gods are invisible*

*which doesn't mean that they don't exist.
They may temporarily inhabit another's form
lacking material bodies of their own. Our nervous systems*

*should function as their receptors
though our nervous systems are often agitated,
sheathed, or in need of fine-tuning*

*The gods decline when they become a one-trick pony.
For holding them in this way
makes the gods and ourselves a little lame.*

*Think of them as metaphors
finally given the proper respect.
And any gods worth their alabaster*

*Or Holy Book must be more subtle
than our beliefs about them.
Our beliefs about the gods*

could make the jovial ones laugh
—comic relief for eternal beings
with a lot of timelessness on their hands

And if truly our lords & masters, we must be
like pets to them—a source of entertainment and joy
yet creatures in need of training

If our Holy Book tells us we've been created
in the like-ness of a god,
then we've gotten this hat on backwards

by converting gods into our own like-ness
which is why the gods worshipped by others
can seem hokey, skewed, primitive, outlandish

The belief there is only one god
—when our hearts are pure—
may bring blessings

from the other gods as well
(blessings that we attribute
to the one we believe in).

—Nothing wrong with this.
But at other times, it seems
to make the other gods jealous

And they rubble
our cities
or scorch the countryside.

*—which also becomes confusing
if our notion of a deity only
resembles Father Christmas, or the Tooth Fairy.*

*It is generally hubris to think
we know what they want
and when we've sacrificed*

*animals or other people
this may be like when our cat
leaves a dead mouse on our pillow*

*A god is not a vending machine
that we might kick or bewail
when it has swallowed our quarters*

*When we serve the gods it may be unknowingly
(Safer to assume they've agendas of their own
while folly to think they're here to serve ours).*

*Praying to or invoking a god
is a way of opening to regions
beyond our own cramped ego structures*

*This was once expressed as
"Praying outside your geography."
And by another poet as*

*"Extending the heart, searchingly
toward Infinity. Hold this a while;
then honor what comes next."*

And when we can't get out
of our own way, sometimes a god might help
by giving us a shove

The gods attend us through threshold experiences
—giving birth, dying, making love or war
or making do under trying circumstances.

For when we're splayed open
or entering uncertain territory
that's when we remember how tiny we are

And when we bargain
and plea with invisible forces.
That's when we remember them...

The gods summon us to awe & surrender
are bearers of amplitude, ushers
of extreme states, the fevered pitch.

They are the primal energies
we keep forgetting, primal energies
we can tap into but never really own.

When we're depressed
or really high, a god
may be breathing on our shoulder

*Some are jealous Fathers, sky gods
like Zeus, Yahweh, or Thor
—thunderers, who live up yonder…*

*Like bad parents, some eat their children,
or reveal by the laws they give
(which sometimes need to be updated)*

*While some steal, or dissolve things,
and reveal by what they take away.
Others have a unique sense of balance*

*and harmony, or are vulnerable,
abducted, betrayed, or crucified
yet manage to return from the dead*

*Another is seductively feminine,
and extravagantly sensual
—like beauty itself.*

*One god limps, makes useful
beautiful things, and is tortured
by a beauty he can never fully possess*

*Janus presides over transitions
and this god has two heads, one
facing the future, and the other the past*

*Both Kali and Pluto have two pairs of arms
—one pair being threatening
and the other pair that seems welcoming*

*Another has thousands of arms, being merciful
toward one and all, while other gods
appear to have their favorites*

*We may, however, be selling them
—and ourselves, short—
in assuming the gods lack a sense of humor*

*What we instinctively love and are good at
(without having to think about it)
may be the work, no the **play**, of a god*

*For the gods don't really work
the ways that we do
—for a god things are easy*

*and there's no sense of time.
"Business as usual"
make the gods yawn*

*But when our asses are on the line
the gods seem to awaken, as if witnessing
a play that has suddenly become interesting.*

*For the gods have seen it all…
Have seen those like you before.
"And if one has great realization*

*the protectors will be scrambling to help you."
Lacking realization, "there is no certainty it will help
no matter how long you enjoin them."*

TWENTY-FIVE

Evoking, or Freshening, the Archetypes

> "Encircled by her arms as by a shell,
> she hears her being murmur,
> while forever he endures
> the outrage of his too pure image..."
> —Rilke

EVOKING, OR FRESHENING, the archetypes—is what poets *do*. And what Rilke is doing as we begin this chapter. It's part of the traditional bardic responsibility to provide a fresh take on myths, as is serving as their custodian, the custodian of a culture's mythic memory—and why in Greek mythology the myths were told, passed on by poets; not a priest-hood. And thus, as Freud once humbly confessed, *"wherever I go, I find a poet has been there before me."*

This said, an impulse weaving through this book is the attempt to reflect what I term "the fresh mythic imprint"—in other words, the specific guise in which the gods or archetypes—are surfacing *today*. And since the myths of Narcissus/Echo and Pluto/Persephone are linked (through the narcissus flower), the following section of the book will attempt to make cultural reflections by way of an extended literary conceit; namely, by reflecting *the multiple ways that we see or are seen, speak or are heard, through the archetypal perspective of these myth's protagonists...*

The myth of Narcissus and Echo seems in a way to be Narcissus's story; at least he is the figure with the fullest arc. But how are things from Echo's point of view? In Rilke's poem "Narcissus," Echo hears her being murmur, but the too pure image that Narcissus has of himself cannot respond to this "murmur of being." There is an erotic disconnect here. And from Rilke's point of view, it is not only Echo who suffers this disconnect; Narcissus must continually endure a shell-like bounded-ness of his own, an encapsulation caused by the confining outrage of a self-image too pure.

In a way, both the myth of Echo and Narcissus and the myth of Persephone and Pluto have something to do with *love—and its difficulties*. Both stories concern a couple, both reflect transformational nuances of death and rebirth, and in both stories the narcissus flower figures prominently. For as he perishes, Narcissus transforms into the flower that now bears his name. And it is her reaching for a hundred-headed version of the narcissus flower that instigates Persephone's descent into her underworld marriage.

Persephone's reaching for the narcissus is one half of a movement whose other half is Pluto reaching for her, as if what she reaches for opens the door to the underworld. But even after her marriage to him, Persephone can't remain available to her husband in a normal way. For the greater part of every year Persephone dwells apart from Pluto, returning to him in the underworld (each winter) as involuntarily as she first entered her marriage, and ostensibly, only because while in the underworld she has eaten a few seeds of a pomegranate.*

Having just written about the pomegranate, and Persephone's involuntary returning to the underworld each winter, I'd like to make a brief, personal confession about something that both delighted and confounded me for several years. And it also helped me to discover the mythic connectivity between the myth of Narcissus (which *ends* with him morphing into a narcissus flower) and the Persephone myth (which *begins* with her plucking a narcissus flower). And this mixture of confusion and delight

---

* Why a pomegranate—who can say? But in regarding the pomegranate, I thought to note an anecdotal incident—one that seems more lovely and mysterious to the extent it's something that I have no means to account for…I'd been living in my current home for 12 years when I first began to write about the Pluto/Persephone myth. That spring a pomegranate plant that I never planted—and didn't know even existed on my property—suddenly burst into flower a few feet from my newly planted vegetable garden. For the next 15 years it continued to show its vermillion flowers each spring—though strangely, never any fruit. Then in March of 2015 North Atlantic Books brought out a Pluto anthology that contained my first published writing on this myth. A few weeks later—just as strangely—the plant showed its first fruit.

lent a personal *urgency* to my engagement with myth(s), an "increased necessity," if you will.

What happened was: *I'd fallen crazy in love.* The lady in question affected me like no one before—or ever since. Her beauty was like Kryptonite to my inflated ego structure. It completely undid me, and shifted my assemblage point as profoundly as had any drug, or decades of Buddhist meditation. Like Beatrice for Dante, or Laura for Petrarch, I'd been ambushed by a beauty that opened me to another dimension of depth—my own heart. Love poems flowed through me, in fact my life had become a love poem. And for the next several years this went on—and off—on, and off...

And the love plot here thickened, especially its on and off again nature, because my beloved—by her own admission—was deeply identified with the goddess Persephone. And like Persephone, for years she disappeared with the coming of each winter, when she'd break up with me for one reason or another. And this yearly loss seemed enormous, wrenching, and incomprehensible, at least to any rationality I still possessed. And it led me to begin to read everything I could about the myth of Pluto and Persephone. For it seemed increasingly apparent that the two of us were now living this myth out, and in our actual, contemporary, California lives.

When she reappeared in the spring from her Underworld sojourns, we'd reconnect, and my heart went back into bloom—much as the green world sprung into bloom with Persephone's return from the Underworld at the end of each winter. And over the course of years, I came to discover how every figure in the myth of Pluto and Persephone also lived inside of me (and the same would prove true for the myth of Narcissus and Echo).

And in the winters of her disappearance, aside from a few tortured love poems, I began to write about mythology—the *seminal* impulse of this book—and to see the living relevance of myth for our contemporary lives. And long after she left my life for good, this has continued to be the case. In the end, I didn't get the girl. But she was that rarity—a Muse with a long shelf life—for in continuing ways she changed my life.

When it comes to *love,* each of the central characters in these two myths suffers some form of erotic isolation, a specific style of erotic tension that arises out of their differing characters, and the ways that other gods have conspired against, cursed, or colluded with them—which is then subsequently played out in the inter-subjective field of their relationship with each other. Like *any* couple, they seem to come from, or inhabit two different worlds—and things become fraught with mythic drama, as the archetypes collide, collude, attempt to love, or bicker within *us*.

In the relationship of Narcissus and Echo, their differences are a *deal-breaker*. Both Narcissus and Echo operate under a curse—Narcissus from Nemesis, and Echo from Hera—and so the relationship never "gets off the ground." Which is—again—perhaps why Freud wisely observed: *"to love is to pawn some portion of our narcissism."* Yet this is also why when relationships "don't work out," we might in performing their autopsy, discover the "curse" of narcissism's limiting, shell-like encapsulations.

Though both myths reflect death / depth experiences of the soul, the actual *relationship* between Pluto and Persephone seems "deeper" than the other mythic couple. (Narcissus merely runs away from Echo, as if she threatens him with "fearful chains." And Echo is incapable of even initiating a conversation with him—about this, or anything else).

While Pluto abducts Persephone into a depth she's never been before. And so, if the relationship between Narcissus and Echo never gets off the ground, the Pluto and Persephone relationship largely takes place *beneath* the ground. And if the myth of Narcissus ends with him transformed into a narcissus flower—a *perennial* that returns each year as the harbinger of spring, the Persephone myth "ends" with her leaving the Underworld, something she will now *do* each spring.

Yet the old Olympian, or even *pre*-Olympian power that conspired to place that seductive narcissus in front of Persephone—Gaia, an even older earth mother than Demeter, and who was in cahoots with Pluto—may have been at it again. For what seems the trumped-up charge of having eaten a few seeds of a pomegranate, Persephone must now *return* to the Underworld each winter, to resume her relationship with the god of death, the god of ultimate depth, a god who has penetrated her, and made her his wife. So in this way the myth really is *interminable*, cyclical as the seasons; it *has* no ending.

As for Narcissus, even in dying, what he morphs into, returns each year as the harbinger of spring. (Which suggests there may be something interminable about narcissism itself). And we can't use the word "interminable" in reflecting these two myths, without it evoking something else...

※

Freud's paper, *Analysis Terminable and Interminable (1937)* was written during the last years of his life, and has been regarded as Freud's "last will and testament"—and thus, a *Plutonic* document; a parting reflection offered to the movement he had fathered, and one informed by the vantage of death's depths.

Clearly, Freud knew that his own end was near. He was 81 years old, and had now suffered through 33 operations on his mouth and jaw, and had been forced to struggle with his smoking addiction,* as well as the fatal illness he had been suffering for over a decade. A few years earlier his 95-year-old mother had died, and he had also recently lost a close friend in Karl Abraham. As if there wasn't already enough on his plate, the Nazis had come to power, hated his "Jewish psychology," and had burned his books.

Freud's life now reeked of death's solemn perfume, and was surrounded by endings. And in *Analysis Terminable and Interminable* he was writing about the issues raised in the *ending of an analysis.* And there were a lot of issues there; issues that remain on the table for anyone engaged in psychotherapy.

Here Freud seems to be struggling with the limitations of any created thing, any system, and specifically the new discipline he has brought to the world. And he recognizes that the qualities, skills, and defenses of the analyst inevitably come into play in determining therapeutic outcomes—for better or worse. He suggests that ideally the analyst should continue his or her self-analysis after the completion of their personal analysis. Yet Freud also recognizes that, more often than not, analysts are too defended to effectively do this on their own, and thus he recommends a reanalysis of the analyst, perhaps at five year intervals, thus making even the analyst's own analysis "interminable."

Though both the most and least successful of therapies inevitably end, the relationship of Pluto and Persephone really *doesn't*. It manages to endure forever—through Persephone's eternal and bi-polar-like swings, her yearly cycling up and down, her transits between Earth and the Underworld. It

---

* In January of 1884—the same year he published his monograph on cocaine—Freud had rather charmingly written to his wife: "Smoking is indispensable if one has nothing to kiss."

endures—even given the rude beginning of their relationship—that matter of the rape. (Though when gods have sex we may need to read between the lines, and note the specific nuance of their style of loving, each of them different in important ways).

The "Plutonic couple" hangs in there with each other, through it all. Pluto and Persephone endure even the perils of a long distance relationship—these partners live not in separate cities, countries, or opposite coasts, but in separate *realms* for the majority of each year. Still, the relationship continues, keeps returning to depths beneath love's flowery seductions, in a never ending story where even the flowers are enchanted and part of the plot—placed there and informed by hidden forces.

At first, Persephone enters a chasm in the earth formed from the narcissus flower she has just unearthed. And as she picks the flower, she *herself* is plucked, raped—and carried down into the underworld by an invisible god—He of Many Names: Pluto, the Greek god death.

Though there's no one "right" way to read or tell any myth, I find the evocative metaphors at the myth's beginning to include: Persephone's naïve lack of awareness of the depths lying beneath her, and what these depths contain. Secondly, the shocking *loss* of that innocence. (And the suggestion, that there is a primordial intelligence in cahoots with Pluto—Gaia—that doesn't *want* Persephone—and by extension, *us*—to remain so innocently naïve toward what's invisible and deep). And lastly, that Persephone enters her underworld marriage to Pluto as an *involuntary descent,* much as our own deepening may be initiated by traumatic events that involuntarily arise, grab us, and pull us down—or these days, bring us to therapy.

In retrospect, such traumatic events may later come to be viewed as "*benevolent* seductions"—*into depth itself;* and perhaps why Pluto was sometimes depicted as having two pairs of arms—one pair that seemed *threatening,* and the other pair in a gesture that seems *welcoming* to us. But from Persephone's more naïve (*kore,* maiden, pre-initiated) view, she isn't *courted* by her husband to be; Pluto's more threatening arms seem to have grabbed her: She's ambushed, raped, *abducted.* And as the poet Robert Creeley once heard her say, "*O love, / where are you / leading / me now?*"

Yet a virtue of such "involuntary descents," is that they can lead us to a depth we might not have gotten to in any other way. Suddenly, we discover we're not in Kansas anymore; not on the flat surface of the Great Plains—nor the flattened plane of life's mundane daily-ness, where we often get to pick and choose, and without such deep, immediate, and unsuspected complications from what we pick. Instead, something immanently shocking, overwhelming, is taking place. Like getting a cancer diagnosis or being pulled down by a shark. We've been singled out, as if stalked by something that seems to have its *own* designs, its own desire for us. Something more powerful than ourselves seems to have us in its grasp. Perhaps we're finally close enough to an agency of Pluto that he can now confer his riches, *the depth of perspective he would bring us to*—albeit kicking and screaming.

I'm suggesting that whenever our traumas, terrors, and vulnerability involuntarily appear, and too seem "overwhelming," we may have *become* Persephone; may be about to lose some portion of our naiveté, may be in the grips of some form of mythic initiation. And Plutonic initiation—Pluto's style of *eros*—is not only "overwhelming," or leads us to feel "carried away," but involves being *pricked, probed, penetrated by what has been hidden or feared*. (Maybe this archetype thus lies behind the contemporary, anecdotal reports of people being abducted—and probed—by aliens; if not the plethora of unwelcome sexual probes come to light in the wake of Trump's *Hollywood Access* tape).

For those of us living in a monotheistic culture (where it is assumed there is only *one* god) the mythic figures from a polytheistic mythology can initially seem rather remote and alien, while presumed to be lacking in relevance to our own contemporary lives. Yet again—as Freud once confessed, "wherever I go, I find that a poet has been there before me." And so we might consider that the poets who transmitted the Greek myths had recognized something lingering and trans-temporal about the gods, goddesses, and other archetypal figures in their mythology. Namely, that such mythic figures as Narcissus and Echo or Pluto and Persephone, are the personification of psychological traits residing in human beings—now as ever.

And thus, with a nod to our inner Persephone, when I've led retreats I've often included a period of "vulnerability practice." During this segment of the retreat we actively *cultivate* our vulnerability, rather than the attempt to ward it off. Which for the ego is a completely counter-intuitive move. And part of why I do this is that all personality types have something that seems uniquely vulnerable and shameful for that particular type. What's being avoided has a Plutonic tinge, becomes conceived in an exaggerated way, as if it might bring annihilation. And so, part of the ego structure begins to shape itself around the avoidance of these vulnerabilities.

A very differentiated topology of these avoidances is found in a largely unknown enneagram, the Enneagram of Avoidances and Deficiencies.* Here, for example, an enneatype 8 tends to avoid his weakness, an enneatype 4 her simple sadness, a 7 his pain, etc. Yet this attempt to avoid a shame-felt vulnerability just adds one more layer of veil obscuring our underlying true nature, a true nature that is not defending against, or avoiding *anything*. So a less negatively tinged word for "vulnerability" is *undefended-ness*. And what I find when I actively court my vulnerability is that it opens my heart to its greater depths.

It leads me to feel less emotionally guarded, less anxious, with nothing needing to be warded off. And when type 4s for example, can *allow* (rather than resist) the sadness that often exists just beneath her surface, it actually becomes a portal to her deeper nature. She becomes a "Queen of the Underworld," no longer a *kore* resisting a descent to her emotional depths. And a similar soul-depth can be experienced by each ego style once they've lessened their aversion to what seems so vulnerably shameful.

As for Pluto, his name comes from *ploutos,* which means "riches" or "wealth." And we seem to inherit these riches not by anything that is *given* or *added* to us, but by what is revealed from what he takes away (whatever we have held most dearly, whatever we've identified with, or thought we couldn't bear to live without). And finally, he seems to take nearly everything away, all that is subject to perishing.

And in this way Pluto is not only the god of death, and the "deepest" god of the Greek pantheon, but the god of *deepest wisdom.* For as the god of death and impermanence, his deconstructive power is such that he can also destroy the habitual cognitive and emotional obscurations that veil the deepest truth. (Of the god's many names, in India he was called *Shiva,* whose third eye was thought to abide in a perpetual state of meditation).

---

* This enneagram is customarily taught in tandem with another enneagram, the Enneagram of Self-Idealizations, for much of the personality structure shapes itself around both what we try to avoid, as well as that which we use to self-idealize. For example, type 8 who's avoiding his weakness, self-idealizes around "being strong," or a type 7 whose avoidance is pain, self-idealizes around "being OK," and "feeling no pain." While a type 4 who in avoiding her sadness self-idealizes around being "authentic." (While in actuality, the avoidance truly makes her somewhat *generic,* as is the case with the characteristic avoidances of each of the personality styles).

And without metaphorically dying to who we have naively been taking ourselves to be, there is no "second birth," no "resurrection" into a more essential form; the butterfly of the soul remains encased in some form of larval shell—or what more recently has been termed "the narcissistic shell."

Destabilizing visitations from below, that the ego may normally defend against, at other times *are* quite overwhelming. Consensual reality becomes a helpless spectator. We are dragged down into the under-worldly spaces, the psychic holes of our deepest wounds and helplessness where we feel the most deficient, like a vulnerable maiden being ravished. There's often an edge of terror. Plutonic initiations up the ante, like enriched *Pluto*nium. They're powerful, powerfully deconstructive (*corrosive* to the ego; and so the ego feels them as *destructive*). We have been grabbed by something that could destroy what we've known as ourselves.

For these *terrifying* reasons, in the ancient world Pluto was usually not spoken of directly. But instead, was referred to by *euphemisms*, as if even speaking his name might attract the god's attention, might lead the god of death to come for us. One of the commonly used euphemisms for Pluto was, in fact, "He Who Comes For Us All." Yet another was, "The Good Counselor" (a nuance reflected not only by Greek mythology, but also in Toltec shamanism when Don Juan Matus tells Carlos Castaneda to always keep Death as a counselor over his left shoulder). If Oedipus wasn't as universal as Freud had thought, Death shows up everywhere, comes for us all.

But as the Greeks seemed to know, Pluto is also the deepest of counselors—a very demanding one, though; a real hard ass who won't let us get away with anything but the deepest truth—*which is all that might remain*, once our deconstructive initiation has gone deep, once Pluto has fully had his way with us. And when Pluto is "doing therapy" with us, it's like he drags us into the neighborhood we were the most frightened to enter, and then if we're lucky, or have the wherewithal to make use of the teaching he's offering, we might come out of that neighborhood transformed, no longer so afraid of the thing that used to scare us. (Such a Plutonic initiation is alluded to in mythic stories where "the pearl beyond price" *lies in the jaws of a dragon,* the terrifying *last* place the ego would ever think to enter—or in my own story, in confronting my fear of public speaking).

Pluto is a "good counselor" in that he first shows us what is not an adequate enough refuge, what is not a large enough peg for us to hang our hat. The world, it turns out, is *deeper than we thought.* And as Persephone discovered, maybe we are too.

It's like our brush with Death, our death or near-death experiences, the encounter with our deepest fears—our "abduction into ultimate depth"—can show us what's really important in life, what's most deeply true, what can be relied upon, and what not. A great light might appear. Goethe's last words: *"mere licht, mere licht!"* ("more light, more light!"). On our deathbeds, a deeper wisdom may beckon—as our self-idealizations and avoidances flee, like rats leaving a sinking ship…

If Pluto had many names and euphemisms, many too are the nuances associated with him: elemental power, depth, and intensity, for this principle intensifies whatever it touches—the instincts, whether libidinal and aggressive, or destructive and regenerative. He oversees the biological processes of sex, birth, and death, and is associated with upheaval, breakdowns, life and death struggles. He could be the rapacious will to power, say like Donald Trump, who turns to shit whatever he touches—or that, which takes us deeper, first by overwhelming and checkmating the ego. (And the shit reference above is archetypally correct). For Pluto is thought to rule *eliminative processes* (all that seems like shit to us, all that we would disown, excrete, piss off, vomit, or cast outside us). If the ego tends to walk naively through life wearing a "Do Not Disturb" sign, Pluto purges… the old, often violently, volcanically, excrementally; just as he transfigures and resurrects.

As Rick Tarnas tells us, Pluto represents the underworld and the underground in all their nuances, whether geologic, criminal, political. Mythically, Pluto is associated with stories involving descent and transformation, and is kindred with all the deities of destruction and regeneration, death and rebirth: Persephone, Inanna, Isis, and Osiris, Kali, Dionysus, Shiva, and Shakti. In a nutshell, as Nietzsche wrote in *Thus Spoke Zarathustra*: *"You must be ready to burn yourself in your own flame: how could you become new, if you had not first become ashes?"*

Psychotherapy itself may be Plutonic, and like gambling or prostitution, an "underworld activity." (Or I find something depth conferring, un-policed, and *enlivening* in conceiving of it in this way). And in fact, the night before C.G. Jung hung out his shingle to practice psychotherapy, he had dreamt that he was opening the largest *brothel* in the world.

In important ways, Pluto and Persephone may inform the imaginal backdrop of *depth psychology*. If the more unsavory manifestation of Pluto is an "underworld figure" (like a mafia don, a predatory psychopath, president, or a lurking pedophile or rapist) then the more noble side of the archetype is the *psychopomp*, a receiver or guider of souls—those more "welcoming" arms.

But the god of the Underworld is an impersonal receiver of souls, harvesting a new generation of humans every 12 to 30 years, which astronomically is the time it takes Pluto's irregular orbits to complete. And in astrology this is sometimes thought to be what determines "a generation." This isn't a warm and fuzzy deity; whereas the compassion of his wife Persephone was thought to attend more to the personal side of death's bewilderment and grief.

Though both the most and least successful of therapies inevitably end, the soul's deepening seems a continual or *cyclic dying*—to whatever we have last taken ourselves to be; and thus *has no* conclusive ending. And the same might be said of the relationship between Pluto and Persephone ("which endures forever—through Persephone's eternal and bi-polar swings, her yearly cycling up and down, her transits between Earth and the Underworld").

The Plutonic *psychopomp* as therapist, though, is but one half of a couple who meet behind closed doors, hidden from view, like in an underworldly vault—or an illicit tryst that is nobody else's business. What they say and do there is "confidential," privileged information. Like what happens in Vegas *stays* in Vegas.

But even if one member of the couple at times is the *psychopomp*, still it takes two to tango, and in any moment the music could change, and suddenly the other partner begins to lead, to take them deeper. These confidential visitations, these cyclic encounters with each other, may lead them each to a dissolution into the same depth, and by doing so, can confer the sovereignty of that depth. For what is pricked, probed, and uncovered may become an initiation into fearlessness, a fearlessness towards the depths of feeling, the depths of grief, and depths of the psyche that are even deeper than death.

TWENTY-SIX

Mythic Dissociation:
The Loss of Transformational Rites
& Loss of the Real Self

A PIVOTAL CONCEPT in this book is Joseph Campbell's notion of "mythic dissociation." Yet to better understand what this means for an individual (or a culture) we first might ask: *what is the function—or functions—of myth?* Campbell believed there were *four* functions of myth. And the first function (which should also animate the other three) "is that of eliciting and supporting the sense of awe before the mystery of being."

And before proceeding further, we might pause...might allow Campbell's phrase to resonate for a moment in our awareness, especially the words "awe," "mystery," and "being." For these words might stop us in our tracks, might turn us to face another direction, another *dimension,* might halt what I variously term "an idiot's momentum" or "walking briskly beneath a ridiculous hat"—which is to say *the vector of the ego,* which tends to be somewhat oblivious toward the numinous, the *Mysterium Tremendum* of being itself. (And *narcissism,* as I employ the term, is in part this obliviousness, this dissociation from being, this "mythic dissociation").

Campbell found that the second function of myth is rendering a cosmological vision of the universe "that will support and be supported by this sense of awe before the mystery of the presence and the presence of a mystery." The third function is "to support the current social order, to integrate the individual organically with his group." And the fourth function of myth is "to initiate the individual into the order of realities in his own psyche, guiding him toward his own spiritual enrichment and realization."

When these mythic functions are active and vivifying, perhaps it is no wonder that Karen Armstrong tells us that "mythology should awaken us to *rapture*." And when they are *not* operating functionally, why Mircea Eliade attributed modern man's anxieties to his rejection of myths and the sense of the sacred. (And it is my view that mainstream, modern psychology has, as a mythic enterprise, done a fairly decent job when it comes to fulfilling the 3rd function of myth; in terms of the other three, not so much…).

Cultures can suffer and become mythically dissociated in various ways. Though the most important and over-arching ways result in the loss of being itself, such dissociation could also take the form of the loss of *any kind of mythic reference at all*. Ironically, this commonly occurs when people are unconsciously *living a myth*, "acting it out" without being able to recognize the myth they are in. (And thus it's been said that when we are unconsciously *identifying* with an archetype, we are then doomed to suffering the *fate* of that archetype).

Another form of mythic dissociation might occur when the myths being employed by a culture no longer speak to the nature of the time, as might happen when a society has shifted from a hunting and gathering culture to an agrarian one, or from an agrarian to an industrial, an industrial to a technological or digital one, etc. Or, say, when facing an ecological crisis.

A mythic dissociation can also occur when a society has largely overlooked, or *too narrowly interpreted* the myths that really *do* speak to what that culture is facing or suffering from—which can result when a culture's poets and other transformational change-agents are not doing part of their traditional job. (As *has* been the case with the myth of Narcissus and Echo; *and what I've been attempting to counter with this book*. For the archetypal figures in *this* myth seem those which we—unconsciously—are currently "acting out").

A mythic dissociation can also occur when the myths have been taken over and interpreted by a priest-hood with their own fish to fry; leaving that culture with a mythology that has grown to be "fishy" in some way. And whether it was a Catholic priesthood in the Middle Ages promising "a remission of sins" for all crusaders fighting against the Saracens (Muslims) during the Crusades, or contemporary Islamic clerics touting a certain entrance into Paradise for Islamic State fighters who die in an allegedly religious campaign, it's the same smelly barrel of fish.

Yet in cultures *not* mythically dissociated, important myths have commonly been enacted as *initiatory rites*—so that their metaphoric themes *don't* become enacted (neurotically) as *symptoms*. And as a psychotherapist working in a mythically dissociated, narcissistic culture, I've attempted to offer at least some initial approximate.

Among the most profoundly transformational of such rites were those celebrated at Eleusis—the Eleusinian Mysteries—rites which were enacted for nearly 2,000 years, and which were based on the myth involving Persephone's abduction by Pluto, the Greek god of death. Unfortunately, a more nuanced understanding of the rites that comprised the Eleusinian Mysteries have largely remained an object of *conjecture*—because revealing the details of these rites were *punishable by death*. And in this way, these Mysteries have largely *remained* a mystery; if not vouchsafed by Pluto.

For nearly two thousand years though, we *have* retained a similar rite celebrating a mythic death and reappearance—the Catholic mass. (It was due to the rise of Christianity, in fact, that the Eleusinian mysteries were closed down in 392 C.E by the Christian Emperor Theodosius I, who saw these rites as inspiring resistance to Christianity. Within 4 years the temple of Demeter and every sacred site in Eleusis had been sacked, leaving behind only ruins and rubble, where for nearly 2000 years transformational rites had been celebrated).

But a problem with ritual—a problem encountered in any religion, or with any spiritual practice, really—is that the ego can get a hold of almost *anything,* such that things can become routinized, or narrowly viewed or distorted, and thus no longer as able to effect a profound shift in awareness.

In this light, it's hard to know what *kept* the mysteries of Eleusis so vital and psychically charged for such a long time. Undoubtedly, the injunction against revealing the details of these rites must certainly have *helped* to preserve their numinosity—but can't in itself fully account for the profound impact of these rites.

Recent scholarship, however, plausibly suggests that this may have been aided by the ingestion of psycho-active ergot, a fungoid growth found on grains—the study of which later led the Swiss chemist Albert Hofmann to first synthesize the hallucinogen LSD.*

---

* See *The Road to Eleusis: Unveiling the Secret of the Mysteries.* Wasson, Hofmann, and Ruck. Berkeley: North Atlantic Books, 30th anniversary ed., 2008. (Parenthetically, this Hofmann *is* Albert, the chemist).

The use of potions for magical or religious purposes was relatively common in ancient Greece. They were often ingested after a fast, as this both intensifies and hastens the effect. And such a fast occurred in the Eleusinian mysteries just prior to the ritual ingestion of the *kykeon*. The *kykeon* was said to include barley and pennyroyal—but we don't know *what else*. We do know that ergot, a fungal parasite of the barley or rye grain, contains ergotamine—a precursor to LSD, as well as ergonovine (which also produces LSD-like effects).

Another theory has been that the Eleusinian rites employed DMT as its *entheogen* (from the Greek, literally meaning "generating the divine within;" i.e., any psychoactive substance that induces a spiritual experience). DMT (N,N-Dimethyltryptamine) is a psychedelic tryptamine molecule with intense effects and rapid onset; hence ideal for collectively induced rites. It can be produced from many wild plants of the Mediterranean, including Phalaris and/or Acacia. To produce a psychoactive reaction these must be combined with a monoamine oxidase inhibitor such as Syrian Rue* (*Peganum harmala),* which also grows wild throughout the Mediterranean.

Though there's been no conclusive modern agreement as to what psychoactive agent(s) *might* have been employed in the Mysteries, what scholars have commonly agreed upon is that the Eleusinian rites seemed to greatly relieve their celebrants' *fear of death*. In our own culture, the *loss* of such a rite—or the failure to create one—has left us with a fearful lack of orientation in facing death, a lack of orientation toward what dies and what doesn't; a lack of orientation toward what we most deeply are, and are not. Which points us back to the problem of *narcissism...*

As we have seen, from the perspective of Narcissus, Echo seems *beneath* him—and thus her love threatens him with "fearful chains." And the same threatened quality might be seen in Persephone, she too (as *kore,* the yet to be initiated maiden self) recoiling from being captured by what seems beneath *her.*

---

* Similar two-part brews employing the seeds of Syrian Rue as the monoamine oxidase inhibitor occur in various *ayahuasca* recipes. I've made such brews myself, and can attest to their potency.

The encounter with death can be frightening, and in different ways for different people. For in a mythically dissociated culture, a culture that has no rites that might better prepare us for death, death can be the ultimate boogieman, a "grim reaper." But Persephone's abduction by the god of death is also an initiation into mystery, one in which she is penetrated *by*—and taken *to*—a greater depth.

Like the old Chinese Zen masters such as Han Shan ("Cold Mountain") who take on the name of the mountain where they live, Hades—as Pluto was otherwise known—names both an invisible *god* and the *realm* where he dwells.

And Persephone's descent into Hades is at once the loss of her familiar vantage, her familiar world; the loss of her accustomed identity. For she must suffer the separation from her mother Demeter, and the loss of her virginal, maiden perspective—which had been naively unaware of the depths lying *within* and *beneath* her—in order to inherit her own sovereignty, and to reign as a co-monarch of depth; no longer as a vulnerable *victim* with no agency, but as the *Queen* of the Underworld. And as such, in her *matured* version, hers is the mythological perspective capable of compassionately welcoming others, who in facing death, are also involuntarily entering the mysterious realm where she's come to reign.

In our modern world, Hospice workers may be the embodiment of *this* aspect of Persephone. Just as anyone who has been raped, molested, abducted, or has experienced an involuntary, terrifying descent into a greater depth, may have embodied Persephone in her earlier, *kore* form. (The sexual violations against women come to light during Trump's presidency, thus casts them as modern day Persephones; much as their years of voiceless-ness seems resonate with Echo).

And in a parallel manner to Persephone, Narcissus's depth-vision leads to the death of *his* former perspective and familiar sense of self, a transformation that leads both to a metaphoric death, and to a metaphoric "flowering." (i.e., his dying and then morphing into the narcissus flower at the myth's end).

Such a metaphoric death, and a flowering rebirth commonly occur in perinatal rebirthing experiences, holotropic breath work and psychedelic experiences (as seen in the research of Rick Tarnas and Stan Grof) and as well in the world's mythic, shamanic, and spiritual traditions. *Here, a new sense of identity emerges as the ego's inflationary regard of the self perishes.*

Yet there's something paradoxical about this. On the one hand we are, each of us, quite special and unique. Yet so is *everyone else*—which narcissism fails to grasp. As Tarnas points out, we can't take our inflationary sense of "specialness" through the death/rebirth experience, which may be ruthlessly humbling to the self we've previously taken ourselves to be. Yet as we emerge from the crucible of such experiences, we again experience our specialness, but not in an inflationary way, as if above all others; but rather, as a unique embodiment of the whole.

And the world itself regains its luster, and is no longer seen as a meaningless and mechanical world of objects with ourselves as the subject. Instead, the world itself is experienced as ensouled and replete with meaning, intelligence, and its own sense of purposeful timing.

For hundreds of years though, a kind of scientific rationalism has led to the loss of such a perspective, and a loss of mythic rites, teachings, and practices that can lead to a shift of vantage, and a transformation of whom—or what—we take ourselves to be. And when a culture lacks such rites and teachings, people are more likely to remain in the collectively shared condition of "taking themselves to be what they are not." In this way, there is not only a lack of orientation in facing death, and a lack of awareness of what *doesn't* die, but (from a Plutonic perspective) a collective case of "mistaken identity."

Our culture itself now largely abides in this mistaken, uninitiated and inflationary condition; a condition where the self-image is what people embellish, defend, attempt to market, and naively take themselves to be. In the process we become dissociated from the depths of *being itself*—whose support and enhancement Campbell tells us, *should be* the first and overarching function of myth.

Yet unfortunately, in a mythically dissociated culture *being* is pervasively shunted aside, while the winged, butterfly-like nature of the soul remains encased by something akin to a larval shell. And amongst the numerous ways I've attempted to define it, "narcissism" *is* this "mistaken identity," this inflationary estrangement from being, this uninitiated, pervasive, and enshelled condition.

TWENTY-SEVEN

Cultural Narcissism:

Idealization and Devaluing, Ethnocentricity,

and the Narrowing of God

As initially seemed the case with the protagonists in these two myths, in a *narcissistic culture* of *un*initiated people, those whom we might otherwise love also tend to be initially experienced as if they were either above or beneath us—so the relational field is seldom *level*—which is the only ground from which a more stable relatedness can be built.

Here we can have an idealized expectation, seeking a partner who is "a good catch," someone who might augment us or bring us to some higher or deeper station, as if they comprise some kind of wish-fulfilling gem. And when we fall in love, it often looks like this, as if we have found a gem that will ever fulfill us—and if so, enjoy it while you can!

For though the ideal might reflect a latent potential in a partner—a glimpse of their essence—the ideal is also an airbrushed version of the real, a version without blemishes...

And so, there is often a disappointing thud that can follow, a kind of buyer's remorse—when the erotic ideal crashes down to earth, and we find ourselves embraced by a partner whose feet are made of clay, a partner who snores...Or watches hours of dingbat romantic comedy—or football and mixed martial arts. Or has a yen for tofu and ghee versus hearty portions of dead animals sizzling on the grill—or whatever savory, or unsavory traits you failed to mention in your wish list to Love's casting director.

Here we can next find ourselves *devaluing* the other—who seems now an outrage to the purity of our erotic or spiritual ideal—as if they are disappointing us now, failing our lofty expectations, bringing us down. This kind of "splitting," of seeing the other (or oneself) in either an idealized or a devalued way, is—as we've seen—a central feature in narcissism (as well as in Borderline Personality Disorder, if not in much of what contemporary psychology would term *pre-Oedipal pathology**).

Yet in Deuteronomy and the biblical book of Joshua, this is also a central feature in *monotheistic ethnocentricity,* where a tribal version of "God" blesses the "chosen people," giving them the spoils of desert warfare—and to Hell with the rest. And today, we can see the same splitting, the same ethnocentric and polarizing perspective, the same righteous (and violently enforced) "purity" being employed on the part of the Taliban, al Qaeda, and ISIS—and a similar "tribalism" in America's political parties.

As with a cultic conception of "God," when it comes to *love,* there seems a tremendous amount of illusion often at work, a great tendency to projections of all sorts, especially this kind of "splitting." And this seems to be the case for many of us, not just people that Western psychology would recognize as having a personality disorder.

And in a narcissistic culture that has lacked adequate rites and practices for working with the Narcissus myth, not only can potential lovers become objectified such that they seem beneath us in a devalued way, but so can the poor, the homeless, animals and plants, people of another political party or religion, refugees, our own less than ideal bodies, the entire third world.

Here, I'm suggesting again that narcissism and its penchant for devaluing is a *cultural* phenomenon, as well as an intra-psychic one. And our cultural narcissism—with its "too pure" self-image, its righteousness, and

---

* In the "etiological mythology" of contemporary psychology, "pre-Oedipal pathology" refers to the enduring legacy left by traumatic ruptures, the psychic wounds that continue to inhibit development, and that were initially suffered by the age of three, or the inception of "the Oedipal phase" of psycho-social development. Freud himself had suffered such a traumatic rupture at this age when his family was forced to leave Freiburg. And as he later said, "I never got over my longing for home." And if we understand "home" in a more metaphoric way, most of us, though to varying degrees, became dissociated from parts of our own true nature at some early stage of our development; if not the loss of an original *being*, an Edenic "Paradise." (Deeply evolved people throughout history have told us however, that this "Paradise" never went elsewhere; it's still available, even if we've become dissociated from it. And aside from transformational gazes and other practices spoken of thus far, further hints for rectifying this dissociation are evoked in this book's concluding section).

its penchant for devaluing others—goes way back, for we already find it in *Deuteronomy*.

Similarly, the westward movement of Europeans into the Americas took place at the expense of the native cultures who were here first, and who seemed "heathen"—and "beneath" us. And this is why, again, that George Washington came to regard the failure to vouchsafe the territorial rights of the nation's native peoples as *the greatest failure of his presidency*. A legacy that has continued…

For the "manifest destiny" of the white man became a mythic banner beneath which wagons rolled west across the plains, displacing the native peoples, and forcing them onto reservations; the American nation's westward expansion as much a form of *cultural narcissism* as was the abduction, and genocidal enslavement of Africans, a devaluing that ironically accounted for much of the nation's *wealth* for over two hundred years (which thus, was not only a manifestation of *cultural narcissism*, but at once, a *negative reception of Pluto*, the Greek god of "riches"—and *death*).

The treatment of its native peoples, its legacy of slavery, and the largely unseen fact that America has been at war *for every decade since its founding*, are the shadowy, historical undersides of a nation that mythically prides itself as "the land of the free, and the home of the brave"… "with liberty and justice for all." And since 1953 (in Iran) our narcissistic entitlement to the oil reserves of the Middle East, has led the U.S. to meddle in the affairs of other countries, depose even democratically elected governments, and wage a series of costly wars that continue even today.

And even today… a tribal, ethnocentric perception of the One God—which initially arose from the Syro-Arabian desert thousands of years ago—finds us still embroiled in mythological warfare (in Iraq, Afghanistan, Syria, and on the west bank of the Jordan River). For exoteric religion, and religiously-tinged political cults have—now and throughout history—exhibited a militant grandiosity (*hubris*) when they have claimed for themselves the one true path to the one true God; and where there has been a devaluing—often lethal—regard for all who are Other. Here too we find a narcissistic "splitting" of what is being idealized and what is being devalued, what is good and what is bad, what is *us* and what is *them*.

And where there has been a collective misapprehension of *God*, how can there *not* be a resulting skewed sense of *identity*? And where there has been a collective misapprehension of *identity*—narcissism—how can there *not* be a resulting skewed sense of God? And regardless of which way we frame it, the unfortunate truth here has given God a bad name. For throughout history, all kinds of crazy inferences have been projected onto God, and subhuman forms of behavior enacted in God's name.

Here, "God" has often been reduced to a tribal god, at best, yet for whom claims are still made that this is the *only* God. Perhaps we shouldn't be allowed to even use the word "God" for a while, at least not without a license that only the truly wise might confer, and perhaps not even then.*

With this in mind, the Judaic and Islamic injunction against constructing or worshipping "graven images" seems initially an understandable, if not a wise custom. Understandable, in that it helped differentiate their own emerging religious sensibility from that of competing Great Mother cults of the desert who commonly made use of religious icons—such as the golden calf mentioned in the Bible.

In this sense, monotheism attempted to offer a new turning of the wheel of truth, a potentially developmental advancement from earlier more animistic religions, and one that would turn away from worshipping idols while—importantly—instilling a detailed ethical code of behavior that was badly needed to whip desert bad asses into shape. As Ken Wilber or Spiral Dynamics might say, the previously prevailing Red *meme* was needing some restraining blue structure(s) to advance to the next level in the spiral.** And at a more profound level, the injunction against "graven images" (or image-worship) might help alert us to God's non-material *boundlessness*, by lessening the human tendency to *concretize the deity*.

But unfortunately, the ethical code that monotheism offered came with its own potential pitfalls, for where you have religious *laws* you have religious *judgment*, with human beings enforcing these laws that ostensibly

---

* Traditionally, such *has* been the case in Judaism, where the Hebrew word for God—yud-hay-vay-hay—is never pronounced out loud. When appearing in scripture the reader substitutes the word "adonai" which means "Lord" or "Master." And among many traditional Jews even the word "adonai" is not spoken outside of prayer services, but instead "HaShem" might be used ("the Name")—or some other euphemism.

** Regarding my various reflections about *memes*, again, see Beck, Don Edward and Cowan, Christopher C. *Spiral Dynamics: Mastering Values, Leadership and Change*. Malden: Blackwell Publishing, 2006. See also Wilber, Ken. *Boomeritis: A Novel That Will Set You Free*. Boston: Shambhala, 2002.

come from God,* thus often giving rise to a punitive religious superego—*an eye for an eye and a tooth for a tooth*—an avenging self-righteousness become conflated with the deity.

For where you have a mythology where the deity resides in Heaven or Paradise, and where the deity is seen as a judge, the back-story of our life on Earth can become that of a test—a test of our resolve, a test of our obedience to our *imagination* of the deity, and of our persevering faithfulness to the laws and beliefs inculcated in us as part of our cultural conditioning, such that when we will face "Judgment Day"—if we have passed these tests—we might be admitted to Heaven or Paradise ourselves.

For as Campbell points out, in this mythology there is a "two-story world," where those on the Earth plane might ascend to Heaven if they perish, for example, in the defense of their religion—a tenet that continues to plague us in the practice of *jihad*. Or perhaps our ascension to God will come "at the end of days," when the deity might come down from Heaven, lifting the righteous –in *rapture*—up to the heavenly abode. There we would finally dwell with God, always and forever, and would be re-united with departed loved ones and fellow believers who have also lived righteous lives.

But the centrality of judgment in such a mythology can cast a shadow over the entire psychic landscape—over our imagination of God, ourselves, as well as over other people(s); as if there's been placed a Cosmic Super Ego smack dab in the center of our mythic imagination. Here we will not only be judged by God at the moment of death, but will tend to be judging toward ourselves and our fellow human beings all along the way. As suggested earlier, such a *mythos*—when not outshined by love—can create a dualistic tension between good and evil, Heaven and Hell, *us vs. them*. (Hence, the then radical, and still timely teaching of my favorite rabbi: *Judge not lest ye be judged*).

And besides, *any* postulation on the part of the conceptual mind as to what God *is*, or what God likes or abhors, would be a narrowing of God, ever running the risk of anthropomorphism and concretizing assumptions about the nature of God.

Similarly, there's a difference between thinking God is metaphorically *like* a father (or a mother, for that matter, or "the Friend") vs. literalizing

---

* Here, I'm alluding not just to Vice President Pence's attempt to create legislation forcing all judges to admit our laws are based upon *the words of God*, but something far older: that shamanic bit of stagecraft Moses brought down from Mount Sinai—i.e., "The Ten Commandments."

the image of God by seeing God *as* a particular this or that, while insisting that any such theological portrayals are the only true way to conceive of, or worship divinity. (This literalism represents a loss of what I've termed "metaphoric thinking." And in this way, God may continue to be "concretized" even if this is not occurring through the worship of *physical* icons or idols. For our "idols" can be literalizing *conceptualizations* as well; and thus a narrowing of what lies *beyond* all our concepts: "a peace that passeth understanding"). And the emphasis upon "the Word" or scripture, has commonly led exoteric, fundamentalist religion to be oblivious to the *trans-conceptual peace* that Jesus pointed to; and instead, with religions promulgating "Holy War"—which *should be* an oxymoron.

A literalizing "narrowing of God" has also resulted when a *single* and ironclad interpretation of scripture is maintained—long beyond the time certain proscribed injunctions might have been timely and valuable for a culture, and its religion. For this has left parts of our world still practicing an ethnocentric, medieval—if not a *Bronze Age* religion; "the old time religion" which gave us the Crusades and the Inquisition, and in persisting, helped "inspire" the events of 9/11.

Yet we might note something *ethnocentrically similar* in hegemonic empires that seek to win out over all others; and both of these are not dissimilar from the fans of a football team who in unison might break into a chant of *"we're number one, we're number one!"*

For both football *fans* and religious *fanatics* share the same etymological root. In both there is an inflationary exaltation that can lift us to frenzy. In such a perspective, life may be reduced to a war between opposing forces: the Redskins vs. the Cowboys and the Raiders vs. the Saints, God vs. Satan, the Righteous vs. the Infidel, Good vs. Evil, the neo-cons vs. al Qaeda, the *Shi'a* vs. the *Sunni*, the American security establishment against Russia, Iran, or whomever the current "enemy," ISIS vs. anyone with different views—in other words, *us* versus *them*.

We may be willing to kill or die for "God;" or bleed in the colors of our team—or our *nation*. Here we are no longer vulnerably alone, but linked to a like-minded membership striving for supremacy. And besides religions, terrorist groups, hegemonic empires or football fans, today we often find the same headset with street gangs, corporations, and increasingly in the U.S. with our political parties.

TWENTY-EIGHT

Narcissism's Apotheosis of Fame & the Loss of Attention, Eros, Empathy, and Altruism

IN A NARCISSISTIC culture we often seem out of touch with the love native to our own being—and so may feel erotically *tentative* at times, as if love is something we fear not *getting* instead of a natural abundance that we have to give.

Kind voices of wisdom have arisen on this lovely planet, which till now—even in the face of a lingering and oblivious ecological idiocy—has sustained our life form so well. They have said, *"if you want to be happy think more of the welfare of others; if you want to be miserable, think only of yourself"* (or say, "America first"). But in a narcissistic culture, people tend to be so self-absorbed that we often don't seem to have much time or attention to give to others.

If you're an American—and not an epidemiologist, or a billionaire who's morphed into a bodhisattva like Bill Gates—you probably don't know that 2 billion people on the planet today don't even have clean water to drink. And why more children are dying from diarrhea each day than AIDS, malaria, and measles combined.

Unless you're already a famous author, good luck in getting someone to actually read your manuscript. Few have the bandwidth. The contemporary publishing climate has grown stressed by competition with a free Internet. Like the studio system in Hollywood, it's become more influenced by group decisions and the mindset of MBAs now, than by editors who'd been English majors. With the diminished role of editors, the mentality is now so risk-aversive, if not so narcissistically insular, that few New York publishers will respond to an author without an agent, and few agents will even bother to respond to a new author's query—unless one has a commanding social media platform—say 50k followers on Twitter. In a way though, it's hard to blame publishing's gatekeepers. They're so bombarded by those (like Echo) who are seeking to be heard, it it must be hard to winnow the wheat from the chaff. Post a 23 year-old intern at the gate—or don't even bother—since most of it is chaff anyhow.

In an age of sound bites, the prevailing attention span seems just adequate for a 30 second video—and these days many people (even our 45th president) have stopped reading books entirely, while getting all their information from TV and the Internet. We're "too busy," too obsessed often, to even listen to our own hearts; too busy for *eros,* for our own hearts to find us.

Or we're so wounded—like Echo—that it's also hard to find the full voice of our heart. Our deeper voice, a voice that might quiver with soulful vulnerability and authenticity, often arises only when we've been overwhelmed in some way, knocked off our horse, our course, when the ego is losing its familiar grip, no longer able to "hold it all together" –which after all, *should* be the job of a *god.* But we've been replacing the gods with something else…

In a narcissistic culture—where people have become dissociated from their own deeper nature (in part because it hasn't been adequately recognized and reflected)—there is thus also the compulsive drive to win notice, to become recognized, to become known or *famous* for something; more so than to know oneself.

However, just as there is a difference between *wanting* love—and actually loving—there is a pivotal difference between *wanting* attention and being *attentive*. Learning to *embody* this pivotal shift is crucial for *the transformation* of our prevailing narcissism and its dissociated sense of lack. (Do not pass go until you've read this paragraph *again*).

For the sense of separation from some needed "it"—whether love, fame, revenge, God, a Caliphate—keeps us living in a waking dream in which we take ourselves to be what we're not, and where we fail to apprehend the glimmer of a unity *already* here. And whether with suicide bombers in Islamic cultures, or the more ample possibilities for narcissistic expression in America, the drive to become known, recognized, or famous for something has become the Great Quest, a kind of counterfeit version of the Grail.

Our tabloids, magazines, and many of our TV programs show us the faces, lives, and possessions of the rich and famous, hundreds of millions of TV screens mirroring our idealization of celebrity. And in the plethora of contemporary "reality" shows, there is often a competition—of contesting chefs, singers, dancers, fashion designers, hair stylists, golfers, Beverly Hills and Manhattan realtors, Hollywood private caterers, apprentice business executives, those wishing to win the love of millionaires—the collective air waves are *filled* with this now–all of them striving to *win recognition,* if not to become rich and famous themselves. These shows are so popular—our cheapened versions of Greek tragedy—not only because these shows are so inexpensive for the networks to produce, but because they reflect so directly the *hubris,* the *pathos,* the collective narcissism of our *own* inner dramas.

The well-recognized voices of rich and famous personalities are also used to sell us products, as if these products could make us famous too—more successful, or more desired. These successful people would seem the *opposite* of Echo, those who have managed to avert her fate, that of languishing un-noticed in lonely valleys and caves.

Fame thus becomes the longed-for balm for the narcissistic wound— the injury done to the soul from not being better heard, recognized, valued. And in a narcissistic culture it seems that so many of us have grown calibrated to pursue our "fifteen minutes of fame," as if it were some kind of elixir. Unconsciously—or with our own collusion—the gods and saints have been replaced by *celebrities.* And so today, many people feel driven to become famous too—for something, *anything.* Instead of the gods, we have *Donald Trump and the Kardashians* (which sounds like a rock band from the depths of Samsara).

And we have come to idealize (or envy) those who have ascended, people who have become "stars," those whom we all recognize. Like the sun, and like Venus, Saturn, and Mars, the gods have *always* appeared as stars. And in a narcissistic culture we have deified the famous, and through fame they live on—Elvis, somehow eternal, a twangy Dionysus in our cult-hood of celebrity.

In a reigning culture that has never been brought low, never been brought to its knees, love poems become an endangered species, echoing in lonely valleys and caves like Echo herself, and far from the engines of commerce that propel the popular culture. We have produced no Rumi, nor a Hafiz. Unlike Russia—suffering a revolution, Stalinist purges, and millions of soldiers dying defending their own soil in the Second World War—we have produced no Anna Akhmatova. And related to the loss of love poems—and the diminution of *eros* as a whole—is our loss of *altruism,* for the notion of "putting others first" tends not to get very much validation or importance in our culture of "me first," "America first," our "looking out for number one." Our culture remains developmentally stymied at either the egocentric or culturally centric perspectives, having failed to progress to world-centric.

For decades our distorted version of "world-centric" had been America's imperialism, whereby the success of our own culture sat upon the shoulders of the rest of the world. And if since 1945 this had been termed a *Pax Americana,* such a Peace resulted in the very thing that President Dwight Eisenhower warned us against at the end of his presidency. Namely, the dangers of a growing "Military-Industrial Complex" that has since led America to spend more on armaments than the other eight or ten most highly armed countries combined. And in truth, this *Pax Americana* gave rise to decades of unwinnable yet unrelenting *wars,* whether cold, hot, or proxy, and whether in or against: Korea, Vietnam, China, Russia, Iraq, Afghanistan, and Syria. And this leaves out more minor "interventions" in Central America, Iran, Somalia, Yemen, and places I can't even remember now. Oh, how could I have forgotten Granada!

Yet here I am not siding with a Trumpian "splendid isolationism." Instead, that there's a largely unexplored middle ground capable of steering between the Scylla of perpetual warfare on the one hand, and the Charybdis of an irresponsible ("fuck you, I've got mine") isolationism on the other hand. Like the sea between treacherous rocks, the conditions of such a passage are constantly changing, so a policy that might have been right in a former decade might not be right for today, or the months and years ahead.

And sometimes, as Jesus suggested, the passage may be as narrow as the eye of a needle. To even *see* it, we may have to offload our own polarizations and selfishness. Our political leaders and strategists—in fact our nation as a whole—might have to get past the polarized tendencies in our own minds. We have to get *wiser*. The greatest military force in the world, when commanded by ignorance, or a two thousand mile wall when commanded by the same, is not going to make us great, is not going to provide our homeland with a true from of security. This isn't to argue against "border security," but it does need to be balanced by the virtues (such as empathy, altruism, and justice) that a great nation, and the leaders of nations, should possess.

Yet the *selfless* empathy of true altruism doesn't even tend to get much airplay in contemporary Western psychology where we've become so alert for any evidence of co-dependency that our vigilance to root out the *counterfeit* versions of altruism leads us to inadequately value the real thing. We wind up throwing out the baby with the bath water. (And the same could be said—going back to Freud—in the attempt of Western psychology to disassociate itself from religion and spirituality).

Yet the practice of altruism lies at the heart of almost every religious tradition—the *caritas* and "good works" of Christianity, the *bodhicitta* of Buddhism, the *mitzvah* of Judaism, Hinduism's *karma yoga*, the *zakat* (tithing and alms-giving) which comprises the third of Islam's "five pillars." Something in the psyche seems to become free from its cramped sense of confinement and self-importance when we put the needs and welfare of others a bit more forward in our minds.

The *lack* of altruism, the lack of a sensitive attunement to others, has led many people in our world to have a frustrated social residue, to feel that they have been "dissed." And this has given rise not only to Trump's base and Brexit, but has also contributed to a lot of the retaliatory violence we've been seeing, whether on the Arab street, or from hate crimes and inner city street gangs in our own country, and in the *mass killings* that have increasing occurred in our elementary schools, high schools, and college campuses.

Between the Sandy Hook Elementary School massacre on Dec. 12, 2012 in which 26 people were murdered and the Valentine's Day 2018 massacre of 17 at a high school in Parkland, Florida, there had been at least 3 dozen *mass* shootings in the U.S. and at least *240 school shootings* nationwide. (Yet with nearly each passing month since, these figures have grown—ever more gruesomely, out of date.) Over half of the mass shooters possessed high capacity magazines, assault weapons, or both. And most of these were *legally* obtained.

Amongst the world's developed countries, this is a uniquely American problem. It's a damning indictment of the role of money in the American political system, and the reluctance of Congress to do anything but smile and curtsy before the powerful gun lobby. The National Rifle Association donated $30.3 million to Trump, plus another $20 million to six Republican senatorial campaigns during the 2016 elections alone. So the needed reforms that are actually supported by the vast majority of American citizens were not to come under Trump's watch and a Republican dominated Senate who wanted to protect the Homeland with *armed teachers* and a giant *wall*. (While the real threat is not murderous Mexicans or Salvadorians—but deranged, heavily armed *Americans*, and American politicians in bed with the gun lobby).

But it is not just those who wield guns, bombs (or tweets) upon their imagined tormentors, who behave as if they've been slighted, disrespected, overlooked, or unheard. Even the less floridly disturbed can face the world with a similar frustrated residue. For when people are suffering in their significant relationships, the *narcissistic wound* is often getting set off, the littlest things seeming huge insults or threats that make us feel we are *not* being loved.

As any therapist who does couples counseling might tell you (see chapter 8) love experienced through such a perspective can be a world of tedious repetition, where the same limitations, the same stupid fights, the same repeating (mythic) pattern keeps happening for people in their love relationships ...as if love has become tainted by neurosis, as if neurosis in itself has a repetitive Echo-like quality, a curse from the gods.

TWENTY-NINE

Who—or What—is Echo?

ECHO HAD BEEN privy to acts of *eros*—between Zeus and his concubines. Yet this led Echo to be duplicitous; to tell Zeus's wife Hera distractive stories that hid the truth of Zeus's infidelities. For this Echo was *cursed* by Hera (the patron goddess of marriage and child-birth). And her curse would be *the inability to initiate conversations.*

Yet when it comes to sexual love, where we have considerable skin in the game, how often are *we* able to tell the truth, the whole truth, and nothing but the truth? And when we can't, what stops us? And how willing are we to endure *the vulnerability of our desire* before we close down, and retreat into lonely valleys and caves?

How readily do we provide even our lovers with the *complete* versions of our "erotic maps," maps that lay us bare by revealing our hidden kinks—precisely what it is that turns us on—or off? And even if we eventually manage to speak up a bit, *why did it take so long? What is it that causes us to lose part of our voice?*

This hindered or missing voice—can we see it not only in the myth that stands behind narcissism, but can we sense it in *ourselves*—and how this missing voice plays itself out culturally, and politically? And if so, what *is* this? And what caused it? Is it shame—that we might be seen as a less than pure image if we told the truth? Is it that someone wouldn't like it, that we might turn someone off, lose political support, or lose the support and love of a dominant figure in our landscape if we told the truth?

Maybe Echo felt she needed to stay on the good side of power—Zeus—and what he represented to her, powerful god that he was. And who in our contemporary world resembles Zeus today—powerful married males whose lives are littered with infidelities?

This very voiceless-ness, that keeps some part of ourselves hidden, bounded, and enshelled—as if inside a closet—*is* Echo. It's also evocative of what James Masterson terms "closet narcissism." (Which I've suggested is also the most common form of narcissism in our culture today). And if so, then Echo may be closet narcissism's paradigmatic figure.

Yet in a narcissistic *culture*—where so many of us have not had our being-ness adequately recognized and supported—then even our elected officials suffer from an Echo-like condition, and find themselves inhibited from speaking the truth.

But archetypal constellations such as those involving Narcissus and Echo can play themselves out in numerous and varied ways. If politically, narcissism's *hubris* prevents us from *living* the truth, then Echo's wounded voice precludes us from *speaking* it. In this regard, it took years and often decades for the women sexually exploited by Donald Trump, Judge Roy Moore, and (allegedly) Judge Brett Kavanaugh to overcome the Echo-like wounded voiceless-ness and shame that is often the lingering, pained residue of sexual abuse.

Yet the perpetrators in these cases, rather than acknowledge their culpability, heaped further shame upon their victims by calling them liars. And this is straight out of the playbook of *hubris*—that is, Aristotle's notion of shaming a victim, and as if this further establishes one's superiority.

Though also like Echo, Trump's apologists tell *distractive narratives* that would deflect attention from the truth—by attempting to re-route our attention toward one Democrat or the other, whenever Trump's latest infraction is revealed. And the cheerleading spin-doctors echoing a narcissistic president—say Kellyanne Conway or Sarah Huckabee Sanders—are thus evidences of an "Echo complex." Yet more crucial is how long Republican legislators continue to remain voiceless, or to merely echo this president—while abrogating their oversight duties, and keeping the nation's political polarization intact.

Echo and Narcissus are a matched pair of archetypes. Like Pluto and Persephone, one comes in the door along with the other. Each are templates floating in the sphere Jung termed the "Collective Unconscious."

They are just in the psychic air we breathe—and have been for thousands of years. And so, if what we won't—or can't—manage to say inhibits us as social beings, best to look deeper into what's going on here, lest we continue to suffer what the myth portrayed as a "mythic curse."

With this in mind, the efficacy of a *couple's therapy* can be judged by the extent to which each member of the relationship has found a voice not previously available, a voice no longer inhibited by wounds from the past. This may signal the release from the archetypal perspective of Echo. It may signal a couple's emerging from the ways they have grown trapped in the Narcissus myth, a myth in which the protagonists are either devaluing or being devalued—a mythic structure within which true relatedness seems perpetually doomed. (Again, as seen in the couple reflected in this book's 8th chapter—though as any marriage counselor would tell you, they are by no means unique).

Psychotherapy itself is predicated on overcoming such a wounded voiceless-ness—going back to Freud's "talking cure." (If we can't even *say* the truth, how can we possibly *live* it? Or put to rest lingering wounds from the past?).

In the myth, Echo feels the thread, the pulse of her desire curling toward Narcissus—and dauntlessly at first, she *chases after him*. Yet before retreating into lonely caves and forest valleys, modern Echoes may have made the "first move" toward a prospective beloved. She may have been the one who first (voicelessly) "winks" on an Internet dating site, or "likes" the other's photo, or the words in another's profile. Echo can hold a torch, and easily "favorite" somebody.

But each of these operations can be done without words, without putting much of her own psychic skin in the game. If in some way like Pluto she's a stalker, then like Persephone, there is also a *wounded fragility* in Echo. And the wound, in some way, is oral. She longs to speak, yet for her there's little room to utter an original peep.

As part of the attempt to validate itself as a legitimate scientific and medical enterprise, the emerging discipline of modern psychology attempted, during the early 20th century, to largely divorce itself from its close cousin—religion, while retaining a less aversive, though still ambiguous relation to myth. The gods and other mythic figures, in essence, became *pathologies*. They became "complexes," repetitive and reoccurring compulsions, or patterns of behavior.

And so, what the ancients called "a curse from the gods" (such as what Echo suffered from Hera) in modern psychological parlance became referred to by different terms. A "repetition compulsion" is one of them. But Echo's reoccurring frustration is, for god's sake, *not* for a penis. It's for an intimate *connection*, and for a fully functional voice that could make that more possible.

But erotic love at times can be messy, wounding, and complicated—even for the gods and other mythic figures. And Echo's traumatic, primal scene arose from a complicated erotic situation—one not even her own, but an erotic triangle involving other figures. In a sense, Echo was an innocent bystander, who got caught between conflicting loyalties—like the child of bickering, adulterous, or divorced parents—*an impossible situation*. And to make matters worse, someone then cuts off part of her voice. It doesn't seem *fair*—and life often isn't—something keenly (and disturbingly) noted by children (and liberals). And the Greek myths faithfully reflect this sense of *tragedy*, perhaps more so than any other tradition.

Echo then—as a figure of "tragic love"—is one of the patron archetypes standing behind enneatype Four. There's the sense of longing—for a distant or unavailable other. And love—when frustrated—can lead to *resentments* (that for Echo, can't quite be *expressed* in the way that others might). So what she does is leave the scene, a retreat into lonely valleys and caves, trailing a hopeless aura, that is also her *aria*, a timeless (and echoing) inner lament: *She feels so un-gotten*. As if the myth, which is also her life, is always more of the same. And everyman Narcissus.

Of her various and subtle facets, Echo is also *love's vulnerability spurned*. She is also *the frustrated eros in any narcissistic encounter*. And in a narcissistic culture, this vulnerable frustration is palpable. For like Echo, so many people are waiting to be heard, to have their being-ness recognized, valued, and embraced.

What the ancients called a *curse* from the gods, we today call a *trauma*, which in German—modern psychology's original language—is etymologically linked with "dream." A trauma is a bad waking-dream we can't seem to wake from. Here we remain shocked, frozen in some way, like in those nightmares where we can't speak, move, or remember. Something isn't working here. Like an amputated leg, we may still feel what *should* be there, but it can no longer be found. Now we are suffering this drama, this dream, this trauma, while playing without a full deck, feeling deficient in some way—until we wake up.

But while presuming to be deficiently or innocently ourselves, *we are every part of the myth of Narcissus and Echo*, this collective dream. Like Narcissus, we are the attempt to preserve a too pure image—and so become estranged from our own being, while being unable to fully receive another in the waking dream we call our lives.

Like Echo, we may bear the psychic residue of couples that have come before us—whether that be our parents, or the betraying philandering of Zeus, or the jealous outrage that Hera displaces onto Echo. And like Echo, we are the traumatized recoil that we've retained from those who have lashed out at us in pain, and the vulnerable residue that remains from our encounters with the narcissism of others; a vulnerability that can then live in uncertainty about the universe's capacity to hear us, to support us or respond to our being, or to our deepest wounds and desires. Like Echo, we are also the wounded inhibited-ness that precludes us from expressing ourselves more fully, and from initiating conversations that we are needing to have.

And so, the unrelenting witnesses of the Me Too movement that have arisen during the Trump presidency seem to be Echo rising up from her wounded, voiceless sojourn in lonely valleys and forest caves…

We are also the concerned mother who would visit fortunetellers. And the far-seeing prophetic voice, which answers her. We are guilty of *hubris*, and are the critical, avenging perspective of *Nemesis* who would punish the crime of *hubris*. *We are all of these facets*—and in the most wakeful part of ourselves, we are like a mysterious pool of water, a pool capable of being a mirror to the divine, or essential world.

Certainly when we are young our parents are like gods to us, and the reproach of a parent can sometimes lead people to close down, to lose part of their own voice. And the same can happen in repressive cultures, whether business, political, or religious. In dealing with important people we may similarly become "tongue-tied" and lose our voice. Guys can get this way in asking pretty girls out for a date. And girls can become tongue-tied as well, if in sometimes differing ways.

In many Islamic countries today, it simply hasn't been safe to speak out... against some of the more questionable notions and policies currently prevailing. In Egypt, Saudi Arabia, Turkey, and Syria for example, journalists and those pressing for reform have often been imprisoned—or worse—for speaking out has become treated as a crime against the state.

And in an American culture that is striving to maintain *its* image of purity—in the guise of political correctness (or while being exported abroad under the banner of "democracy") we similarly have failed to adequately speak out—or even to recognize—some of the more questionable notions prevailing in our own society, not to mention the policies we've attempted to foist upon other parts of the world. For example, the U.S. has made Devil's Bargains in the Middle East with autocratic governments with long histories of human rights violations against their own people—which flies in the face of our nation's core values. This was actually part of the critique made against the U.S. by al Qaeda, and unfortunately, in this instance at least, the critique was a valid one.

In countries such as Egypt this has contributed to a looming instability—and part of the upheaval that has been destabilizing the Middle East as a whole. Though Egypt had been virulently anti-Semitic between 1948 and 1968 during which its entire Jewish population had been forced to flee due to human rights violations, it subsequently became something of a stabilizing anchor in the turbulent sea of the Arab world's relationship to Israel, as well as in the American "war against Terror." But with the Mubarak regime in Egypt ousted by an *Arab* population that had *also* just endured 30 years of human rights violations, there's no guarantee that Egypt's continued support of America's foreign policies will continue into the future.

And this instability has recently been the case in *many* of the poorer countries of that region—which have the largest youth bulges, and the most wide-scale unemployment. *Like Echo, here are voices that have yet to be fully heard from.* But in an age of camera-packing cell phones, in an age of You Tube and Facebook, the long history of human rights violations—that the U.S. government has often turned a blind eye to as part of its Devil's Bargain—will no longer be swept so easily under the Middle Eastern carpet. Our Devil's Bargain may come back to haunt us. (Just as the Devil's Bargain the Republican Party made with Trump is *already* haunting us. In a sense, narcissism *itself* is a Devil's Bargain, one made with the fake parts of the self).

Already the regime of Tunisian President Zine el-Adidne Ben Ali has been toppled. And the same has happened to the Gaddafi regime in Libya. For years the regime ruling Syria has been engaged in the brutal anguish of civil war. And the same might be said of Turkey in its ongoing conflict with the Kurds. Will Jordan be next—or Saudi Arabia? How many cycles of instability will continue to erupt in Iraq, Lebanon or Yemen?

And in speaking of Iraq, Lebanon, and Yemen, will *Iran* continue to fund and foment discord in neighboring countries as it jockeys for power and influence in an ever-shifting political landscape? Yet when Trump casts the Shi'a in Iran as being the sole source of world terror, while cozying up to the Sunnis in Saudi Arabia and offering them over a hundred billion dollars of armaments (while also relocating the U.S. embassy in Israel to Jerusalem, and allowing the unholy triumvirate of Israel's Benjamin Netanyahu, Saudi crown prince Mohammad bin Salman, and Jared Kushner to shape America's foreign policy in the region) what are the implications for healing the Continuing Middle East Crisis?

Will the whole Middle East fragment into a divisive war of Sunni vs. Shi'a—with Russia thrown into the stew to thicken the plot? And should the old regimes continue to fall, which way will these countries go? Will we see a pan-Arab youth movement, aided by Facebook, spreading democracy to the region? Or will they fall into the hands of Islamist rule, or yet further decades of autocratic rulers, who have their own side deals with hegemonic empires?

At times, the inability to speak out has been evidenced not only in Islamic nations ruled by dictatorial regimes that have iron-fistedly held the reins of power for three or four decades but by our own legislative bodies, by our profession of journalism,* and in the reluctance to become a "whistle blower" within any governmental or corporate culture. In retrospect, we can see this now in the run-up to the Iraq war, where relatively few journalists, and even fewer members of congress were willing to speak out in questioning the premises leading us to war. And as for whistleblowers, Trump's cabinet—principally Attorney General William Barr and Secretary of State Mike Pompeo—had been sent forth to make them as voiceless as possible. This, at the behest of America's own autocratic leader, and as part of the scandal that would lend strength for his impeachment.

When it comes to *public speaking*, much of American culture has suffered from an Echo-like speech impediment, for the fear of public speaking has arguably become *America's most common phobia*—again linking the state of our culture to this myth. (And the 5th chapter in this book reflected my own experience of this).

For decades, the U.S. government had been unable to speak—to Cuba or Iran. And even today the two parties in the U.S. government are largely unable to speak to *each other*, and so haven't managed to co-create a more optimal agreement regarding health care. Instead, the party in power has tried to ram its own policy down the throats of the other. The Obama regime passed its Affordable Care Act largely without Republican support. And Trump's Republican legislators have repeatedly tried to repeal and replace it without any Democratic support. Yet with this the case, *who are these people taking themselves to be?* (Whether with individuals, nations, or political parties, such a polarized stance—such an inability to collaborate with others has its own *hubris*—which obscures a deeper truth, and makes true *dialogue* impossible). And so, whenever there are things that we are not yet able to

---

* Though I've found some historical fault on the part of journalists, recently this has been far from the case. In fact, there's good reason that Trump has viewed the press as his enemy. For more and more our journalists have grown emboldened, and are appearing less like *Echo*, and more like *Nemesis* in their willingness to confront governmental *hubris*. As defenders of our democracy, I now *bow* in their direction. And in a political landscape where boundaries are so persistently violated by acts of tribal *hubris*, the boundaries between fact and fiction—and between comedy and tragedy—have grown increasingly thin. And thus, *never has there been a better time to be a journalist—or a comedian*. Trump has offered a career's bottomless treasure chest for both. And if, as Jung had said, "without necessity nothing budges," it may be that Trump's presidency has created an "increased necessity" for American culture to emerge further, not only from its polarization and narcissism in general, but from its collective Echo Complex in particular.

talk about, things which continue to bear a historical wound, *that,* again, is Echo.

That is the Echo who has suffered the curse of Hera, but apparently that was even true in some way when Echo was telling Hera all those stories. For Echo couldn't find a way to talk to Hera about what she knew to be true, and so suffered from a lack of voice *in the first place;* just as Narcissus was plagued by an arrogant inability to love even *before* the curse placed on him by Nemesis, as it was his arrogance and inability to return the love of others that led one of his jilted lovers to cast a prayer to highest heaven asking that Narcissus be doomed to ever fail in love.

From this point of view, the curses encountered in this myth—whether stemming from Hera or Nemesis—offered a means of *personifying* psychic impediments widely suffered by humanity. What we think of as personal neurotic symptoms caused by "failures in the early holding environment," the Greeks viewed as having a more transpersonal etiology, as something emanating from the *gods,* or the archetypal realm. This gave them a way of metaphorically rooting their personal experiences into a larger context than that of their families of origin—or the various categories of *psychopathology.* In this way, their psychology—unlike ours—never had largely severed its connection to the *transpersonal* dimension; it never became so "person-centered," so personalistic—or dare I say it, so *narcissistic.* Unlike ours, it never became so fixated on "the wounded child."

That wounded child in all of us—needs to be compassionately held, in order to recover from our loss of voice; the echoing legacy of traumas still being carried from the past.

Yet this emphasis on childhood wounding needs an augmentation in its perspective, lest our prevailing forms of psychology remain somewhat infantilizing. And for that, modern psychology itself needs to heal from its spiritual divorce—in order for it and the clients it would serve to evolve into a further spiritual maturity.

Just as contemporary members of the Republican party must reclaim their noble, ancestral roots, and evolve beyond the regressive state of merely echoing a King Baby, a narcissistic president.

May all beings find the missing part of their voice.

THIRTY

Narcissism as Spiritual Dissociation:

the Estrangement of Psyche from Spirit

BELIEVING THAT WHO we *are* is what was done to us in early childhood seems an operating premise in much of contemporary psychology—an art and a science still apparently in its infancy. But such a view, at best, only manages to reflect one aspect of our human nature—the conditioned nature of our personality structures. It fails to equally understand and adequately mirror our *essential* nature, and to account for –or model and help point out—forms of awareness no longer being shaped by our conditioning. At times, this can keep our mainstream forms of psychology ego-bound, and ego centered. (But isn't that the problem of narcissism itself?).

Much of our professional psychology has washed its hands of the responsibility to model, reflect, and support a more primal mode of awareness, or relegated this responsibility to the spiritual traditions, if to anyone. In this way our mainstream forms of psychology are often not only mythically dissociated, but *spiritually* dissociated—and are thus less capable of addressing the needs of a population that is *similarly* dissociated.

Such a psychology, unknowingly, contributes to the current perspective of *victimization* (which is what you're left with, not only when you believe that who you are is what was done to you in early childhood, but also when you have a psychology derived from the *medical* tradition, a psychology based upon *pathology*—psychology's version of "original sin").

And from such a perspective, Western psychologists—and I among them—have been trained to be hunters and stalkers—of psychopathology—for that's what we've largely been trained to diagnose and treat; while increasingly relying upon psychopharmacology as the treatment of choice. (At times these medications can be a god-send, but they tend to be *way* over-proscribed, and this "medicalization" often seems to reflect the lack of more skillful therapeutic means—skillful means that might prove to be more *empowering* for the client population that we treat).

Whether the *Bible*, the *Koran*, or Mao's *Little Red Book*, most forms of fundamentalism rely upon some form of scripture, a "holy book" which is thumped and referred to as its ultimate and authoritative guide. Though in the case of American mental health professionals, it is highly unlikely that the *Diagnostic and Statistical Manual of Mental Disorders*—the "bible" of American psychiatry—ever *has*, or ever *will*, lead to a *metanoia*, "a transformative change of heart," a spiritual awakening. (Though the insurance companies also believe in this bible, and will not pay for treatment unless framed by its pathologizing lens).

The 900 plus page doorstop that was the *DSM-IV* provided the definition of Narcissistic Personality Disorder that the *DSM-V* retained in forming its estimate of the disorder in the American population (0 to 6.2 percent). And this ostensibly definitive guidebook listed "Religious or Spiritual Problem" almost as an after-thought—in the "v-codes" near the end of the book, amongst "Other Conditions that May Be a Focus of Clinical Attention," and just prior to "Criteria Sets and Axes Provided for Further Study." (Is this the kind of *language*, the kind of *priority*, the kind of *literature* with which to speak of the *soul*, or to help bring it home from the unrecognized exile in which it suffers?).

Of its 943 pages, the *DSM-IV* devoted a total of *two sentences* to the entire "category" of religious and spiritual problems. And it's hard to know whether this reflects how little it *understands* about religious and spiritual problems, or how marginally it holds their *significance*. But at least psychiatry's official manual recognized there *might* be some kind of problem here, perhaps one worth some further study. It could have been worse—though not much. Our profession of psychology could be *completely* spiritually-dissociated; there could be *no* category indicating that our contemporary psyches and culture have been suffering due to religious or spiritual problems—though this has been the case for much, if not all of human history, and continues to be the case, even today.

And thus our psyches (and culture) might well benefit from an alternative perspective, one that is spiritually informed and soulfully nuanced vs. one that is based on pathology—a version of curing that had its modern origins in Viennese consulting rooms treating hysteria—a syndrome that no longer exists; and in Swiss hospitals treating schizophrenia.

For the ancient Greeks, however, their psychology wasn't *pathology-centered*. Nor was their psychology, mythology, and spirituality dissociated from each other. They were all of a single fabric, and recognized the gods as distinct perspectives arising in one's mind-stream and thus shaping the unfoldment of daily life. The very recognition of "distinct perspectives arising in one's mind-stream" dethrones at once the fiction of a singular *self-hood* and a singular *godhead*—as well as the *hubris* of egoic centrality ("where id is, there shall ego be")—much like Copernicus's recognition that the Earth is not the center of the universe. This leads me to wonder: *Is there something about monotheism that makes monotheistic cultures less able to recognize—or treat—its own narcissism?* (A condition that views *oneself* as the center of the universe). Perhaps we might profit, not only from the perspective and skillful means contained in the world's mystical spiritualities, but also from a psychology that James Hillman roots in "the poetic basis of mind, whose imagination is structured by mythical configurations."

For the Greeks, there were *many* gods, each with their own attributes and pitfalls of passion—like we human beings ourselves. But with the loss of the pagan gods, we have lost the differentiation once provided by a wide *panoply* of divine beings, and the different divine qualities they evoked; parts of our humanity have lost their shimmer and link to divinity. What is "holy" becomes marginalized by professional psychology, as if it's all hokey and non-quantifiable. Or religiously, it often becomes reduced to the terms, imagery, and doctrines of a particular mythology, one with a single victorious deity.

If Judaism and Islam evidence a distrust of the image, a lack of iconic or pictorial figure ("thou shalt make no graven images") then in a largely Christian, narcissistic culture, people seem to believe that "image is *everything*"—and our TV ads further promote this. But all the imagery here refers back to the self. And so a good amount of our attention becomes employed in either trying to draw a favorable attention toward a fictional, idealized image of self, or avoiding the fear of a wounded humiliation—the fear of being seen as a bad image—like someone with a speech impediment. In such a culture people often take their sense of identity in any moment from one of these extremes: identifying with a self that is either inflated, or shamefully inhibited, and voiceless in some way; yet both are "enshelled," in different ways. Thus, there's a lack of awareness, let alone acceptance, for the full range of ourselves—which then translates into a lack of awareness/acceptance of the full range of others. We've learned to place ourselves, each other—and even "God"—in cramped little boxes.

THIRTY-ONE

The Ascent and Crash of the Box & What's Been Left Behind

THE BOX-LIKE CONFINES that result from *identifying* with the self-image, as well as the attempts to embellish or defend it, have several effects. Aside from sustaining a fundamental and widely shared *identity-confusion*, this also encapsulates, fills, structuralizes, and *obscures* the underlying spaciousness of the mind's essential nature. It may also lead to *hypocrisy*, when people—or governments—then try to pass off an overly pure image as being who they are.

A similar identity-confusion can then play out in our regard of other people. For when we're disoriented toward our own deeper nature, we're going to have a distorted view of others. And if we wind up deifying those whom we "look up to" and have placed into idealized boxes—then just as surely, we wind up devaluing them when those we've been celebrating then reveal feet made of clay, feet that don't fit within the idealized box we've erected.

When this "ascent and crash of the box" happens in our love relationships, the previously idealized other becomes devalued, and we have a relationship that suffers from erotic instability, love's confusing and destabilizing mood swings. When some scandal happens with preachers or spiritual teachers, people feel horribly betrayed, may lose their sense of *basic trust* entirely, grow estranged from spirituality itself—or go looking for a new "miracle man." And when the "ascent and crash" happens with more recognized public figures, it gives rise to an obscenely overblown news frenzy. We then are flooded with a procession of fascinating and sordid details,

Internet updates which both delight and appall: Monica's blue, semen-stained dress; the shocking number of Tiger's mistresses, Donald Trump's appalling latest tweet or scandal…

Now we have Greek Tragedy on the hoof, and a presidential blowjob, another president's presumed entitlement to grab women's bodily parts, a golfer's flings out of wedlock—or whatever the latest celebrity scandal—trivializes our collective awareness by captivating our media for several news cycles, as if the dominant happenings in the universe.

In a narcissistic culture where our own true nature has been inadequately recognized, people wind up striving for their "15 minutes of fame," and the attainment of celebrity itself becomes an unconscious life-mission. And if your name already has some kind of "brand recognition," why not run for public office? You can figure out the details of this governing stuff later…Morons are already doing it. (But these days, you may need to share the debate stage with 16 or 20 *other* candidates).

Yet it is not just celebrities for whom an inordinate amount of attention goes into altering and promoting one's image, while hiring publicists or spin-doctors who might airbrush away metaphoric blemishes, helping them to appear in a more favorable light. The American nation itself spends billions of dollars on cosmetics, and cosmetic surgeries. We often spend more time trying to work on our "look" before attending a party, than attending the soul inside the clothes. And if in a narcissistic culture women have come to feel insecure about their looks, their weight, their ageing, their intelligence, and at times can still feel like second-class citizens who aren't being taken seriously—somewhat like Echo; then men are generally *several degrees* more relationally clueless, and often—like Narcissus—are emotionally unavailable, moving through our lives with a shell shielding our hearts.

In such a culture, it is not only public civility, but *eros*—our sense of relatedness—that limps on teetering, uncertain legs. As opposed to many other cultures, in most American cafes or bars (unless drunk or stoned, or the bar is gay) most people one finds interesting will seldom meet your gaze. It's as if there's something *threatening* about having the bounded-ness of our ego structure penetrated by another's gaze. (Or is it a vulnerable shame about our need and desire for greater intimacy?). Whichever it is, people tend to interact socially from an *enshelled* condition—this enshelled condition being one of the most salient characteristics of narcissism itself.

And from this enshelled condition, this bounded island of an isolate selfhood, there's not only a lack of *eros,* but of empathy, and altruism. The richest nation in the history of the Earth then finds itself engaged in a frenzied, hostile, polarized debate about whether it should guarantee healthcare for its own citizens. This is something most other developed countries have managed to provide—more inexpensively, and without all the hoo-ha. Here in the U.S. it's been "every man for himself," a lingering Calvinism, especially amongst conservatives. Out of this there develops an increasing gap between the "haves" and the "have nots," and between the *image* and the *reality.*

This has given rise to a specialized profession: those whose job it is to "spin," to manipulate the image, those who distort the truth toward their own ends. Check out the Fox News Channel, and see what I mean. For this isn't "the news" so much as *a point of view;* quite ironic for a station that prides itself for its objective purity—that of being a "no spin zone."

In a narcissistic culture, Truth, Reality itself—our own very *being*—also become "second class citizens," forever being ignored, or left behind (*not just blue collar workers*). And in the case of Donald Trump, Truth has been completely disenfranchised, replaced by "alternative facts," as if what's *real* has been relegated to an Echo-like status, grown lonely and neglected. What is then valued is not our real selves, or real needs, but our party or *meme* affiliation, and our *image*—or *product.* In this corporate age in fact, the self that is put forward is often treated as a *commodity,* one that we might *market.*

If the Internet has "leveled the playing field," it also transmits so much "noise" today that worthy projects, books, films, and artists often have a *harder* time gaining notice. So many are competing for their 15 minutes of fame that marketing, advertising, and the appeal to demographics then replace substance—not only in the arts, but in broadcasting, publishing, social media, and in the political arena as well. Authenticity is lost, and we manipulate, we learn to project, we buy, we vote—for the *image.*

The United States has become an image-based, lobbyist-driven, and spin-doctored culture, with Madison Avenue and Washington's K Street its Mecca and Jerusalem. But the images we have been offered aren't reminders to worship at the countless (and countlessly overlooked) shrines of the real world. Instead, these images often evoke what feels missing in us, or how we've been left behind—while then touting images of products, policies, politicians, or self-help books that could "make us great again."

Like we really *should be Number One, but haven't been given our due!* This is not only narcissism's lament—but its war cry: an *entitlement* that feels *spurned, neglected, unfairly treated*. And from terrorist groups, to Brexit, to Trump and his base, there have been unbroken echoes of this sensibility. And it gravitates toward a swampy, spiritual and moral numbness whose grandiosity promises much, while providing no real relief.

The falsehoods of polarization, special interests, and demagoguery simply become the new normal. And what continues to fall through the cracks is not only Truth, but the jewel of an *authentic self*—which like Cinderella, has been overlooked and neglected...

CINDERELLA

Off to the ball,
her sisters
dressed to the nines

& strutting their stuff
having learned the ways
of a fallen world

Nobody recognizes
Cinderella. Or that her sisters
are wearing false pearls...

And in our own lives
at what point
do we notice

the soul's
true jewel
has been left

dressed in rags
glowing
amidst the ashes?

VI.
Coming Home:
The Music of What Happens

THIRTY-TWO

The Music of What Happens

> "What is found now is found then.
> If you find nothing now, you will simply end
> Up in an apartment in the City of Death"
> —Kabir

BEFORE HE WAS to be tried for heresy—and disappeared—Meister Eckhart said that there is nothing in the world that resembles God so much as silence. And yet, as Meister Eckhart's brother in silence John O'Donohue writes in his book *Anan Cara: a Book of Celtic Wisdom*, "silence is one of the great victims of modern culture."

O'Donohue said that we live in a visually aggressive age where everything is drawn outward toward the sensation of the image, a "continued netting of everything" where "that which is deep and lives in the silence within us is completely ignored." He said there is "a sinister eviction taking place; people's lives are being dragged outward all the time." And thus, "one of the reasons so many people are suffering from stress is not that they are doing stressful things but that they allow so little time for silence."

This eviction of the soul from its silent depths—and its being dragged outward—are key components of the "mythic dissociation" and "idiot's momentum" discussed in this book. The over-emphasis upon the image, the resulting dislocation of the real self, as well as the "netting of everything" (the netting of stags—Narcissus's favorite pursuit) unmistakably link our eviction with narcissism, a curse-like force that propels us across a flattened Waste Land with little time or space for our own depths, and a consequent failure to recognize those depths in our own wounding, others, or in the world at large.

To the extent that we have been seduced or captured by this momentum, we live in exile from our deeper nature, and from the imageless God hiding silently, spaciously, behind our word "God," if not behind our own eyelids. (Here again, we have two different notions of God, and why Meister Eckhart said "the ultimate and highest leave-taking is leaving God for God"—i.e., leaving one's *notion* of God for an experience of That which transcends all notions). And as the Upanishads tell us, we *are*, truly, "That."

But following some of our inherited, yet spiritually dissociated notions, we often continue to long for what God might confer—while perpetuating a trajectory that continues to keep God veiled to us, veiled and removed to a "Hereafter." And with God posited in a Heavenly Hereafter, we've become disoriented toward—and "dislocated" from—the silent and spacious threshold *to* God, which lies in our own *presence.*

Unless we're facing a particularly challenging situation, witnessing the birth of our first-born, or winning some version of the lottery, the naïve soul customarily thinks that the present moment isn't particularly significant—and so isn't really worth giving our whole-hearted attention. Thus, what's actually arising to meet us often seems disposable in some way—like the beggar or wounded animal in a fairy tale*—a "meaningless interval between intermittent harvests," just a throwaway moment awaiting something *better* to arrive.

The prevailing and unquestioned assumption often seems to be that Reality itself isn't really worth showing up for *most of the time.* And with this being the case, Reality itself seems only too willing to mirror our own assumptions and expectations back to us; not revealing its full splendor to such oblivious and devaluing creatures.

---

* One of the most commonly re-occurring motifs of fairy tales is that of a failing kingdom with a dying king and his three sons. From this Waste Land setting, the three sons set off on a mission to find a source of renewal. Each son on their separate journeys comes to a crossroad, where they encounter a wounded animal or a beggar. The first two sons see nothing here worth stopping for. It is only the "foolish" son, the *dummling*, who stops for the wounded or starving creature, and gives it something to eat. Upon which, the wounded one changes its form, and becomes a kind of soul guide who leads the third son to the very thing that was sought.

In this way, *what is* tends to be experienced without any vivid luster, as if something is deficient or missing in Reality itself. (Though any lack here really lies in the quality of our attention and its "view"—which is often that of facing the moment as if attending a party in which there are no interesting guests). Since the culture we live in tinges and shapes our perception of the world, it is easy to lose sight of the fact that there even *is* an alternative…

Fionn and his band of warrior-hunters, all of them poets, were sitting by the headwaters of the Blackwater in Sliab Luachra, all of them at ease after a great battle fought and won yesterday and before what they were sure would be the greatest of all boat hunts proposed for the morrow.

'A question,' Fionn said. 'Each of us true to himself, what is the music we best like to hear in all the world?'

'The savage, beautiful music of an otter's face,' Oscar said.

'The music of hounds, far off and foamy, just before the stag turns and stands at bay,' Cailte said.

'The screech the screech the screech the screech the squawk and croak croak croak of a heron overflying a mirroring inlet of sea,' Diarmaid O Duibhne said.

'A victory of wild geese all broken up and braying at full height and at full, flapping wingspan, all of this at the first touch of land,' Conan Maol said.

'A whole night in a cave and, as though it had just invented hearing, the sound of a drop of water falling into a well I too would have fallen into had I kept going,' Oisin said.

'A curlew that has been two months away on her breeding ground, the first call of that curlew from her home shore in early August,' Goll mac Morna said.

'The music of Cliodhna's wave washing its broken divinity over my bare feet,' Lughaidh Lagha said.

'And you, Fionn," Oscar asked, 'what music most pleases you?"

'The music of what happens,' Fionn said.*

---

[*] Moriarty, John, *Invoking Ireland,* p.104. Dublin: Lilliput Press, 2005

The above is a passage from the *Fianna* cycle of Irish mythology, hearkening back at least 1500 years, and possibly as long as 2,500 to 3,000 years ago, when iron tools and weapons were first beginning to replace those made of bronze in Europe. The *Fianna* was an elite society of warrior-hunters, and in order to be admitted into its ranks a succession of *initiations* was required. One had to demonstrate athletic prowess—jumping over a branch as high as one's forehead, bending under another as low as one's knee, and to be able to draw a thorn from one's foot without breaking stride. Admission also required the completion of an apprenticeship in poetry, and as I've mentioned earlier, that one treat women well.*

For it may be that lacking these three modes of initiation, a culture will tend to lack body/mind integration, lose its poetic capacity to think in a less literal, more metaphoric way, and not adequately value the feminine—in the process losing vital portions of its collective intelligence.

In an initiated society of hunters who have retained their shamanic roots, notable powers of *attention* were evident, and highly valued. This is clearly reflected in the above quoted passage— where we might stand in awe at the vividly recalled details of the natural world, and the sheer perception of beauty on the wing. This is not an *anti*-nature mythology, such as the one which arose from the Syro-Arabian desert 3500 years ago. And here what's valued—by the *leader* of this band—is Reality itself, or as Fionn himself beautifully phrased it, "the music of what happens."

But when we're sleep-walking through life and dragged forward by an unconscious momentum that fails to perk up for Reality—for *the music of what happens*—our filter of devaluing obliviousness can dull the perception of everything we encounter. It can shade the way we perceive and relate to other people who (if they are not being idealized) may become objectified as not worth fully showing up for. And such was the perspective Narcissus exhibited toward Echo as well as his previous lovers. And Narcissus, whether in his ancient myth, or as he shows up in our contemporary lives, certainly doesn't treat women very well—or for that matter, anybody.

But the "lens" of this devaluing object relation also shades and distorts the way we come to regard *ourselves*—who too often seem unworthy of bringing a keen attentiveness. Without realizing it, we may be

---

* O hOgain, Daithi, *The Lore of Ireland*, p.228. Woodbridge Suffolk: *Boydell Press*, 2006

following—almost continuously—a perfect recipe for cheating ourselves of an original gift.

> Kabir says: "What is found now is found then
> If you find nothing now, you will simply end
> Up with an apartment in the City of Death.
> If you make love with the divine now,
> in the next life you will have the face
> of satisfied desire." (versioned by Robert Bly)

If we don't wake up to the open secret—the riches available in the present moment—then we "simply end up with an apartment in the City of Death." In fact, when we're *not* present, we've deadened ourselves, and are *already* not here—as if we've already taken up residence in that apartment Kabir alludes to, and tries to wake us from.

This deadening loss of spiritual vitality leaves us in a Waste Land where we fail to recognize the present as the gateway to the divine. This deficient experience of the soul then gives rise to "the grasping impulse." Since something seems lacking, and since we're looking for "it" elsewhere than the here and now, we want to import something *else* into our territory. Maybe a little chocolate, a hot lover, or a red convertible would do the trick. 50,000 followers on Twitter might be nice, or a zillion thoughts, one right after the other. Maybe the petroleum resources possessed by other nations are what we really need—and thus worth fighting for. Maybe a presidential candidate who promises "change." Maybe a bomb—or an AR-15 assault rifle advertised "for all your needs." A little of something else (other than what is actually happening or already here) begins to seem like a good idea, as if it might make things better, like an amendment to a soil, or a *soul* that feels lacking.

And in this way our often unrecognized narcissism (that comes equipped with an ungratified devaluing feature) can keep us involved in a near-constant process of egoic activity, an idiot's momentum that fails to fully receive what Reality is already sending our way—while we continue to feel deficient, left behind, frustrated, anxious, pissed off, or bored—and resultantly, keep reaching for something else. For in a narcissistic, consumer society, rather than searching for the grail of our own deeper nature, our quest becomes a never-ending search for the "something else."

THIRTY-THREE

Mind, Space, and the Dislocation of the Essential Self

IN FIRST ENCOUNTERING his visionary pool, Narcissus exhibits a schism, a split in the self. Since the beautiful image—the self being longed for—seems "out there" to him, we might say that he had become locked out of his own Body House, his own *Bodhi* Mind, his attention become oblivious to his own essential *presence*. (And further, that the problem of narcissism *is* this lack of presence, this lack of *"self-realization,"* this inability to realize the value—and *beauty*—that is innate within the self).

And thus, in treating narcissism (that is, in treating the majority of clients who walk into my consulting room) I often find it necessary to re-orient the other's attention in such a way that they become *more* absorbed—but not in an *image* or an *objectification* of the self (which otherwise had been occurring, usually taking the form of an *ideal* image that the client, like Narcissus, can never quite grasp).

Instead, what I've found useful is redirecting awareness to the client's own sense of *presence*, that their fundamental "dislocation" has failed to adequately *recognize*, or *value*.

The emergence of an ego, the formation of an assumptive, separate self, is a *developmental achievement; a necessary station in development.* (And in the developmental model provided by Spiral Dynamics, this first emergence of a self—as distinct from the tribe—only *begins* with the Red *meme;* the third of Spiral Dynamics eight developmental stages, and one of six "first-tier *memes"*—which is a "tier" who all believe that their perspective is the one best, or "true" point of view).

There is thus a significant difference between having *developed* an ego structure, and being so encapsulated by that structure that we've become *imprisoned* by it, losing the capacity to freely come and go from its vantage, and losing our access to the boundless (while ever questing for what seems to be *missing,* or bracing ourselves against what we fear might happen next).

Here, along with the failure to access a natively available freedom and its more spacious and expansive view, there's been a loss of *basic trust.* And if the natural flow of Reality can't be trusted, *we're really on our own here*—orphaned from our origins, and jerking around anxiously, like a junkie, or a fish out of water, and with a sense of loss like the first mythic couple in Genesis… as if we've become banished from an Eden, a Paradise that's been lost.

And exiled from a metaphoric Eden, we begin to long for what (only seemingly) is no longer here, what can no longer be found. And such a forlorn, orphaned perspective can become what is living our life. And in fact, to the extent that the developmental "achievement" of ego consciousness is seldom followed by *further less egocentric developmental stages,* it becomes inflexibly established as a culture's *consensual reality.* And such a "reality" can be not only deficient and anxious, but walled-off, erotically unavailable, politically polarized, imperious, militant, and *fiercely defended…*

Teachings that would dethrone the ego and its prevailing world-view become seen as "heretical" (by the Blue *meme)* or banished, devalued, marginalized in some way. They become seen as hierarchical, sexist, and authoritarian (by the Green *meme)* or too woo woo and unverifiable (by the Orange *meme)* to be practical for a world that we think of as "real."

Our myths then become filtered through a narrow, exoteric view; and religion becomes ethical and moralistic, no longer mystical. Our psychology becomes divested of "spirit." And we have police-state prohibitions against mind-altering drugs—yet a vast increase both in prisons, as well as prescription drugs deemed legal; many of which would treat our existential *anxiety,* if not our *terror*—an anxiety, a terror, that is the inevitable bi-product of our *loss of presence.*

For presence—to the human soul—is like water to a fish; the native "environment" in which it flourishes. And like a fish out of water, when we become dissociated from presence, we begin to anxiously thrash on the shores of our lives, to feel agitated and bereft.

The collective *anxiety* that inevitably follows our spiritual dissociation is legally acceptable. In fact, political parties as well as the advertising industry play upon this anxiety to market their feeble cures for it. While drugs also deemed legal are often prescribed for this widely occurring condition. Yet for the growing dependency upon anti-anxiety drugs, our collective anxiety of late only seems to be dramatically *increasing*.

The alarming, vivid reflection of this occurred in February 2016, when *The American Journal of Public Health* reported that the number of Americans filling anti-anxiety prescriptions had increased 67% between 1996 and 2013. (Apparently, while the incidence of narcissism had been on the rise, so had our anxiety—and as well our opioid addictions). Overdose deaths from these drugs have also increased. Benzodiazepine-based prescriptions for anti-anxiety drugs such as Valium and Xanax now account for 30% of the deaths from prescription drug overdoses.

Here, a "scientific," and often spiritually disoriented form of therapy (on the part of the Orange *meme*) has attempted to treat what is often a *spiritual* problem with *psychopharmacology*—rather than teaching people some rather simple things that would allow them to access the more parasympathetic, less anxious part of their own autonomic nervous system.

Here I'm not suggesting that anti-anxiety drugs are "bad," in fact it's a good thing that we now have them available as back up. What I *am* suggesting is that they should be more conservatively proscribed —as a treatment of *last resort*—not the first thing that is reached for, an often disempowering band aide that substitutes for a patient's deeper development and self-mastery.

Since anxiety is a natural outgrowth of the *loss* of presence, it isn't surprising that in nearly 40 years of private practice as a psychotherapist that I can't recall a single highly motivated client suffering from anxiety—and willing to put in the time—who hasn't found relief from their anxiety through some version of *the practice of presence.*

But this requires that psychotherapists themselves have access to their own presence, adequately value it, *and know how to teach its access to their clients*. It requires psychotherapists to figuratively take off their medical aprons, and be less the gateway to pills, and more the *psychopomp*, "the guide of souls."

I find it strange that teaching a therapy client how to be an active partner in shifting their own assemblage point, while deconstructing the ego's point of view (grown to become a culture's consensual reality) has commonly been so *overlooked* by modern psychology's prevailing mainstream. And I find it equally strange that throughout history we've seen so many examples of spiritually developed people —those whose vision pierced the veil of their culture's consensual reality—who have either been largely ignored and marginalized, or hunted down and condemned; poisoned like Socrates, imprisoned like Nelson Mandela, assassinated like Martin Luther King, publicly executed like Hallaj, crucified like Jesus.

Lacking such an *enlightened* perspective, our *own* anxious hopes, fears, plans, self-idealizations, avoidances, and ruminations all seem to occur within a self-enclosed mental envelope that forms around an *image* of the self—which is who or what we are taking ourselves to be—while we are seldom fully present, or better attuned to the actual unfolding of reality.

These hopes, fears etc., further shape our sense of *psychic space,* making the space more claustrophobic, encapsulating our view, and in a way that increases a sense of separation from life as a whole. And enshelled now and apart from the rest of life, something feels existentially "missing"—which is the ego's plaintive, forlorn lament. And then we feel driven by compulsive, compensatory activities that attempt to fill in the ego's sense of deficient emptiness. And without some halting of this claustrophobic and driven momentum, these features make it nearly impossible for the ego to feel *supported by,* or even to recognize "actuality."

Here the ego's identification with its own separate *image* becomes a barrier to what lies beyond that image—which is Reality itself, but also, the experience of (unconfined) psychic *space*. For as the contemporary spiritual teacher A.H. Almaas (Hameed Ali) has pointed out, the self image "is what fills the space, what structuralizes it; so only an individual who can let go of identification with the self image will be able to experience space."*

---

* Almaas, A.H. *The Void,* p.85. Berkeley: Diamond Books, 1986

The gazing practices evoked in this book are thus intended to shift awareness from the identification with the self-image, thus making accessible the experience of unconfined psychic space, which is also the portal for wisdom to arise. Such practices give us the skillful means through which we can shift our own assemblage point; and in such a way that we not only become more familiarized with non-conceptual space, but assisting in the recognition that we can actually *take refuge in it*—refuge in our own deeper nature—which is the ultimate, and best refuge of all. (Though this shift also represents the death or deconstruction of the egoic perspective, the "death of Narcissus").

And it would be further empowering to employ such practices *in conjunction* with actively noting and working with the forms of ego-encasement that naturally present themselves in the course of our daily lives—i.e., the very "encasements" that have been filling and obscuring this spaciousness.

For here both "spiritual" and "psychological" approaches can work in concert, rather than continuing the commonly prevailing "divorce" of one from the other. And I'll give an example of how psychological insight can be de-constructively employed—revealing the mind's underlying essential spaciousness—in the following sub-chapter…

※

Uncovering:
Pulling the Sheets on an Object Relation

The broadest, yet most succinct definition I've been bringing to narcissism is "taking oneself to be what one is not" (all the identifications and object relations that obscure presence, Buddha-nature, "pure awareness" itself). I've thus found it helpful to train those whom I work with *how to better recognize* the object relations currently at play, in the issues that their daily lives lead them to face.

The client is reminded that object relations contain three components—three components very *different* than the three found in *rigpa*—and are then asked to see if they can identify all three of these components in their current dilemma.

As suggested in the latter part of this book's 8th chapter, the first of these facets lies in being able to identify *the self image component* of an object relation. This is revealed by undertaking the following inquiry: "*Who, or what, are you taking yourself to be here?*"

The second component of an object relation is revealed by asking: "*Who, or what—are you taking the world to be here?*" And the third component is revealed by asking: "*What is the **emotional tone** running through the first two concretized assumptions?*"

For example, someone currently struggling with their inner critic might come to recognize that who they are taking themselves to be is "a shamed, inadequate person being judged." And who they are taking the other or the world to be is "an entity who is being critical and judging them." And the emotional tone running through these two concretizations might be frustration, anger, or some semblance of an anxious, shame-filled, vulnerable inadequacy.

And just as we might come to see that in varying moments we might be each and every figure in the myth of Narcissus and Echo, we come to see that each of the three components of an object relation are *also* part of us. Though in terms of the latter, we are usually projecting the second component of an object relation onto the rest of the world. Which in turn taints our vision of the world in a way that can undermine our sense of *basic trust*.

These three inquiries, by their very nature, tend to shift awareness into a more objective, or witnessing mode—what Western psychology terms "the observing ego," or what Freud termed "even hovering attention" (the style of awareness Freud touted for analysts). These inquiries can also help us to more vividly recognize the cognitive structures (or object relations) we've become encapsulated by, and that have been limiting awareness.

And once these object relations have become more *visible*, more conscious and better *recognized*, we begin to be freed from our *fusion* with them. And then, quite naturally, such object relations may begin to dissolve, or self-liberate on their own.

And as these cloud or shell-like structures begin to dissolve, what is left, vividly cohering, is awareness itself, a spacious, undivided, un-encapsulated awareness; a spacious awareness that not only has a heightened capacity for cognizance (or *gnosis*) but has an innate sense of *contentment* and *ease*, without anything external needing to be manipulated, improved, or imported.

But if a mind that is encapsulated (and *lacks* spaciousness) impairs intuition—while making us anxious, and heedless to our deeper nature—then this isn't something *only* manifested by people deemed to be narcissistic, or those suffering an anxiety disorder. *Nearly everyone in our culture is more or less encapsulated and oblivious in this way—probably for the majority of each day.*

For this reason, when the majority of a culture is largely deviated or dissociated from essential nature, one of its outcomes—narcissism—becomes so global and widely occurring that it spreads not only through *much of the population,* but it also spreads *beyond the discrete boundaries of conventional diagnosis.*

For narcissism, as I'm reflecting it here, is not only a *personality disorder*—which is how it is viewed by the *DSM 5;* it could also be viewed as an *identity disorder,* as well as an *attention disorder.* In the broadest sense, narcissism is the "Mother of all Disorders," just as the "narcissistic wound" (of not having our true nature recognized and valued) is the "Mother of all Wounds."

And to the extent narcissism has become so pervasive in a culture, its diagnosis can be less than fully useful when *only* employed as a diagnosis for individuals. For it's a "dis-ease" nearly all of us are suffering now, though in various ways, and to varying degrees.* Which is why significant portions of this book have attempted to reflect narcissism's broader and historical, if sometimes unrecognized outlines, and in particular how these contours manifest *culturally.*

For if spiritual teaching and psychotherapy both contain some element of a critique of the ego's point of view, the individual ego does not arise in a vacuum separated from everything else—though the ego *tends to experience itself as encased inside a vacuum and separate from everything else.*

And so, a re-visioning of narcissism must include a cultural critique of the environment which spawns and propagates it, a critique of a culture's prevailing assumptions, motivations, idealizations, and aversions, a

---

* Just as there's a variance in *severity* between suffering some of narcissism's traits, and a full-blown Narcissistic Personality Disorder, there's a variance in *the traits recognized* by one *meme* of psychologists, and those recognized by another. My view has been that there's really quite a wide *spectrum* in narcissism—from a horrifically toxic version at its most extreme (as in a *malignant narcissism* portrayed by Fromm as "the quintessence of evil")—to what's now become normative, "the narcissism of everyday life." (The *DSM5* recognizes neither). There's been dueling views of *the same syndrome*—and thus, widely ranging estimates of its prevalence.

critique of what it values and ignores, a critique of its approach to religion, psychology, and government, a critique of its regard of the non-human world, *a critique of its point of view.*

Similarly, a re-visioning of narcissism would almost have to provide a more nuanced and "heretical" view of the myth standing behind it, one provided by a less ego-centric *meme.* For a narrow, limiting, *meme*-bound view of the myth has narrowly impacted both our *conception* of narcissism, and how it might be *treated* (which then *remain bound* by the narrow perspective of "first tier *memes*").

And when the *DSM* tells us that narcissistically disordered personalities in America could be as insignificantly low as 0% of the population, it might be evident to even a moderately observant layman that here narcissism *is being narrowly conceived.* Which is why this book has been arguing for a *larger,* more inclusive "net" for narcissism, not the smallest imaginable. In fact, as police chief Brody famously said in the movie *Jaws: You're gonna need a bigger boat!*

And since narcissism is really a larger, more inclusive phenomenon than is commonly recognized, what seems to aid *the transformation of narcissism,* also aids *much else* that collectively ails us. And this is also why treatment plans that include teaching therapy clients how to shift the nature of their customary, fixated awareness—through such means as inquiry, meditation, or various forms of transformational gazes—turn out to be quite efficacious for nearly everyone, regardless of the diagnostic category into which they've been lumped.

All of us, to the extent we are identifying with, or encapsulated by our ego or personality structures, could be thought of as having a *personality disorder,* or for that matter an *identity disorder*—that is, a confusion about *who we really are.* And bored, agitated children in classrooms are only a small fraction of the population whose attention is distracted, who suffer from an "Attention Deficit Disorder."

Narcissism, as I've come to regard it, is the composite of *several* disorders, several forms of deficiency that ensue from the loss of presence, the loss of being—and the failures of the holding environment to adequately *mirror and support* that presence, that being.

This loss of presence, this loss of being, this condition of narcissism…is very similar, if not *identical,* to what Joseph Campbell termed "mythic dissociation." (Which he variously reflected as the failure to "elicit and support the sense of awe before the mystery of being." The failure to "support and be supported by this sense of awe before the mystery of the presence and the presence of a mystery." The failure to awaken "a sense of awe and mystery and gratitude for the ultimate mystery of being." A failure to say "yea to the world as it is").

In this light, we might view narcissism's *entitlement*, its lack of *empathy*, its loss of *humility* and its resulting *grandiosity*, merely as the unfortunate symptoms of an earlier, and more primal loss, the loss of one's essential nature, the loss of being-ness itself.

This is a primal loss that can become hard-wired into the personality structure far earlier in its onset than adolescence or early adulthood. (Though in cultures, it's what *keeps* them adolescent). And culturally, this condition in turn *conditions us*…is just in the air we breathe. And it's been *with us* forever. For this is also the condition Buddhists term *Samsara* and at once, the very condition alluded to in humanity's mythic exile from the Garden of Eden.

And so, this loss of an "Edenic being"—and a composite of these disorders—is endemic and epidemic in American culture at large; not just in our politics. For when you turn on the TV, go online, or even should you read the *DSM5*, there's not much here that's mirroring and supporting the soul's deeper nature, its being, its presence. So narcissism—"taking ourselves to be what we're not," a dissociation from the soul's true nature—is also not just a problem of 0 to 6.2 percent of our population.

For this disoriented, multiply-disordered condition is shared by *you* and *me*—and every *he*, *she*, or *them*—if to differing degrees. Like Narcissus—all pronouns, all personality styles, *all of us at times*—are a bit agitated, anxious, and *confused*. (This book—in its better moments—a guide for the perplexed).

For nearly all of us live much of each day as if exiled from Eden, like a fish out of water, or a plant uprooted from the ground (of being). And sadly, much of the time, so distracted by "the ten thousand things" that we fail to recognize the beauty that exists around us, within us, and within each other…

This is the "bad news" of a bewildered, orphaned condition, which is reflected daily on our TV screens, in the world's needless suffering, its various theatres of cruelty and ignorance, in the products and policies that promise much, while failing to deliver us from the discontents of our exiled condition.

I know it sounds bleak. But I've saved the best for last...

Here's the *good news* that has yet to be offered—whether on Fox News, CNN, in the *DSM,* or on the Home Shopping Network: Beneath our mythically dissociated, culturally transmitted, polarized, self-absorbed and shared obliviousness, there's a sacred, timeless, essential nature... just waiting for us to discover it.

THIRTY-FOUR

Egoic Will as a Feature of Mythic Dissociation

Our egos, so much of the time, are quibbling with life *the way it is*. Like other battles this book has evoked, this is a battle that can never be won. For when our own wills are pitted against nature in this way, against the will and flow of Reality—that is, against what is actually taking place—then we can only come away from this encounter feeling frustrated and unsupported, while assuming that we are failing in our lives due to a weakness in our will, or from life's deck being stacked against us.

The truth here, though, may not be that life's deck is stacked against us, or that our wills are too *weak*. Rather, we're often running the wrong *kind* of will, a fussy, controlling, *egoic* will. In every moment life is actually serving us our next course, but we seem to have special requirements, and want life served to us "our way." We're like Goldilocks constantly quibbling with the porridge before us now, holding back until we find something that's "just right."

But unfortunately, so much of life simply doesn't come that way. And so, we tend to experience a considerable amount of "glitch" as we encounter life, a considerable amount of frustration with life *as it is*—which continually seems to veer away from the image of our self-constructed ideal. And for this reason we experience a considerable amount of dissatisfaction and suffering that isn't actually *necessary*.

There's certainly a poignant element of *grief* that just seems built into life—for example, the fact that (if we're *lucky*) we're going to get old, develop diseases of various kinds, and eventually die. And death will also come to everyone that we love, everyone we care for. Everything upon this schoolhouse Earth, everything that has a form, is only temporary and on loan...

But there's also a great deal of suffering that isn't *compulsory*, that isn't actually necessary for us to go through—the kind of suffering that psychotherapists and spiritual teachers attempt to alleviate. And *this* kind of suffering largely involves some kind of disorientation or unskillful-ness in the way we *react* to reality, some way that we're being un-necessarily oblivious, controlling, polarized, or resistant toward what is actually unfolding. When you put it under a magnifying glass, the actual *cause* of a good amount of our suffering stems not from the object or event *itself*, but from our *reaction* to it.

I may have wanted it not to rain today, so that I can play golf. I may wish that someone would see or treat me differently than they do, and as long as I can't accept the rain, or the fact that Suzie or daddy doesn't relate to me differently than they do, I'm going to suffer because of it. Yet if I can hold this all more spaciously and simply accept the rain (and that perhaps the universe had something else in store for me to do today) or can simply allow Suzie or daddy to have their own experience *exactly as it is*, then I find, surprisingly often, that any *suffering* drops out of the equation, for I'm no longer having a battle of wills with *what's so*, no longer experiencing life from inside a frustrating object relation, nor being impeded from experiencing the fullness of my own being.

This issue of egoic will—the disorientation toward Reality as it is currently displaying itself—is one of the (many) features of our "mythic dissociation." For as Joseph Campbell once said, the first function of myth is "awakening in the individual a sense of awe and mystery and gratitude for the ultimate mystery of being. In the old traditions—the very old ones—the accent was on saying yea to the world as it is."*

The mythological passage I've quoted from the Irish *Fianna* cycle would thus be a good example of the "old tradition"—and you can't top the Irish for mingling wisdom with poetic flair. For in the old Irish tradition, "poet" and "seer" (those who possess a visionary, prophetic capacity) had been inseparably linked, with the same Irish (Gaelic) word (*"file"*) used for them

---

* Campbell, Joseph. *Pathways to Bliss: Mythology and Personal Transformation*, p. 104. Novato: New World Library, 2004.

both; and why even today, the Irish continue to value their poets in a way that most cultures haven't.*

Like a member of the *Fianna* ducking a branch, in Ireland I have stooped, lowering my head—in order to enter mythological structures such as the megalithic passage tomb at Newgrange. It was built approximately 5,200 years ago, making it over 600 years older than the Giza pyramids in Egypt.

If history ("his story") is a story most commonly told by the male victors, we have largely lost an awareness of the truly ancient and sophisticated mythological traditions of *pre*-Christian Europe, which are the oldest mythological traditions in the world. The earliest cave art from Europe for example, pre-dates Christianity by 38,000 years (while fundamentalist Christian sects such as the Unification Church tell us that the universe was created by God only 6,000 years ago). Though in truth, next we had the Neolithic, the early planting cultures, followed by the great Bronze Age traditions, which in turn were followed by the Indo European warrior traditions, and then the Greek followed by the Roman, and only then do we get the Christian tradition, followed by the Arthurian quest mythology in the 12th century.**

But to return to Ireland, the astronomical knowledge of those who built the tomb at Newgrange was such that at precisely the Winter Solstice the light of the rising sun enters the roof-box at Newgrange and illuminates the passage of the inner chamber. While culturally, in being a Celtic, island nation—one that retained the roots of a strong and ancient oral tradition—in the Irish soul a pagan, pre-Christian mythopoeic sensibility was never entirely paved over as it had been through most of Europe. And it makes Irish culture uniquely rich and distinctive. For this sensibility lives on and remains visible, not only in such monuments as Newgrange, but in song, myth, poetry, story-telling—alive in the vocal, lyrical exuberance of the Irish people themselves.

But in cultures *lacking* a mythopoeic orientation that might remind us to perk up toward the mystery actually unfolding here and now, we at times become like a tomb that's been sealed over and can't receive the living

---

* O hOgain, p.426-430
** Campbell, Joseph. *Transformation of Myths Through Time*, p. 214; though Campbell here references the cave paintings at Lascaux, I reference the still older Cave of El Castillo in Northern Spain, which according to radiocarbon dating is just over 40,000 years old.

daylight. We've officially entered Kabir's "apartment in the City of Death." In this way "Reality" (with a capital "R") and *ourselves* seem to be *two different entities,* although this is not really the truth. It's merely as if the ego is wearing a full body condom that acts as a shield, a shell, a membrane of separation that cuts us off from the rest of Reality, from what is transcendent, and from the possibility of being infused by the unconfined conduit of presence. In the process of this dissociation we have ceased to identify with what is most real in ourselves. Such a fixated condition might be seen as a *spell, trance, or curse*. And wasn't that the very condition of Narcissus, who lived under the curse placed upon him by Nemesis?

Today it seems that most of us are living at the effect of such a curse or trance—one that not only hinders our capacity to love or experience beauty, or to feel supported by the actual flow of reality, but also blocks the cause-less joy of simply being *alive*.

This "trance of narcissism" inhibits our capacity to know and experience ourselves in a deeper way, and the effects of this trance would be more readily noticeable if the majority of other human beings weren't *similarly* entranced. If in a nutshell this is the "bad news," then what are we to do about this problematic state of affairs?

Awakening from our entrancement can happen *right now*—in *any* moment. This is good news. Yet *staying* awake in a largely slumbering kingdom will require all the commitment, will, and perseverance we can possibly muster. In fact, like all ideals, this is more like something to aim for, rather than something likely to be fully achieved. And even then, no single tool is going to be adequate for the *enormity* of the undertaking. And aside from transformational gazes, meditation and prayer, empathic mirroring, cultivating vulnerability, processing early wounds and their defenses, solitude in nature, intimate relationships that recognize and support being-ness, inquiries that deconstruct object relations, and other strategies suggested thus far, something that I have found helpful in beginning to free attention from this fixated condition is what I've come to call "the little two step."

THIRTY-FIVE

Two Roads &
the "Little Two-Step"

Before introducing the reader to the practice of "the little two step," it might be helpful to preface it, by first introducing two concepts. Which I'm about to do—yet in two different ways…

In the spiritually insightful introduction to his new translation of the *Bhagavad Gita,* Stephen Mitchell (in paraphrasing Jesus) suggests that the essence of Judaism is "to love God with all your heart, and to love your neighbor as yourself"—just as the essence of Hinduism is "to let go."

These two statements, he tells us, "are different entrances into the same truth which is the beginning and end of all spiritual practice." These two statements—these two approaches to the same truth—have long been identified as the *via positiva* and the *via negativa*…

The *via positiva* is a "holy affirming," a great and impartial generosity of heart extended to all that is. Its stance would embody an inclusive *YES* to all that is objectively arising, seeing "this too" as part of the mysterious unfoldment of the Universe, Divine Will, or the Tao. In this way, the *via positiva* is a progressive *identification* with more and more of the manifest world, eventually leading to the realization of non-separation, or as it's been expressed in Hinduism, in a phrase that keeps re-surfacing in this book: *"Thou art that."*

One of the spiritually efficacious virtues of the *via positiva* is that it effectively side steps the *aversive* impulse, as well as the tendency to be *heedless,* or *devaluing* toward our experience, other people, and towards Reality itself. (To me, these virtues suggest that the *via positiva* may be especially helpful in the transformation of narcissism; though as we will see, the same could be said for the *via negativa*).

The *via positiva* is a "perking up" to what's right in front of our face. This *is* it! To assent to and fully *embrace* the other, the object—or "what is"—that's the essence of the *via positiva*. We might frame this as a kind of impartial love, or as "a recalibration of the will," maximal open-ness, or simply, the complete absence of resistance or aversion.

In contrast, the *via negativa* has been termed "a holy negating," for it is saying *neti, neti*—no to this, and no to that, a progressive *dis-identification* from more and more of the manifest world. Here awareness is employed somewhat like a machete, and the deconstructive intent is to continually chop away all the beliefs, assumptions, identifications—all the cognitive structures that *obscure* our reception of God, ultimate Truth, Reality itself. (The *Dzogchen* term *Trekchö** in fact, means *to chop*, or *thoroughly cut through;* and precisely with the above intent).

The spiritually efficacious virtue of the *via negativa* is that it helps to deconstruct the *clinging* impulse. And as our clinging to conceptual structures or outcomes is relinquished, the underlying sense of peace, the underlying sense of space ("non-deficient emptiness") becomes shiningly evident. Paradoxically, when we *let go of everything,* we are no longer *separate* from everything.

And thus, the *via negativa* also leads to non-separation, or "Thou art that." In different moments, or for different people, one or the other of these approaches may prove to be more useful, but both *vias,* both roads, lead to the same boundlessness, the same undivided immanence.

Here's the other, less prosaic way I'd think to say it...

> I know of a road that says "no," only "no"
> to every hillock, every rounding curve,
> "no" to everything it passes...
>
> This road is like a man
> who wants to hear from his King
> and with such fervor, he just can't bear

---

* The allusion to *Trekchö* thus stands behind the title of Chogyam Trungpa's seminal 1973 book, *Cutting Through Spiritual Materialism.*

even the emissaries from the Palace
—and for long stretches, all
seem but "emissaries"

Yet there's another *via*
which says only "yes"
to everything arising:
cloudy days and lizards,
road-kill and jalopies farting petrol…

This road is like a woman
for whom all things are a door
that only opens, always "yes"

to Nubians, Puerto Ricans, every
crack in the pavement,
barking dog
and happenstance
seems to find its way
into her eager assent

Remarkably, these two roads
like lovers following opposite directions
happen to meet at the end of their journey

And there they were married
long ago
before there were doctrines

The "little two step" is a *via positiva* approach. This is a practice that begins to recalibrate our *attention* and our *will* so that we can begin to leave ego consciousness behind—by coming into the immanence of *presence*.

It's as if presence is a dimension of being that the ego can't quite enter, and so it's a good way to say "goodbye" (at least temporarily) to the perspective of the ego and its sense of fixation—its grasping, aversion, and heedlessness, its "idiot's momentum," its being stanced in either the past or the future, its attaching to either pleasure or pain—in other words, its sense of mundane, bounded confinement.

If as Mircea Eliade had suggested, that since the Middle Ages the West has lost something in terms of initiatory rites and practices, then we would no doubt profit by going back to what Joseph Campbell calls "the old tradition"—that of saying "yea" to the world as it is presently displaying itself. And saying "yea" to the world as it is presently displaying itself, *is precisely what enables us to enter presence.*

This, in fact, would comprise an important, largely missing "initiatory" element; one that is essential to the transformation of narcissism. I've thus found it fitting to begin bringing this book to a close by discussing in greater detail the practice of presence—or at least a version of it.

Like a golf pro who spends much of his time on the driving range recalibrating the tendency to slice or hook on the part of his students, I spend a good amount of time in the consulting room recalibrating the lack of presence in those who work with me. And as an adjunct to individual or couples sessions, at a certain point in my work with people I've invited them to join periodic retreats held throughout the year that attempt to provide some of the initiatory elements that our culture has largely failed to develop or provide. These are retreats that center on *the practice of presence,* and where the simple (not *easy*) intent is to spend *every* moment in a long weekend *opening fully to the present moment;* and *especially* those moments when attention might lapse: during a retreat's transitions, its rest periods, walking to the next event; and its work periods, or whatever you do in the bathroom.

One of the virtues of the practice of presence is that it enables us to activate a central pivot found in all mystical religion, without requiring that we buy in to the particular ethnic and cultural accretions that may surround any particular religious denomination. And here I've found "the little two step" to be a model exercise.

There is nothing particularly novel about "the little two step" in that a developed person—in those moments he or she is functioning in a "developed" way—is naturally embodying a style of attention more or less along its lines, i.e., an attentive and allowing mindfulness, completely absent of attachment or aversion. It is a simple, foundational practice that provides a basic re-orientation toward Reality—yet at the same time, it can profoundly shift what Toltec shamanism refers to as "the assemblage point."

There is nothing "extraordinary" that the little two step makes available to us—in that it merely realigns our vision in the direction of what Tibetan Buddhism's *Mahamudra* teachings refer to as "ordinary mind"—a mode of awareness which shares something in common with the band of warriors led by the mythical Fionn MacCumhaill; a mode of awareness that is not dissociated from the senses, from nature, from our *own* deepest nature. It gives us two simple steps that can enable us to enter presence, and by so doing, helps us to better attune to "the music of what happens."

But to the extent that we may have been previously running a more heedless, driven, aversive, or oblivious mode—an attentional style that has literally "lost its senses"—what is truly "ordinary" (read "natural" or "innate") does turn out to be quietly "extraordinary" in a way.

As I prepare to describe this simple exercise, I somehow feel called to point out what may or may not be obvious: if you just read the words that follow, the *description* of this exercise—without actually practicing it in earnest—it won't seem like much. It won't do much for you, or be any more fulfilling or nourishing than reading the menu in a restaurant, while failing to actually eat the meal.

In other words, if we don't slow down the trajectory of grasping, aversion, or indifference—what I term "idiot's momentum"—if we just keep speeding along looking to acquire more conceptual information, looking for something external to fill us, entertain us—or something to judge or get into an argument with—we will wind up being obscured towards something that could be an *antidote* to the ego's narcissistic, devaluing, or oblivious stance toward reality.

The little two-step goes like this: *Begin with where you are.* Simply and fully take in what you are actually *seeing* now—by disengaging from the stream of thoughts and employing your eyes in an unfiltered way, *as if they were a movie camera objectively panning the horizon of where you actually are.* Spend a few moments simply viewing your immediate environment in as objective a way as you can, without allowing interpretation or judgment to deflect your fresh reception of the visible world. Here all you are doing is seeing, pure seeing, completely empty of any bias, attachment, heedlessness, or aversion…

Next, allow your awareness to fully let in what you are actually *hearing* now, the sounds of this moment, sounds, pure sounds, sounds both near and far. *It's like you're listening now the way a tape recorder would listen*—completely absent of any interpretation or judgment. *Allow yourself to hear the world on its own terms.* To note both its sounds and its silences. Simply listen to "the music of what happens."

Then, begin to freshly note what you are kinesthetically sensing in your body, whatever flutters of sensation there might be—whether heat, frictive agitation, density, or stillness. And note your posture, your skeletal alignment, and the muscular tension that may be present if your skeletal structure isn't aligned on top of your sit bones—all of this received emptied of judgment, you're just wanting to register whatever is here.

(And if you do happen to note a muscular tension in your body, do feel free to shift your posture, such that each of your spinal disks become like golden coins, each one resting upon, and supporting each other. Relax into this innately available spinal structure…and allow it to support you, without your muscles having to do any work at all).

Lastly, begin to allow yourself to simultaneously receive *all three* of these senses, the visual, auditory, and kinesthetic. And with this receptive composite of your sensory experience, there's nothing you have to *do* about any of it, just receive. *All of this is "step one"—to allow the composite of your actual sensory experience to be a kind of meditation object with which you are making contact—and to turn up your receptivity toward it.*

It's actually not a small thing to be able to isolate and activate the "control knob" of our receptivity toward Reality. It gives us another option than our more egoic, knee-jerk reactivity toward our experience, and toward life as a whole. And it's often easier to "recalibrate the will" if we start by becoming more receptive to these sensory perceptions, which seem to have a more objective basis, and thus tend to be less initially fraught with attachment or resistance than is often the case with our hopes, fears, and the more emotional parts of our experience.

Though once our will has begun to become more pliable and receptive towards these sensory experiences, the *entirety* of our experience—including the more emotional parts—can be included in our receptive sensing of the present moment, until nothing whatsoever is being resisted, grasped, or ignored. Then, *unlike* narcissism's enshelled nature, we've become more porous, more permeable, an open system.

Once you have noted what your actual experience *is* right now, the **second** step is to *allow it to be there*. To begin to value and validate (versus ignore, second-guess, or resist your experience) so that it can begin to unfold, and actually take you somewhere—like the wise "fool" in a fairy tale, who has let go of the reins and allows himself to be led by the horse.

Part of our disorientation to presence has been that our (supposedly) rational minds tend to be so active, that we normally don't fully digest our experience, we don't stay with it long enough for it to settle, we don't provide enough *space* before we're already lurching forward toward the next mental event.

The combination of *recognizing* what our current experience *is* and then merely *allowing* it to unfold has been referred to as "choice-less awareness." Here we aren't attempting to fiddle with, manipulate, or *control* our experience. We're merely aware of *what is*. And thus, this form of awareness short-circuits the three Lords (or ruts) of egoic consciousness—these three "ruts" being the tendency to either *grasp onto* what is appearing, to be *indifferent* (ignorant or heedless) toward what is appearing, or to be in active *aversion* to what is appearing.

At first what you become aware of, what your actual experience *is*, may not feel that profound or fulfilling, and so there may be an almost built-in tendency to devalue it, to think *"this can't be right, I ought to be experiencing something more significant than* **this**. *This exercise is bullshit, it doesn't do anything for me."* But remember, this exercise involves learning to go with, and allow the experience you are *actually having*, instead of devaluing or rejecting it in favor of a quest for something more "ideal."

Once you are more focused toward what your actual experience *is*, continue to relate to it more nakedly—with a minimum of interpretation, or judgment. Each time you can identify what is actually happening now and then "go with it," it will take you to a new subway stop, a new "cross-road," a new movement in the soul. And again you apply the little two-step. You notice what the new "now" is like—and then you say "yes" to *that*.

By practicing this style of attention, the psyche gets to go where it needs to go (or to more fully embody where it already *is*). Our obscurational tape loops get a chance to unravel all the way to the end, until there is no longer anything filtering our experience.

We're finally receiving it straight on.

This reception of our psychic flow is actually quite similar to what unfolds in doing *EMDR*, a protocol that has proven quite helpful in dealing with trauma, and in getting people hooked up again to their own inner guidance. It is also quite *different* than what is going on much of the time, where our psychic movement is more choppy—either distracted by thoughts of the past or future, dwelling upon hopes or fears, pleasure or pain, or being invalidated by the critical part of the mind.

On a psychological level, the little two-step also enables us to penetrate areas of the soul that we might normally defend against or ignore, and hence never complete with or succeed in better understanding. And so these "tape loops" can continue to usher us around, obscuring our perception.

But if you will continue to simply note what is actually being experienced in the present moment (which is "step one") and then say "yes" to it, *whatever* it is (which is "step two") a couple of things are likely to happen. First, you will begin to move through successive psychic layers, and will begin to penetrate—or release—whatever has been buffering your experience.

Here you might note *exactly what it is* that arises in your mind-stream which characteristically takes you *out* of presence. Perhaps it's a fear, or a part of the self that feels deficient, and that normally we might recoil or dissociate from in some way. Yet if we can say "yes" to that too, then even our characteristically avoided experiences can in themselves become *portals into presence*. (And in terms of EMDR, this is generally where *interior guidance* begins to kick in, and to outshine the traumatic residues that have been shadowing our perception; though we might need to go through several "subway stops" first).

Secondly, at a certain point, your *will* and the flow of *Reality* will begin to become more fully congruent, as what you are actively aligning with becomes none other than what is actually *occurring*. As your will becomes congruent with Reality in this way, more and more you yourself and the present moment will become the same entity—the experience of "one taste"—as if some kind of barrier wall has dissolved, the barrier wall of ego structure itself.

Now the ego's fussiness toward reality, and its attempt to pick and choose—or control the uncontrollable –can fall by the wayside. (What a relief!). More and more you will become an awareness without a shell, an awareness without a psychic membrane separating you from what is actually taking place. As this separative membrane dissolves, what is left will be a sense of spaciousness mingled with awareness. And you may recognize that "just this" is quite enough. Now—becomes the only game in town. Now, there's no longer some part of you having an experience while another part of you ignores or rejects it, or longs for something external that seems to be missing, something more "juicy."

There will be an experience of contentment, without anything external needing to be changed or imported. You will realize that when we are fully present for *what is* then nothing essential is really "missing." You will have reconnected with your own native presence.

THIRTY-SIX

Who *Isn't Dissociated from Presence?*

WHEN NOT AGITATED or stressed, almost any dog, cat, or animal, whether domesticated or wild. Soaring hawks... effortlessly circling, upheld by the thermal currents of the sky... And meditators... resting in the space between their thoughts...

Beaming grandparents... in the presence of their grandchildren. Or anyone fully attentive to a lover's touch... People who've taken the marriage vow "for better or worse" to its ultimate extension, and find that the personal beloved was but a portal to a vaster beloved, and that now they are married to life...

Athletes when they're "in the zone," and the game seems to slow down... Golfers, when all their "swing thoughts" have fallen away; and the intuitive genius inside the body—fully trusted—becomes what is swinging the club. (No longer "trying to kill it," just a relaxed, rhythmic swing fully completed... launches the ball farther and straighter than expected—and surprisingly, is often more than enough).

Accomplished performance artists—say the late Robin Williams on an improvisational riff, or anyone experiencing some form of mastery. Something has disappeared; gotten out of the way. And in that absence, brilliantly attuned elves seem to be doing their work...

Surfers in "the green room." People unafraid to fully embrace their weeping, and the poignant tidal conversations between their grief and their joy... Lovers of great wine, wrapping their whole mind around a flavor wave that might carry them for over a minute, before leaving them nowhere in particular. Lovers of even a greater wine, a spiritual "wine" whose waves have neither beginning nor end…

Yogins and yoginis, people whose bodies are like mountains deeply resting, but who are not asleep. Zen masters who have said "***every** day is a good day!*" Native American warriors who have said *"**this** is a good day to die!"*

Anyone deeply listening to the world, and its silences… People in praying from the depths of their broken-ness—who discover a greater depth that is seamless and unbroken… Or anyone, once their narcissistic shell has begun to crack open, release, or dissolve. It seems to come to them, like a Sabbath, an ease from striving…

Anyone deeply in love…Or those receiving an epiphany… Grateful people. Humble people. Ecstatic people. People who are inspired—or nearly breathless after a good run… Or any healthy tree or plant. They're not grasping, nor in aversion. And wide open, it comes to them all, faithfully suffusing them with a causeless contentment.

For however overlooked, presence is all surrounding, buoyant and supportive. A non-conceptual spaciousness where nothing is lacking and nothing in excess; it's the sufficient and subtle formlessness that gives rise to all forms. It's life's original gift. And is never not availably here…

EPILOGUE

Echoing the Whole

> "In every culture, we find the myth of a
> lost paradise, in which humans lived in
> close and daily contact with the divine "
> —Karen Armstrong,
> *A Short History of Myth*

THE "PARADISE LOST" in which humans once lived in close and daily contact with the divine is *still* available—and always *has* been. As elsewhere suggested in this and other books, such a paradise or heaven is not a literal, or even "astral" where-ness. It's a *metaphor* for a kind of *awareness*—from which, most of us have grown to be dissociated. Nearly all the problems evoked in this book are the outgrowths of this dissociation; a "mythic dissociation" that Joseph Campbell first coined, and that I've attempted to more fully mirror in this book.

The purpose of all spiritual training—if not the intent of most mythologies—is to rectify this state of dissociation and to re-enter a trusting kind of *participation mystique* with life. And yet, it may be one of religion's consoling illusions to expect that without sufficient spiritual orientation and training during life, that our deaths alone—or our mythic membership with some chosen group—will manage to deliver us to some version of paradise or Heaven. For as Kabir has told us:

> "What you call Salvation belongs to the
> time before death.
> If you don't break your ropes while you are alive
> do you think that ghosts will do it after?
> The idea that the soul will join with the
> ecstatic just because the body is rotten—

that is all fantasy."
(trans. Robert Bly)

The death that is the true resolution of narcissism is thus not the literal death of the body, and seldom does this "death" happen once and for all. Like "paradise" or "heaven" itself, this death is *metaphoric*, and the work of a lifetime—"the death of Narcissus." This is a *good* death… into a grace-filled *depth*—one that timelessly predates, outshines, and outlives the egoic perspective.

For the perspective of the ego, though a developmental *achievement*, is not the be-all, nor should it be the end-all of development. Though in a narcissistic culture, development tends to become *arrested* here, leaving us in some version of a Waste Land.

The transitive "death" of what we have taken ourselves to be, and the "rebirth" to what we most deeply are, is thus the deepest and ongoing pivot of our life, a shift into an ever-freshening, unbounded presence. This transitive shift of perspective does not occur in the future, no matter how brightly imagined. Right now is the only access point we will ever have to the "eternal Kingdom." For as Kabir says,

"What is found now is found then. If you
find nothing now you will simply end
up in an apartment in the city of death."

Another great poet—Rilke—writes of "this clumsy living that moves lumbering / as if in ropes through what is not done." And it is our lack of orientation in "breaking our ropes" and toward what these ropes keep us from more fully recognizing and embodying, that *blinds and binds* us to the perspective of narcissism, while keeping us dissociated from an undying, unborn (innate) awareness.

The belief in Jesus Christ as our own personal savior—or the belief in the eventual victory of one religion over all others, or the *belief* in anyone or anything—may offer consolation as we face our lives and our deaths, but such belief alone does not necessarily "save us" from living in illusion toward the Great Matter, or become the guarantor that our dissociation from the holy of holies has come to an end. In fact, to the extent that all *beliefs* are at some remove from the moment-by-moment unfolding of Reality itself, they all have something a little psychotic about them.

And this "psychotic" dissociation from Reality has led to all the religious, psychological, and political suffering this book has attempted to evoke and mirror. It has led to our religiously "inspired" holy wars—a malignancy of fundamentalism, the self-righteous duality of "us against them." Similarly, this dissociation has led to the polarizations of our political parties, and their resulting gridlocks. And the dissociation from an innately dwelling awareness—a non-dual "true nature"—becomes the breeding ground for our narcissism, our confusion about who we really are. For we have taken ourselves to be something other than *this,* something apart from Reality *itself,* having identified instead with an image of self that can seldom, if ever, embody and reflect the freshly arising vastness of being.

In the epidemic of our collectively shared and culturally transmitted state of dissociation, we have become orphaned from an original blessing; a birthright innately contented, that doesn't need to be added to or embellished. Nor do we have to vanquish the beliefs of others, in order for it to endure, now and forever. *What is most real cannot be destroyed,* for it is "unborn" and has never not been. Thus, it doesn't require from us that it be defended or fought over.

It is accessed not by some feat of addition—not by the acquisitive importations of addiction or fame, nor by imitative piety, nor expansionistic struggle with other people or nations—but by a radical kind of *subtraction.*

"Beneath every stone," and in the gap prior to thought, "it" is already here, awaiting discovery, like a neglected beauty we have failed to notice. It exists in the peaceful spaciousness of a silent mind no longer launching itself toward the future, in recoil toward the past, or heedlessly ignoring the subtle riches of the present.

Yet even "the present" is a concept. There is really nothing, no thing there—nothing having to do with time at all. But this "nothing" is marvelous, a shimmering, radiant *nothing* that *lacks* nothing. It is timeless—boundless and bountiful—an original inheritance that may be overlooked, but never truly lost—for it *is,* and has never not been.

Our deepest nature *is* this radiant no thing (the very "nothingness" that wisdom told Nisargadatta he actually is). Its beauty is a fatal attraction—to what we've otherwise taken ourselves to be. And it may be reflected by a clear pool of water in a myth; or by the clear pool of another's eyes. It may be mirrored in the spaciousness of a blue cloudless sky.

It may be found in a field, a field of *basic trust*, like Jesus' " lilies of the field." Or a field of awareness emptied of judgment—such as Rumi's "field beyond right and wrong." It is heard in "the music of what happens."

All these *metaphors*, all our *senses*, in fact *our lives themselves* are part of this music. And they too have arisen from this spaciousness, this thing-less field, this ground of being; prior to any willful bidding of our own. And the wise are those who attempt to offer themselves back to its supportive and invisible arms; and not merely at the time of death.

This "radical subtraction" by which the eternal is revealed and lived *is* a kind of death—but not to anything real. Nor does it require the death of those we presume to be enemies. It is ourselves who must die the death of Narcissus—the death of the egoic perspective. This "death"—and the flowering that arises from it—has always been the goal of mystical religion, if we may speak of something innately present and always available as being part of a goal.

Just as the man attached to riches may not fit through the metaphoric needle's eye, neither can those clutching to conceptual relics, however "holy." At best scripture should be the adornment to realization, not stand in its stead. Otherwise, we'll continue to hear it half-cocked, striding earnestly at best, but beneath a ridiculous hat from long ago.

Karen Armstrong reminds us that there is never a single orthodox version of a myth—as circumstances change, we need to tell our stories differently in order to bring out their timeless truths, for "every time men and women took a major step forward, they reviewed their mythology and made it speak to the new conditions."

Reflecting the story of Narcissus and Echo "differently"—in order to bring out the myth's timeless truths—is what I have attempted to do in this book. For I have tried to reflect the story's "fresh mythic imprint"—that is, the varied and nuanced ways its mythic figures are alive in us, and in our world *today*. In reflecting them, I've attempted to free the myth from the narrow way it has commonly been held—as a kind of cautionary tale on the dangers of "self love."

In different cultural epochs, certain myths seem not only more *pertinent* for a culture, but also *in need* of being told and viewed differently—a fresh *re-visioning*. If I have found this to be the case with the myth of Narcissus and Echo, or to a lesser extent here with the myth of Pluto and Persephone or some of the other mythic structures I've evoked in this book, these are by no means the only possibilities.

Barry Spector has done an important cultural service by offering us fresh reflections of unconscious facets of the American psyche by using a completely *different* myth—that of Dionysus.* Stephen Mitchell also has performed—for many decades now—an ongoing type of karma yoga in giving us fresh re-visions, new and spiritually attuned translations for a wide swath of the world's sacred literature.

And though the Parsifal myth arose out of, and as a response to the psychic needs of medieval Europe, it still has much to say to us today. This would be evident for anyone who has had the good fortune to be present while Martin Shaw brings that mythic material alive through his oral presentations.**

Numerous writers, including but by no means limited to Cynthia Bourgeault, have attempted to give us a fresh take on facets of the Christian *mythos*. And numerous clear-eyed Sufi teachers and authors have done the same for Islam. Wisdom is wisdom—from whomever it arises—even if it seems "heretical" to religious or psychological orthodoxy.

If we have truly entered a new cultural epoch—or *in order for us to do so*—**all** the myths we've inherited as part of our cultural legacy may be, from time to time, in need of a fresh re-visioning. For as I've suggested, if a mythic reorientation doesn't happen, or soon enough when one is needed, we become more subject to suffering a Terror yet to come, whether from a frenzied enemy also following an outmoded mythic sensibility, or equally ominous ecological, political, or financial melt-downs.

Karen Armstrong also reminds us that mythology should awaken us to *rapture*, and if a myth ceases to do that, "it has died and outlived its usefulness." This "awakening to rapture" was something needing to be reflected in the myth of Narcissus and Echo. For without a different way of viewing

---

* See Spector's *Madness at the Gates of the City: The Myth of American Innocence*. Berkeley: Regent Press, 2010.
** See Shaw's *A Branch from the Lightning Tree: Ecstatic Myth and the Grace in Wildness*. And also his subsequent *Snowy Tower*, and *Scatterlings: Getting Claimed in the Age of Amnesia;* each book in this trilogy published by White Cloud Press (www.whitecloudpress.com).

the vision that led to Narcissus's metaphoric death, something would be ever lacking in our approach to the *healing* of narcissism, for we would lack reference to the style of vision that puts narcissism out of its misery; we would lack orientation to the fullness and rapture of being—which lurks, often undiscovered, beneath the narcissistic shell.

Untransformed, the perspective of narcissism—the perspective of egoic encasement, or what we might rechristen as "Self-Absorbed Diminished Awareness Syndrome"—does not awaken us to rapture. And for those no longer children it has "outlived its usefulness." And aside from the lessons he might cause us to learn, a childish, corrupt, and narcissistic president is *worse* than useless.

And something similar should be said of ethnocentric, mythological warfare conducted in the name of "God." Such a perspective must now be subtracted from our mythic, religious imagination. If it is not, our religious imagination (and political vision) will remain stuck, nearly back in the Bronze Age, having failed to evolve. And the employment of modern weaponry in the service of an archaic interpretation of myth—or a divisive form of politics—can only be catastrophic.

The habit of recoil or indifference toward *what is,* our habit of always reaching for something *else,* as if this very moment were somehow lacking—all that, and more, cannot fit through the needle's eye—where, having emptied ourselves enough to pass through it, our *own* eyes might recognize a world presently shimmering in beauty and depth.

For here, the lilies of the field already, and forever, sway in the wind... As if to an ancient music—that mysteriously, is always graceful and fresh...

AFTERWORD

The Gifts of Narcissus's Pool

NARCISSUS'S MYTH HAS continued to be viewed in the light of a moral tale about the dangers of "self love," less frequently as a myth of *transformation*.

Yet when it comes to mythic figures and archetypal *images,* best not to be a reductionist.

For like ourselves, every archetype has its own light-giving qualities, and its own shadow. And what we see in them may be reflecting our own minds—for better or worse…

In retrospect, I woke up early every morning—for *years*—by gazing into the reflective depths of this book, or what had just come to me the previous day, before realizing that this form of visionary entrainment *is* Narcissus's visionary pool. Were there "narcissistic features" in this? No doubt.

Yet spending so many years writing a book that had been undertaken without a publisher's advance or support seemed to require that the book itself support, guide, and mirror my efforts, reflecting my own depths as they came into view, and the insights arising from these depths.

I must have read and re-read this book five hundred times in its different incarnations, as it was gestating—before its deeper nature revealed itself and cohered; and before I was finished with it, and it with me. For each of us seemed to have been progressively transforming the other. And it may be that a certain kind of *healthy* "self absorption" provides some of the staying power *necessary* for such a long-term project.

You put everything you have into something; everything that you know, everything that you are. And though the object of your fascination begins to have *a life of its own*, you can't help but see yourself in it. And the same might be said for any ongoing, creative project—such as nurturing a child.

Narcissism has become a bad word. Yet if all artists and poets are said to be innately narcissistic, unless they're malignant or devaluing toward others should we blame them for this, and reduce their creative, *visionary absorption* to "narcissism" and leave it at that?

When a poet looks into the eyes of his or her Muse that may be Narcissus's pool. When in Genesis, God looks upon the world He's just created, and finds that it is good, that too may be Narcissus's pool. When the "godless" Russian cosmonauts first gazed upon the planet Earth from outer space, and found something about this astonishing, that may be Narcissus's pool. Anytime *we* manage to look at the world with fresh eyes, as in doing transformational gazes like *trespasso,* or *Dzogchen's* sky-gazing, that may be Narcissus's pool.

When a meditator comes to a one-pointed absorption upon the meditation object, and "the ten thousand things" fall away—*even oneself*—that may be the effect of Narcissus's pool. (And actually, as in most of these examples, what *transforms* narcissism's encapsulated vision).

The French refer to orgasm as *la petite mort*. But *what* is it here that undergoes "a little death," as pleasure mounts overwhelmingly, and we begin to shudder, gasp, dissolve, losing all control, bursting apart at the seams?

Whenever love's various intensities, beauty, creative absorption, or self-realization's clear vision have outshined the ego structure, leaving us wide open, and "confusing" us with everything else, these Neptunian *dissolutions of the ego into a greater depth* are the gifts of Narcissus's pool.

Works Consulted or Recommended

Almaas, A.H. (Hameed Ali). *The Point of Existence: Transformations of Narcissism in Self-Realization.* Berkeley: Diamond Books, 1996

Almaas, A.H. (Hameed Ali). *The Void.* Berkeley: Diamond Books, 1986

Ali, Ayaan Hirsi, *Infidel.* New York: Free Press 2007

American Psychiatric Association: *Diagnostic and Statistical Manual of Mental Disorders,* 4th Edition, Text Revision. Washington, D.C., American Psychiatric Association, 2000

American Psychiatric Association: *Diagnostic and Statistical Manual of Mental Disorders, 5th Edition.* Washington, D.C., American Psychiatric Association, 2013

Armstrong, Karen. *A Short History of Myth.* New York: Canongate, 2005

Armstrong, Karen. *The Battle For God.* New York: Knopf, 2000

Barks, Coleman and Khan, Inayat. *The Hand of Poetry: Five Mystic Poets of Persia.* New Lebanon: Omega Publications, 1993

Beck, Don Edward and Cowan, Christopher C. *Spiral Dynamics: Mastering Values, Leadership and Change.* Malden: Blackwell Publishing, 2006

Begg, Ean. *The Cult of the Black Virgin.* Brooklyn: Chiron Publications, 2006

Berry, Patricia. *Echo's Subtle Body.* Dallas: Spring Publications, 1982

Blackburn, Paul and Economou, George. *Proensa: An Anthology of Troubadour Poetry.* New York, Paragon House, 1986

Bly, Robert. *The Kabir Book.* Boston: Beacon Books, 1977

Bly, Robert. *The Sibling Society.* New York: Vintage Books, 1996

Brannon, Peter. *The Ends of the World: Volcanic Apocalypses, Lethal Oceans, and our Quest to Understand Earth's Past Mass Extinctions.* New York: Harper Collins, 2017

Brill, Steven. *Tailspin: The People and Forces Behind America's Fifty-Year-Fall—and Those Fighting to Reverse It.* New York: Knopf, 2018

Campbell, Joseph. *Myths to Live By.* Toronto: Bantam Books, 1973

Campbell, Joseph. *Pathways to Bliss: Mythology and Personal Transformation.* Novato: New World Library, 2004

Campbell, Joseph. *Transformation of Myths Through Time.* New York: Harper Perennial, 1990

Campbell, Joseph. *The Inner Reaches Of Outer Space.* Novato: New World Library, 2002

Capellanus, Andreas. *The Art of Courtly Love.* New York: Columbia U Press, 1960

Castaneda, Carlos. *The Power of Silence.* New York: Simon and Schuster, 1987

Castaneda, Carlos. *The Wheel of Time: The Shamans of Ancient Mexico, Their Thoughts about Life, Death and Universe.* Los Angeles: LA Eidolona Press, 1998

Chayes, Sarah. *The Punishment of Virtue.* New York: The Penguin Press, 2006

Clarke, Richard A. *Against All Enemies: Inside America's War on Terror.* New York: Free Press, 2004

Cousineau, Phil. *Once and Future Myths.* Berkeley: Conari Press, 2001

Donner, Florinda. **BEING-IN-DREAMING:** *Florinda Donner in conversation with Alexander Blair-Ewart. Dimensions Magazine,* February, 1992

Eliade, Mircea. *Rites & Symbols of Initiation: The Mysteries of Birth and Rebirth.* New York: Harper, 1965

Ferguson, Niall. *The Great Degeneration: How Institutions Decay and Economies Die.* London: Penguin, 2012

Frum, David. *Trumpocracy: The Corruption of the American Republic.* New York: Harper, 2018

Green, Joshua. *Devil's Bargain: Steve Bannon, Donald Trump, and the Storming of the Presidency.* New York: Penguin Press, 2017

Gimbutas, Marija. *The Living Goddess.* Berkeley: University of California Press, 2001

Grimm, *The Complete Grimm's Fairy Tales.* New York: Pantheon, 1944

Grun, Bernard. *The Timetables of History.* New York: Simon and Schuster, 1975

Harari, Yuval, Noah. *Sapiens: A Brief History of Humankind.* New York: Harper Collins, 2015

Hillman, James. *The Dream and the Underworld.* New York: Harper & Row, 1979

Hillman, James. "The Gods, Diseases, and Politics." *Parabola Magazine*, Winter, 2004

Johnson, Chalmers. *Nemesis: The Last Days of the American Republic.* New York: Henry Holt, 2006

Johnson, Chalmers. *Sorrows of Empire.* New York: Henry Holt, 2004

Johnson, Chalmers. *Blowback: The Costs and Consequences of American Empire.* New York: Henry Holt, 2000

Jung, C.G. and Kerenyi, C. *Essays on a Science of Mythology.* Princeton: Princeton/Bollingen Paperbacks, 1963

Kelly, Kevin W. *The Home Planet.* Boston: Addison Wesley, 1988

Kerenyi, Carl. *Eleusis: Archetypal Image of Mother and Daughter.* Princeton: Princeton/Bollingen, 1967

Lasch, Christopher. *The Culture of Narcissism: American Life in an Age of Diminishing Expectations.* New York: W.W.Norton & Co.; Revised edition, 1990

Lowen, Alexander. *Narcissism.* New York: Macmillian, 1983

Lewis, Bernard. *The Crisis of Islam: Holy War and Unholy Terror.* New York: Random House, 2004

Lewis, Charles. *935 Lies: The Future of Truth and the Decline of America's Moral Integrity.* Public Affairs, 2014

Markale, Jean. *Courtly Love: The Path of Sexual Initiation.* Rochester, Vermont: Inner Traditions, 2000

Marti, Biddy. *Women and Modernity: The (Life)Styles of Lou Andreas Salome.* Ithaca: Cornell University Press, 1991

Masterson, James F. *Psychotherapy of the Disorders of the Self.* New York: Brunner/Mazel, 1989

Masterson, James F. *The Emerging Self: A Developmental, Self, and Object Relations Approach to the Treatment of the Closet Narcissistic Disorder of the Self.* New York: Brunner/Mazel, 1993

McCants, William. *The ISIS Apocalypse: The History, Strategy, and Doomsday Vision of the Islamic State.* New York: ST. Martin's Press, 2015

Mitchell, Stephen. *The Bhagavad Gita: A New Translation.* New York: Three Rivers Press, 2002

Morell, Michael. *The Great War of our Time: The CIA's Fight Against Terrorism From Al Qa'ida To ISIS.* New York: Twelve, 2015

Moriarty, John. *Invoking Ireland.* Lilliput Press, 2005

Nasr, Amir Admad. *My Islam: How Fundamentalism Stole My Mind—and Doubt Freed My Soul.* New York: St. Martin's Press, 2013

O'Donohue, John. *Anam Cara: A Book of Celtic Wisdom.* New York: Harper Perennial, 2004

O hOgain, Daithi. *The Lore of Ireland: An Encyclopedia of Myth, Legend and Romance.* Woodbridge: The Boydell Press, 2006

Ovid. *Metamorphoses.* Penguin Classics; Reprint Edition, 2004

Paglia, Camille. *Sexual Personae.* New York: Vintage Books, 1991

Pape, Robert A. and Feldman, James K. *Cutting the Fuse: The Explosion of Global Suicide Terrorism and How to Stop It.* Chicago: U. of Chicago Press, 2010

Pausanias. *Guide to Greece, Vol.1 and 2.* New York: Penguin, 1984

Phillips, Adam. *On Balance.* New York: Picador, 2011.

Rashid, Ahmed. Taliban: *Militant Islam, Oil & Fundamentalism in Central Asia.* New Haven: Yale U. Press, 2001

Rashid, Ahmed. *Descent into Chaos: The United States and the Failure of Nation Building in Pakistan, Afghanistan, and Central Asia.* New York: Viking Adult, 2008

Reilly, Rick. *Commander in Cheat.* New York: Hachette, 2019

Riedel, Bruce. *What We Won: America's Secret War in Afghanistan 1979-89.* Washington: Brookings, 2014

Riedel, B. *Deadly Embrace: Pakistan, America, and the Future of the Global Jihad.* Washington: Brookings, 2011

Rilke, Rainer Maria. *The Complete French Poems of Rainer Maria Rilke.* Translated by A. Poulin, Jr. Saint Paul: Graywolf Press, 1986

Robin, Corey. *The Reactionary Mind: Conservatism from Edmund Burke to Donald Trump, 2nd Edition.* Oxford: Oxford University Press, 2017

Rosenthal, Gary. *The Museum of the Lord of Shame.* Richmond: Point Bonita Books, 1997

Rosenthal, Gary. *The You That is Everywhere: Love Poems.* Richmond: Point Bonita Books, 2000

Rosenthal, Gary. "The Enneagram of Avoidances, Deficient Emptiness, and the Plutonic Paradox of Space." *Enneagram Monthly,* February 2006

Rosenthal, Gary. "Regarding Space, Regarding Depths." *Enneagram Monthly.* March, 2006

Rosenthal, Gary. "The Terror of Deficient Emptiness." *Enneagram Monthly*. March, 2006

Rosenthal, Gary. "History, Mystery, and the Otherworldly Foot." *Enneagram Monthly*. March, 2006

Rosenthal, Gary. "The Loss of the Four-armed God." *Enneagram Monthly*. March, 2006

Rosenthal, Gary. *An Amateur's Guide to the Invisible World*. Richmond: Point Bonita Books, 2020

Rosenthal, Gary. *Love Poems: The Great Neglected Tradition—an interview with Gary Rosenthal by Mark Rudinsky*. www.garyrosenthal.net/interview.html

Rosenthal, Gary. *Waking from an Age of Amnesia*. Richmond: Point Bonita Books, 2020

Rumi, Jalal al-Din (Author), Barks, Coleman and Moyne, John (Translators). *The Essential Rumi*. HarperOne, 2004

Shah, Idries. *Tales of the Dervishes: Teaching Stories of the Sufi Masters over the Past Thousand Years*. New York: E.P. Dutton, 1970

Shaw, Martin. *A Branch from the Lightning Tree: Ecstatic Myth and the Grace in Wildness*. Ashland, Oregon: White Cloud Press, 2011

Sky, Ema. *The Unraveling: High Hope and Missed Opportunities in Iraq*. New York, Public Affairs, 2015

Smith, Huston. *The World's Religions*. San Francisco: HarperOne, 1958, rev. ed 1991

Snyder, Gary. "Piute Creek" from *Riprap and Cold Mountain Poems*. Counterpoint Press, 2009

Spector, Barry. *Madness at the Gates of the City: The Myth of American Innocence*. Berkeley: Regent Press, 2010

Spengler, Oswald. *The Decline of the West*. Oxford: Oxford U. Press Paperback, 1991

Tarnas, Richard. *The Passion of the Western Mind*. New York: Ballantine Books, 1991

Toms, Michael. *An Open Life: Joseph Campbell in Conversation with Michael Toms*. New York: Harper Perennial, 1990

Tulku Urgyen Rinpoche. *As It Is, vol. I & II*. Boudhanath: Rangjung Yeshe, 1999, 2000

Von Franz, Marie Louise. *An Introduction to the Psychology of Fairy Tales*. New York: Spring Publications, 1970

Von Franz, Marie Louise. *Shadow and Evil in Fairytales*. Dallas: Spring Pub., 1980

Wasson, R. Gordon, Hofmann, Albert, and Ruck, Carl A. *The Road to Eleusis: Unveiling the Secret of the Mysteries;* 30th anniversary ed. Berkeley: North Atlantic Books, 2008

Whyte, David. "Tilicho Lake," from *Where Many Rivers Meet*. Langley: Many Rivers, 1990

Weiss, Michael, and Hassan, Hassan. *ISIS: Inside the Army of Terror*. New York: Regan Arts, 2015

Wilber, Ken. *Boomeritis: A Novel That Will Set You Free*. Boston: Shambhala, 2002

Wilber, Ken. "The Pre/Trans Fallacy" from *Sex, Ecology, Spirituality*. Boston: Shambhala, 1995

Wolff, Michael. *Fire and Fury: Inside the Trump White House*. New York: Henry Holt and Co., 2018

Wood, Graeme. "What ISIS Really Wants." *The Atlantic* (magazine), March 2015

Yeats, W.B. *A Vision. Kessinger Publishing*, 2003

Zakaria, Fareed. *The Post American World*. NY & London: W.W. Norton & Co., 2008

I also wish to acknowledge the television show *Charley Rose*, the widely ranging curiosity of its host, and the collective reflection of our *zeitgeist* as provided by those Mr. Rose interviewed while this book was being written.

I bear a similar appreciation—for the same reasons—to Fareed Zakaria, both for his timely, balanced writing on the issues of our day, and for his own television show.

And lastly, appreciation is due Rachel Maddow for passionately curating the reportage of the world's investigative journalists—and her skill at connecting the dots—during an age when the world's democracies have been under threat.

About the Author

Gary Rosenthal is a bard—in the old Irish sense. He initially studied psychology at the Jung Institute-Zurich, and formerly has also lived as a Buddhist monastic, worked on offshore fishing boats, and as a fire lookout ranger in the White Mountains of New Hampshire. He lives in the San Francisco Bay area where for many years he's been a licensed marriage and family therapist, led groups, and consulted with clients throughout the world.

Gary is the author of *The You That is Everywhere*, a collection of ecstatic love poems whose back-cover blurbs include praise from fellow poets David Whyte and Coleman Barks. His poems have appeared in numerous anthologies including 365 *Nirvana Here and Now: Living Every Moment in Enlightenment*, and *What Book!? Buddha Poems from Beats to Hip Hop*, a national book award winner (1999).

Written while still a graduate student, his non-fiction psycho-spiritual writing first appeared in the anthology *Spiritual Choices*, co-edited by the transpersonal philosopher Ken Wilber. Excerpts of his writing on the Pluto/Persephone myth appeared in North Atlantic Books' *Pluto: New Horizons for a Lost Horizon*. In addition to an audio-tape—*Love and the Poetic Tradition*—which arose from the keynote address he gave to the International Enneagram Conference in the year 2000, Gary is also the author of a chapbook, *The Museum of the Lord of Shame*, as well as another full-length poetry collection, *An Amateur's Guide to the Invisible World*. Forthcoming works include: a collection of writing from—and about—the perception of "Transpersonal Will" (*The White Latifa and its Citadel: Radical Allowing, Discipline, and the Poetry of Essential Will*); and a new poetry collection, *Waking from an Age of Amnesia*.

In gratitude for purchasing this book, Point Bonita Books would like to gift its readers with free "bonus material" from Gary that you can download at www.pointbonitabooks.com/bonus

www.ingramcontent.com/pod-product-compliance
Lightning Source LLC
Chambersburg PA
CBHW030133170426
43199CB00008B/53